COUNSELING BOYS AND MEN WITH ADHD

The Routledge Series on Counseling and Psychotherapy With Boys and Men

VOLUMES IN THIS SERIES

FORTHCOMING

COUNSELING BOYS AND MEN WITH ADHD

GEORGE KAPALKA

Routledge
Taylor & Francis Group
New York   London

Routledge
Taylor & Francis Group
270 Madison Avenue
New York, NY 10016

Routledge
Taylor & Francis Group
27 Church Road
Hove, East Sussex BN3 2FA

© 2010 by Taylor and Francis Group, LLC
Routledge is an imprint of Taylor & Francis Group, an Informa business

Printed in the United States of America on acid-free paper
10 9 8 7 6 5 4 3 2 1

International Standard Book Number: 978-0-415-99344-9 (Paperback)

Library of Congress Cataloging-in-Publication Data

Kapalka, George M.
    Counseling boys and men with ADHD / George Kapalka.
       p. ; cm.
    Includes bibliographical references and index.
    ISBN 978-0-415-99344-9 (pbk. : alk. paper)
    1. Attention-deficit-disordered children--Counseling of. 2. Attention-deficit-disordered youth--Counseling of. 3. Attention-deficit disorder in adults--Patients--Counseling of. 4. Men--Counseling of. 5. Boys--Counseling of. I. Title.
    [DNLM: 1. Attention Deficit Disorder with Hyperactivity--therapy. 2. Adolescent. 3. Adult. 4. Child. 5. Counseling--methods. 6. Men--psychology. 7. Psychotherapy--methods. WS 350.8.A8 K17c 2009]

RJ506.H9K37 2009
618.92'8589--dc22   2009011031

Visit the Taylor & Francis Web site at
http://www.taylorandfrancis.com

and the Routledge Web site at
http://www.routledgementalhealth.com

Contents

Series Editor's Foreword

Attention deficit hyperactivity disorder (ADHD) is a serious mental health problem affecting boys and men throughout many parts of the world. According to a recent report issued by the National Center for Health Statistics and authored by Pastor and Reuben (2008), nearly 12% of all boys in the United States will be diagnosed with ADHD by age 18, and boys are more than twice as likely as girls to be afflicted with the disorder. For at least a third of these boys, the symptoms of ADHD will continue into adulthood (National Institute of Mental Health, 2008). Numerous studies published by the World Health Organization have confirmed that ADHD is a common problem for boys and men that cuts across various continents, posing serious service challenges for health professionals in many countries (e.g., World Health Organization Regional Office for Africa, 2002; World Health Organization Regional Office for Europe, 2007). In short, ADHD among boys and men is a widespread problem that has generated international concern.

In response to the many educational, emotional, and social problems associated with the disorder, ADHD has received extensive attention over the past several decades. ADHD is a popular topic for discussion in the media, organizations dedicated to supporting people and families affected by ADHD have blossomed, and numerous interventions designed to treat the symptoms of ADHD have been developed and administered to millions of boys and men throughout the world. Nevertheless, there are many misconceptions about ADHD, how to assess for ADHD in boys and men who are suspected of having the disorder, and how to treat those who truly have ADHD. Accurate information about ADHD is necessary so that the legions of boys and men who are affected by the disorder can receive effective treatment to help them function adequately in their personal relationships and in school and the world of work.

Fortunately, Dr. George Kapalka of Monmouth University has devoted his many talents to studying, understanding, and helping boys and men with ADHD throughout his illustrious career. I had the pleasure of meeting Dr. Kapalka many years ago when I attended one of his superb conference presentations on ADHD at a time in my life when I was trying to become more knowledgeable about the disorder. I was so impressed with the thoroughness and authoritative nature of Dr. Kapalka's presentation that I have followed his career and have often called him for advice about counseling my own male clients whose difficulties included problems with attention and hyperactivity. As a result of my frequent contacts with Dr. Kapalka, I have learned that he has conducted a series of highly sophisticated empirical studies on ADHD and its treatment, completed numerous publications and conference presentations on the subject, and developed a private practice that includes extensive service to boys and men with ADHD and similar problems of adjustment. Consequently, when I decided to start the *Routledge Series on Counseling and Psychotherapy with Boys and Men*, Dr. Kapalka was one of the first people I asked to consider writing a book for the series. Recognizing the widespread occurrence of ADHD and its detrimental impact on boys and men, and concerned about the many misconceptions practitioners and the public have about the disorder, I realized that publishing a book devoted to the subject of ADHD is this series was warranted, and that Dr. Kapalka would be the perfect person to write it. To our good fortune, Dr. Kapalka accepted my invitation to contribute to the series, and his book, *Counseling Boys and Men with ADHD: A Guidebook for Professionals,* is the latest achievement in Dr. Kapalka's long line of work on ADHD.

Counseling Boys and Men with ADHD provides professionals with everything they need to know about ADHD in males. Dr. Kapalka has sorted through the mountainous literature on the etiology, epidemiology, and course of ADHD to paint a vivid picture of what ADHD is and how it affects of the lives of countless boys and men. He then describes in detail the multifaceted assessment procedures that must be followed in order to properly diagnose boys and men with ADHD. In his discussions about interventions for ADHD, Dr. Kapalka carefully reviews the empirical support for various approaches to treatment, thereby separating effective interventions from useless (if not harmful!) fads that have been applied with ADHD. Across all of these topics, Dr. Kapalka accentuates what it is like to be *male* and to have ADHD, empathically describing the impact of ADHD on male roles, and how masculinity ideology and expectations can influence both the expression of and response to ADHD. Consequently, *Counseling Boys and Men with ADHD* gives us a uniquely male perspective on ADHD and how we can help boys and men with ADHD to live more satisfying lives.

I sincerely thank Dr. Kapalka for his efforts to help us more fully understand this important topic.

Mark S. Kiselica, Series Editor

The Routledge Series on Counseling and Psychotherapy
with Boys and Men
The College of New Jersey
May 1, 2009

REFERENCES

National Institute of Mental Health (2008). *Attention deficit hyperactivity disorder*. Retrieved on May 1, 2009 at http://www.nimh.nih.gov/health/publications/attention-deficit-hyperactivity-disorder/complete-index.shtml

Pastor, P. N., & Reuben, C. A. (2008). Diagnosed attention deficit hyperactivity disorder and learning disability: United States, 2004–2006. National Center for Health Statistics. *Vital Health Statistics, 10* (237), 2008.

World Health Organization Regional Office for Africa (2002). *Disorders of childhood and adolescence*. Retrieved May 1, 2009 at http://www.afro.who.int/mentalhealth/related_diseases/childhood_adolescence.html

World Health Organization Regional Office for Europe (2007). FLORENCE DECLARATION: *Mental wellbeing of children in Europe: Plans and perspectives*. Retrieved on May 1, 2009 at http://www.euro.who.int/mentalhealth/declarations/20070828_2

Preface

Attention deficit/hyperactivity disorder (ADHD) is the most frequently diagnosed psychological disorder in childhood and adolescence (American Psychiatric Association [APA], 2000). According to figures published in the *Diagnostic and Statistical Manual of Mental Disorders* (*DSM-IV-TR*; APA, 2000), 3% to 7% of school-age children are diagnosed with this disorder. Because the U.S. population just reached 300 million, and school-age children represent approximately 24% of the population (U.S. Census Bureau, 2003), this means that approximately 2 to 5 million children in the United States are diagnosed with this disorder.

The *DSM-IV-TR* (APA, 2000) suggested that ADHD is a disorder that occurs primarily in boys by as much as a 9-to-1 boy-to-girl ratio. Although some researchers have suggested that the ratio may be closer to 3-to-1 (Barkley, 2006), higher ratios are evident in other epidemiological data (e.g., Bird, 2002). Thus, it can be estimated that 1.8 to 4.5 million boys and male teens in the United States are diagnosed with ADHD.

Not only is ADHD more prevalent in boys and male teens but male children and adolescents with ADHD are more likely to be brought for mental health treatment (Barkley, 2006). This difference exists because male children and teens typically exhibit more difficulties with self-control and greater severity of disruptive symptoms at home and in school. As a result, parents and teachers need assistance in addressing these problems and seek help from mental health and education professionals.

Forty percent to 60% of individuals with ADHD will continue to exhibit the full range of ADHD symptoms as adults (Barkley, 2006). Based on the U.S. census data, it can be estimated that 1.2 to 3 million of children and teens with ADHD will be affected by the disorder into adulthood, and males constitute up to 90% of that population. Thus, it is clearly evident that most adults with ADHD are males.

The symptoms of ADHD are characterized along two dimensions: hyperactivity/impulsivity and distractibility/disorganization. Boys and teens typically present with significant symptoms of hyperactivity and/or impulsivity and often act out in school and at home. They have difficulties following commands and directions, and they tend to be argumentative and disruptive in classrooms and during many day-to-day household activities (e.g., at meals and during family outings). Accomplishing tasks associated with daily routines, such as getting dressed and doing homework, is difficult for boys and teens with ADHD because their limited attention span, poor frustration tolerance, and inadequate impulse control often divert them away from the activity.

In addition, because impulsivity is a common dimension that under-lies many of the symptoms, males with ADHD often exhibit difficulties with self-control and are known to be defiant and aggressive. Parents, teachers, spouses, and coworkers find these behaviors very frustrating, and males with ADHD frequently experience conflicts with close family members (especially parents, siblings, and spouses), teachers, and coworkers (especially supervisors).

Some males with ADHD are not impulsive, defiant, or aggressive; they instead present with limited attention span, disorganization, difficulties completing tasks, and forgetfulness. As children, these males usually do not exhibit problems with acting out, but they often have academic difficulties and fall behind their peers in common academic skills (e.g., writing, reading, and mathematics). Disorganization can be a particularly troubling symptom, and males who exhibit this problem usually have difficulties keeping track of their assignments, books, notebooks, and other materials. As a result, they frustrate their parents, teachers, supervisors, and spouses and are frequently reprimanded for being so absent minded.

It is common for boys and male teens with ADHD to have difficulties with social adjustment. Because their self-control and impulse control tends to be poor, male children with ADHD are frustrating to their peers during social interactions. For example, when joining a peer group, boys with ADHD often attempt to take over leadership and want to impose on others their preference for what activity the group should perform. In addition, boys with ADHD frequently exhibit problems sharing and are often explosive when they do not get their way. Consequently, many boys with ADHD have difficulties making friends and maintaining good peer relationships.

Adult males with ADHD continue to exhibit most of the same problems male children and teens exhibit. They usually have difficulties meeting the demands of employment, and they change jobs frequently. They have problems keeping up with routine household maintenance (e.g., remembering to pay bills), and they are often seen by others as being irresponsible. If the impulsivity persists into adulthood, adult males with ADHD exhibit problems making decisions and sometimes exercise bad judgment. They are described as being difficult spouses and partners, and they typically have poor parenting skills.

Because boys, male teens, and adult males with ADHD exhibit problems in so many areas of day-to-day functioning, they are commonly exposed to the experience of failure. Parents, teachers, and other caretakers of boys and male teens with ADHD usually find themselves reprimanding and correcting them, and because so many boys with ADHD exhibit behavioral difficulties, they regularly get yelled at and punished by adults. Adult males with ADHD tend to have conflicts with their spouses and find parenting their own children to be difficult. As a result, it is common for males with ADHD to exhibit low self-esteem, limited academic motivation, anger, and hypersensitivity. These secondary difficulties further exacerbate the primary symptoms of ADHD, thus making it even more difficult for males with ADHD to relate well with their parents, teachers, spouses, coworkers, and peers.

Males with ADHD are at risk for developing other problems as well. About one half of males with ADHD exhibit symptoms of other psychological disorders, commonly including depression, anxiety, oppositional defiant disorder, and conduct disorder (Barkley, 2006). These comorbidities are even higher for adult males with ADHD, and three quarters of them are diagnosed with another mental disorder. Adolescent and adult males with ADHD are at risk to engage in criminal behaviors and to abuse drugs. Furthermore, they are likely to have significant educational problems: About one third of boys with ADHD are retained in school at least once, about one third receive special education, nearly half receive at least one suspension, 10% to 33% either drop out of or are expelled from school, and only 10% complete college (Hinshaw, 2002).

Because boys and male teens with ADHD constitute the largest segment of minors brought for mental health treatment, and adult males with ADHD increasingly seek treatment to help them adjust to life's demands, clinicians need to be well versed in the techniques to treat this disorder. Although many resources exist that review the disorder's etiology and treatment, most focus on the benefits of the use of medications to address the core symptoms. Coverage of nonmedical treatments is usually limited to parenting interventions, and most books for clinicians do not devote much space to other counseling interventions. In addition, resources for clinicians usually do not address the specific needs of males with this disorder. Consequently, this guidebook is intended to fill this void in the professional literature and provide a review of counseling, educational, and medical interventions that are specifically oriented toward the needs of the population of boys, male teens, and adult men with ADHD.

The guidebook is divided into five sections. Section 1 reviews issues of symptom description, etiology, and course, and Section 2 reviews assessment and differential diagnosis, particularly focusing on the symptoms that boys, male teens, and adult men commonly exhibit. Behavior, academic, social, and occupational problems evident at home, in school, at work, and in social settings are reviewed. Core (primary) symptoms are differentiated from secondary symptoms to help clinicians appreciate the complexity and diversity of various symptom groups that contribute to the overall impairment that males with ADHD exhibit. Epidemiology and course are also discussed, particularly focusing on the progression of symptoms from boyhood into the teen years and adulthood. The guidebook then provides a review of instruments that clinicians with varying levels of mental health training can use to assist with the diagnosis of the symptoms of ADHD. Finally, diagnostic issues are discussed to assist in performing differential diagnosis.

Section 3 presents a comprehensive discussion of the techniques that mental health professionals use most frequently. Specific counseling techniques that can be used to address the core symptoms and the associated features of the disorder are discussed from a practical, applied perspective, focusing on the application of each intervention to boys, male teens, and men. Individual counseling, group counseling, and parenting strategies are reviewed. In addition, specific techniques are discussed to involve spouses and partners of men with ADHD in treatment and help the spouses and partners develop a collaborative relationship that will assist the male with ADHD in improving his ability to attend to daily tasks of maintaining employment, managing a home, and being a parent.

Section 4 reviews educational interventions especially appropriate for boys, teens, and men with ADHD in academic settings. This section should be of particular value to school mental health professionals (including school counselors and school psychologists) and other mental health professionals who frequently work in academic settings. Classroom behavior management techniques are reviewed, specifically focusing on the application of behavioral principles to the classroom. Instructional modifications are also reviewed to help boys, male teens, and college students with ADHD function better within the classroom, including a discussion of changes to the physical arrangement of the classroom, the use of specific instructional methods, and the implementation of techniques to improve students' ability to attend to classroom activities and stay on task.

The information provided in Section 5 of this book informs nonmedical practitioners about how to collaborate with medical professionals about using medications to treat boys, male teens, and men with ADHD. Psychostimulants and nonstimulant medications are discussed with regard to their use, established efficacy, common adverse effects, and monitoring. The use of alternative medicine strategies is also reviewed in Section 5, including a balanced and research-based review of the available data about the effectiveness of herbal and nutritional supplements in reducing the symptoms of ADHD. The clinician will become better prepared to guide males with ADHD (and their parents and/or partners or spouses) toward treatments that may be effective while discouraging those that are likely to be ineffective and may be harmful.

This book is a practical and scholarly guide that will be a valuable resource for mental health and education professionals who serve boys, adolescent males, and men with ADHD in a variety of settings, including community mental health agencies, schools, private practice, and other institutions. These professionals include psychologists, counselors, and social workers within public and private mental health facilities and education professionals, including school counselors and school psychologists. This guidebook is also designed to help graduate students in psychology, counseling, and social work to develop skills to work with this population of patients and clients. Finally, this guidebook will also be useful to supervisors who work with developing mental health professionals and need resources to help their supervisees advance the skills they need to work with boys, male teens, and men with ADHD.

Etiology, Epidemiology, and Course

1

Symptoms of ADHD

In 1885, a German physician named Heinrich Hoffman wrote about some interesting patients that he saw in his practice, including the case of "Fidgety Phil," which he found particularly intriguing (Stewart, 1970). This description is commonly regarded as the first important reference to a boy with hyperactivity. Because Phil could not remain still for any significant period of time, he exhibited significant management difficulties and proved to be very frustrating to those who came in contact with him. Since that time, hyperactivity has been considered to be among the most common, and troubling, behavioral symptoms of childhood.

In addition, since the early 20th century, physicians have also recognized that some children (especially boys) exhibit significant problems with being able to sustain attention. Still (1902) described some three dozen children (the boys outnumbered the girls by a factor of about 3 to 1) he encountered who had significant difficulties with maintaining focus and who also exhibited symptoms of notable overactivity. These two dimensions of symptoms were accompanied by problems with aggression, defiance, and emotional overreactivity. Thus, for over 100 years, we have recognized that children who exhibit problems with overactivity and difficulties sustaining attention present with significant emotional and behavioral difficulties and that these problems are evident mostly in boys.

The syndrome we know today as attention deficit/hyperactivity disorder (ADHD) has been known through a variety of terms. Still (1902) remarked that children with this syndrome exhibit a major "defect in moral control." In the 1920s, these symptoms were presumed to be secondary to "postencephalitic" behavior disorder (Ebaugh, 1923), because children previously infected with encephalitis were noted to be particularly likely to exhibit these problems. This label eventually morphed into "minimal brain damage," because brain damage due to known or unknown causes was presumed to be responsible for the symptoms. As it became evident that brain damage may not necessarily underlie the syndrome, the term was then replaced by "minimal brain dysfunction" and eventually "hyperkinetic impulse disorder" (Laufer, Denhoff, & Solomons, 1957). Gradually, as the diagnostic terminology continued to move away from presumed etiology to terms that are simply descriptive of the symptoms, in the third edition of the *Diagnostic and Statistical Manual of Mental Disorders* (*DSM-III*; American Psychiatric Association [APA], 1980), the term "attention deficit disorder" was officially approved, and the diagnosis specified whether a particular person exhibited a variant with or without hyperactivity. The fourth edition (*DSM-IV*; APA, 1994), introduced the comprehensive term "attention deficit/hyperactivity disorder," a moniker that continues to be the official name of the syndrome at this time.

To diagnose ADHD per *DSM-IV* requirements, clinicians assess two dimensions of symptoms: hyperactivity/impulsivity and inattention. Depending on the specific variant evident in a given person, ADHD can be diagnosed as "predominantly hyperactive-impulsive type," "predominantly inattentive type," or "combined type." Individuals who present with enough symptoms from either (or both) clusters to negatively affect their adaptive functioning but not enough symptoms to meet all diagnostic criteria in either cluster can be diagnosed with ADHD "not otherwise specified."

Although the diagnosis of ADHD requires symptoms of the disorder to be present in a person before age 7 (APA, 2000, p. 92), there is no presumption in the diagnostic system about whether the symptoms remain into adulthood. The epidemiology and course of ADHD are discussed in more detail in the next chapter, but for now it must be noted that there is a significant number of boys with ADHD who do not "grow out" of the disorder and who continue to exhibit symptoms long after becoming adult men. These symptoms then become apparent in the course of usual adult lifestyle, including the workplace, intimate relationships, social adjustment, and so on. Thus, when reviewing symptoms of ADHD, one must consider the symptoms that are usually evident not only in childhood and adolescence but also in adulthood.

Boys, male teens, and men with ADHD commonly exhibit a variety of problems across different settings. In accordance with the *DSM-IV-TR* diagnostic guidelines, these symptoms fall along the dimensions of hyperactivity/impulsivity and inattentiveness, and they are often referred to as the "primary" or "core" symptoms, because they are presumed to be directly caused by the underlying etiology. A boy with ADHD, however, is a member of his family, his class, and his peer group, and his interactions with his parents, siblings, teachers, and peers are negatively affected by the core symptoms. Similarly, a man with ADHD is also a member of his peer group, his own family (which now usually includes both the current spouse and children and the continued relationship with his family of origin), and the workplace. In these settings, boys and men with ADHD commonly develop secondary symptoms that stem out of the primary difficulties and further exacerbate their difficulties with adaptive behaviors. Thus, any comprehensive discussion of the symptoms of ADHD must take into account both primary and secondary symptoms, across many settings, and must consider various age groups across which symptoms may be apparent.

CORE SYMPTOMS

Boys and men with ADHD exhibit difficulties along two behavioral dimensions: those of hyperactivity/impulsivity and distractibility. These are presumed to be separate clusters, and impairment in at least one of them is required for diagnosis, but patients sometimes exhibit symptoms that overlap and may fall into either cluster. In addition, various settings where symptoms are apparent must be reviewed, because symptoms in each cluster may present differently in diverse settings and situations. Various age groups must also be considered, because the presentation of symptoms from each category commonly changes with age.

Hyperactivity/Impulsivity

Many boys and men with ADHD exhibit impulsivity, but sometimes these symptoms may, at first glance, be overlooked. Individuals with ADHD often act with little forethought, exhibiting a knee-jerk reactivity to environmental events. The experience of an urge is universal. We all feel urges and impulses to do things and say things. When our ability to control these impulses is intact, we are able to process an urge and evaluate the consequences of our behaviors before we decide how to act or what to say. An impulsive individual, however, converts an impulse into action with limited cognitive processing. Thus, boys and men who are impulsive often say and do things that, in retrospect, they recognize they should not have done or said. For them, controlling their urges to say and do things is a major struggle.

Many boys who are impulsive are also hyperactive. Hyperactive boys usually exhibit a "driven by a motor" quality, a restlessness, and a need to constantly move about. Impulsivity and hyperactivity are closely related. Human beings constantly experience urges of various types. Some of these urges are impulses to say something, and others are impulses to move or do something. Those boys who have difficulties suppressing their urges to move are described as hyperactive. Thus, hyperactivity is one expression of the larger problem: a boy's difficulty to control his impulses.

Although impulsive boys are also likely to be hyperactive, adult men are less likely to continue to exhibit hyperkinetic behaviors. As discussed in the next chapter, boys who exhibited significant hyperactivity as children commonly lose some of the "driven by a motor" quality by middle adolescence, and hyperactivity as a symptom in adult men is more rare. A few adult males, however, retain the symptoms of hyperactivity long into their adult years.

Impulsivity and hyperactivity present differently in various settings and across different age groups. It is important for clinicians to review the patient's functioning in these settings to determine whether hyperactivity and/or impulsivity are present in different aspects of life. Such review is necessary to make the diagnosis, because the *DSM* requires the presence of the symptoms in at least two settings to make the diagnosis (APA, 2000, p. 92).

Home. Some symptoms of impulsivity are relatively obvious and easy to recognize. For example, a young boy will run out into the street to chase a ball, forgetting to look whether a car is coming his way. Although this behavior is typical of very young children, by the time boys reach school age, they are expected to use sufficient self-control to be able to suppress the impulse to chase the ball into the street and recognize that they need to first stop and look to see if doing so is safe. Boys with ADHD find this difficult, and so they may place themselves in danger because they seemingly act without thinking.

Of course, impulsivity is evident in day-to-day behaviors that do not necessarily reflect danger. Boys with ADHD have quick reactions and often act without thinking. This is evident in many decisions they make; for example, problems suppressing the impulse to continue playing when it is time to start doing homework, or difficulties accepting that it is time to stop watching television because it is time to start getting ready for bed. Boys who are impulsive frequently have difficulties accepting tasks that are not "fun"; for example, performing house chores or following a morning routine to get ready for school. Consequently, boys with ADHD frequently argue with their parents. This results in a number of secondary reactions, discussed later in this chapter.

Boys who are hyperactive exhibit additional management difficulties. They have problems sitting still at meals. They tend to use high levels of physical activity during play and can be very noisy. They are likely to roughhouse with siblings, which often results in conflicts. All in all, parents often find these behaviors frustrating, and therefore boys with ADHD frequently get reprimanded, scolded, and punished.

When boys become teens, hyperactivity usually becomes less apparent, but impulsivity may persist. Teenagers primarily display the symptoms of impulsivity in their decision making. Impulsive adolescents are more likely to make decisions with little forethought and may exhibit poor judgment, including spontaneously breaking house rules (e.g., going out of the home to see friends at inappropriate times, such as close to bedtime), frequently changing their mind about activities and interests, agreeing to partake in an event and deciding not to do it at the last minute, performing mischievous behaviors on the spur of the moment, and so on. Of course, the presence of these symptoms does not necessarily constitute the evidence of any psychological disorder. When impulsive behaviors and decisions are performed so frequently that the teen's day-to-day existence becomes adversely affected to a significant degree, however, problems with impulsivity may be apparent.

Like teens, adult men are less likely to exhibit symptoms of hyperactivity, but they may continue to exhibit impulsivity. Although to some degree teenagers may be impulsive because they enter a stage in their life when they test limits and experiment with the degree to which they can make their own decisions, men are presumed to have grown out of this developmental phase and usually are able to exercise more mature judgment. Thus, when notable impulsivity and poor judgment are evident in adult men, they may indicate clinical significance. Impulsive men continue to exhibit behaviors that are often regarded as immature: They have difficulties saving money and frequently neglect their financial obligations because they spontaneously decide to take trips, attend events, remodel the home, and so on, usually with little notice and preparation. In general, they frequently change interests, plans, and pursuits. The clinician must again be cautioned that a limited amount of these symptoms does not constitute psychopathology. In fact, adults who are able to maintain some spontaneity are often regarded as fun people, because they allow their life to be somewhat unpredictable. When an adult male, however, is so spontaneous and unpredictable that he seems to have difficulties living up to adult responsibilities, it is likely that clinically significant impulsivity is evident.

Although teens and men are less hyperactive, some do exhibit a high degree of hyperkinesis, which may present as restlessness during times when others in the family seem able to remain relatively still, such as during meals or when watching television. Rather than gross motor overreactivity, this restlessness can take the form of significant fidgeting with hands and feet, often accompanied by a subjective sense of restlessness or difficulties remaining seated (Murphy & Barkley, 1996a).

Out-of-Home Settings. Boys who are hyperactive/impulsive often exhibit difficulties in outside settings. When boys with ADHD accompany parents during shopping trips (e.g., in the supermarket), they are easily affected by what they see on the shelves, and they commonly place items into the shopping basket that caught their interest regardless of whether their parents allowed them to do so. When boys with ADHD see an item they want, they expect a parent to get it, and they usually tantrum when they do not get their own way. Hyperactive boys are also known to wander (or run) away from their parents in stores, requiring a chase that results in a power struggle to bring them under control.

In restaurants, boys with ADHD often present with similar problems. They find it difficult to sit still, and they impulsively wish to order items from the menu that their parents do not approve of. They tend to wander away from the table and require parents to chase after them. They are often loud during meals, and their parents often feel embarrassed.

Attendance at religious services is particularly difficult for boys with ADHD. In a church (or a similar place of worship) parishioners are usually expected to sit still, remain quiet, and follow the protocol of the services (stand during appropriate times, repeat certain phrases with the entire congregation, etc.). Boys with ADHD find it difficult to sit quietly for long periods of time, particularly during an event that does not hold their interest. Consequently, boys with ADHD typically stand out during religious ceremonies and annoy others with their loud and restless behaviors. Again, parents become embarrassed, and a conflict with the boy is likely to ensue.

As noted before, teens and adults with ADHD are less likely to exhibit significant hyperactivity, but impulsivity may continue to be evident. They may exhibit poor control over spending habits and seem unable to resist temptation when faced with an item they desire, even when they obviously cannot afford it. They may change plans on the spur of the moment, even if the planned event was previously agreed to and involved significant commitment of time and effort from others. They may agree to go to a specific place and come back at a specific time and then change their mind without notice about the destination or time to return, which may be very frustrating to parents and spouses. As previously noted, others will generally tend to describe the behaviors as immature and unpredictable.

Some teens and men may retain the motor restlessness they exhibited when younger and still have difficulties attending settings where it is necessary to remain quiet and still (such as religious events, theater performances, etc.). In addition, teens and males who present symptoms of impulsivity and hyperactivity often like activities that require high motor output, such as extreme sports. In fact, the preference for physical activities that involve some physical danger and risk taking has been reported as common among teens and males with ADHD (Drechsler, Rizzo, & Steinhausen, 2007). Risk-taking behaviors may also be exhibited in day-to-day behaviors. For example, men with ADHD are much more likely to have poor driving records and are prone to motor vehicle accidents (Barkley, 2006).

School and Work. Boys who are impulsive and hyperactive have difficulties remaining still during lectures and tend to be disruptive in the classroom. At times, they may leave their desk and interfere with other students' efforts to pay attention in class. Young boys with ADHD, those who are in kindergarten, first grade, and second grade, are also known to call out without raising their hand. When a teacher asks a question of the class, boys with ADHD who know the answer experience a strong urge to respond, and because their impulse control is poor, they find it difficult to suppress that urge. Thus, whereas other children raise their hand to indicate that they know the answer, boys with ADHD call it out right after they hear the question. Teachers usually do not appreciate this behavior and reprimand those students.

Boys who are hyperactive/impulsive are especially known to present with difficulties in settings with less structure. During lunch, on the playground, in the gym class, or during music and art classes, boys with

ADHD easily become overstimulated by the amount of activity, sound, and movement that is going on around them, further reducing their ability to exercise self-control.

Teenagers and men with ADHD may continue to be fidgety and impulsive. As a consequence, their abilities to succeed in high school and college may be significantly compromised. They may feel restless in classes and have difficulties sitting through lectures and presentations. When trying to complete assignments, they may find it hard to remain in one place long enough to do any significant amount of productive work. They may change their mind frequently about what field of study they want to pursue or what classes they want to take. They may frequently drop out of classes or fall behind because of missing assignments. Generally, boys with ADHD are much more likely to leave high school without graduating (Hinshaw, 2002) and are much less likely to complete a college education (Johnston, 2002).

Impulsive men also present safety risks within the workplace. When performing tasks that require safety precautions, they may impulsively skip a step or decide to do a portion of the routine differently, thus compromising their ability to perform the task safely. Indeed, men with ADHD are often described as accident prone, are more likely to be involved in accidents at work, and are at a higher risk for work-related injuries (Barkley, 2006).

Peer Relationships. Boys with ADHD often exhibit difficulties while interacting with their peers. Impulsive children have difficulties sharing their toys. Boys with ADHD often find it hard to suppress their impulse to possess and control the toy entirely, and they feel encroached upon when another child wants to play with that toy. They are likely to overreact and consequently are perceived by their peers as bossy and controlling.

During play activities, boys with ADHD often like to remain in charge and have difficulties accepting that rules must be arrived at by consensus. When another child suggests a rule that the boy with ADHD disagrees with, he has difficulties resisting the impulse to resist and often becomes argumentative. When the dispute is not resolved to his satisfaction, a boy with ADHD is likely to "take his ball and go home." Peers are likely to avoid interacting with a boy who exhibits such behaviors.

Boys with ADHD also have difficulties joining an existing social activity. When seeing a group of friends talking or playing, a boy with ADHD is likely to barge in and try to take over the activity. Peers often resent such behaviors and tend to avoid playing with such a child. All in all, boys with ADHD are known to exhibit difficulties making friends and are often rejected by peers (Asarnow, 1988).

These problems tend to persist into the teenage and adult years, and peer rejection is considered to be predictive of long-term difficulties in social relationships (Parker & Asher, 1987). Indeed, boys and men with ADHD seldom form long-lasting friendships and are often uncomfortable in group settings. Teens and adults with ADHD may avoid social settings, such as social gatherings and parties. When there, they may feel that they need to outperform others in their attempts to be liked. Although they are often described as bossy and controlling, individuals with ADHD generally tend to become followers rather than leaders of social groups, because they strive hard to be accepted by others. For this reason, teens and men with ADHD are at a significant risk of succumbing to peer pressure, particularly with regard to experimenting with substances or taking part in mischief and behaviors that break laws.

Distractibility/Disorganization

Another dimension of symptoms of ADHD pertains to difficulties sustaining attention. It is important, however, to recognize that distractibility is not the lack of ability to pay attention. Rather, it is the reduced ability to filter out distractions in the environment that interfere with sustaining attention on the primary task. Thus, one cannot say that boys with ADHD do not pay attention. Rather, they pay attention to *everything* around them, thus constantly diverting their focus from a primary stimulus (e.g., a teacher talking in the classroom) to distractions around them (e.g., noises in the hallway, a classmate moving about at his desk, etc.).

Boys who are distractible usually are also disorganized. As a result, they have difficulties keeping track of their things, and they frequently lose toys, homework assignments, books, and so on. Distractibility and disorganization are conceptually related. Mental effort is required to be able to sustain attention and filter out distractions. It takes similar mental effort to remember to do something or memorize where an item was placed. Those boys who have difficulties with these mental activities frequently have problems with both distractibility and disorganization.

As with symptoms from the hyperactive/impulsive cluster, symptoms of distractibility and disorganization are usually evident across various settings.

Home. Problems with distractibility and disorganization are often more subtle. These involve difficulties keeping track of one's possessions and generally appearing to be disorganized. Those boys often misplace toys, clothing, and other items of interest. Because they easily get distracted or sidetracked, they need a lot of supervision to complete their morning routine, homework, and so on. They often do not exhibit the level of independence that parents expect, and therefore parents often find these boys frustrating to manage.

As boys become teens and men, their responsibilities and expectations increase. Distractibility and disorganization, however, impair their ability to exhibit age-appropriate responsibility and follow-through. They may easily lose track of deadlines to complete assignments, file appropriate documents (such as tax forms), or pay bills. They may forget to renew their car insurance, registration, or driver's license. They may misplace important personal things, such as date books, calendars, checkbooks, and other documents. When parents or spouses attempt to help, they usually become frustrated because the items in question (such as bills or legal documents) may be lost or accidentally discarded. These problems often lead to significant conflicts within the family and a diminished level of independence evident in the functioning of the teen or male with ADHD.

School and Work. Boys who are distractible and disorganized also present with academic difficulties. Because they lose focus during class, they miss portions of the class content and may derive limited benefit from the teacher's lectures and classroom activities. They lose track of their assignments and require a significant amount of redirection to remain on task. When it is time to write down their homework assignment, boys with ADHD often miss what is being assigned and forget to bring home necessary books, handouts, and notebooks. The disorganization they exhibit is often frustrating to their teachers. The book bags, desks, and lockers of boys with ADHD are often very messy and unkempt. It is common for boys with ADHD to lose track of what they have in their book bag or desk and to retain items in there long after they are no longer necessary. In frustration, some teachers have been known to dump the contents of the desk of a boy with ADHD on the floor, in an attempt to teach him to become more organized. Unfortunately, this only embarrasses him and produces no benefits. Rather, the boy probably learned to dislike his teacher, and school in general, even more than he did before.

Teens and adult males usually continue to exhibit these difficulties, and consequently their ability to complete further education is adversely affected. Teens with ADHD are more likely to exhibit academic failure and drop out of school more frequently than teens with any other psychological disorders (Barkley, 2006). Much of this is due to their continued impairment in their abilities to organize and track their responsibilities, and they miss assignments and deadlines. Even when they attempt to perform assigned work, distractibility affects their ability to remain on task and read, write, or otherwise complete academic tasks productively. These problems continue to impair males with ADHD as they enter college, and males with ADHD have been shown to maintain an academic grade point average (GPA) that is generally 1 point lower than that of controls (Barkley, 2006). By some accounts, only 5% of males with ADHD complete college (Weiss & Hechtman, 1993).

Often, work functioning is similarly problematic. Males with ADHD change jobs frequently and are likely to get dismissed because they forget to perform assigned tasks, misplace work-related materials, and generally fail to attend to their responsibilities. Because they have difficulties remembering rules and routines, they are more likely to perform tasks inappropriately, sometimes resulting in injuries. Consequently, males with ADHD are less likely to advance in the workplace and generally earn less than individuals without ADHD (Barkley, 2002). Men with ADHD are more likely to be unemployed and experience financial hardship. These problems affect not only their socioeconomic status but also their personal and family life.

SECONDARY SYMPTOMS

What is it like for males with ADHD to go through life with symptoms of this disorder? Their existence is usually filled with much stress and conflict. Some symptoms (especially those in the impulsive cluster) predispose them to interpersonal conflicts and related difficulties, and all symptoms of ADHD are likely to affect self-esteem and motivation. It is important for clinicians to screen clients for these additional dimensions of symptoms that commonly accompany the core symptoms of this disorder.

Poor Frustration Tolerance

Those boys and men who are impulsive often exhibit limited ability to deal with frustration. When a person, any person, faces a situation that did not come out as planned or one where preferred action is not possible, that person experiences an internal feeling of frustration, an urge that may be accompanied by a thought such as "I don't like this." Day-to-day life frequently places one in such situations: A sibling is playing with a toy or a game that you would like to play with, a parent is not allowing you to continue playing and tells you to start doing something else, or a video game activity does not come out as you expected and you did not achieve the score you hoped for. Boys who are not particularly impulsive gradually learn to accept such situations as part of normal life. Boys with ADHD, however, have difficulties dealing with this frustration and usually display it more strongly and openly by defying the parent or exhibiting an emotional outburst (such as throwing the game controllers across the room).

Those boys who retain a significant degree of impulsivity into the teenage and adult years usually continue to exhibit significant problems with frustration tolerance. This is especially evident in their relationships with parents and spouses. Healthy adjustment in interpersonal relationships requires the recognition that compromises are necessary and the acceptance that one cannot get his own way all the time. Teens and men with ADHD often are described as selfish, because they have difficulties suppressing the urge to express their frustration when things do not go their way. This predisposes them to conflicts and places much stress on their interpersonal relationships.

Defiance

When a boy is playing with a video game and a parent says, "Stop playing because it's time to do your homework," the initial reaction of most boys will be to resist the change and continue with the activity that they are enjoying at the moment. Those who have good impulse control will experience that internal urge to resist, but before they choose a response, they will process the situation and recognize that resisting will result only in a negative outcome (e.g., getting yelled at). Consequently, they select a reaction *after* thinking through their alternatives. Instead, those who are impulsive have difficulties delaying the reaction to perform such processing, and *before* thinking about it, they express the negative urge through protests, arguments, and downright defiance. Indeed, males with ADHD who are impulsive are usually also described as defiant. Although it is common for impulsive males to be described as "strong-willed," in reality the more accurate term would be "weak-willed," because the defiance is really a symptom of limited self-control to suppress an internal urge.

Defiant boys tend to get into frequent conflicts with figures of authority, because parents and teachers usually do not appreciate oppositional reactions. This pattern often continues into adulthood and causes significant work-related difficulties. Males with ADHD often argue with coworkers, supervisors, and employers. When told to perform something they do not like, impulsive males often express their dislike and may refuse to do what they are told. As a result, it is common for males with ADHD to change employment frequently, usually when a boss gets tired of the arguments, protests, and defiance and decides to replace the employee.

Problems With Control Over Emotional Discharges

When boys with ADHD face a situation where an emotional reaction was invoked, their limited self-control makes it hard for them to suppress that reaction. This is especially evident when negative feelings were awakened, such as when they became frustrated or saddened. Boys with ADHD are frequently described as "angry children." This is a misnomer. They are not quintessentially angry. Rather, they are reactive, in that they have difficulties suppressing the initial urge to react, and they externalize whatever they feel inside. Because boys with ADHD are often on the receiving end of the anger response, however, they sometimes do become angry children. Because boys with ADHD are more likely to get scolded and punished, they learn to expect that those around them usually give them a hard time.

Teens and males with ADHD often continue to be quite reactive. This predisposes them to overreact in situations when they become frustrated. At work, men with ADHD are likely to become involved in arguments and altercations. They are often described as volatile and are more likely to be fired. As a result, their problems with maintaining employment exacerbate further. With spouses, they are likely to argue and are often described as explosive. This contributes to the strain they experience in interpersonal relationships.

In fact, males with ADHD are likely to act out aggressively when they are angry and frustrated, and they are generally regarded by their peers as more aggressive (Hinshaw, 2002). There is a reciprocal relationship between ADHD and aggression. The more aggressively a man behaves, even when the display of negative emotion remains verbal rather than physical, the more likely he is to be rejected by peers. This, in turn, further predisposes males with ADHD to act aggressively when they expect that their colleagues and coworkers will reject them. This self-defeating loop often contributes significantly to the overall functional impairment of males with ADHD.

Problems With Regulation of Mood

Difficulties with self-control that boys with ADHD commonly experience permeate several areas of their daily functioning. One of these relates to their ability to modulate the expression of negative affect. When upset, boys with ADHD are likely to express those feelings with much greater intensity, sometimes losing control over their emotions. This is evident throughout their development. For example, angry young boys with ADHD may exhibit severe tantrums that require physical restraining by the parent. When older, boys with ADHD are likely to hit or throw things when they are upset. It is common for boys with ADHD to trash their room when they are punished or restricted. Parents are often surprised at the intensity of these outbursts, especially because between these episodes, boys with ADHD usually do not display the "chip on their shoulder" attitude commonly associated with boys who are chronically agitated or depressed.

In school and with peers, this tendency to exaggerate the expression of negative affect presents similar difficulties. Boys with ADHD are more likely to lose control and get into physical altercations with peers. Some of these altercations may occur when the amount of provocation is relatively limited, for example, when boys are playfully teased. Similarly, when angered by their teachers, boys with ADHD may become so agitated that they throw something that is within their reach or turn over a desk. Because teachers cannot tolerate such behaviors, these boys are much more likely to receive serious punishment, including detentions, suspensions, and expulsion from school (Barkley, 2006).

As adults, males with ADHD often continue to exhibit this emotional overreactivity in various aspects of their life. They are more likely to get into severe conflicts (at times including physical fights) with coworkers. Often, this causes them to be fired. Similarly, their relationships with adult peers tend to be similarly volatile, and males with ADHD are much more likely to get into physical fights. This tendency is especially evident when they become upset in an environment that overstimulates them, such as at a party or in a club with loud music and noise all around them.

Because males with ADHD express negative emotions more intensely, their personal relationships are negatively affected. Men with ADHD are much more likely to exhibit marital conflict, and they end up divorced (Weiss & Hechtman, 1993). As fathers, men with ADHD tend to be more rigid and less accepting of their children's transgressions, however minor they may be. Consequently, their relationships with their children are often strained and distant (Lifford, Harold, & Thapar, 2008).

Low Self-Esteem

Whether or not they are impulsive, boys with ADHD usually experience academic difficulties. Because the symptoms of the disorder affect the ability of boys with ADHD to complete their work, their grades usually suffer. For example, they commonly lose track of assignments, misplace books and handouts, and find it difficult to remain focused through the length of time required to complete assignments. Over time, repeated experience of academic failure becomes internalized. Boys with ADHD may not recognize why they seem to get lower grades, but they do recognize that they do not seem to succeed as easily as many of their peers, and they often conclude that they are not very smart. Indeed, boys with ADHD commonly exhibit lower self-esteem than their nonaffected peers (Bird, 2002).

Low self-esteem is a significant risk factor for additional emotional and functional difficulties. Although only about one fifth of the boys with ADHD exhibit comorbid depression, by the time they become adults (Barkley, 2006), 50% to 66% of males with ADHD exhibit a comorbid depressive disorder (dysthymia or major depression; Ramsay & Rostain, 2008). Although the exact cause-and-effect relationship of this progression has not been established, it is reasonable to expect that low-self-esteem, already evident in childhood, gradually becomes exacerbated by the continued experience of failure in interpersonal, academic, vocational, and social settings, and the internalization of these failures contributes to the development of depression.

Low Motivation

As discussed previously, boys with ADHD are more likely to incur academic failure and adverse consequences, such as detentions, suspensions, and expulsion from school. These experiences affect their self-concept and self-esteem, and boys with ADHD often feel "dumber" than their peers. As boys with ADHD internalize these feelings, their sense of self-efficacy becomes compromised. Boys with ADHD often conclude that they cannot succeed academically, and their motivation to try hard to do their homework and study becomes increasingly limited. Often, parents and teachers of boys and teens with ADHD are surprised by the inadequate effort that these students exhibit. It is important to appreciate that this lack of motivation developed over many years. As symptoms of ADHD gradually made it more and more difficult to complete academic work, lower grades ensued, and a decrease in self-esteem followed. These factors are exacerbated by the emotional reactivity and volatility that males with ADHD commonly exhibit, thus resulting in frequent conflicts and a sense of disapproval and rejection. Over time, these factors combine and result in limited motivation to achieve.

As boys and teens with ADHD mature into adulthood, these patterns continue. Limited academic achievement signals to the male that he should not expect to pursue further schooling, because he may not do well in college. As males with ADHD enter the workforce, they find that they get into frequent conflicts with bosses and coworkers, and in addition they may find many work tasks difficult (especially those that require organizational skills and sustained focus) and frustrating. Their personal and social life may also be filled with failure and conflicts. All in all, males with ADHD are likely to conclude that it is not worth it to try to achieve and improve their life, and studies have shown that males with ADHD are likely to exhibit symptoms of learned helplessness (Ramsay & Rostain, 2008).

SUMMARY

Boys and males with ADHD exhibit both primary and secondary symptoms associated with this disorder. Core symptoms are those that stem directly from the underlying etiology, and they include hyperactivity/impulsivity and inattentiveness/disorganization. Symptoms that fall into these clusters result in significant functional difficulties across many settings, including home and family, school and workplace, and peer relations.

In addition, symptoms of ADHD usually result in secondary difficulties that progressively become apparent with age. Impulsive males tend to exhibit problems with defiance, limited self-control, emotional overreactivity, and limited abilities to regulate their affective expression. As they continue to experience frequent conflicts, failure, and rejection, low self-esteem and limited motivation commonly become apparent. Clinicians need to screen for all of these primary and secondary symptoms to gain a comprehensive understanding of the difficulties that boys, male teens, and men with ADHD commonly exhibit.

2

Epidemiology and Course

Much has been written about the epidemiology and course of attention deficit/hyperactivity disorder (ADHD). Some reports in the media have accused mental health professionals of overdiagnosing ADHD. In addition, confusion remains over the disorder's course—some report lifelong impairment, whereas others seem to mostly "grow out" of symptoms by late adolescence. It is important for mental health professionals to examine these issues to form accurate expectations.

EPIDEMIOLOGY

Because ADHD has been recognized for several decades, it is helpful to review diagnostic trends to determine whether the prevalence has remained consistent. In addition, ADHD has traditionally been considered to emerge primarily in childhood and adolescence. Consequently, diagnostic criteria are written to reflect primarily problem behaviors that are specific to those age groups. As a result, males who continue to exhibit impairment into adult years may no longer meet the disorder's diagnostic criteria, even though functional difficulties may still be apparent. Also, it has been believed that boys do, in fact, grow out of the disorder with age. Thus, epidemiological data are likely to be different across age groups, and the discussion must focus separately on pediatric and adult data.

Pediatric Data

ADHD was first included in the *Diagnostic and Statistical Manual of Mental Disorders* (*DSM-III*; American Psychiatric Association [APA], 1980), as attention deficit disorder (ADD) with and without hyperactivity. The *DSM-III* estimated the prevalence of ADD with hyperactivity to be about 3% of prepubertal children (p. 42) and estimated the ratio of boys to girls to be about 10 to 1. The *DSM-III* did not include prevalence data for ADD without hyperactivity or ADD, residual type. In the *DSM-III-R* (APA, 1987), diagnostic criteria for hyperactivity/impulsivity and distractibility/disorganization were incorporated into one diagnosis (ADHD), and prevalence was again reported to be about 3% of children (p. 51). It was suggested that, according to clinic samples, the disorder is six to nine times more common in boys, but it was acknowledged that community samples revealed less drastic sex differences and that the disorder was three times more common in males.

In the 1990s, the *DSM-IV* (APA, 1994) adopted the two-cluster model of ADHD that is still used today. The prevalence was estimated at 3% to 5% of school-age children (p. 82), and the male-to-female ratio was reported to range from 4:1 to 9:1, depending on type of sample (community vs. clinical). The current version of the *DSM* (*DSM-IV-TR*; APA, 2000) estimates the prevalence as 3% to 7% of school-age children (p. 90), and the sex ratio is estimated at 2:1 to 9:1, depending on the type of symptom presentation ("predominantly inattentive" type has less pronounced sex differences) and setting. After a review of the progression of prevalence as reported in the successive editions of the *DSM*, it is apparent that estimates have increased, although not dramatically. The lower end of the estimate remains to be about 3% of school-age children, as reported originally in the *DSM-III*, although the *DSM-IV-TR* acknowledges that the range may extend up to 7%.

Researchers have pondered the reasons why such an increase may be apparent. Barkley (2006) suggested that this change is due to the inclusion in the *DSM-IV* of a new subtype of ADHD, "predominantly hyperactive-impulsive" (PH-I) type. Prior to the *DSM-IV*, ADD was typically diagnosed as occurring with or without hyperactivity, and inattention was assumed to be present in both variants. By allowing ADHD to be diagnosed without inattentiveness, prevalence may increase. This appears to be only a partial explanation, however. Readers will note that when the PH-I type was included in the *DSM-IV*, estimates varied from a low of 3% (no change from prior *DSM* data) to a high of 5% (an increase from prior *DSM* versions) of school-age children. When the *DSM-IV-TR* was released, the diagnostic criteria were not changed, but the prevalence was reported as varying from 3% (as with all prior versions of *DSM*) to 7% (further increase of 2% since the *DSM-IV*) of school-age children. Thus, although the increase is small, there is evidence of a further rise in the diagnosis of ADHD from the *DSM-IV* to the *DSM-IV-TR*, with no changes in diagnostic criteria. Readers should note, however, that just because the upper limit of the range has changed, this does not necessarily indicate that the median rate of diagnosis is any different. These results merely indicate that some of the epidemiological studies reviewed in preparation of the *DSM-IV-TR* revealed prevalence in the higher range. Unfortunately, because the

DSM did not cite these studies, there is no way to tell what data were reviewed to arrive at those figures.

Some studies have specifically examined the prevalence of ADHD, PH-I type. Brown et al. (2001) reviewed epidemiological studies that used a variety of diagnostic criteria, including those that diagnosed ADHD in accordance with *DSM-IV* subtypes. Results revealed a median prevalence of 6.8% for any subtype, 3.2% for inattentive subtype, and 2.9% for combined subtype. This means that the PH-I subtype accounted for less than 1% of all cases. Similar data are available from studies that used International Statistical Classification of Diseases and Related Health Problems, 10th Revision (ICD-10; World Health Organization, 1992), which allow for diagnosis of ADHD based on hyperkinetic symptoms only. Two studies that used this approach revealed prevalence of this subtype to fall around 1% (Bird, 2002). Thus, it is apparent that the PH-I subtype of ADHD is most rare, and its inclusion in the *DSM-IV* may account for only about a 1% rise in the prevalence of ADHD.

Non-*DSM* epidemiological data reveal much wider variability in rates of ADHD. Before 1980, no consistent diagnostic standards existed for ADHD, and results of those studies are likely to be unreliable. Consequently, when rates of prevalence are reviewed, only data using *DSM-III* (or subsequent) diagnostic criteria are included. Studies that used *DSM-III* criteria obtained prevalence estimates that ranged from about 2% to 3% (Bird, 2002), but some studies have suggested that ADD may be present in up to 20% of school-aged children (DuPaul, 1991). Studies that used *DSM-III-R* diagnostic criteria reported a similar range, from a low of about 2% (Bird, 2002) up to a high of about 22% (DuPaul, 1991). It is apparent that these estimates varied widely, although aggregate data seemed to suggest that most epidemiological estimates using *DSM-III* or *DSM-III-R* criteria hovered around 5% or 6% (Bird, 2002). Although it may be expected that using *DSM-IV* diagnostic criteria may result in increased rates of diagnosis, available data seem to indicate that most studies report a median prevalence of about 5% (Bird, 2002). Thus, for more than two decades, the rates of diagnosing the disorder have remained rather stable, and our current estimates of median prevalence actually are slightly lower than those reported in the 1980s. Thus, any suspicion that there is widespread overdiagnosing of ADHD appears unfounded.

In addition, since the 1980s clinicians and researchers have pondered the cutoff points used to make diagnostic classifications. The *DSM* system identifies the symptoms necessary to make the diagnosis but does not specify how high above the mean the symptoms must be evident to make the diagnosis, and establishing the cutoff on assessment measures (e.g., those discussed in Chapter 4) where normal function ends and impairment begins was left to clinicians and researchers. Through the 1980s and 1990s, the clinical cutoff has been established at 1.5 standard deviations above the mean, and anyone scoring above this cutoff was regarded as exhibiting symptoms severe enough to potentially warrant the diagnosis. Barkley (2006) has long argued, however, that this cutoff overclassifies children and artificially inflates diagnostic rates. Instead, he has proposed that a cutoff of 2 standard deviations above the mean is necessary to make an accurate diagnosis of ADHD. Using these limits, prevalence of 2% to 9% has been reported when using *DSM-III-R* criteria, and rates of 7% to 9% have been reported when *DSM-IV* diagnostic criteria are employed (Barkley, 2006). The *DSM-IV-TR* (APA, 2000) reports prevalence of between 3% and 7% and is explained to be derived by "expert consensus" (Ramsay & Rostain, 2008). Using these data, it can be estimated that somewhere between 1 in 15 and 1 in 30 school-age children meet the diagnostic criteria for the disorder.

ADHD is a disorder that is recognized in many countries around the world. Canadian data have reported that the prevalence of ADHD in Canada is similar to that in the United States (Barkley, 2006). One Australian study also reported a similar mean prevalence of about 7% (Graetz, Sawyer, Hazell, Arney, & Baghurst, 2001), whereas studies in New Zealand have shown prevalence between 2% and 7% (Barkley, 2006). European rates vary widely, from a low of about 1% in the Netherlands (Kroes et al., 2001) to a high of about 17.8% in Germany (Baumgaertel, Wolraich, & Dietrich, 1995). Asian data also vary, from about 6% in China (Leung et al., 1996) to a high of about 29% reported in parts of India (Bhatia, Nigam, Bohra, & Malik, 1991). Although the exact interpretation of this data is difficult, one conclusion that can safely be made is that ADHD is a worldwide phenomenon and has been found in every country in which it has been studied (Barkley, 2006).

In addition, it must be remembered that just because 3% to 7% of children in the United States exhibit symptoms of ADHD, these children do not necessarily receive needed treatment. In one study, although almost 9% of youngsters age 8 through 15 were reported to meet the diagnostic criteria for ADHD, less than half were receiving treatment (Froehlich et al., 2007). It is true that symptoms of ADHD are the primary reason why a child or adolescent is brought in for mental health treatment, and ADHD is the most prevalent pediatric mental health disorder found in clinical samples and accounts for nearly one third of all visits for mental health treatment in the pediatric population (National Center for Health Statistics, 1994). Still, when actual numbers are reconciled with the estimated national prevalence (as reported in the *DSM-IV-TR*), at best only 50% of children with diagnosable ADHD have received any form of treatment (Angold et al., 1998), and only 24% have received any form of school services (Jensen et al., 1999). Thus, it is apparent that rather than overdiagnosing the disorder, clinicians seem to undertreat it.

Adult Data

Examining the prevalence of adult ADHD is difficult. To begin with, it must be determined how such prevalence should be established. Prevalence data are usually reported by calculating the proportion of individuals in a given sample that meet the diagnostic criteria for this disorder. Such studies are rare. Weyandt, Linterman, and Rice (1995) found that when they used the cutoff of 1 and a half standard deviations above the mean, 2.5% of adults in a community sample met the diagnostic criteria for ADHD. When the cutoff was adjusted to fall at 2 standard deviations above the mean, the prevalence rate dropped to 0.5%. In another sample, however, 4.7% of adults were found to meet the *DSM-IV* diagnostic criteria with a cutoff of 2 standard deviations (Murphy & Barkley, 1996b). Either way, however, it is apparent that adult prevalence is lower than that reported for school-age children.

Another way to estimate the adult prevalence is to examine the rates of continuation of a formally diagnosed pediatric ADHD into adulthood. Once again, estimates vary. When full diagnostic criteria are used, 5% (Johnston, 2002) to 50% (Claude & Firestone, 1995) of children previously diagnosed with the disorder still meet the diagnostic criteria in adulthood. There is considerable dissatisfaction with the use of *DSM* criteria to diagnose adult ADHD, however, because the symptom descriptions were written to reflect behaviors common to children and adolescents rather than adults. Indeed, Weiss and Hechtman (1993) reported that 66% of adults previously (in childhood) diagnosed with ADHD still exhibited functional difficulties stemming from continued symptoms, although most no longer met the *DSM*'s full diagnostic criteria for ADHD.

Sex Differences

Over 100 years ago, when Still (1902) wrote about the disorder that eventually became known as ADHD, he already noted that males outnumbered females by a ratio of 3 to 1. Over the years, although the name of the disorder changed many times and our understanding of it increased, most researchers continued to find these sex differences. In current pediatric data, the ratio of boys to girls with ADHD is reported to be between 3:1 and 10:1 (Bird, 2002), and most boys with ADHD outnumber girls about 5:1 to 9:1 in samples referred for clinical treatment (Barkley, 2006). Consequently, it is apparent that boys present with symptoms of this disorder more commonly than girls do and are brought for treatment much more frequently.

To further understand this trend, researchers must examine the symptom patterns. Much research has found that boys are more likely to present with hyperactive/impulsive symptoms and related impairment. For example, boys with ADHD are much more likely to exhibit "externalizing" symptoms (Barkley, 2006), and boys (much more so than girls) with ADHD are likely to exhibit conduct problems in school (deHaas, 1986). More recent meta-analyses confirmed these findings and revealed that whether community, school, or clinical samples were studied, boys were more likely to be disruptive, hyperactive, and aggressive (Gaub & Carlson, 1997). Other studies similarly found that girls had about half the rates of comorbid disruptive disorders (such as con-duct disorder or oppositional defiant disorder) and rule-breaking behav-ior (Barkley, 2006).

Conversely, researchers (e.g., Biederman et al., 2002) have found that girls with ADHD are more likely to present with distractibility and related difficulties, including greater cognitive deficits. It is interesting, however, that even though the girls in the sample exhibited slightly lower intellectual functioning, they were at lower risk for learning diffi-culties and exhibited fewer overall problems in school. Thus it is appar-ent that even though boys with ADHD seem to exhibit symptoms of inattentiveness less frequently than girls with ADHD do, when boys do exhibit those symptoms, they are more impairing and result in more significant functional difficulties.

There are many reasons for these sex differences. Some of these rea-sons may be related to biological differences that predispose males to more developmental and medical complications. ADHD is far from being the only pediatric mental health disorder that affects boys to a greater degree. In fact, the majority of psychological disorders listed in the *DSM* are more prevalent in boys, and for those disorders that are more common in adult females, rates during childhood are similar in males and females, indicating that males seem to exhibit an earlier onset of these disorders. In other aspects of development and health, similar differences are apparent. Most pregnancies result in a male embryo, but male fetuses are miscarried more frequently. Male infants are more likely to be born with birth defects. Seven out of the 10 more common childhood infections are more prevalent in boys. Boys are more likely to suffer from learning disorders, and male teens are more likely to com-mit suicide. As one reporter put it, males are really the "weaker sex" (Legato, 2006).

Sex differences in the human brain have been identified by many researchers. Males have a higher proportion of cortical white matter (myelinated axons) and cerebrospinal fluid, whereas females have a greater proportion of the cortex devoted to gray matter (somatodendritic tissue) (Gur et al., 1999). Differences in the size of corpus callosum have also been identified (Pinker, 2002). In addition, in men, the percentage of gray matter is higher in the left hemisphere, the percentage of white matter is symmetric, and the percentage of cerebrospinal fluid is higher in the right hemisphere. In women, no asymmetries have been iden-tified. These differences may account for the differences in cognitive functioning of the two sexes, for example, better verbal skills in women and better spatial skills in men. Men generally devote more energy to modality-specific functions, including motor control, whereas women devote more energy to integrative and subcortical functions, including the processing of emotions. Female brains seem to distribute processing across diverse regions of the brain, whereas male brains are notably more compartmentalized in processing. Some researchers have suggested that this organization of the brain makes it easier for women to perform multitasking, whereas men seem to do better when they are able to devote all mental energy to one task at a time (Moir & Jessel, 1989).

As children, girls exhibit superior sensory processing and tend to engage more readily with adults. On the other hand, boys do not like to observe as much, do not exhibit a strong preference for interpersonal engagement, tend to talk more, and are more active. As children become adults, cyclic rhythms of female hormones seem to affect processing of emotions, whereas greater amounts of testosterone in men have been correlated with more aggression (Moir & Jessel, 1989), although findings of research studies in this area are inconsistent. Other findings, however, suggest that males may be more biologically predisposed to aggression. For example, stimulation of the amygdala in males seems to result in more aggressive behaviors, whereas stimulation of the amygdala in females seems to result in anxiety. Similar differences in the functioning of the hypothalamus have also been identified, and consistent sex differences in sizes of various hypothalamic nuclei seem evident. In addition, a consistent, inverse relationship has been found between aggression and serotonin levels in both men and women. Moreover, female brains seem to have greater levels of serotonin than male brains do. One reason for this difference may be that female brains have significantly lower levels of transporter molecules involved in the reuptake of serotonin (Jovanovic et al., 2008).

All in all, results of brain studies suggest that males are more predisposed to aggression, devote more brain power to motor control, and are more comfortable processing tasks that do not require extensive integrative functions. These tendencies are evident in the expression of the symptoms of ADHD. As described previously, males with ADHD tend to be more aggressive and are much more likely to present with hyperactivity. Conversely, because attention is an integrative function that requires the coordinated use of several brain regions, it seems logical that the female brain would be more predisposed to these difficulties.

Of course, biological factors cannot be examined separately from environmental influences. The nature–nurture controversy has been debated for generations, and today it is clear that mutual interaction between the two is responsible for human development (Siegel, 1999). Although a genetic blueprint for development is present at birth, these genetic instructions must be activated during specific developmental windows. Thus, socialization, particularly including the influence of caregivers, is a crucial component that affects both biological and psychological development.

Boys and girls are driven by intense emotional experiences during early development (Robertson & Shepard, 2008). As boys develop, their parents provide the primary source of learning, followed by teachers and peers. They shape the boys' identities by modeling behaviors and preferentially responding to those behaviors deemed appropriate by them from each sex. Thus, boys get socialized in accordance with a "boy code" (David & Brannon, 1976). As summarized by Robertson and Shepard (2008), boys "should be stoic and must not show weakness by sharing pain or displaying grief"; "should demonstrate daring, bravado, and an attraction to violence"; and "should not express tender feelings such as dependence, warmth, and empathy" (p. 16). It is clear that the "male" expression of the symptoms of ADHD is consistent with those expectations.

It is interesting that when prevalence of adult ADHD is examined in clinical samples, it is apparent that the ratio of males to females is closer to equal (Johnston, 2002), despite the fact that prevalence rates in nonclinical samples heavily favor males. It is clear that females (with any psychological disorder) are more likely to self-refer and seek treatment, whereas males with ADHD (or other psychological disorders) are more likely to resist mental health treatment. Boys, male teens, and men are socialized to suppress open expression of vulnerable emotions, and social norms that reinforce these rules can be particularly insidious. Boys are socialized to inhibit emotional language development, and the consequences of breaking these rules can be severe: Males who express tender feelings too openly are seen by others as weak and emasculated. This starts early in life—fathers tend to suppress the use of words that convey sadness, pain, or fear when speaking with their sons—and is reinforced further by cruel consequences boys experience from their peers—boys, male teens, and men who openly express sadness, pain, or anxiety are often referred to as weak and are usually rejected.

As with children and adolescents, men and women present symptoms differently. Males are more likely to present with restlessness and impulsivity and exhibit continued disruptive behaviors, reckless driving, problems with substance abuse, difficulties with self-control, poor judgment, explosiveness, and aggression. Conversely, women who are impulsive are less likely to express it aggressively and instead exhibit more problems with inappropriate spending habits, sexual acting out, and unplanned pregnancies. Men and women who continue to exhibit symptoms of inattentiveness tend to exhibit similar impairment, such as forgetting things, lacking responsibility in attending to bills and work duties, losing things easily, and having difficulties sustaining attention during reading and academic tasks.

Adults with ADHD are also much more likely to exhibit comorbid disorders; by some accounts, three out of four adults with ADHD exhibit another diagnosable psychological disorder (Biederman, 2004). Patterns of these comorbidities reveal that men and women commonly present with different associated symptoms. Although depression is common in both men and women with ADHD, men are socialized to suppress verbal expression of these feelings and therefore are much more likely to present variants associated with agitation, anger, and aggression. Conduct problems are also much more common in males with ADHD, and men more commonly exhibit problems with the law and substance abuse. For this reason, clinicians working with males with ADHD must recognize that not only is the pattern of core symptoms somewhat different but the presentation of comorbid disorders and associated features are also dissimilar. Consequently, clinicians treating boys, male teens, or men with ADHD must specifically be prepared to address the symptom pattern that is especially common in males with ADHD.

COURSE

ADHD is classified in the *DSM* system as a disorder that is usually first evident in infancy, childhood, or adolescence. In fact, criterion B in the diagnostic criteria (*DSM-IV-TR*; APA, 2000) requires symptoms that cause impairment to be present before the age of 7 (p. 92). Thus, the expectation is that the symptoms of this disorder are first evident early in childhood. Accordingly, epidemiological studies have indeed primarily focused on the pediatric population and described the impairments that are commonly evident in various functional settings relevant to that age group (as discussed earlier and in the previous chapter).

In addition, those children with very early onset of symptoms, especially with significant severity, usually exhibit more impairment along the way. For example, Rappley et al. (1999) studied 223 children diagnosed with ADHD by age 3 and found severe functional impairments in many areas, along with a higher degree of comorbid disorders and more physical injuries than are typically associated with children with ADHD. Other studies have shown that children age 2 to 4 who are diagnosed with ADHD appear to present more serious overall impairment than children with other disorders diagnosed in that age group (Connor, 2002).

The most typical age of onset is difficult to determine, but studies have shown that the disorder is most frequently diagnosed when children are enrolled in school and problems with disruptive behaviors within the classroom or problems with the ability to attend to academic tasks become apparent (Barkley, 2006). When boys are brought in for treatment, it usually becomes apparent that symptoms in other settings have been present for some time—the boy's behaviors at home have been difficult to manage for some time, he acted out when taken to a store or a church, he fought with peers and siblings, and so on— but the parents attributed these problems to his "just being a boy" and attempted to deal with them on their own. Thus, it seems that the presentation of difficulties in school is a tipping point that prompts most parents to seek help for their son.

Progression of Symptoms Into Teenage Years

Research studies have suggested that symptoms of ADHD are likely to persist into the teenage years. Barkley (2002) reviewed prospective studies that followed children with ADHD for 4 to 10 years. Results of these studies revealed that 70% to 80% of children diagnosed with ADHD continued to qualify for the diagnosis at the follow-up age (ranging from

14 to 19). Thus, only 2 or 3 for every 10 boys diagnosed with ADHD no longer exhibit full-blown symptoms when they become teenagers. In addition, clinicians should remember that even those teens who no longer meet full diagnostic criteria for the disorder may still exhibit residual symptoms that affect their functioning at home, in school, or with peers and may still benefit from treatment to help them adjust to those remaining difficulties.

As boys get older, symptoms from each of the two main diagnostic clusters progress differently. Hyperactivity has been shown to decrease with age. Although exceptions are common, most boys with ADHD who were hyperactive as children tend to become less hyperactive as teenagers. Although these boys may remain fidgety, their ability to remain seated generally improves, and their problems with sitting through meals, behaving in stores and churches, and remaining at their desks in the classroom generally diminish (Hinshaw, 2002). This does not mean, however, that symptoms of hyperactivity disappear altogether. Many teens continue to express feelings of restlessness that are expressed through fidgeting, finding it hard to feel comfortable, and craving a high level of physical stimulation. Thus, it can be said that the "outer" hyperactivity diminishes, whereas the "inner" hyperactivity remains.

Although hyperactivity tends to diminish, impulsivity tends to remain. Young boys express impulsivity through calling out, performing dangerous behaviors (such as running out into the street), interrupting peers, not awaiting their turn in games, and generally intruding on others. Teenagers generally learn not to call out answers in settings where it is obvious that such behavior is inappropriate (such as the classroom), but they continue to interrupt adults and peers in other ways, including having difficulties taking their turn when speaking and intruding into conversations and activities. Even more important, impulsive teens frequently exhibit poor judgment that results in dangerous behaviors, including reckless driving, criminal mischief (such as shoplifting or trespassing), experimentation with psychoactive substances, and risky sexual behaviors (Barkley, 2006). Thus, clinicians treating youngsters with ADHD should expect that impulsivity seen in childhood is likely to remain into the teenage years, although the specific expression may change.

Of all the symptoms of ADHD, distractibility and disorganization are most likely to continue into the teenage years with little change in presentation (Barkley, 2002). Teenagers with ADHD are still likely to make careless mistakes in their work, daydream during classes, forget directions, misplace necessary items (such as books and assignments), lose personal items, fail to follow through on required tasks (such as homework or house chores), forget about prearranged activities, and so on. As a result, teens with ADHD who are distractible and disorganized are still likely to exhibit notable impairment in school and in various aspects of personal, social, and home life.

Progression of Symptoms Into Adulthood

When Laufer, Denhoff, and Solomons (1957) wrote about "hyperkinetic" symptoms, they noted that in the vast majority of cases, those symptoms resolve in adulthood. Because the diagnostic criteria listed in the *DSM-IV* primarily provide examples of symptoms that are common to children and adolescents, it is apparent that the *DSM* system similarly expects most clients with ADHD to be children or adolescents, and as McGough and McCracken (2006) pointed out, the *DSM* system "begrudgingly" accepts that adults may also be diagnosed with this disorder. A substantial body of evidence, however, now exists that suggests that a major portion of children with ADHD continues to exhibit full diagnostic criteria into adulthood. For example, Kessler et al. (2005) found that 36% of patients previously diagnosed with ADHD as children still meet the full diagnostic criteria as adults. Analysis of epidemiological data reveals similar findings. As reviewed previously, about 3% to 7% of school-age children are reported to be diagnosed with ADHD. By comparison, 2% to 5% of adults are reported to meet the diagnostic criteria (Ramsay & Rostain, 2008). Thus, a synthesis of these findings reveals that between one third and one half of boys diagnosed with ADHD are likely to continue to exhibit full-blown symptoms into adulthood.

Men who were diagnosed with ADHD as boys and teens, however, are likely to continue to exhibit significant functional impairment, even if they no longer meet the full diagnostic criteria. For example, Biederman, Mick, and Faraone (2000) revealed that even though many children with ADHD no longer meet the full diagnostic criteria in adulthood, they still exhibit sufficient impairment to require treatment. Mental health clinicians must be prepared to treat men with residual symptoms and recognize that even if full diagnostic criteria for ADHD are not met, significant impairment can still be present.

One additional issue that must be considered is whether those adults who no longer meet full diagnostic criteria have improved because of the gradual remission of the symptoms or whether the men have developed sufficient compensatory strategies to address those symptoms. There is some evidence to support both possibilities. As reviewed in the next chapter, the most widely accepted etiological explanation focuses on the understanding of the differences in brain structure and function that are evident in individuals with ADHD. These differences mostly involve the frontal lobes and dopaminergic functional pathways. Frontal lobes, however, are the last portions of the brain to mature, and they undergo significant growth during adolescence. Perhaps not coincidentally, some symptoms of ADHD (e.g., hyperactivity) diminish during the same developmental period. It is plausible that as the frontal lobes mature, self-control over motor impulses is increased, thus resulting in the observed decrease in hyperactivity.

It is also likely that some boys and teens with ADHD develop compensatory skills along the way that help them cope with any residual symptoms. As reviewed by Ambroggio and Jensen (2002), there are numerous studies that verify the effectiveness of medical and psychosocial treatments. Although long-term follow-ups are rare, Hechtman and Abikoff (cf. Ambroggio & Jensen, 2002) revealed that children (mostly boys) who remained in treatment (combined counseling and medication or medication alone) improved significantly and maintained those improvements over the duration of the treatment, and subsequently the Multimodal Treatment of Adolescents (MTA) study (MTA Cooperative Group, 1999) revealed that both psychosocial and medication treatments significantly improved symptoms of ADHD during the duration of treatment, which lasted more than 1 year. The improvements were specifically noted in classroom behavior, aggression, and social skills, and the ratings of children in treatment by teachers, parents, and peers revealed significant improvement in functioning in those areas. It is evident, therefore, that boys with ADHD who receive treatment improve their ability to learn, exercise self-control, and interact with peers. Although long-term follow-ups are lacking, it is reasonable to expect that those boys and teens who participate in long-term treatment to manage the symptoms of ADHD learn social, academic, and self-control skills along the way, thus helping them become better prepared for adulthood. Although such compensatory skills may not be sufficient to eliminate all ADHD-related difficulties, they may nevertheless be of enough benefit to decrease the overall degree of impairment that the adult male with ADHD may still exhibit.

When men continue to exhibit ADHD-related impairment into adulthood, the expression of the symptoms may change. As discussed earlier, hyperactivity is likely to diminish, and residual presentation may include fidgeting and restlessness. In adulthood, these symptoms are not likely to be as problematic, but restlessness may still produce an inner sense of general discomfort. By contrast, impulsivity often continues to be a significant problem for men with ADHD (Barkley, 2002). Impulsive men still show difficulties with social relationships and tend to be disliked by their peers. In addition, impulsivity impairs judgment and is often evidenced in behaviors that result in adverse personal, occupational, legal, and health-related consequences, including poor decision making, truancy from work, excessive spending and poor financial planning, reckless driving, and accidental injuries (Barkley, 2006).

Similarly, inattentiveness and disorganization are likely to continue into adulthood (Barkley, 2002). Men with these symptoms often have difficulties completing work-related or academic assignments, meeting financial obligations, organizing and keeping track of their possessions, and attending to a variety of day-to-day responsibilities associated with normal adult life. Consequently, their family relationships are often strained, and their work achievement significantly lags behind their peers without ADHD (Ramsay & Rostain, 2008).

Finally, one more factor needs to be considered. Men who exhibit residual symptoms of ADHD generally experience more stress and strain in their everyday life. As a result, they are more likely to experience frequent conflicts with coworkers, supervisors, peers, and significant others. They are also likely to be less accomplished and successful. Undoubtedly, men are aware of those factors, even if they do not exhibit extensive insight into the underlying causes. Consequently, men with ADHD or residual symptoms are very likely to exhibit comorbid psychological difficulties that further complicate their overall symptom profile. By some accounts, three out of four adult men with ADHD present with symptoms of at least one more psychological disorder, most common of which is depression (Ramsay & Rostain, 2008). In fact, some researchers who have examined the adult outcome of children with ADHD reported that it is the symptoms of those comorbidities, even more than the adult symptoms of ADHD, that are mostly responsible for the overall impairment of adults with ADHD. As discussed in Chapter 5, clinicians must be vigilant to comprehensively diagnose all symptoms that are apparent and adequately plan to address all those symptoms in treatment.

SUMMARY

The prevalence of ADHD has changed over the years as diagnostic criteria evolved. In addition, researchers now recommend that more stringent cutoff criteria need to be used to avoid classifying children who do not exhibit sufficient levels of impairment. In accordance with current diagnostic criteria (as listed in the *DSM-IV-TR*), and using a cutoff of 2 standard deviations above the mean when measuring each major cluster of symptoms, current prevalence of ADHD is reported to fall between 3% and 7% of school-age children. The prevalence of ADHD in adults is less clearly established, but some recent research has suggested that between 2% and 4% of adults meet the criteria for the disorder.

The course of the disorder has been debated for many decades. Fifty years ago, children were expected to grow out of the disorder by late adolescence and adulthood. Recent findings, however, reveal that 70% to 80% of children with ADHD continue to exhibit the disorder in adolescence. Once again, adult outcome data are rarer, but it is now generally accepted that about half the men who were diagnosed with ADHD as children or adolescents still meet those diagnostic criteria in adulthood, and a significant portion of the remainder still exhibits residual symptoms that still produce significant impairment. The expression of symptoms changes over the years, and hyperactivity is less common, but impulsivity and inattentiveness/disorganization commonly persist. In addition, males with ADHD are more likely to exhibit comorbid psychological conditions that significantly exacerbate the overall functional impairment.

3

Etiology

Just as our understanding of the symptoms, epidemiology, and course of attention deficit/hyperactivity disorder (ADHD) has evolved over the past several decades, our understanding of the etiology has similarly changed. Once, ADHD symptoms were viewed to be caused by inappropriate interactions between a boy and the world around him—his parents, teachers, maybe even his church (Rafalovich, 2001). According to theorists like Klein and Anna Freud, the latency stage, which was believed by Freud to occur between 6 and 12 years of age, is a time when children may develop restlessness, mischief, and social detachment. Klein (1963) wrote, "The motor discharges which the little child achieves through fidgeting often become condensed at the beginning of the latency period into definite stereotyped movements which are usually lost to view in the general picture of excessive mobility which the child presents" (p. 144). Thus, fidgeting is viewed as a physical overcompensation for the emotional state of anxiety.

Similarly, impulsivity was thought to be the product of the child's unsuccessful struggle to obtain satisfaction from his parents, and distractibility was a result of neurosis and was caused by a fragmented ego caused by the interactive dynamics of the family system and its effect on the development of an infant (Rafalovich, 2001). Psychoanalytic treatment aimed to help the family members obtain insight into their behaviors and help them understand the meaning of the child's symptoms, allowing the deviant experiences to be interpreted, analyzed, and reconstructed. Thankfully, in face of the resounding failure of this approach, most clinicians today do not use the psychodynamic theory to try to understand the etiology of this disorder.

Instead, the vast majority of clinicians today recognize that the symptoms of ADHD stem from well-documented neurophysiological differences evident in the brains of children with ADHD, and learning

processes further contribute to the development of conflicts and problem behaviors. Consequently, this chapter will review those two etiologies to help the practitioners gain insight into the causes of the disorder's
symptoms. Understanding the processes that underlie the symptoms
will help readers develop an appropriate framework to conceptualize
the treatment strategies that are most likely to result in effective symptom reduction.

NEUROBIOLOGICAL FORMULATIONS

To grasp the pathophysiology of ADHD, one must identify the regions
of the brain that are involved in controlling the brain functions that
underlie impulsivity, hyperactivity, inattentiveness, and disorganization. It is usually helpful to divide the discussion into two parts, because
hyperactivity and impulsivity are the product of interconnected brain
functions, and inattentiveness and disorganization are similarly related.

Hyperactivity and Impulsivity

The cerebral cortex, sometimes known as the forebrain or telencepha-
lon, makes up the largest portion of the human brain. The cortex is
responsible for most cognitive functions and sensory processing. Each
of the two lateral hemispheres of the cortex is divided into four lobes:
frontal, parietal, occipital, and temporal. The frontal lobes are most relevant. The posterior (closer to the top of the head) portions are involved
in motor control, whereas the anterior (closer to the forehead) portions
control inhibitory functions and the "executive skills" of planning and
making decisions.

Humans are impulsive by nature. This means that every moment our
brain generates a large number of impulses. Some of these impulses are
thoughts, and some others are urges to say things or perform some movement. As various portions of the brain generate those impulses, those
urges are relayed into the anterior portion of the frontal lobes to perform
decision making and determine whether the urge should be converted
into action. Thus, when the frontal lobes are not fully activated, are
smaller, or otherwise do not function to capacity, the urges that are sent
to them are not processed sufficiently, and too many of them become
quickly converted into behaviors. In this context, it becomes clear that
impulsivity and hyperactivity are closely interrelated—hyperactivity is
merely the reduced ability to control motor impulses, so that too many
of them become converted into overt behaviors. In other words, hyperactivity is really motor impulsivity.

Anterior frontal lobes not only process motor urges but also play
an important role in decision making. When we decide on a course
of action, it is usually beneficial to review alternatives (based on prior
learning and experiences), organize the decision-making process into

discrete steps, and implement the solution. These are commonly known as executive functions and, according to Barkley (1997a), require the use of verbal and nonverbal working memory; self-regulation of affect, motivation, and arousal; and planning. Thus, interference with the normal function of the frontal lobes potentially results not only in hyperactivity but also in a deficit in executive functions.

Brain areas that lie under (and are surrounded by) the cortex also play an important role. The basal ganglia, a collection of nuclei located on the inside on the cortex, close to where the frontal lobes meet the temporal lobes, are particularly relevant. Basal ganglia are relay stations in the process of control over motor functions. Specifically, they are involved in the control of motor urges. Thus, when a motor urge is not controlled and is converted into motor action (as happens when a person exhibits a tic, a compulsion, or motor restlessness), basal ganglia failed to suppress that urge.

The cerebellum is also an important part of the motor system. It stores functional motor units—highly specific sequences of movements that must be performed in concert and in the proper sequence when any complex movement (such as walking, sitting, running, writing, lifting an object, etc.) is performed. The cerebellum is closely connected with the frontal lobes and basal ganglia. When a movement is performed, the urge to carry out that action is processed by the frontal lobes and the basal ganglia, and when those brain parts "decide" that the action should take place, appropriate functional motor units are recalled and impulses are sent into the peripheral nervous system, via the efferent pathways, to control the muscles responsible for performing the behavior. When the behavior seems uncoordinated or poorly planned, appropriate functional units have not been stored or are not recalled properly.

To understand why the complex brain system responsible for motor control and executive functions may malfunction, let us consider one more aspect. Brain function occurs by the coordinated action of brain cells, or neurons. Neurons work by "firing," or transmitting messages. Neurons are not actually connected to each other but separated by small spaces called synapses. For one neuron to communicate with another, a chemical messenger (a neurotransmitter) must be released into the synapse and affect the postsynaptic neuron. Although there are some neurotransmitters that are found throughout the entire brain, others are more localized and are involved in the processing of discrete brain functions. The frontal lobes (especially the aspects of frontal lobe function discussed herein) are primarily controlled by the action of dopamine. Thus, levels of dopamine are likely to affect the extent to which motor control and executive functions are appropriately performed.

Inattentiveness and Disorganization

Inattentiveness and disorganization are brain functions that also involve the frontal lobes (Stahl, 2000). To filter out distractions, one must

suppress the urge to attend to an event that comes into one's awareness, such as a sound that is heard or an item that comes into view. This
requires self-control. In addition, when one strives to organize his or
her things, keep track of possessions, and plan to complete assignments
or perform assigned responsibilities, the use of executive functions is
also necessary. The organization of thoughts and the ability to filter
out distractions are, however, more purely cognitive tasks that do not
require the use of the motor system and therefore do not require the
activation of basal ganglia and the cerebellum. Indeed, it is apparent
that different portions of the frontal lobes are involved in attention and
concentration, and those parts of the brain have been found to be primarily activated by both dopamine and norepinephrine. Consequently,
changes in the levels of either of those neurotransmitters may have an
effect on inattentiveness.

In addition, another subcortical part of the brain is crucial to consider. The reticular formation, also known as the reticular activating
system (RAS), is an oblong bundle of nerve cells located within the
brain stem. The RAS is extensively connected with various portions
of the brain, including all cortical lobes. The RAS can conceptually be
understood as the "gas pedal for the brain," because it plays a major role
in activating the brain to sustain a baseline level of arousal. If the RAS
does not activate sufficiently, the brain (including the frontal lobes) will
not function at capacity, and symptoms of distractibility will be much
more likely.

There are various reasons why the RAS may have difficulties activating the brain. One of these may be related to the corpus callosum,
a longitudinal fissure densely packed with connections between neurons. Much of brain action involves communication between various
brain areas, and those messages must be transmitted through the
corpus callosum. Thus, if the corpus callosum exhibits any difficulties in efficiency or capacity, deficits in brain functions are likely to
be apparent.

As discussed previously, regions of the frontal lobes that are involved
in motor control and executive functions (such as planning) appear to be
regulated primarily by dopamine, whereas regions that are involved in
arousal and the control of attention are regulated by both dopamine and
norepinephrine. The RAS activates the brain by releasing dopamine in
its substantia nigra and tegmentum regions, and dopaminergic projections activate regions of the frontal lobes, basal ganglia, cerebellum, and
other brain areas not directly related to ADHD. The RAS also releases
norepinephrine in the locus coeruleus, and projections activate portions
of the frontal lobes responsible for attentional control, as well as other
brain structures that may play an indirect role in attention, including
portions of temporal and parietal lobes (Mirsky, 1987). Consequently,
it is apparent that the neurophysiological control of the brain functions
that underlie symptoms of ADHD primarily involves those two catecholamine neurotransmitters.

Summary of Research Findings

Although it is helpful to localize the brain regions that may be involved in the production of symptoms of ADHD, it is necessary to review the findings of neuropsychiatic research in order to examine whether individuals with ADHD do, in fact, present abnormalities in these areas. Brain research studies have identified both structural and functional differences in individuals with ADHD. Each of these categories needs to be reviewed separately.

Neuroanatomical Abnormalities. As reviewed by Swanson and Castellanos (2002), four major studies performed in the 1990s, all of which used magnetic resonance imaging (MRI) scans, consistently revealed that children with ADHD (mostly boys) exhibit smaller basal ganglia. Furthermore, a striking consistency is evident in these findings: The studies revealed a uniform decrease of about 12% with an effect size of about 0.75. Those studies also revealed that the cerebellum of children with ADHD was similarly smaller, and all four studies revealed said size differences in the same regions of the cerebellum (inferior posterior lobe, lobules VIII-X of the vermis). As discussed earlier, the basal ganglia and cerebellum play key roles in the control of motor functions. It is apparent that the findings of these studies support the hypothesis that these brain structures are involved in the production of the symptoms of hyperactivity.

Research studies have also identified significant differences in the frontal lobes. Three studies have shown that three regions of the frontal lobes—the anterior cingulate gyrus (linked to the control of executive functions), the left dorsolateral region (involved in working memory and cognitive functions), and the right frontal region (linked to alertness and focusing)—have similarly been found to be smaller in ADHD groups. Once again, significant consistency was observed between these studies, with a decrease of about 10% and an effect size of about 0.70 being uniformly reported (Swanson & Castellanos, 2002). Furthermore, additional findings revealed that these same regions of the frontal lobes were smaller only in individuals with ADHD and not in participants with learning disabilities (without ADHD). Consequently, it is apparent that regions of the frontal lobes also show particular abnormalities that seem specific to individuals with ADHD.

Studies investigating the size of the corpus callosum have also revealed notable findings. Although some lateral inconsistencies were revealed, two research teams reported that anterior and posterior regions of the corpus callosum were smaller in ADHD groups, and these differences were not apparent in other clinical groups (Swanson & Castellanos, 2002). Additional studies by other groups of researchers also confirmed these findings (Barkley, 2006). Thus, it is likely that abnormalities in the corpus callosum contribute to the production of the symptoms of ADHD.

Neurophysiological Abnormalities. Over the past several decades, researchers have used a variety of functional brain scan techniques to investigate brain activity in patients with ADHD. Single photon emission tomography (SPECT) scans revealed that individuals with ADHD exhibited lower than normal blood perfusion in the striatum and frontal/prefrontal regions (especially on the right side), indicating a lower level of activity in those areas (Barkley, 2006; Swanson & Castellanos, 2002). These findings were supported by studies that used functional magnetic resonance imaging (fMRI). In addition, when individuals were given stimulant medications (which increase dopaminergic transmission), the blood perfusion of the striatal regions returned to normal levels.

Studies that used positron emission tomography (PET) scans revealed somewhat variable findings, and a number of brain areas showed underactive metabolism in the brains of individuals with ADHD, but not consistently. The one finding that was consistent across three different studies, however, was that the frontal lobes, especially the left anterior region, showed significant underactivity.

Results of electroencephalogram (EEG) studies have revealed findings that are also somewhat variable, but quantitative EEG (QEEG) measures have consistently shown that individuals with ADHD exhibit increased slow-wave (theta) patterns and decreased fast-wave (beta) activity in the frontal lobes, again indicating reduced frontal activation. Evoked response potential (ERP) studies have shown smaller amplitudes that are believed to be the result of smaller prefrontal activation. Once again, studies have shown that these deficits resolve when individuals with ADHD are given stimulant medications (Barkley, 2006).

Since Wender (1971) proposed the "dopamine hypothesis," investigators have suspected that ADHD symptoms are secondary, at least in part, to a deficit in the dopaminergic brain functions. Current understanding of brain function confirms that the brain structures responsible for the control of motor, executive functions, and attention are activated by catecholamine transmitters, especially dopamine and norepinephrine. In fact, recent research findings point specifically to deficits in three of the brain's four dopaminergic pathways (mesocortical, mesolimbic, and nigrostriatal) as well as in the prefrontal norepinephrine pathway (Stahl, 2000). Studies of individuals with ADHD lend further credence to these hypotheses. Examination of cerebral spinal fluid reveal that children with ADHD exhibit lower levels of dopamine (Halperin et al., 1997), and other studies of blood and urine metabolites similarly implicate dopamine and norepinephrine, although not consistently (Barkley, 2006). Studies, using flouro-dopa PET scans, with adults also confirm these findings and reveal that adults with ADHD exhibit lower dopaminergic activity in the frontal lobes (Ernst et al., 2003).

Molecular genetic research has identified some of the genetic factors that underlie these neurotransmitter deficiencies and suggest an explanation about why individuals with ADHD exhibit lower catecholamine-related function. Deficits in dopamine transporter genes have been identified in children with ADHD and their probands. The DAT1 gene on chromosome 5, the DRD4 gene on chromosome 11, the DRD5 gene on chromosome 16, and the DBH transporter gene have specifically been implicated (Barkley, 2006; Swanson & Castellanos, 2002). These genetic factors likely result in reduced dopaminergic activity in key areas in the brain, including the majority of the dopaminergic system. Because dopamine is a precursor for norepinephrine, it is plausible that dopaminergic deficits also result in noradrenergic deficiency.

THE PHYSICAL ENVIRONMENT

Since Zubin and Spring (1977) discussed the applicability of the diathesis-stress model to our understanding of schizophrenia, mental health researchers and clinicians have extended it to the understanding of other psychological disorders. The model posits that certain individuals are born with a genetic vulnerability toward a disorder, and environmental factors (such as trauma, stress, and other life events) exacerbate this vulnerability and activate the development of the disorder. The greater the underlying vulnerability, the less stress is needed to trigger the process. Conversely, where there is smaller genetic contribution, greater stress is required. In extreme situations, maximum vulnerability requires virtually no stress to produce a disorder, and minimum vulnerability does not result in development of the disorder unless the stress becomes extreme. Most cases, however, fall between these two ends of the continuum.

The environmental stress and trauma may be physical in nature. For example, brain trauma, especially one that involves hypoxic–anoxic insults (where the brain is deprived of oxygen for a significant period of time), has been shown to increase the vulnerability for developing ADHD (Cruickshank, Eliason, & Merrifield, 1988; O'Dougherty, Nuechterlein, & Drew, 1984), and ADHD is more common in children with seizure disorders (Hesdorffer et al., 2004). Similarly, symptoms of ADHD commonly accompany injuries and lesions in the frontal lobes, especially the prefrontal cortex (Fuster, 1997).

Pregnancy and birth complications have also been shown to increase the risk for ADHD. Teenage mothers are more likely to give birth to children with ADHD, and pregnancies that result in long and difficult delivery also increase the risk (Claycomb, Ryan, Miller, & Shnakenberg-Ott, 2004). Fetal distress, toxemia, and low birth weight are similarly associated with ADHD (Breslau et al., 1996), as is maternal smoking and alcohol use (Barkley, 2006). Some researchers suspect that physical trauma, especially associated with pregnancy and birth, is responsible for 14% of all cases of ADHD (Whittaker et al., 1997). Pregnancy during which the mother experiences significant psychological distress has also been shown to increase the risk for ADHD. Although most of the research is correlational, maternal anxiety and distress appear to be associated with increased risk that the offspring will develop ADHD (Barkley, 2006).

Research with monozygotic twins, including those reared apart, further supports the diathesis-stress model. As expected, the vast majority of studies report findings that monozygotic twins are likely to present similar risk—either both twins develop ADHD or neither of them do. Sharp et al. (2003), however, identified 10 discordant pairs, where one twin developed ADHD and the other did not. Analysis of these pairs revealed that the affected twins experienced birth complications (e.g., breech delivery) and were smaller at birth.

All in all, findings of a large number of studies that examined brain structure, brain function, genetics, and correlates of developmental and physical trauma reveal that ADHD is, indeed, a neuropsychiatric disorder that, in accordance with the diathesis-stress model, likely results from the inheritance of genetic vulnerabilities and exposure to environmental events. Because the vast majority of boys with ADHD do not present with a history of significant physical distress, however, other environmental stressors that likely contribute to the development of the disorder must be examined.

PSYCHOLOGICAL FACTORS

Boys with ADHD exhibit symptoms of hyperactivity/impulsivity and inattentiveness/disorganization. As discussed previously, these symptoms have an early onset and generally persist through childhood, and boys with ADHD display difficulties across different settings, including problems within the home, at school, and in the peer group.

Of these problems, those within the home are the earliest to develop, because boys with ADHD begin to show symptoms in infancy and early childhood. As the boys start to become fussy, irritable, cranky, and impulsive, parents find the experience of raising such children quite stressful. Boys with ADHD have much more conflicts with their parents (Johnston & Mash, 2001), and mothers, in particular, find it more difficult to supervise them and attend to their needs (Tallamadge & Barkley, 1983). Because mothers are still generally the primary custodians, boys with ADHD generally spend more time with their mothers, and the conflicts that ensue between them tend to be frequent and pervasive. As a result, negative expectations develop in the boy as well as the parent—the boy learns that he frequently gets yelled at and punished and seems to always get in trouble, whereas the parent learns to expect the worst from the boy and begins to approach interactions with an "edge," an anticipation that contact with the boy will be difficult and often will not produce desired outcomes. Over time, these negative expectations result in an internalization of mutual negative feelings, and all future interactions are even more likely to result in conflicts. Consequently, ADHD has been associated with disturbances in family and marital functioning, including disruptions in parent–child and mother–father relationships, an increase in levels of parenting stress, and a reduction in parents' sense of efficacy (Johnston & Mash, 2001). These disturbances, in turn, are stressful on the boy and exacerbate the developing symptoms of the disorder.

When conflicts persist, parents often seek to minimize them at any cost. Patterson (1982) identified a coercive family process in which parents, when faced with difficulties obtaining compliance from their child, often give up when the child begins to argue and protest. Such a process is well documented with parents of boys with ADHD. When parents become frustrated, they often do not use consistent, appropriate parenting interventions (Donenberg & Baker, 1994). At times, they overreact, and at other times they give up in frustration and do not follow through on threatened consequences. As a result, boys with ADHD commonly experience secondary gain—the more they act out, the more they get their way. Parents of boys with ADHD have also been shown to ignore many misbehaviors and exercise limited monitoring of their children's behaviors (Burt, Krueger, McGue, & Iacono, 2001), perhaps out of frustration or in an attempt to sidestep conflicts. In addition, negative patterns of interaction that exist between boys with ADHD and their parents result in few opportunities for the boys to receive rewards and positive consequences (Barkley, 2006). Thus, the boys rarely experience situations where positive behavior and utilization of appropriate self-control result in positive consequences.

Cognitive factors also contribute to these problems. Barkley, Guevremont, Anastopoulos, and Fletcher (1992) found that behavioral problems associated with ADHD may be related to distorted cognitions and unrealistic beliefs sustained in parent–child conflicts. These distortions, shared by both parents and boys with ADHD, include feelings that one is ruining the other's life. Other distorted cognitions include expectations of perfectionism and self-blame and a lack of understanding of proper limits of autonomy and fairness. As a result, parents and children alike manifest more anger and more negative communication patterns during their discussions, including insulting remarks, authoritarian demands, complaints, and defensiveness.

The stress of parenting a boy with ADHD may intrude on other members of the family. This may create negative reactions from family members and may have a disruptive influence on other relationships within the family, including structural changes, transgenerational coalitions, scapegoating, and intermember triangulations. Barkley et al. (1992) reported that a family with a child with ADHD may have altered family boundaries that rearrange the power hierarchy, which further exacerbates the stress that the whole family (including the boy) is experiencing.

Relationships between mothers and their sons with ADHD are much more directive and negative and less socially interactive. Because boys with ADHD are less compliant and more negative in their reactions, mothers are more likely to respond with irritation and hostility (Fletcher, Fischer, Barkley, & Smallish, 1996). In turn, the boys' responses tend to mirror the parents', and so if the mothers' reaction is negative, the boys will respond negatively as well. Over time, this pattern becomes learned and deeply entrenched. Weinstein et al. (1998) additionally noted that boys with ADHD have a major impact on parents' self-worth, and parents tend to blame their children or themselves for the difficulties they experience. If parents develop feelings of guilt, they may withdraw and, as a result, make the boys feel unloved and rejected.

SUMMARY

Although the exact causes of ADHD are still unknown, most clinicians now agree that children with ADHD are born with a genetic predisposition for functional brain deficits associated with dopaminergic and noradrenergic neurotransmission. Genetic studies have identified several transporter gene markers, and neuroanatomical and neurophysiological scans consistently reveal that individuals with ADHD exhibit abnormalities in the size and level of activity on the frontal and prefrontal lobes, basal ganglia, and cerebellum. The resultant underactivation is responsible for the difficulties in self-control, impulse control, and sustained attention that individuals with ADHD exhibit.

In accordance with the diathesis-stress model, a comprehensive formulation of the etiology of ADHD must recognize the interplay of biological vulnerabilities with environmental and psychological factors. A small portion of boys with ADHD may have experienced physical stress (birth difficulties, other head trauma, etc.) that contributed to the development of the disorder. The vast majority, however, likely developed ADHD when deficits in brain function resulted in early behaviors that were difficult for the parents to attend to and manage, and the boys then encountered parenting styles that included significant conflicts, blame, and rejection. The resulting stress significantly exacerbated the emerging symptoms and contributed to the development of the disorder.

Assessment and Diagnosis

4

Assessment

As reviewed in previous chapters, symptoms of attention deficit/hyperactivity disorder (ADHD) fall along two major dimensions: hyperactivity/impulsivity and inattentiveness/disorganization. Because it is common for boys and male teens to exhibit many behaviors that fall into these categories, clinicians need to use techniques that will help them classify the degree of severity of those symptoms. To prevent overdiagnosing, clinicians must use measures that will help them rate the relative degree of impairment in these areas. Standardized assessment tools allow clinicians to determine symptom severity by comparing them to normative data.

In Chapter 2, the topic of the need to establish proper cutoff criteria was reviewed. Clinicians are encouraged to consider what level of severity they require to make a diagnosis. Although using a cutoff of 1 and a half standard deviations above the mean has been considered standard, researchers have suggested that a cutoff of 2 standard deviations is more appropriate to avoid misclassification (Barkley, 2006). The measures discussed in this chapter allow clinicians to decide what cutoff criteria will be used, and clinicians are encouraged to give this matter careful consideration.

There are various types of assessment techniques that can be used to diagnose the symptoms. Each offers advantages and disadvantages. In addition, some of these have been standardized only on children and adolescents and some only on adults. The following discussion should help clinicians determine which techniques are most appropriate to serve the needs of their clients.

BEHAVIORAL CHECKLISTS AND INVENTORIES

A variety of checklists and behavior rating scales have been published. Many of those are intended to assess a wide variety of symptoms and guide the clinician about the presence or absence of symptom categories that need further follow-up. For example, the Behavioral Assessment System for Children (Reynolds & Kamphaus, 2004) and the Child Behavior Checklist (Achenbach, 2001) include symptoms from many dimensions (including mood disturbance, anxiety, aggression, etc.) in addition to those that may be directly relevant to the diagnosis of ADHD. Although such measures are helpful as general screening tools, they do not provide adequate specificity and are not sufficiently cross-validated to the *Diagnostic and Statistical Manual of Mental Disorders* (*DSM*) to allow their use as diagnostic measures. For this reason, the present review will focus only on those behavioral inventories that specifically focus on symptoms of ADHD and are designed to help clinicians rate the degree of symptoms in the clusters listed in the *DSM-IV* (American Psychiatric Association, 1994).

In addition, a wide variety of checklists have been designed to closely correspond with the *DSM-IV* criteria but have not been validated. Many of these were published in books about ADHD (e.g., Barkley, 2006) or are available on the Internet. Clinicians are cautioned about using these instruments. Although they may possess good face validity, the vast majority do not document sufficient psychometric properties (reliability, validity, norms) to be useful when making a diagnosis. As best, these can be considered rough screening tools, and consequently those instruments are not reviewed herein.

Appropriate behavioral inventories can be useful to help quantify the degree to which the child is presenting symptoms. Information from multiple reporters is usually gathered to allow clinicians to check whether various sources (such as self-report, parent report, teacher report, etc.) report similar degrees of impairment. In addition, some instruments are designed for use with children and adolescents only, whereas others are appropriate for use with adults. Clinicians should examine these instruments to determine which meet the specific needs of the clients for whom they are intended.

Conners Scales

The Conners scales have been around for decades and are well known in the clinical community. Although the version intended for use with children and adolescents has been around since the 1970s, the version for adults has been published more recently. Both are reviewed next.

Conners Rating Scales (CRS). The CRS is intended for children and adolescents and is currently in its third edition (Conners, 2008). The current edition provides a choice of self-report, parent-report, and teacher-report forms, in a long form (consisting of about 100 items each) or a short form (consisting of about 40 items each). The short forms allow for easy hand-scoring by using scoring grids to sum up items for various subscales, including Inattention, Hyperactivity/Impulsivity, Learning Problems, Executive Functioning, Aggression, Family Relations, and

Peer Relations. Not all scales are used by all forms, although most scales overlap between the three reporters. Two composite scales are also calculated: the ADHD Index and the Global Index.

The long forms provide more detail for each scale and allow for the calculation of validity scales (Positive Impression, Negative Impression, and Inconsistency Index) that can be used to interpret the accuracy of the obtained results. The long forms are primarily intended to be scored online or with the available software. Electronic scoring produces a comprehensive printout that not only includes the scores on each scale but also generates interpretive reports.

The CRS allows intuitive interpretation of scores by using standardized *T*-scores with a mean of 50 and standard deviation of 10. Thus, clinicians can easily determine how far above the mean a given score lies and whether a cutoff of 65 (1 and a half standard deviations) or 70 (2 standard deviations) will be used as a basis for the diagnosis. In addition, the manual reports that the scales have been cross-validated against the *DSM-IV*, and so the inattention and hyperactivity/impulsivity dimensions closely correspond to the *DSM* criteria for those symptoms. The remaining scales can be used to provide information about comorbid disorders, such as oppositional defiant disorder, conduct disorder, or learning disorders.

The CRS is a mature instrument that offers extensive evidence of reliability and validity, and it appears to be psychometrically sound. Normative data are based on a sample of 3,400 assessments from 1,200 teachers, 1,200 parents, and 1,000 self-report protocols. Parent and teacher forms are intended to assess behaviors in children and adolescents, aged 6 through 18 years. Self-report forms are meant to be administered to children aged 8 years and older. The composition of the sample appears to reasonably resemble U.S. normative data, and separate norms are reported by sex. Each form is scored by comparing it to normative data within the same age group (in 1-year increments) and same-sex peers, which is a definite plus.

Conners Adult ADHD Rating Scales (CAARS). Because the previous and current versions of the CRS are intended for use with children and adolescents, a parallel instrument was developed for use with adults. The CAARS has been around for about a decade (Conners, Erhardt, & Sparrow, 1999) and is available in long, short, and screening forms to be used for self-report and observer (e.g., a spouse) report. The short forms have 26 items, the long forms have 66 items, and the screening forms have 30 items each. All the forms can easily be hand-scored by using scoring grids.

The long forms provide scores divided into nine subscales, including Factor-Derived Subscales (Inattention/Memory Problems, Hyperactivity/Restlessness, Impulsivity/Emotional Lability, Problems With Self-Concept), *DSM-IV* ADHD Symptoms Subscales (Inattentive Symptoms, Hyperactive/Impulsive Symptoms, Total ADHD Symptoms), the ADHD Index, and the Inconsistency Index (a validity scale). The short forms provide only the four Factor-Derived Subscales, the ADHD Index, and the Inconsistency Index. The screening forms provide only the three *DSM-IV* ADHD Symptoms Subscales and the ADHD Index. In addition to hand-scoring, all forms can be scored online or with the available software that provides the scores for each scale and an interpretive report.

As with the pediatric scales, the CAARS is scored by using standardized *T*-scores, allowing clinicians to determine what cutoff they desire to use to classify the severity of the symptoms. The *DSM-IV* subscales have been cross-validated against the *DSM-IV* diagnostic criteria for ADHD symptoms. The remaining subscales can be used to provide information about comorbid disorders.

Although the CAARS is a newer instrument, it appears to exhibit sufficient reliability and validity, and it seems to be psychometrically sound. Normative data are based on a sample of about 2,000 assessments (about 1,000 each for self-report and observer report). Age group data are available (18–29, 30–39, 40–49, and 50+ years of age), and each record is scored by comparing it to normative data in the appropriate age group. Separate norms are also reported by sex, allowing males to be assessed by comparing the scores to same-sex peers.

McCarney Scales

Some clinicians prefer to use the McCarney scales because they are shorter and are more specifically geared toward educational settings. Two versions are available, one for school-age children and adolescents and another for preschoolers. Both are reviewed next.

Attention Deficit Disorders Evaluation Scale (ADDES). The ADDES has been around for decades and is now in its third edition (ADDES-3; McCarney, 2003). The current edition provides a home version that consists of 46 items and a school version that consists of 60 items. Two scales are calculated, one each for inattentive and hyperactive/impulsive behaviors. Both forms can be hand-scored but are primarily intended to be used with computer software that generates an individualized printout of goals, objectives, and specific interventions to be implemented by teachers in the classroom. A prereferral checklist version of the ADDES-3 is also available.

The ADDES-3 uses less-intuitive scoring that resembles the standard scores of the Wechsler tests of intelligence: "Standard Scores" use a scale with a mean of 10 and standard deviation of 3, and "Quotients" use a scale with a mean of 100 and a standard deviation of 15. Although this may take some getting used to, clinicians still can easily determine what cutoff they choose as the basis for the diagnosis. As with the Conners scales, the ADDES-3 manual reports that the scales have been cross-validated against the *DSM-IV*, and each scale closely corresponds to the *DSM* criteria for ADHD symptoms.

The ADDES-3 is also a mature instrument that offers sufficient evidence of reliability and validity, and it appears to be psychometrically sound. The instrument was standardized on nearly 4,000 students, and normative data provide separate norms for students with ADHD as well as nondiagnosed students. It is intended to assess behaviors in children and adolescents aged 4 through 18 years. Each form is scored by using normative data within the same age group and same-sex peers, and a Spanish version is available for Spanish-speaking students and households. This is a definite benefit to clinicians who work with that population.

Early Childhood Attention Deficit Disorders Evaluation Scale (ECADDES). The ECADDES (McCarney, 1995) is a sister instrument to the ADDES (described earlier). Similarly, it includes a home version and a school version, each of which consists of about 50 items. As with the ADDES-3, two scales are calculated, one each for inattentive and hyperactive/impulsive behaviors. The forms can be hand-scored but are primarily intended to be used with computer software that provides goals, objectives, and suggested interventions.

The ECADDES uses the same standard scores as the ADDES-3 (with a mean of 10 and standard deviation of 3) and also provides percentiles. The manual reports that the scales have been cross-validated against the *DSM-IV,* and each scale closely corresponds to the *DSM* criteria for ADHD symptoms.

The ECADDES offers evidence of reliability and validity. The instrument was standardized on almost 3,000 students, and normative data provide separate norms for students with ADHD as well as nonclinically diagnosed students, but the instrument is now more than a decade old, and the norms may be becoming outdated. It is intended to assess behaviors in females aged 24 through 83 months and males aged 24 through 78 months. Scores are provided separately by age group and sex, and a Spanish version of the home form is available for Spanish-speaking households.

ACTeRS

The Attention Deficit Disorder–Hyperactivity Comprehensive Teacher's Rating Scale (ACTeRS) is also a well-established instrument that is available in parent and teacher forms (Ullmann, Sleator, & Sprague, 2000). Each version consists of about 20 items, and a 36-item self-report form is also available. Four scales are calculated: Attention, Hyperactivity, Social Skills, and Oppositional Behaviors (the fourth scale is not calculated for the self-report form). The parent form also includes an additional scale that focuses on early childhood behaviors. The forms can be hand-scored, and computer software is available that generates scoring and interpretive reports.

ACTeRS provides only percentiles and no standard scores. Thus, clinicians desiring to determine separate cutoff criteria for 1 and a half and 2 standard deviations above the mean must convert those z-score cutoffs to percentiles (93rd and 98th percentiles, respectively). The manual reports that the Attention and Hyperactivity scales have been cross-validated against the *DSM-IV* and correspond to the *DSM* diagnostic criteria, and the Oppositional Behaviors scale can be useful to assess comorbid symptoms, such as those of oppositional defiant disorder.

ACTeRS offers evidence of reliability and validity, and it appears to be psychometrically sound. The instrument was standardized on about 2,400 students, from kindergarten through eighth grade. Although norms are available by sex, unfortunately the norms do not provide data by age group, a major drawback of the instrument (Erford & Hase, 2006). A Spanish version is available for Spanish-speaking households.

Brown ADD Scales

The Brown Attention-Deficit Disorder Scales (Brown ADD Scales) are available in child (Brown, 2001) and adolescent and adult (Brown, 1996) versions. Various forms are available, each including 40 to 50 items, that can be completed by clinicians, parents, and teachers. A self-report form is also available. The instrument provides ratings of symptoms divided into six factors: Organizing, Prioritizing, and Activating to Work; Focusing, Sustaining, and Shifting Attention to Tasks; Regulating Alertness, Sustaining Effort, and Processing Speed; Managing Frustration and Modulating Emotions; Utilizing Working Memory and Accessing Recall; and Monitoring and Self-Regulating Action. The forms can be hand-scored, and computer software is available that provides scoring and interpretive reports.

Like the Conners scales, the Brown ADD Scales provide *T*-score standard scores and percentiles, allowing for intuitive interpretation on a scale that is familiar to many clinicians. The six factors are not as directly linked to the *DSM-IV* as those of other scales reviewed herein, and several factors appear to measure primarily symptoms of inattentiveness. In accordance with Barkley's (1997a) model, however, the factors also provide scores for executive functions and working memory. Still, analysis and synthesis of the factor scores are needed to determine whether *DSM-IV* diagnostic criteria are met. Brown offered his own model of understanding the symptoms of ADD (Brown, 2005) that closely resembles Barkley's model, but clinicians need to recognize that the *DSM-IV* criteria for ADHD are much more focused than either Barkley's or Brown's models, and both models are primarily useful in promoting further research of the disorder rather than providing guidelines for establishing a *DSM-IV* diagnosis.

The Brown ADD Scales offer some evidence of reliability but not in every age group. In addition, little data on validity related to specific diagnosis of ADHD are available. One study (Rucklidge & Tannock, 2002) found that using the scales to diagnose ADHD resulted in few false positives but far too many false negatives (suggesting good specificity but poor sensitivity). At this time, the Brown ADD Scales may be useful as a screening measure, but they are not sufficiently validated to be useful as tools to diagnose ADHD. The instrument is normed on individuals in four age groups (ages 3–7, 8–12, 13–18, and adult), and normative data are available by age and sex, but each age group was composed of fewer than 200 participants, and therefore the normative data are much less comprehensive than those on which other instruments reviewed herein were normed. In addition, little data are available about the locations from which participants were drawn, and therefore it is questionable whether the norms are relevant and useful (Mandal, 2000).

CONTINUOUS PERFORMANCE TESTS

Rather than provide a rating of behavior that was presumably observed by the reporter (a parent or a teacher), continuous performance test (CPT) techniques attempt to measure symptoms directly. CPTs usually expose the test taker to a computer-administered, repetitive task and measure various aspects of the performance within a timed trial. As such, they provide an opportunity to measure aspects of behavior that may be difficult to observe directly or ascertain during a regular clinical interview.

CPTs differ with regard to the specific behavior modality being assessed. Visual CPTs produce visual stimuli to which participants must produce simple responses, and the speed and accuracy of these responses are measured in real time. Some boys, male teens, or men, however, may present more difficulties with auditory rather than visual tasks. In those cases, auditory CPTs may be a better choice. These generate auditory stimuli that require the respondent to identify the occurrence of certain sounds. Both types are reviewed next.

Conners' Continuous Performance Test

The Conners' CPT was developed in the 1980s and was restandardized about 20 years later (Conners, 2004). It is a visual test that provides letters that flash on the screen, one at a time, in intervals of 1 to 4 seconds apart, and the respondent has to click the mouse button (or the space bar) as soon as every letter comes up with the exception of the letter X. The test takes about 14 minutes and is subdivided into six blocks, and each block presents the letters in interstimulus intervals of 1, 2, or 4 seconds. Each block consists of 20 letters. The test is intended for individuals aged 6 and older, and a child version (for children aged 4 and 5) is also available from the publisher. The test measures hit and omission rates, as well as commission rates, defined as trials that result in providing a response to the letter that is supposed to be omitted (the X). Generally speaking, the omission rates provide a measure of inattentiveness, whereas the commission rates provide a measure of impulsivity. The test additionally measures the hit rate and its standard error, variability, detectability, perseverations, hit reaction time block change (and its standard error), and hit reaction time inter-stimulus interval change (and its standard error). The computer generates an extensive printout that can be coded to score the performance based on ADHD samples or nonclinical norms.

The current edition is normed on nearly 2,000 individuals divided into age groups (ages 6–7, 8–9, 10–11, 12–13, 14–15, 16–17, 18–34, 35–54, and 55+). It is curious that the gender composition of the normative sample is split about equally for both sexes for individuals up to age 18, but for individuals aged 18 or older, the sample is nearly three-quarters female and slightly less than one-quarter male. Given that males with ADHD significantly outnumber females, the choice to select norms that do not reflect the epidemiology of the disorder is rather curious.

The Conners' CPT provides standard scores that use *T*-scores with a mean of 50 and standard deviation of 10, allowing clinicians to easily set a cutoff of 65 (1 and a half standard deviations) or 70 (2 standard deviations) as the basis for the diagnosis. Using the default scoring option, however, to "optimize overall hit rates," the program's built-in scoring algorithms minimize false positives but provide unacceptable specificity. Thus, the manual suggests that various scoring options can be used on the same data to produce results that will, separately, minimize false positive as well as false negatives.

First, the software can be configured to score the obtained data to minimize false positives, which uses nonclinical samples and sets the base rate to 65%. The overall function can then be reviewed, and when it falls within the clinical range, false positives are reported to be reduced to merely 5%. Because this procedure produces an unacceptable rate of false negatives (45%), however, another scoring round should be performed, selecting the algorithm that minimizes false negatives. This algorithm uses clinical samples and again sets the base rate at 65%. It reduces the incidence of false negatives to only 5% but increases the rate of false positives to 57%. Thus, clinicians who desire to use the Conners' CPT as a diagnostic tool are encourage to use both procedures to make sure that the obtained score passes both criteria before a diagnosis based on the test results is established.

The Conners' CPT provides a lot of useful information, including norms that are referenced by age and sex. It provides evidence of sufficient reliability, and its psychometric properties appear to be well established. The need to perform scoring in accordance with two different diagnostic algorithms, and the requirement to compare both to separately minimize false positives and false negatives, however, limit the practical utility of this instrument.

Test of Variables of Attention

The Test of Variables of Attention (TOVA) (Greenberg & Kidschi, 1996) is another well-known CPT. Rather than using letters, it provides shapes that need to be responded to when they occur in a particular place on the screen. The test takes about 22 minutes to administer and consists of two 11-minute trials, the first presenting the stimuli infrequently (prompting omission errors) and the second presenting it more quickly (prompting commission errors). For an additional cost, the test can also be set to provide auditory stimuli. The test primarily evaluates the accuracy of correct identification and the speed of responding. The clinician must purchase, in addition to the software, a microswitch that is required to be used by the participants during the administration. The publishers claim that this switch minimizes latency associated with the different hardware and operating systems, but others have questioned that assumption (Barkley, 2006). The test provides measures of inattention, impulsivity, response time, and response variability.

The current edition was normed on about 1,500 individuals divided into age groups (ages 4–20 in annual increments, ages 20–70 in 10-year increments, and ages 80+). Norms are available by age group and gender, with approximately equal representation of both sexes.

Like the Conners' CPT, the TOVA provides standard scores using *T*-scores with a mean of 50 and standard deviation of 10 and percentiles. The software provides one scoring algorithm that is meant to maximize hit rates and specificity, but the manual reports that the risk of false positives and false negatives is about 20% each. In addition, psychometric data are derived from unpublished studies, thus providing no peer-review verification of the accuracy. Although the TOVA continues to be popular with some clinicians, most researchers have suggested that it is primarily useful for research purposes or general screening and should not be used to base a diagnosis of ADHD in clinical settings.

Integrated Visual and Auditory CPT

Like the Conners' CPT, the Integrated Visual and Auditory (IVA) CPT (Sanford & Turner, 1995) also requires the respondent to press a button for specific characters, but the test uses numbers (1 and 2) and integrates both visual and auditory stimuli (where the numbers are spoken) by presenting both interchangeably (through the speaker in the computer). The test takes about 13 minutes.

The IVA provides scores for errors of omission and commission, as well as response speed and response speed variability. Results for auditory and visual stimuli are presented separately, allowing for comparison between the two modalities. Full-scale impulsivity and attention quotients are also calculated. In addition, a fine motor regulation scale is calculated from excessive mouse clicks. Three validity scales are included that assess for neurological and/or learning problems, poor motivation or motor fatigue, and lack of comprehension. The printout of results does not provide any interpretive notes, but additional software can be purchased that produces an interpretive report.

The test was normed on nearly 500 individuals ranging in age from 5 to 90 years, and the interpretive report provides standard scores and percentiles by age and sex. As with the TOVA, psychometric data are derived from unpublished studies. For example, Sanford, Fine, and Goldman (1995; cf. Barkley, 2006) reported a rate of false negatives of 8% and a rate of false positives of 10%. Although these results seem promising, it appears that they have not been published or replicated. In addition, the test was normed in the early 1990s, and the norms are becoming outdated. Although the IVA provides an important dimension not included in the other tests (auditory stimuli), clinicians are encouraged to approach the scores with caution, and any diagnosis of ADHD should not be based solely on the results provided by the IVA.

Gordon Diagnostic System

The Gordon Diagnostic System (GDS; Gordon, 1983) is similar to the other visual CPTs, but it is available only in a self-contained portable unit that includes the computer and the monitor. In a 9-minute trial, three tasks are administered, two for attention and one for impulse control. In the vigilance task, nondistracting and distracting tasks are presented. In the nondistracting tasks, the respondent must press a button when a certain combination of numbers flashes on the screen. In the distracting portion, target digits are shown surrounded by distracting numbers. A third task aims at impulse control and requires inhibition of responding. Separate adult, child, and preschool versions are available, and parallel forms are also included to reduce practice effects when retesting.

The GDS provides a printout that includes raw data and percentiles of correct responses, incorrect responses, and failures to respond. Normative data, based on approximately 1,000 boys and girls, are available for children aged 3 through 16 years. Norms are also available for adults, but these data are based on small samples, and the test has been found to have poor sensitivity for individuals older than age 14 years (Oehler-Stinnett, 1998). Psychometric properties appear to be well established. Rates of false positives have been reported to be about 2%, but rates of false negatives have ranged from 15% to 35%, indicating poor specificity (Gordon & Mettelman, 1988). Clinicians are encouraged to use it primarily for screening or as a research tool and not as the basis for rendering a diagnosis of ADHD.

FORMAL PSYCHOLOGICAL ASSESSMENT

Instead of using focused instruments specifically designed to measure symptoms of ADHD, some clinicians prefer to administer (or refer clients for) formal psychological testing. A comprehensive psychological evaluation usually includes tests of cognitive aptitude and personality functioning, which are sometimes supplemented by tests of academic achievement. Tests of cognitive function generally provide a profile of cognitive abilities and may include an intelligence quotient. Tests of educational achievement measure acquired knowledge and academic skills. Personality measures can be useful to assess aspects of personality that may reflect symptoms of ADHD.

It is important for clinicians to have appropriate expectations about psychological tests. On the one hand, these instruments provide a significant breadth of information that can identify a wide variety of problems that require clinical attention. On the other hand, much research into these techniques has revealed that formal psychological testing is of limited value in diagnosing ADHD, and no ADHD-specific profile of scores has been established for any of these tests (Barkley, 2006). Consequently, it is important for clinicians to understand that these instruments provide useful information, especially about comorbid conditions, but any results that may be suggestive of ADHD should be followed up with the administration of techniques specifically focused on ADHD symptoms and cross-validated with the *DSM-IV* diagnostic criteria. Several such measures were described in this chapter.

Tests of Cognitive Aptitude

Measures that assess cognitive aptitude are often referred to as intelligence tests, although it is more accurate to say that *intelligence* is a comprehensive term that describes a subset of cognitive aptitude, and not all tests of aptitude are tests of intelligence. Still, the most widely administered cognitive aptitude tests are the Stanford-Binet Intelligence Scales and Wechsler tests of intelligence.

It is common for boys and male teens suspected of ADHD to undergo a psychological evaluation that includes the administration of these tests. For example, if the student is being evaluated for eligibility for special education services, a routine assessment performed by the school's child study team will usually include one of those instruments. As mentioned previously, however, no specific profile of scores reflective of ADHD has been established, and therefore the diagnosis of ADHD cannot be made from the results obtained from these tests.

Wechsler Tests. The Wechsler family of intelligence tests is the most commonly used, and it includes versions for preschoolers (Wechsler Preschool and Primary Scales of Intelligence, Third Edition [WPPSI-III]; Wechsler, 2002), children and adolescents (Wechsler Intelligence Scale for Children, Fourth Edition [WISC-IV]; Wechsler, 2003), and adults (Wechsler Adult Intelligence Scale, Fourth Edition [WAIS-IV]; Wechsler, 2008). Wechsler tests offer an extensive profile that includes scores for every subtest administered, as well as composites that measure Verbal Comprehension, Perceptual Reasoning, Working Memory, and Processing Speed and an overall Full Scale Intelligence Quotient.

Some of the subtests were once thought to measure distractibility, and on the previous edition of the Wechsler tests, the Freedom From Distractibility Factor score was calculated from scores on the Arithmetic, Digit Span (participants must repeat a series of numbers that was just stated by the test administrator), and Coding (a graphomotor task that requires participants to sequentially reproduce 10 symbols, in varying order, under a time pressure) subtests. Although some studies have showed statistically significant correlation between this factor score and measures of inattention (Klee & Garfinkel, 1983), results of research have also revealed that this score was not able to discriminate children with ADHD from nonclinical samples or those with learning disorders, and the false positive rate was estimated to fall between 48% and 77% (Anastopoulos, Spisto, & Maher, 1994). Consequently, these subtests have been reassigned to other factors in the newest version of the test.

These results provide a good example of both the benefits and the shortcomings of the use of intelligence tests in assessing ADHD. On the one hand, specificity is very poor, and therefore a diagnosis of ADHD cannot be made based on results from these tests. The results, however, provide a comprehensive breadth of scores that can signal the presence of other disorders, including learning disabilities.

Stanford-Binet Intelligence Scales. The Stanford-Binet Intelligence Scales, currently in its fifth edition (Roid, 2003), is an alternative to the Wechsler tests, but it has much in common with them. The test is designed to provide assessment of individuals from age 2 to late adulthood, and different subtests are administered to different age groups. Like the Wechsler tests, the Stanford-Binet offers an extensive profile that includes scores for every subtest; composites for Fluid Reasoning, Knowledge, Quantitative Reasoning, Visual–Spatial Processing, and Working Memory; and an overall Full Scale Intelligence Quotient.

The Stanford-Binet, even more than the Wechsler tests, is specifically designed to assist in the diagnosis of learning disorders, and large portions of the test manual are devoted to this issue. Guidelines are provided to help determine what score profiles may suggest learning problems, and research is cited to back the claims that the test offers desirable specificity when making these classifications. The Stanford-Binet has not undergone as much independent research as the Wechsler tests, however, and therefore many of the findings have not been replicated. As with the Wechsler tests, the test is psychometrically sound and offers extensive, nationally representative norms. It is a good alternative to the Wechsler tests, especially on retesting. For example, to minimize an inflation in test scores commonly associated with repeated administration of the same test, individuals previously tested with the Wechsler tests can be retested with the Stanford-Binet. In addition, the Stanford-Binet is generally regarded as having a "lower floor" and a "higher ceiling" than the Wechsler tests. Because the subtests provide more items at both ends of the range of difficulty, the Stanford-Binet is a particularly good choice to assess individuals suspected of low or high cognitive functioning.

In summary, as with the results of Wechsler tests, the results of the Stanford-Binet provide a comprehensive breadth of scores that can signal the presence of other disorders, especially learning disabilities, but the subtest and composite scores are not helpful in assessing the severity of symptoms of ADHD. ADHD cannot be diagnosed based on the scores obtained from the Stanford-Binet.

Tests of Academic Achievement

When educational functioning and skills must be assessed, it is helpful to supplement tests of aptitude with tests that reflect the current level of academic knowledge and skills. Tests of achievement fall into various categories. Some focus on a wide range of academic skills and abilities, whereas others are more specific and focus only on reading, mathematics, or another discrete academic skill. In addition, some tests that assess a specific ability are further subdivided into portions that measure various aspects of that skill. For example, a reading test may have separate sections that assess word attack skills, phonics, and so on.

A comprehensive review of academic achievement tests is beyond the scope of this chapter. Two tests will be briefly described, however, to illustrate the ways in which tests of academic achievement are commonly used to supplement tests of aptitude. Although these techniques do not specifically relate to the diagnosis of ADHD symptoms, they can be very helpful when assessing the presence or absence of learning disorders that commonly accompany the symptoms of ADHD.

Wechsler Individual Achievement Test (WIAT). The WIAT, currently in its second edition (WIAT-II; Wechsler, 2001), is divided into eight subtests that provide scores for four academic content areas—reading, mathematics, written language, and oral language. An overall score and a screener score are also provided. The test was normed on over 1,000 students and offers evidence of good psychometric properties, and the second edition is intended for use with individuals aged 4 through 85 years. Both age and grade norms are provided for individuals who completed education of up to 4 years of college. The extension into adulthood will be of particular interest to those who are evaluating adult males with ADHD and want to assess whether learning disorders may also be present.

In accordance with the special education laws of most states, a diagnosis of learning disabilities may be rendered when there is evidence of a significant discrepancy (usually at least 2 standard deviations) between an aptitude score (e.g., derived on a standardized intelligence test, such as the Stanford-Binet and the Wechsler tests) and a corresponding achievement score. Calculations are necessary to statistically compare the aptitude and achievement scores and identify the discrepancy. To improve the accuracy and sensitivity of this procedure, intercorrelations between the measure of aptitude and the specific test of academic achievement must be accounted for in the procedure. Although research data exist that provide intercorrelations between (primarily) the Wechsler tests and various achievement tests, calculating discrepancy scores that account for these intercorrelations can be tedious, cumbersome, and very time-consuming.

The Wechsler tests greatly simply this task by cross-referencing the Wechsler tests of intelligence with the WIAT-II, and the scoring and interpretive software generates expected WIAT-II subtest and composite scores based on the obtained Wechsler IQ score. The expected and actual WIAT-II scores are then compared, and the clinician can establish the necessary minimum discrepancy (e.g., 2 standard deviations). The software then flags the significant discrepancies. Although this technique has some critics, it is still used by the majority of states, and clinicians who wish to assess whether a boy, male teen, or man suspected of having ADHD may also present with a learning disorder will find the convenience offered by the Wechsler tests very useful.

Woodcock-Johnson. The third edition of the Woodcock-Johnson III battery (WJ-III; Woodcock, McGrew, & Mather, 2001) is intended for individuals aged 2 to 90 years and offers a comprehensive assessment of achievement and aptitude. The WJ-III renders a wide multitude of scores, including 18 individual subtest scores and more than 10 cluster scores. It is a mature instrument that offers extensive evidence of sound psychometric properties, and it is normed on a large, nationally representative sample. It has become the de facto standard educational achievement battery administered by child study team professionals in schools.

Because the current version offers two separate batteries, one each for cognitive (aptitude) abilities and academic achievement, the available scoring and interpretive software calculates the discrepancy discussed earlier, streamlining the process of diagnosing learning disorders. Although the aptitude scores have been found to correlate highly with the Wechsler intelligence scores (Flanagan, 2001), however, subtests and scores between the two instruments are not interchangeable, and the validity of the WJ-III as a measure of intelligence is not well established. In addition, comparative rates for cross-referencing discrepancies between the Wechsler and WJ-III methods are similarly unknown, and therefore there is no guarantee that any individual identified with significant discrepancy through the Wechsler method (described earlier) would similarly be diagnosed by the aptitude-achievement discrepancy calculated from the WJ-III scores. To address this problem, the publisher provided data that allowed for manual calculations of WJ-III–WISC-III discrepancies (Schrank, Becker, & Decker, 2001). This procedure, however, is tedious and not widely used. In addition, the WISC-III has since been updated to the WISC-IV, and data for manual calculations of WJ-III–WISC-IV discrepancies are not yet available. Clinicians are cautioned against relying solely on the WJ-III discrepancies, especially when the WJ-III cognitive aptitude score is significantly different from the Wechsler IQ score or when the Wechsler IQ score is not available.

Tests of Personality

Boys, male teens, and men referred for psychological evaluations are usually administered at least some instruments that measure aspects of their personality. As with tests of academic achievement, a wide variety of instruments is available. Some of these instruments focus on specific personality characteristics, whereas others offer much broader assessment. In addition, some techniques measure personality characteristics by using objective measures, for example, counting specific (usually, yes–no) responses to a list of questions, whereas others provide the examinee with stimuli that are nonspecific and require the participant to construct a response by projecting some meaning into these items. Both approaches have some benefits and drawbacks, and most representative examples of each are briefly reviewed next.

Objective Tests. Inventories that assess aspects of personality through responses to a large list of questions are among the most popular of all psychological tests. Use of the Minnesota inventories is especially common, including the adult (Minnesota Multiphasic Personality Inventory–2 [MMPI-2]; Hathaway & McKinley, 1989) and adolescent (Minnesota Multiphasic Personality Inventory–Adolescent [MMPI-A]; Butcher et al., 1992) versions. The MMPIs provide a multitude of scores, including 5 validity scales, 10 main clinical scales, and a wide number of content and supplemental scales. The MMPI-2 is widely used in clinical, forensic, and vocational assessments and is supported by decades of active research.

Various computer-generated interpretive reports are available that provide diagnostic impressions based on statistical analyses of clinical and validity scales and the examination of the patterns of the elevation of the three clinical scales with the highest scores. In some cases, this pattern is suggestive of the diagnosis of ADHD, and the software will identify ADHD as one possible diagnosis. Clinicians must be aware that as with all psychological tests discussed thus far, no specific profile of scales has been identified that differentiates ADHD from other disorders with sufficient sensitivity and specificity, and therefore the diagnostic suggestions in the interpretive reports must be treated as being only tentative and cannot become the basis of any diagnosis of ADHD. The MMPIs, however, can be very valuable in providing additional clinical information that can potentially identify symptoms of comorbid disorders.

Similarly, the Millon tests are widely used by clinicians and currently include an adult (Millon Clinical Multiaxial Inventory–III [MCMI-III]; Millon, Millon, Davis, & Grossman, 1996) and two adolescent (Millon Adolescent Clinical Inventory [MACI]; Millon, Millon, Davis, & Grossman, 1993; and Millon Adolescent Personality Inventory [MAPI]; Millon, Green, & Meagher, 1982) versions. Shorter than the MMPIs, the Millon inventories provide fewer scores and similarly generate interpretive reports with the available software. The Millon tests are popular in many clinical settings and are considered to be more focused on identifying psychopathology. In addition, because Theodore Millon is the author of the portion of the *DSM* diagnostic system that describes personality disorders, the Millon instruments are particularly useful when clinicians wish to assess the presence of one of those disorders.

As is the case with the MMPIs, interpretive reports generated from the Millon test scores provide diagnostic impressions based on statistical analyses of the scales. Although the obtained results may sometimes be suggestive of ADHD, clinicians must again remember that no specific profile of scales on any of the Millon tests has been identified that sufficiently differentiates ADHD from other disorders, and therefore any diagnostic suggestions cannot become the basis of the diagnosis of ADHD. Results from the Millon inventories, however, can be valuable in providing additional clinical information that can potentially identify a wide variety of symptoms, especially those symptoms that accompany personality disorders.

Projective Tests. Projective measures predate objective tests and have been around for more than a century. In projective tests, the participant generates a response that must then be interpreted to determine its clinical significance. Early projective tests included word associations, drawing techniques, and responses to a series of pictures. Various versions of the House–Tree–Person technique and Thematic Apperception Test are still in use by some psychologists, especially those who are psychodynamically oriented. Clinicians should be warned that these techniques suffer from lack of evidence of sufficient psychometric qualities, and most have not been normed (or the norms are so old that they are currently irrelevant).

One exception is the Rorschach inkblot test. It is a technique that has been around for many decades, and five different scoring systems have been developed and standardized. Of these, the Exner (2002) system is by far the most comprehensive and psychometrically robust, and various scores and dimensions of the Exner system have been empirically investigated and have been found to be reliable and valid. In addition, the system is based on reasonably current normative data.

The Rorschach test provides a wide variety of indices that assess personality and the processing of emotions. Some of the indices are directly relevant to symptoms of ADHD and provide information about the degree of impulse and self-control, particularly when the participant is faced with emotion-provoking stimuli. The Rorschach test, however, presents with the same shortcoming as all other psychological tests described in this section—limited sensitivity and specificity with regard to symptoms of ADHD. Thus, results from the Rorschach test can be very useful only to provide initial information about possible symptoms that require more focused assessment and cannot be used to establish a diagnosis of ADHD.

NEUROPSYCHOLOGICAL ASSESSMENT

Neuropsychological tests are usually administered when a person is suspected of having some specific brain dysfunction, for example, one that may be the result of a head trauma. The vast majority of these techniques require significant training to administer and interpret, and most psychologists who administer these techniques identify themselves as neuropsychologists.

Whether a boy, male teen, or adult male requires a neuropsychological evaluation depends on a variety of factors. Most males in treatment for ADHD-like symptoms will not need a neuropsychological evaluation, because other measures specific to the dimensions of ADHD symptoms, many of which were described earlier in this chapter, are able to sufficiently guide the diagnosis. Other males, however, may come into treatment with a history of physical trauma that may require a diagnostic work-up, or they may suffer from neurological disorders (e.g., seizures) that possibly may be producing neuropsychological deficits. In those cases, clinicians should consider a referral to a neuropsychologist. In addition, some males seeking treatment may have previously undergone neuropsychological evaluations, and consequently clinicians will benefit from at least some familiarity with neuropsychological tests and batteries.

As is the case with other psychological tests, some neuropsychological instruments are grouped into established batteries, and others are usually used as stand-alone tests to seek information about a specific aspect of neuropsychological functioning.

Neuropsychological Batteries. The Halstead-Reitan Battery (H-R), last updated in the 1980s (Heaton, Miller, Taylor, & Grant, 1991), assesses a variety of brain functions, including sensory (visual, auditory, and tactile) and motor skills, verbal skills, spatial and sequential reasoning, and higher mental processes that involve analysis, judgment, attention, concentration, and memory. Although some of these functions are at least conceptually related to ADHD, clinicians are cautioned that a review of these dimensions vis-à-vis *DSM-IV* diagnostic criteria for ADHD revealed that the H-R was not able to meaningfully tap into symptoms of ADHD, and neither the Halstead Impairment Index nor the score for the General Neuropsychological Deficit Scale were able to meaningfully differentiate individuals with ADHD (Barkley, 2006).

Another major instrument is the Luria-Nebraska Neuropsychological Battery (LNNB; Golden, Hammeke, & Purisch, 1979). Shorter and easier to administer, the LNNB is a comprehensive set of tests designed to assess brain function in accordance with the influential theories of Luria (1976). The LNNB generates 14 scores for sensory and motor abilities, speech, reading, writing, memory, arithmetic, intellectual processes, and the functioning of each lateral hemisphere. As with the H-R, some of these subtests assess areas of function that relate to the symptoms of ADHD. Investigations of the LNNB, however, revealed that none of the scores obtained from the LNNB were related in any meaningful way to ADHD symptoms (Shaughency et al., 1989). Consequently, although neuropsychological batteries are useful to assess brain function and identify specific deficits associated with brain damage, they have not shown any utility in diagnosing symptoms of ADHD.

Specific Neuropsychological Tests. In addition to these batteries, a vast array of neuropsychological instruments is available to assess specific brain functions. Some of these tests focus on executive functions. For example, the Wisconsin Card Sorting Test (WCST; Grant & Berg, 1948/2003) measures frontal lobe and executive dysfunction. Some studies have reported that significant differences in the WCST scores were seen in individuals with ADHD as opposed to nonclinical samples. Other studies have revealed, however, that the WCST accurately diagnosed symptoms of ADHD in only 50% to 71% of cases and, conversely, verified the absence of the disorder in only 49% to 56% of cases. In addition, false negative rates ranged from 61% to 89%. Thus, it is clear that this test does not exhibit sufficient sensitivity and specificity to be used to diagnose ADHD.

Tests of self-control have also been investigated. For example, the Stroop Color and Word Test (Golden & Freshwater, 2002) has been around since the 1930s and is well established as a measure of self-control and mental flexibility. Because individuals are required to inhibit automatic responses, this test has been hypothesized to be a good measure of impulsivity, related to commission errors on CPTs. Indeed, studies have revealed that individuals with ADHD perform more poorly on this test, and the Stroop test may discriminate individuals with ADHD from nonclinical individuals (Frazier, Demaree, & Youngstrom, 2004). A meta-analysis of studies that investigated the use of the Stroop test (Homack & Riccio, 2004), however, revealed that the test does not exhibit sufficient specificity or predictive power, and the risk of false positives and false negatives is unacceptably high. Thus, this instrument should not be used to diagnose ADHD.

Cancellation tasks attempt to assess symptoms of inattentiveness. Respondents usually are asked to mark through target letters or figures that are embedded among distractors, usually under time pressure. For example, the d2 Test of Attention (Brickenkamp & Zillmer, 1998) asks individuals to correctly identify the letter *d* with two dashes anywhere around it while ignoring similar letters (*p*, *b*, and *q*) or other *d*s that have more or less than two dashes. The performance is rigorously timed across 14 short trials. The d2 test provides both standard scores and percentiles for the total number of letters processed and also errors of omission and commission. Additional indices related to attention are also calculated.

The test provides normative data for children and adolescents aged 9 through 18 (in 2-year intervals) and adults (aged 19–39, 40–49, and 50–59). Normative data for children and adolescents are provided separately by sex, but both sexes are grouped together in adult norms. In addition, the norms are based on German samples, and only small studies have thus far been performed in the United States to cross-validate the instrument.

Validity data for the d2 test reveal that the test is able to sufficiently differentiate individuals with schizophrenia, dementia, epilepsy, and ADHD from normal controls. The study samples, however, are exceedingly small (sometimes fewer than 50 individuals), and the test's ability to differentiate symptoms between various disorders that impair attention has not been established. Thus, although the d2 test is promising, currently it can be used only to perform general screening, and diagnosis of ADHD cannot be made based on the results of this test.

BRAIN SCANS

As covered in the previous chapter, various forms of brain scans have been used in research to identify the specific structural and functional brain differences associated with ADHD. For this reason, patients sometimes inquire about whether these same scanning techniques can be used to verify the presence of these deficits in a specific individual to aid in rendering the diagnosis of ADHD.

Magnetic resonance imaging (MRI), functional magnetic resonance imaging (fMRI), single photon emission tomography (SPECT), and positron emission tomography (PET) scans have all been used in research, but they are not useful in diagnosing ADHD in specific individuals. Although each of these techniques has identified specific patterns characteristic of ADHD, no cutoff criteria have been established for when a difference apparent on the brain scan is clinically significant. Comparing individuals with ADHD with normal controls reveals that, as a group, the affected individuals exhibit changes, but individual variation is common among both clinically affected and nonaffected individuals, and some overlap is evident. Statistical methods that evaluate group findings are able to discern consistent patterns, but such procedures cannot be used on scans of a single individual. In addition, most of these brain scans are prohibitively expensive, and insurance plans will not cover the cost.

In research, electroencephalogram (EEG) studies have revealed inconsistent findings, but quantitative EEG (QEEG) measures have identified a specific pattern of beta and theta activity in the frontal lobes typical of individuals with ADHD. These techniques are cheaper (the usual cost is $300 to $700), and some neurological professionals perform these scans in their office. Consequently, some professionals recommend the use of QEEG examination in the diagnosis of ADHD (Monastra, 2008). Noted researchers in this area, however, are skeptical about the utility of QEEG results to diagnose ADHD, and they recommend against its use for this purpose (Barkley, 2006). Review of studies reveals that the positive predictive power (an abnormal QEEG correctly predicting a diagnosis of ADHD) has been reported to be as high as 98%, but the negative predictive power (a normal QEEG correctly predicting non-ADHD individuals) has been reported to be only 76%. This means that 24% of children with a normal QEEG profile still go on to be diagnosed with ADHD by other means. In addition, when the ability of a QEEG to differentiate children with ADHD from those with other childhood disorders (e.g., learning problems) was examined, 20% to 35% were misclassified. Such high rates of incorrect diagnosis are unacceptable. Indeed, after several exhaustive reviews of relevant literature, Barkley and colleagues have continued to recommend against the use of the QEEG to diagnose ADHD (e.g., Loo & Barkley, 2005). Nevertheless, some professionals continue to recommend this procedure and misrepresent its benefits. Clinicians should warn clients to be wary of this unscrupulous practice.

SUMMARY

Although brain scans (including the QEEG) are not useful to diagnose symptoms of ADHD, instruments are available that assess and classify the symptoms of this disorder. Some behavioral checklists and inventories have been developed to specifically assess the degree of hyperactivity/impulsivity and inattentiveness/disorganization. Data are usually collected from observers (such as parents or teachers), but self-report forms are also commonly available. When clearly anchored to the *DSM* criteria, some of these measures offer good psychometric properties and sufficient protection against false positives and false negatives to be useful in rating the severity of the symptoms of ADHD. In addition, the behavioral measures reviewed herein allow clinicians to establish more conservative cutoffs (2 standard deviations above the mean) to prevent overclassification. Variants for boys, male teens, and men exist, and most clinicians will likely find these instruments to be valuable.

CPTs attempt to measure symptoms of ADHD more directly by presenting repetitive tasks via computerized administration. Although most of these instruments focus on visual tasks, some also measure auditory performance. Although these tests are promising, and popular with researchers, clinicians generally find that these tests are not quite as accurate as behavioral inventories, and sensitivity and specificity are sometimes insufficient. Some tests allow the clinician to use a variety of scoring algorithms to separately minimize false positives and false negatives, and those instruments generally offer the most promise and clinical utility.

Formal psychological testing is not usually effective in rendering the diagnosis, but comprehensive psychological assessment is beneficial when the clinician is assessing a wide variety of symptoms and functional problems. Psychologists commonly use various combinations of tests of aptitude, academic achievement, and personality. Each of those categories contributes valuable information, and a comprehensive battery is usually able to identify a variety of problem areas that require attention. If those areas include the symptoms commonly associated with ADHD, clinicians are encouraged to supplement the results of a psychological test battery with a behavioral inventory or a CPT.

Neuropsychological evaluations are generally performed when it is necessary to assess the presence of brain damage. Although many techniques assess executive functions, memory, concentration, and mental flexibility and control, these techniques have not been shown to possess sufficient sensitivity or specificity to be used to diagnose ADHD. As noted by Barkley (2006), referral for neuropsychological evaluation to diagnose ADHD is unnecessary and not cost-effective. If brain damage or organic dysfunction is suspected, however, results of neuropsychological tasks can be invaluable in diagnosing these problems. If problems with symptoms associated with ADHD are reported (and other conditions that may produce such symptoms have been ruled out), clinicians can supplement ADHD-specific measures (such as behavioral inventories or CPTs) to increase the accuracy of the diagnosis.

5

Differential Diagnosis

After our review of the symptoms, etiology, course, and assessment instruments, it is necessary to consider the most effective methods, in addition to the measures discussed thus far, through which appropriate information can be gathered to allow a rigorous differential diagnosis. This is generally accomplished through clinical interviews. To appropriately focus these interviews, however, the clinician must plan to inquire about the sufficient breadth of information that will be necessary to perform the diagnosis. Thus, diagnostic criteria in the *Diagnostic and Statistical Manual of Mental Disorders* (*DSM-IV*; American Psychiatric Association [APA], 1994) must be reviewed, as these will guide the process of gathering relevant data.

DIAGNOSTIC CRITERIA IN *DSM-IV-TR*

The *DSM* system requires clinicians to use both inclusion and exclusion criteria when making a diagnosis. The inclusion criteria are usually considered first, after which exclusion criteria must also be met.

Inclusion Criteria

Since 1994, the *DSM* system considers symptoms of attention deficit/hyperactivity disorder (ADHD) to fall along two dimensions: hyperactivity/impulsivity and inattention (which also includes disorganization). In criterion A, the *DSM-IV-TR* (APA, 2000) first lists examples of symptoms of inattention and disorganization:

    a. often fails to give close attention to details or makes careless mistakes in schoolwork, work, or other activities
    b. often has difficulty sustaining attention in tasks or play activities

    c. often does not seem to listen when spoken to directly
    d. often does not follow through on instructions and fails to finish schoolwork, chores, or duties in the workplace (not due to oppositional behavior or failure to understand instructions)
    e. often has difficulty organizing tasks and activities
    f. often avoids, dislikes, or is reluctant to engage in tasks that require sustained mental effort (such as schoolwork or homework)
    g. often loses things necessary for tasks or activities (e.g., toys, school assignments, pencils, books, or tools)
    h. is often easily distracted by extraneous stimuli
    i. is often forgetful in daily activities (p. 92).

Clinicians should note that these activities include examples of difficulties that may be evident in boys, male teens, or men of any age, although many researchers feel that the current *DSM* criteria favor boys rather than teens or men. In addition, the examples include behaviors that, by definition, will be present across various settings, such as home, school, or work (more on that later). The *DSM* system defines two additional criteria that must be met. The symptoms from the list must consistently be present for at least 6 months. In this way, occasional problems would not qualify someone to be diagnosed, and the level of severity must be sufficient to result in maladaptive behaviors that are inconsistent with the client's developmental level. For example, it is common for young boys to exhibit a short attention span and a high degree of energy and activity. Before clinicians consider a clinical diagnosis, they must consider to what degree those behaviors exceed what is normally expected in that age group and for that sex. This is where the assessment tools reviewed in the previous chapter become very valuable. Several of those instruments are specifically focused on the symptoms in the list and cross-referenced with *DSM-IV* criteria. In addition, those instruments that provide good psychometric qualities and are normed by age (preferably in 1-year intervals) and sex provide the opportunity for clinicians to rate the relative severity of the behaviors listed by comparing them to what is "normal" for boys in that age group. Thus, when clinicians set appropriate cutoffs (e.g., 2 standard deviations above the mean) for when the behaviors exceed the norm, they follow the spirit of the *DSM* system and prevent overclassification.

In criterion A, the *DSM-IV-TR* also lists examples of symptoms of hyperactivity/impulsivity:

    a. often fidgets with hands or feet or squirms in seat
    b. often leaves seat in classroom or in other situations in which remaining seated is expected
    c. often runs about or climbs excessively in situations in which it is inappropriate (in adolescents or adults, may be limited to subjective feelings of restlessness)
    d. often has difficulty playing or engaging in leisure activities quietly

e. is often "on the go" and often acts as if "driven by a motor"
f. often talks excessively
g. often blurts out answers before questions have been completed
h. often has difficulty awaiting turn
i. often interrupts or intrudes on others (e.g., butts into conversations or games) (p. 92).

The *DSM* identifies Item a through Item f as symptoms of hyperactivity and identifies the remaining items as symptoms of impulsivity, but it is clear that some overlap exists between those two categories, and the *DSM* has consequently placed both on this unified dimension. As with symptoms of inattentiveness/disorganization, the *DSM* requires the consistent presence of symptoms for at least 6 months and a level of severity that both is maladaptive and exceeds what is expected for the appropriate developmental level. As discussed previously, use of appropriate instruments can help clinicians make the diagnosis while avoiding overclassification.

By allowing clinicians to diagnose ADHD when sufficient presence of symptoms is evident in either (or both) dimensions, the *DSM-IV* recognizes three different types of ADHD: predominantly inattentive type, where sufficient symptoms of inattentiveness/disorganization (but not hyperactivity/impulsivity) are present; predominantly hyperactive-impulsive type, where the reverse is true; and combined type, where sufficient symptoms are present in both categories.

Clinicians should be aware of one final issue about this method of classification. Although the *DSM* allows for the three subtypes just discussed, prevalence data suggest that some of these types are much less common. For example, the predominantly hyperactive-impulsive type is rarely seen in treatment samples and, by some accounts, constitutes less than 15% of all cases of ADHD (Lee et al., 2008). Conversely, the predominantly inattentive and combined types are more equally distributed in samples that have been studied. Consequently, clinicians who identify a client with sufficient symptoms of hyperactivity/impulsivity should carefully screen whether symptoms of inattentiveness/disorganization are also present, because children who present with symptoms from only the former cluster seem to be rare. On the other hand, no good data are available about the prevalence of the predominantly hyperactive-impulsive type of ADHD in adults.

After reviewing the symptom clusters, clinicians must next determine the onset of those symptoms. By definition, ADHD is considered to be a disorder in which symptoms are present at least in part because of significant neurodevelopmental factors. Inherent in this assumption is the expectation that symptoms of ADHD should start at an early age rather than have a sudden onset later in childhood. Accordingly, criterion B in the *DSM* requires symptoms to have been evident prior to age 7 and that the severity was sufficient to cause functional impairment by that age.

When diagnosing boys or teens with prominent symptoms of hyperactivity and impulsivity, clinicians can easily confirm this criterion, because parents of children with a long history of these symptoms generally notice them early in life and are able to verify early onset. Boys and teens who present with inattentive symptoms and no history of significant hyperactivity or impulsivity, however, may not come to the parents' attention until later in childhood, for example, when they start to attend grades that require harder work and more organizational abilities. In those cases, it is important to direct parents to consider whether there were early signs of problems in these areas that may not have been recognized at the time. If parents deny this, and it is apparent that significant symptoms started after age 7, the clinician cannot diagnose ADHD (with the exception of the "Not Otherwise Specified" option discussed later in this chapter).

Determining whether criterion B is met in adult clients is much more challenging. Although some adults may remember whether they started to present symptoms in early childhood, some may not have a clear recollection. For this reason, it is usually desirable to have access to some collateral information. Obtaining this information can be accomplished by requesting permission to contact family members (such as parents or siblings) or reviewing historical data (such as report cards from school).

Criterion C requires symptoms of the disorder (those identified in the two dimensions in criterion A) to be present in at least two different settings, causing at least *some* impairment. Although the *DSM* provides examples of only three settings (home, school, and work), most clinicians extend this criterion to also include out-of-home settings (e.g., when boys accompany parents to a store) and social situations (e.g., where the boy or teen is playing with peers). Thus, when gathering relevant history, clinicians must inquire about a variety of settings and whether impairment in them was apparent at least to some degree. When the client is an adult, collateral data should usually be sought to verify whether this criterion is met, unless the client is able to describe examples from his own recollection that verify these problems. Clinicians should also note the *DSM*'s specific wording: Criterion C requires at least *some* impairment rather than *clinical* impairment.

Conversely, criterion D requires *clinically significant* impairment in social, academic, or occupational functioning. This criterion was developed to ensure that candidates for the diagnosis present significant functional impairment in at least one setting where the symptoms, if severe enough, would be expected to be maladaptive. This usually means that boys and teens with ADHD should present with significant problems evident in school, and men with ADHD should present with significant occupational difficulties.

The *DSM* allows for some flexibility, where criterion D can be met by evidence of problems in social settings (i.e., with peers). Clinicians, however, should also consider whether the symptom profile is consistent with what is expected from individuals with ADHD. Significant inat-tentiveness/disorganization or hyperactivity/impulsivity, especially when evident since early age, *should* generally be expected to cause functional difficulties at school. If symptoms persist into adulthood (as needs to be the case to meet criterion A for adult clients), these *should* usually cause occupational problems. Consequently, clinicians who encounter boys, teens, or men who do not seem to exhibit significant problems at school and/or work need to consider whether the symp-toms are severe enough to warrant a diagnosis. In those cases, careful differential diagnosis is especially needed to identify the clinical syn-drome that may be present.

Exclusion Criteria

If the client meets the inclusion criteria described earlier, the exclu-sion criteria must then be examined before the diagnosis can be made. Criterion E in the *DSM* states that for individuals to be diagnosed with ADHD, they cannot exhibit symptoms that are present only during the course of an otherwise diagnosed pervasive developmental disorder (PDD) or psychotic disorder (e.g., schizophrenia). Although the exclu-sion related to psychotic disorders is rarely questioned, the exclusion related to the subcategory of PDD, which includes autism and Asperger's syndrome, is one of the most controversial aspects of the *DSM* criteria for ADHD.

The *DSM* follows the principle of parsimony, where symptoms should be accounted for by as few syndromes as possible. Children with vari-ous forms of PDD commonly also exhibit symptoms of ADHD, but the presumption is that the specific PDD already accounts for those symp-toms, and the etiology responsible for causing that disorder is already known to result with symptoms that resemble ADHD. Thus, a separate diagnosis of ADHD is not needed.

Many researchers, however, have questioned this exclusion. For example, Pennington and Ozonoff (1991; cf. Tannock, 2002) compared children with ADHD and autism head-to-head and found that although some overlap was evident, children with autism (and not ADHD) revealed greater deficiencies in memory and cognition, whereas children with ADHD (and not autism) revealed greater problems with motor and self-control. In addition, there were children who exhibited both, suggesting that ADHD and autism are separate clinical syndromes that can exist independently and sometimes co-occur.

One area of particularly heated debate is whether ADHD can coexist with Asperger's syndrome. Strictly following the *DSM* criteria, the two cannot be diagnosed together, because Asperger's syndrome is a disorder classified within the subcategory of PDD. Research results reveal, how-ever, that the two disorders may either coexist or exist separately, and indi-viduals with both disorders seem to exhibit a much greater overall level of impairment (Goldstein & Schwebach, 2004). Thus, some clinicians have argued that future versions of the *DSM* should eliminate this exclusion (Holtmann, Bolte, & Poutska, 2005). At this time, although the two diagnoses are still "officially" mutually exclusive, many clinicians who see symptoms of both disorders apply both diagnostic labels.

Criterion E also requires clinicians to assess whether the symptoms of ADHD occur exclusively while the client is also presenting symptoms of another mental disorder that better accounts for those symptoms. For example, individuals with mood disorders often exhibit agitation, restlessness, impulsivity, or problems with distractibility. Similarly, clients with anxiety and dissociative disorders and adults with personality disorders may also exhibit similar problems. Generally, the *DSM* discourages diagnosing individuals with both syndromes, unless the course is somewhat different (e.g., symptoms of a mood disorder wax and wane episodically, whereas symptoms of ADHD remain more consistently). Issues involved in diagnosing another disorder, or a comorbid disorder, are discussed in more detail later in this chapter.

ADHD Not Otherwise Specified

When clinicians encounter a client who seems to exhibit most of the symptoms of ADHD but does not meet at least one of the diagnostic criteria, a diagnosis of ADHD Not Otherwise Specified (NOS) can be assigned. In those cases, mental health professionals need to consider what criteria will be relaxed and whether the individual in question still requires a diagnosis. Clinicians are encouraged to follow a decision tree to guide them when making such a decision.

First, criterion A should be examined. It is difficult to argue that individuals who exhibit fewer symptoms than required in criterion A still exhibit a disorder that resembles ADHD. Consequently, if criterion A is not met, it is not likely that any variant of ADHD, including NOS, is present.

Next, criterion D should be examined. Is there significant impairment in social, academic, and/or occupational functioning to warrant a diagnosis? If not, it is likely that the client's symptoms do not qualify for a diagnosis of ADHD. Criterion C should also be considered. For example, if the symptoms are evident only at home, ADHD NOS may be present, but clinicians should look whether other disorders (and/or difficulties in familial relationships) better account for the symptoms.

Next, criterion E should be examined. If the symptoms that are primarily apparent coexist with symptoms of a mood, anxiety, or another major disorder, it is likely that the other disorder already accounts for the impairment, and a secondary diagnosis of ADHD may not be needed. If, however, symptoms are present that cannot sufficiently be accounted for by the other disorder, ADHD may also be diagnosed.

Clinicians should then consider criterion B. If sufficient symptoms are present that meet all of these criteria but the onset cannot be documented as starting prior to age 7, ADHD NOS may be a good choice.

ASSIGNING THE DIAGNOSIS

To make a diagnosis of ADHD, clinicians must collect information of sufficient depth and breadth to determine whether *DSM* criteria are met. As is often the case when mental health professionals begin treatment, the initial phase is focused on collecting information and assigning a diagnosis.

Some clinicians may ask why assigning a diagnosis is important. Some may feel that it is sufficient to get a description of the symptoms and treat those without the need to use diagnostic labels. Mental health professionals are not advised to follow this approach, however. As discussed later in this chapter, symptoms that resemble ADHD may not necessarily be caused by the same etiology that is associated with ADHD. Following rigorous and empirically supported diagnostic algorithms allows clinicians to be confident that a diagnostic label is assigned with sufficient sensitivity and specificity. And because there is a significant amount of research that examines the etiology and treatment of most disorders listed in the *DSM*, assigning a correct diagnosis allows clinicians to draw on that literature to understand the nature of the disorder and effective treatments associated with it. Conversely, there is little data available that examine the etiology and treatment of symptoms that are not part of a specific diagnostic syndrome, thus providing clinicians with little guidance about understanding the etiology and selecting treatment approaches that are most likely to be effective.

To collect information necessary to assign a diagnosis, clinicians generally use a variety of methods, including clinical interviews, available records, and data obtained from assessment instruments. The use of these approaches will be examined specifically, as these are related to the differential diagnosis of ADHD.

Clinical Interviews

It is common for clinicians to devote the first contact with any client to the collection of information. To diagnose any disorder, clinicians must assess current symptoms, the degree and length of impairment, precipitating factors, and relevant personal and family history. Diagnosing ADHD, however, is somewhat unique, because it requires clinicians to establish a time frame of the onset of symptoms and verify that impairment occurs across different settings. For this reason, it is common for clinicians who suspect that a client may exhibit symptoms of ADHD to gather information from various reporters.

When the client is a boy or a male teen, it makes sense for the clinician to initially meet with the parents. In the vast majority of cases, parents identify the need for treatment and initiate the referral. It is helpful for clinicians to allow parents to freely discuss their concerns without feeling the need to filter what they say. For this reason, it is helpful to hold the initial session without the boy or teen present. This also allows the clinician to query parents about aspects of family history that may be relevant but may be difficult to discuss in front of their son (e.g., conflicts or stressors that have been affecting the family). In this case, after devoting the first session to the parents, the clinician can devote the second session largely to meeting with the boy or teen. This scenario allows the clinician another benefit—because the parents have already identified their concerns, the professional can lead the diagnostic interview with the client to cover all areas of concern that were identified by the parents.

In some cases, especially when the referral takes place in school, the professional (e.g., a school counselor or a school psychologist) should interview the student's teachers and other individuals who may have firsthand knowledge of the student's behaviors and his academic history (e.g., administrators or members of the child study team). In addition, school counselors and psychologists should also reach out to the student's parents to gather important information and establish a working relationship with them.

When the client is an adult, a different approach is necessary. Because adults usually self-refer, the clinician can devote the first session to gathering symptom descriptions and historical information directly from the client. If the clinician feels that the initial interview did not render sufficient information to review all relevant diagnostic criteria, the professional can request permission from the client to contact available family members. Meeting with a parent or a sibling usually can be helpful when it is necessary to review developmental history and childhood behaviors. Meeting with the spouse or significant other can also often be helpful to allow the clinician a broader view of current problems. Although not all clients agree to allow the professional to contact family members, many do, and valuable information can be gathered that greatly improves the chance of rendering an accurate diagnosis.

Whether the interview is performed with the client, a teacher, or a family member, it is important that the information that is obtained reviews the client's functioning in various areas, some of which are discussed next.

Presenting Symptoms. Initially, the clinician should be prepared to gather data about what brings the client into treatment at this specific point in time. Because symptoms of many disorders tend to wax and wane at least to some degree, and most clients exhibit symptoms for some time before treatment is initiated, it is helpful to know "why now?"—that is, why this specific point in time has resulted in the referral. Perhaps the symptoms have gradually been exacerbating, and the severity became too much to handle. Or a recent episode convinced the client, the parents, or the spouse that "enough is enough." Asking this question of the client as well as his family members usually renders valuable information that helps the clinician understand the specific expectations that bring the client into treatment. In other words, clients and family members will usually seek help for the most pressing symptoms and concerns, and if those are addressed from the start, clients are more likely to remain in treatment.

Along with gathering information about the profile of symptoms, clinicians should develop a timeline for the development of impairment. This will help clinicians determine whether symptoms of ADHD started before the client was age 7 years (as required in the *DSM*) and whether those early symptoms produced at least some impairment in functioning. In true ADHD, that is, ADHD that stems from the neurobiological etiologies described in Chapter 3, there should not be a clear point at which symptoms became apparent, and the symptoms should have begun very early in childhood and should continue to be evident as the boy gets older. In those cases where the symptoms seem to have been precipitated by a specific event (e.g., divorce), and relatively unimpaired functioning was evident beforehand, ADHD can generally be ruled out, and other diagnoses are more appropriate (e.g., adjustment disorder).

Prior Treatment. Clinicians assessing symptoms will benefit from asking about prior attempts at treatment. This may render very valuable information. For example, if prior treatment was attempted but the client dropped out of treatment, it may be helpful to ask whether the client (and/or the family) felt that the treatment was helpful. If not, the clinician should be aware that attempts to provide treatment that is similar to that which previously failed are likely to result in the client's dropping out of treatment again. If the client and/or family members were resistant to some aspects of the treatment that the clinician feels need to be attempted again, discussing these issues at the onset of treatment will allow them to be worked through, with the hope of improving the family's commitment to treatment.

Review of prior treatment may also provide useful information about other symptoms that the client exhibited in the past. Although in many cases prior treatment was attempted for symptoms similar to those that precipitated current referral, sometimes that is not the case, and understanding what symptoms and problems the client exhibited in the past will help the clinician arrive at a more comprehensive understanding of the client and the family.

In addition, reviewing family history of mental health symptoms and treatment is also helpful. Generally, information about close biological relatives is most useful, and clinicians may specifically query the client and family members about any difficulties exhibited by siblings, parents, and aunts and uncles. When it is explained that this information may carry some data about genetic links and may improve the accuracy of the diagnosis, most clients usually willingly provide these data.

School History. In some cases, the presenting symptoms will automatically lead the client and/or family members to disclose school-related problems. In other instances, when school problems seem a little less pressing than those evident at home, the clinician may need to specifically ask about school history. Because the diagnosis of ADHD requires impairment in at least two settings, it is important to specifically review how the client is doing in school with regard to academic issues (grades, study habits, homework compliance, remaining on task during assignments, etc.) as well as behavior control (remaining in the seat, blurting out answers, etc.). Not only should these issues be reviewed, as they are evident in current functioning, but data about the progression of these problems from the beginning of school should also be sought. Those boys and teens who seemed to initially make a good adjustment to school but start to exhibit significant problems in later grades may not exhibit symptoms of ADHD, and they need to be evaluated for other disorders, for example, learning problems.

Adults who come into treatment should also be asked about their school history. Men with ADHD may report disliking school and getting in trouble from an early age or losing interest and gradually disengaging. Clinicians should attempt to focus the conversation on the client's subjective experience in school and on whether the male had experienced difficulties doing academic work and remaining focused on studying or had problems regarding getting in trouble for being too active. The answers may help the clinicians develop a timeline of impairment and may also indicate whether a diagnostic follow-up to rule out learning problems will be needed.

Work History. Men referred for treatment should be interviewed about their work history. Clinicians should especially look for problems with maintaining employment and making frequent changes in jobs. It is helpful to ask the man how many jobs he has held in a lifetime, what is the longest time he held the same job, and what is the longest period he had been out of work. These questions should be followed up by a discussion of the usual reasons why he left a job and whether it was mostly voluntary or because he was dismissed. This will provide valuable information that can verify the presence of occupational impairment.

Even if the man seems to exhibit work history that is not filled with frequent job changes, clinicians should still ask whether he has problems performing work tasks, remembering work assignments, getting along with bosses and coworkers, and so on. Even though these problems may not have resulted in his being fired, they can indicate work-related functional impairment.

Family History. When a boy or teen is brought in for treatment, symptoms have often persisted for quite some time and may have caused significant strain within the family. Professionals should get a sense how the symptoms affected changes in family functioning, and these issues must be addressed when planning appropriate treatment. In addition, information about family history provides additional data that aid in the diagnosis. It is important to ask which parent is the primary disciplinarian and whether the client exhibits similar problems with both parents. Sometimes this may not be the case. As noted before, Tallamadge and Barkley (1983) found that children with ADHD tend to be more compliant and less disruptive with their fathers than with their mothers.

Because in most homes mothers are still the primary disciplinarians who attend to most day-to-day tasks, their interactions make it more likely that conflicts with the boy will ensue. Clinicians should query about this pattern when they gather information about family conflicts.

As discussed before, in cases where true ADHD is apparent, it will be evident that difficulties exhibited by the boy precipitated changes in the family (e.g., friction between parents). In many cases, however, parental conflicts may accompany (and even predate) the symptoms of ADHD. In those cases, clinicians must determine the relative contribution of the family conflicts. If the client's behaviors are there even when parents do not argue and seem independent of the family conflicts, parental discord may contribute to, but probably does not cause, the symptoms. On the other hand, when family conflicts are severe, and the boy or teen exhibits a lot of anger about the family problems, it is likely that problem behaviors may be closely related to those family conflicts, and the diagnosis of ADHD may not be appropriate.

Adults who come into treatment should be asked about their current family history (i.e., the relationship between the male and his current spouse or significant other). Men with ADHD usually experience conflicts with their spouse about a lack of responsibility, the inability to attend to his share of family tasks (such as paying bills or attending to the mechanical upkeep of the house), poor driving habits, and so on. The areas that cause conflicts will signal to the clinician what aspects of adult functioning the client finds difficult.

It is also helpful to ask adults about their family of origin. Many men will remember some of the difficulties they had as boys and teens— severely fighting with their siblings (e.g., when refusing to share their toys), getting in trouble for not doing their chores, fighting with parents about homework, and so on. This information can help the clinician develop the timeline for the onset of symptoms.

Medical and Developmental History. Clinicians should routinely ask about their clients' medical history. Symptoms of ADHD may be secondary to medical disorders such as thyroid dysfunction, cardiac disease, or neurological problems, although it is rare. In other cases, symptoms may have started after physical trauma (e.g., an accident). Those are further discussed later in this chapter. Professionals should seek to ascertain this information about boys, teens, and adults alike. Because it is not uncommon for men who come into treatment to have gone a long time without a medical checkup, it is prudent for mental health professionals to refer them for one at the onset of the treatment.

Information obtained from reviewing the developmental history may be equally enlightening. Delays in major milestones may signal other disorders that may be associated with ADHD. For example, significant delays in physical development may signal ongoing neurological problems, and delays in speech and academic tasks may signal learning disorders. Some clinicians find history-gathering instruments to be helpful. For example, the Warshak Inventory for Child and Adolescent

Assessment, Second Edition (WICAA-2; Warshak, 1995) is a 16-page checklist that allows parents to provide detailed information about developmental, behavioral, medical, school, and social history. Parents are usually asked to complete this form at home and bring it to the next session. The instrument is convenient and allows the clinician to quickly identify problem areas and aspects of development that are notable. Although adult clients are usually unable to accurately provide this information based on their own experience, when parents are available (especially the mother), the clinician can request that the client ask them to complete this form. Clinicians generally find the information contained within it to be very valuable.

Use of Psychoactive Substances. Questions about the use of alcohol or drugs are an important part of any competent intake assessment. In cases of teens and men suspected of ADHD, this information is absolutely crucial. As evident in epidemiological data, teenage boys with ADHD are much more likely to experiment with alcohol and drugs (Tercyak, Peshkin, Walker, & Stein, 2002) and are more likely to smoke cigarettes (Tercyak, Lerman, & Audrain, 2002). This extends into adulthood, and men with ADHD, especially those who exhibit problems with executive functions, are at much higher risk for developing substance use, abuse, and dependence problems (Tapert, Baratta, Abrantes, & Brown, 2002).

When problems with the use or abuse of psychoactive substances are discovered, the clinician must consider whether ADHD-like symptoms are secondary to the use of alcohol or drugs or whether they predate the onset of drug or alcohol problems. If the former is apparent, a diagnosis of ADHD is probably inappropriate. Regardless, a clinician who discovers that a client exhibits substance abuse or dependence problems must address this in treatment, either by directly addressing these problems in treatment or by referring the client to a substance abuse professional.

Assessing for problems with substance abuse or dependence must also include the review of whether the client's close family members (parents or spouse) exhibit these difficulties. Boys or teens whose parents (usually the father) exhibit substance-related problems may be exhibiting a behavioral reaction that is complicating diagnostic clarity. Clinicians must once again determine whether ADHD-like symptoms have been present for a long time (since early childhood) or whether the onset of the problems became more apparent as the parent's substance-related problems (and the family conflicts that usually accompany those issues) exacerbated.

Social History. Boys and teens with ADHD are commonly rejected by peers and usually have few friends. When with other kids or teens, they tend to get into conflicts because they do not like sharing toys and find it difficult to go with the flow during many activities, especially rule-governed sports or games (Barkley, 2006). Mental health professionals should routinely screen for those problems by asking parents questions that specifically flesh out information about behavior with peers and social adjustment. In addition to asking questions about free-play activities, clinicians should also inquire about the boy's behavior in organized settings, such as sport teams or Boy Scout troops.

Clinicians should similarly query men suspected of ADHD about those settings, adjusting the questions to age-appropriate activities. Clinicians need to ask about the client's interests and whether the client is maintaining active contact with friends. Frequent changes in friendships or lack of active engagement in social activities may indicate a reaction to long-standing rejection by peers that is now being presented as a lack of interest. Clinicians should also be aware, however, that loss of interest in social activities may also be a symptom of other disorders, for example, depression. Thus, when social withdrawal is apparent, careful differential diagnosis is needed.

Problems With the Law. Boys, teens, and men who exhibit a high degree of impulsivity commonly present with histories of mischief and involvement with police. At a client's young age, this may involve the client taking something from a store (such as candy) without telling his parents, especially when he asked and the parents refused to buy it. As boys become teens, impulsive individuals tend to become involved in shoplifting and mischief, including trespassing. For some teens with ADHD, these problems become more severe with age, and the juvenile justice system becomes involved (Chemers, 2002). These patterns often continue into adulthood, and men with ADHD are much more likely to have a history of criminal behaviors and legal problems (Johnston, 2002).

Asking about a history of legal involvement is an important aspect of the diagnostic interview, but the clinician must ascertain whether impulsivity and poor judgment, rather than conscious disregard of rules and laws, underlie the behaviors. When a young boy impulsively takes an item from a store, little premeditation is likely, and this behavior probably signals poor impulse control. As boys grow up, and the degree of the transgression increases, clinicians must determine whether the act was performed on the spur of the moment (or when encouraged by peers) or if the act was planned and otherwise performed with full awareness of the degree of the violation of rules and laws. The former is probably a sign of impulsivity and may be a symptom of ADHD. The latter, especially when accompanied by a history of aggression, is more likely to represent behaviors typical of conduct disorder. Of course, in some cases the two disorders can coexist.

Review of Records

In addition to gathering data through clinical interviews, many clinicians find that reviewing relevant records provides useful information. For example, it is common for professionals to receive records of prior treatment or those that pertain to academic settings.

Treatment Records. In cases where the client previously received treatment, it is often helpful to request a release to obtain those records. If time is a factor and waiting for the records is not practical, it may be beneficial to obtain permission to speak with the other professionals. In some cases, this information may reveal data that are consistent with the problems reported at this time. In those instances, the data from the other clinician will verify that the problems occurring now are long-standing. In other cases, a significant difference may be apparent. Prior treatment may reveal much lesser severity of the problem, in which case the clinician must determine whether developmental progression associated with time is solely responsible for the exacerbation or whether additional factors (e.g., changes within the family) may be associated with the exacerbation of symptoms. In other cases, problems reported by the other clinician may be different from those occurring at this point in time. Such a scenario would not typically be expected with clients suspected of ADHD, as symptoms are presumed to start early and continue to be evident through childhood, at least into adolescence.

When adult men come in for treatment, the clinician might find it difficult to determine the onset and progression of symptoms. Because the *DSM* requires evidence of symptom-related impairment prior to age 7 years, efforts must be made to ascertain the history of functioning at a younger age. When the man discloses episodes of mental health treatment earlier in life, the clinician's ability to get the records or contact the other clinicians may help establish what symptoms occurred earlier in life and to what degree they affected the man's functioning at the time.

Sometimes medical records may also carry valuable information, especially when the client is an adult. Clients who previously have been in treatment may not remember the specific reasons why the referral was made. Because it is common for pediatricians to make referrals to mental health professionals when problems with their patients are evident, pediatric data may provide information about the reasons why a referral was made, and the pediatrician may have made notes about behaviors that were observed to be problematic (e.g., excessive hyperactivity).

Medical records can be especially useful when the client reports prior treatment with medications but does not remember the specific compound that was prescribed. Because the majority of psychotropic medications are prescribed by pediatricians (Olfson, Marcus, Weissman, & Jensen, 2002), doctor's notes will usually reveal the choice of medications and the dosage. In cases where various medications were tried and multiple changes were needed, clinicians can further inquire about the reasons why this was needed. These changes can signal important information, for example, limited compliance with treatment or the presence of symptoms that did not respond to the treatment attempted at the time.

Academic Records. The *DSM* requires the presence of clinical impairment in academic, occupational, or social settings to establish a valid diagnosis of ADHD. As discussed previously in this chapter, it is presumed that true ADHD will produce impairment in school from a rather early age. Indeed, the vast majority of children with ADHD exhibit significant impairment in school (Barkley, 2006). Consequently, clinicians, in addition to gathering information from parents and close family members, should focus their efforts on obtaining at least some academic records that can independently verify the presence of significant school problems.

The records that are usually easiest to obtain are the school report cards, especially when the client is a boy or a teen. When reviewing report cards, professionals should focus not only on academic grades but also on the specific comments provided by the teachers, including the ratings of study skills and social adjustment. Often, especially in early years, the assigned grades may not yet reflect problems in school, but the teachers' comments may reveal problems with distractibility, disorganization, impulsivity, excessive activity, lack of compliance with homework, and so on. When report cards are available from the start of school, clinicians can trace the onset and progression of the symptoms, further aiding in the diagnosis.

In addition to providing report cards, parents sometimes also provide results of standardized tests administered in school. These test results carry less information about symptoms of ADHD. Although parents may suspect that low scores reflect problems with distractibility or poor study habits (which also may be caused by distractibility), the test results do not provide a narrative description of the behavior during the testing, and therefore it is not possible to determine the exact cause of the drop in scores. Low scores may reflect a presence of learning problems, especially when all scores seem average or higher with the exception of one academic area (such as mathematics).

School records may also include information provided by the child study team. If the student has exhibited sufficient problems to warrant classification and special education services, members of the child study team must have performed evaluations and developed an individualized education plan (IEP). Although the specific requirements vary from state to state, the evaluations usually include a report from the school social worker, who typically meets with the parents (often visiting them at home) and reviews developmental and family data. In most cases, the report of a psychological evaluation is also required, and it contains information about the child's cognitive functioning (usually obtained from an intelligence test) and personality (usually obtained from an observation or a screening measure). In some states, the evaluations of the child study team also include a report from a learning disabilities teacher consultant, who administers a battery of academic achievement tests. If symptoms of impulsivity, hyperactivity, inattentiveness, or disorganization were evident during any of those procedures, the reports are likely to contain those data.

IEPs can also be helpful. Updated every year, IEPs are multipage documents that list all the goals and objectives (behavioral and academic) that have been established for the student. Clinicians can review the IEP to see whether any of the goals and objectives appear to have been set to address symptoms associated with ADHD. If this is not evident, however, clinicians should not automatically assume that ADHD-like symptoms are not present. Because some school professionals primarily include in the IEP those goals and objectives that they are able (and willing) to address, it is not unusual for some behavioral needs to be excluded.

When the client is an adult, the clinician can get very valuable information by reviewing the school records. Because a timeline for the onset and progression of symptoms must be established, and evidence must be gathered about significant impairment that occurred in school, work, or social settings, school records can help clinicians verify whether significant problems were present when the client attended school. Although most adults do not think about obtaining their school records, some of their school records may still be available many years after graduation. States differ widely on what records must be maintained and for how long, and clinicians may want to investigate record-keeping provisions for their own state in order to provide appropriate guidance to their clients.

Assessment Instruments

In addition to gathering information from clinical interviews and available records, mental health professionals must decide whether to use some of the assessment measures described in the previous chapter. Once again, a decision tree may be useful.

In those cases where a review of data obtained from clinical interviews clearly reveals that *DSM* diagnostic criteria are met, the use of diagnostic instruments may not be needed. This may be the case when the onset of symptoms, the level of impairment, and the presence of symptoms in various settings are clearly established from independent sources. When the client is a boy or a teen, the clinician can establish these things by interviewing the client, parents, and teachers or by interviewing the client and the parents and reviewing records that provide reliable verification of the diagnosis. When the client is an adult male, these things can be established in similar ways, and the spouse can also be an important source of independent information.

Even in those cases, however, clinicians may still consider the administration of a standardized instrument that is cross-validated with the *DSM* diagnostic criteria. For example, if a referral is made to consider the use of medications, many physicians require an objective measure to verify sufficient severity of the symptoms. In addition, if educational interventions are needed (as discussed in Chapters 11 and 12), parents will make a stronger case for educational modifications if evidence of the disorder can be verified by a standardized, valid, and reliable measure.

In those cases where clinical interviews revealed information that suggests the presence of ADHD symptoms, but the level of severity is not clearly established, the use of an appropriate instrument can be very helpful. In Chapter 4, four categories of instruments were reviewed. Psychological and neuropsychological tests are not particularly useful when ADHD-like symptoms must be rated, and they are best used when broad-based assessments are needed, for example, to rule out comorbid conditions or neurological problems.

Instead, clinicians should consider the use of *DSM*-anchored behavior rating scales and continuous performance tests (CPTs), because techniques in those two categories provide the most evidence of assessing ADHD symptoms with sufficient sensitivity and specificity. In fact, as evident in the review in Chapter 4, it is apparent that behavioral rating scales provide superior psychometric characteristics than the CPTs and are better able to identify and differentiate symptoms of ADHD. Thus, when data from clinical interviews need to be supplemented by the use of an instrument, clinicians are encouraged to choose a behavior rating scale. To further improve the accuracy of the data, clinicians should ask for at least two forms to be completed, one by the teacher and one by the parent, and a self-report may also be helpful. For adult clients, a self-report and at least one other informant should be sought.

If data obtained from the behavior rating scales fall at or above the cutoff of 2 standard deviations above the mean for the relevant symptom clusters, this information should be sufficient to assign a diagnosis with confidence. If the data fall close to but not above said cutoff, however, clinicians may consider the administration of a CPT. If the data from the CPT identify the presence of ADHD, clinicians may then consider assigning the diagnosis, provided appropriate steps were taken to maximize the accuracy of the CPT results (as discussed in Chapter 4). If the CPT results are inconclusive, and the client presents a level of impairment that is significant enough to warrant a clinical diagnosis, ADHD NOS may be considered.

RULE-OUTS AND COMORBIDITIES

Most researchers and mental health professionals recognize that symptoms of ADHD are commonly accompanied by other difficulties. For example, boys, male teens, and men who are impulsive are commonly also defiant, and an overlap with mood disturbance is also common, especially in adults (Ramsay & Rostain, 2008). Symptoms of ADHD also commonly co-occur with learning problems and substance abuse or dependence (Barkley, 2006). Clinicians need to be aware that individuals with ADHD are likely to also present symptoms of other disorders that need to be properly diagnosed and treated.

Symptoms of ADHD overlap with those of other disorders, however, and sometimes it may be difficult to distinguish whether symptoms of overactivity or distractibility are secondary to ADHD or other conditions (e.g., depression). Because an accurate diagnosis is necessary to select proper treatment, clinicians need to be able to appropriately differentiate the symptoms of various disorders. If one disorder accounts for all the symptoms, only that label should be assigned. On the other hand, all symptoms that impair functioning must be accounted for, and therefore in some cases multiple diagnoses may be needed.

Disruptive Disorders

It is widely accepted by scientists and clinicians that boys, male teens, and men with ADHD often present with difficulties with aggression, oppositional behaviors, and conduct problems. By some accounts, up to 84% of children and adolescents with ADHD also present with an oppositional or conduct disorder (Barkley, 2006). Some researchers have suggested that problems with self-control underlie all of these disorders, thus explaining the comorbidity (Lynam, 1998). Clinicians need to be able to determine whether one disorder accounts for all the symptoms or whether multiple diagnoses are needed.

Oppositional Defiant Disorder (ODD). Individuals who present with symptoms of ADHD, especially variants that include the hyperactive/ impulsive cluster of symptoms, commonly exhibit comorbid defiance and argumentativeness. The overlap between the two is well documented, and it is likely that problems with impulsivity underlie difficulties with judgment as well as problems controlling one's reaction to frustration (Burns & Walsh, 2002). Thus, poor self-control commonly results in combined symptoms of ADHD and ODD, especially in males.

The reverse situation, however, may present a greater diagnostic challenge. If problems with self-control are evident only in situations where the client has difficulties controlling his feelings of frustration, the clinician must determine whether other symptoms exist to justify the diagnosis of ADHD. If symptoms of impulsivity or agitation do not appear present outside of frustrating situations, it is likely that a diagnosis of ODD (without ADHD) is appropriate.

Conduct Disorder (CD). Symptoms of CD primarily include behaviors such as severe aggression, destruction of property, serious violations of rules, and violation of laws (through theft, truancy, etc.). When these disorders are present, their symptoms cannot be accounted for by ADHD, because the vast majority of individuals with ADHD do not perform these behaviors. Only 1% to 3% of children with ADHD are also diagnosed with CD (Pfiffner et al., 1999), and when clinicians encounter a simultaneous presentation of symptoms of ADHD and CD, both diagnoses should be made.

CD, however, is more likely to occur in the context of a history of comorbid ADHD and ODD. When ADHD (hyperactive/impulsive or combined type) and ODD are present together, about half of those patients later go on to be diagnosed with CD in adolescence (Wilens, Biederman, et al., 2002).

When professionals encounter clients who present symptoms of all three disorders, careful consideration must be given to which diagnostic labels should be assigned. Presence of symptoms of ADHD, especially when it is clear that these symptoms are long-standing and apparent in situations that do not violate rights or laws, should justify the diagnosis of ADHD. Clinicians should consider, however, whether it is necessary to additionally diagnose ODD, CD, or both. As discussed earlier, significant defiance and argumentativeness signal the possible presence of ODD. Many professionals, however, believe that the *DSM* criteria for CD subsume many of the symptoms associated with ODD, and because CD is considered to be the more serious (and comprehensive) diagnosis, CD should be diagnosed instead of ODD.

Not all clinicians follow this approach, however, and some believe that symptoms of ODD and CD are distinct and may or may not occur together. Indeed, this appears to be the approach that the *DSM* is suggesting, because the diagnostic criteria for the two disorders do not include exclusion criteria for each other. In addition, Barkley (2006) argued that children with ADHD and CD represent a severe variant of ADHD that results in a greater disruption of rule-governed behavior (as evidenced by symptoms of CD) and results in much poorer outcome (e.g., more problems with substance abuse and criminal behaviors). He also admitted, however, that symptoms of ODD and CD are hard to distinguish in many cases, and the two most commonly occur together. Clinicians need to make their own decision about which of the two methods of approaching this issue seems most logical and appropriate.

Learning Disorders

Although Chapters 11 and 12 of this volume are devoted to school-related issues relevant to ADHD, a brief discussion herein is necessary to review diagnostic considerations. The overlap between ADHD and learning disorders has been studied for some time, but no definitive data yet exist about its prevalence. Barkley (2006) argued that much of the data gathered before the 1990s used cutoff criteria that were not stringent enough (1 and a half standard deviations above the mean) for diagnosing both ADHD and learning disorders. This resulted in a high overlap that sometimes has been reported to be about 50%. More recent investigations have been using higher cutoffs (2 standard deviations) for both disorders, and the resulting data report much less overlap. For example, DuPaul and Stoner (2003) comprehensively reviewed the topic and suggested that only about 20% of individuals with ADHD have a comorbid learning disorder. Still, these data indicate that clinicians should expect that one out of every five clients with ADHD will present with a diagnosable learning disorder.

As discussed in Chapter 4, learning disorders are still primarily diagnosed by identifying a significant aptitude-achievement discrepancy. Symptoms of ADHD are likely to impair academic achievement at least to some degree. For example, distractibility makes it hard for individuals with ADHD to focus when reading or writing, and these individuals report that it takes them longer to perform most academic tasks (DuPaul & Stoner, 2003). Still, that some tasks will be harder and performance will be affected is not sufficient to diagnose a learning disorder. To suspect the presence of a learning disorder, the clinician should see a clear-cut impairment in academic functioning in at least one academic area.

Of all learning problems, difficulties with reading and writing are the most common in individuals with ADHD. Indeed, some researchers have suggested that the brain changes associated with ADHD symptoms are also partially responsible for these academic problems (Levine, 2004). As children progress from lower grades into mid-elementary grades, and then middle school and beyond, reading and writing abilities become the primary modality through which new material is introduced. Students who are weak in those areas are at a clear disadvantage in all academic areas, and their grades will likely drop across most subjects. When mental health professionals encounter clients who seem to be exhibiting problems keeping up with their work, they should specifically focus at least a portion of the clinical interview on reviewing whether reading, writing, or mathematics seems especially difficult. This topic needs to be raised with adults as well, because learning problems may persist into adulthood. When it becomes apparent that a client is struggling with reading, writing, or math, clinicians should refer him for a psychological evaluation.

Substance Use Disorders

Many years of systematic review of the co-occurrence of ADHD and substance use disorders have revealed that individuals with ADHD are about twice as likely to use or abuse psychoactive substances than the general population (Barkley, 2006). In addition, as may be expected, the risk is highest for male teenagers and young men (Ramsay & Rostain, 2008). When clients disclose regular use of psychoactive substances, clinicians should attempt to determine whether presenting symptoms seem to occur primarily when the person is under the influence or whether symptoms persist even when the client is clean and sober. In the former case, a substance use disorder will probably result in substance-induced symptoms that may include impulsivity, hyperactivity, poor self-control, or distractibility. In the latter case, both ADHD and a substance use disorder may be present.

Clinicians should be aware of the types of symptoms various substance categories are likely to produce. Stimulants (such as cocaine and amphetamine) often generate hyperarousal, impulsivity, and impairment in self-control. Depressants (including alcohol) usually result in evidence of distractibility, disorganization, and a decrease in energy. Hallucinogens (including marijuana) and opiates (such as heroin and pain killers) present with similar symptoms, although a greater sense of well-being while the individual is under the influence will be apparent. Inhalants and PCP often result in a wide variety of symptoms, including a mix of stimulant and depressant effects that are often accompanied by significant volatility. When performing a differential diagnosis, professionals need to determine whether the substance use is the primary problem, in which case a secondary diagnosis of ADHD would not be made, or whether the symptoms of ADHD existed first, and the client likely uses psychoactive drugs to medicate himself and cope.

Mood Disorders

Mood disorders commonly coexist with ADHD. Up to 32% of children with ADHD present a comorbid depressive disorder, and up to 13% are diagnosed with some variant of bipolar disorder (Biederman, Newcorn, & Sprich, 1991). In addition, mood disorders commonly mimic symptoms of ADHD, for example, depression is associated with distractibility, and some variants of depressive symptoms include motor restlessness, and manic symptoms typically include impulsivity. Consequently, clinicians must be able to differentiate symptoms of ADHD from those that accompany mood disorders.

Depressive Disorders. The *DSM* system identifies two primary depressive disorders: dysthymia and major depression. Both share common symptoms, although the level of severity required to diagnose major depression is generally much greater. In addition, dysthymia is a chronic disorder where symptoms must persist for at least 2 years (1 year in children), whereas major depressive disorder (MDD) is an episodic disorder that generally comes and goes. When screening clients who present with symptoms that may indicate depression, clinicians must establish whether the disturbance appears to be episodic or whether the symptoms seem to be chronic. Certainly, if ADHD is being considered as a diagnosis, the symptoms are not expected to come and go (although minor, temporal variations in severity are common).

Symptoms of dysthymia may include irritability, fatigue, and poor concentration. Clinicians need to determine whether motor restlessness and distractibility are the result of depression or ADHD. If these symptoms seem to accompany a chronic presentation of depression that also includes sadness, fatigue, and low self-esteem, dysthymia generally may be the more accurate diagnosis. If the chronic sadness seems to have started sometime after symptoms of ADHD were already apparent, it is possible that both disorders may be present. In addition, if significant hyperactivity and impulsivity are evident that do not seem to be accompanied by agitation, then their presence may also indicate that symptoms of both disorders are present. Probably the most difficult situation occurs when symptoms of dysthymia and ADHD, predominantly inattentive type, are present. In those cases, it may be difficult to determine whether the distractibility and disorganization are due to depression or ADHD.

Symptoms of MDD are generally more severe but are usually episodic, and periods without mood disturbance may be apparent. MDD usually presents with a much greater level of impairment, including changes in physical functioning (especially prominent disturbance in sleep and appetite). In severe cases, suicidal tendencies may be present. In addition, agitation, restlessness, fatigue, and inability to pay attention may also be present and will likely be more severe than is typically seen in clients with ADHD. Especially when accompanied by significant changes in sleep and appetite, these symptoms are more likely to be symptoms of MDD than ADHD.

ADHD and MDD can also coexist. When symptoms of both disorders are present, symptoms of ADHD are usually chronic and start very early in life, whereas symptoms of depression will usually have a more clearly delineated onset and will tend to come and go. In cases where symptoms of ADHD include hyperactivity and impulsivity, it may be easier to differentiate those from symptoms of MDD (and diagnose both disorders when both sets of symptoms are present). As mentioned earlier, however, when symptoms of MDD and ADHD, predominantly inattentive type, are present, it may be difficult to determine whether the distractibility and disorganization are due to depression or ADHD.

Bipolar Disorder. Bipolar disorder is diagnosed when the client exhibits a history of at least one episode of "classic" or mixed mania or when there is a history of MDD and at least one hypomanic episode. Manic symptoms generally include an increase in activity and impulsivity, together with a sense of elation or significant agitation. Changes in sleep and speech patterns are also common. Mixed episodes are characterized by manic symptoms (that commonly include agitation rather than elation) accompanied by symptoms of depression. Hypomanic episodes are evident when symptoms meet the general character of mania but are less severe and lesser impairment is evident.

Symptoms of classic mania—excessive pursuit of pleasure, grandiosity, severe flight of ideas, decreased need for sleep, and rapid or pressured speech—can usually be differentiated from symptoms of ADHD with little difficulty. Those symptoms are not associated with ADHD, and therefore when they are present, bipolar disorder will probably be the more accurate diagnosis. Because manic symptoms are episodic, there will be times when the symptoms of mania are not clearly apparent. If symptoms of ADHD are apparent during those times, both diagnoses can be made.

When hypomanic or mixed episodes are evident, the diagnosis becomes more difficult. Clients who present with significant agitation and restlessness may mimic symptoms of ADHD. In addition, mood disturbance is also commonly accompanied by difficulties with concentration. When hyperactivity and impulsivity are apparent, it is important to determine whether they occur exclusively during episodes of mood disturbance. If that is the case, a diagnosis of bipolar disorder is more appropriate. If the symptoms seem to persist even in times when prominent mood symptoms are absent, it is possible that symptoms of both disorders may be present.

Because symptoms of mood disturbance may not wax and wane as prominently in children and adolescents as they do in adults, some clinicians find it difficult to differentiate symptoms of mixed or hypomanic episodes from those of ADHD. Some research findings have reported that children and adolescents with bipolar disorder present with significantly greater levels of violence than do children with ADHD. Although this may be true in some cases, some children and adolescents with ADHD are also known to present with a lot of aggression. Clinicians are encouraged to perform a rigorous review of the symptoms of ADHD and bipolar disorder, including symptom presentation, onset, and course, and use those data, rather than the degree of violence, to assign the diagnosis.

Anxiety Disorders

Anxiety disorders are also common in individuals with ADHD, and studies report that 25% to 35% of individuals with ADHD also present symptoms of at least one anxiety disorder (Tannock, 2000). Symptoms of anxiety can usually be differentiated from symptoms of ADHD with little difficulty. When symptoms of both disorders co-occur, however, each may change the expression of the other (Barkley, 2006). For example, individuals with ADHD and anxiety tend to exhibit less impulsivity (Barkley, 2006), and comorbid ADHD and anxiety may result in more aggression (Tannock, 2000).

The *DSM* category of anxiety disorders is broad and includes disorders with diverse symptoms, including obsessive compulsive disorder, post-traumatic stress disorder, and other anxiety disorders, such as panic disorder, generalized anxiety disorder, or phobias. These should be considered separately.

Obsessive Compulsive Disorder (OCD). Because OCD and ADHD result in different symptoms, it is not common to confuse the two disorders. When cognitive obsessions are present (e.g., fear of getting sick), especially if they are accompanied by behavioral compulsions (such as excessive hand washing), those symptoms do not resemble the classic symptoms of ADHD, and the two can usually be differentiated rather easily. Some 3% to 5% of children with ADHD may exhibit symptoms of OCD (Barkley, 2006), however, and when the two co-occur, clinicians may sometimes find that compulsions present similarly to motor restlessness, and distractibility may be secondary to cognitive obsessions. Careful assessment of symptoms of both disorders will be needed to determine whether symptoms of OCD fully account for ADHD-like impairment or whether comorbidity between the two is present.

Post-Traumatic Stress Disorder (PTSD). When there is evidence that the client was exposed to severe trauma at some point in his life, mental health professionals should consider whether PTSD symptoms have developed as a result. PTSD among children is unlikely, however, and one study revealed that only 7% of children that have been traumatized develop PTSD (Wozniak et al., 1999). Still, examining those individuals who developed PTSD, researchers found that 14% to 46% have a history of ADHD (Weinstein, Steffelbach, & Biaggio, 2000). Thus, it seems that having ADHD predisposed the person to subsequent PTSD when severe trauma was experienced. The relationship between PTSD and ADHD in adults has not been investigated, although if the Weinstein et al. data extend to adults, men with PTSD are more likely to have a prior history of ADHD.

Hyperarousal and agitation that commonly accompany PTSD may resemble motor restlessness, and sometimes they may be confused. Individuals with PTSD, however, also present with hypervigilance and exaggerated startle response, which are symptoms that are not associated with ADHD. Therefore, when those symptoms are present, a diagnosis of PTSD may be more appropriate. In addition, if there is evidence that hyperactivity/impulsivity and/or inattentiveness/disorganization preceded the trauma, the client may be one of approximately 1% to 6% of individuals with ADHD who develop comorbid PTSD (Barkley, 2006).

Other Anxiety Disorders. Children who exhibit symptoms of generalized anxiety, panic attacks, or specific phobias may also appear restless. It is important to examine the underlying feelings that accompany motor overactivity. Similarly, individuals are likely to report difficulties with focusing when they are anxious or afraid. If episodes of restlessness or distractibility seem to occur exclusively when a subjective feeling of anxiety is present, an anxiety disorder may sufficiently account for those symptoms. If ADHD-like symptoms occur at times when anxiety is not experienced, however, both disorders may need to be diagnosed.

In addition, clinicians must also remember that it is not uncommon for children with anxiety to present with comorbid symptoms of depression. In fact, Pfiffner et al. (1999) reported that about 23% of clinic-referred boys had comorbid symptoms of anxiety and depression. Thus, it is possible that triple comorbidity may be apparent: depression, anxiety, and ADHD. In these complex situations, mental health professionals must carefully assess the symptoms, timeline, and accompanying features to determine which symptoms may be associated with which disorders.

Adjustment Disorders

Environmental factors should always be considered as a potential primary source of the disturbance. Individuals who were exposed to stressful events (e.g., family conflicts or divorce) often exhibit a variety of emotional and behavioral difficulties that commonly include problems with paying attention, poor academic performance, low motivation, and poor self-control. Although these symptoms may appear to be characteristic of ADHD, a careful review of environmental factors may reveal that the symptoms started only after the stressor. To rule out the contribution of such environmental factors, the clinician must make a careful review of personal and family history. If environmental factors appear to sufficiently explain the symptoms, an adjustment disorder, rather than ADHD, may be the correct diagnosis.

It is possible that a client exhibits both ADHD and an adjustment disorder. This may occur in cases where symptoms of ADHD predate the onset of the stressor, and the event exacerbated (but did not initiate) related impairment. In cases where the stressor is long-standing, however, teasing the two apart may be difficult. For example, if a clinician encounters a boy or teen who grew up with severe family conflicts all of his life, it may be difficult to determine whether those conflicts are responsible for the behaviors or whether ADHD symptoms exist independently. Generally, the category of adjustment disorder is reserved for reactions to discrete stressors that have a clearly delineated onset and are presumed to resolve over time. When stressors exceed those criteria, a diagnosis of adjustment disorder may be inaccurate.

Clinicians should also note that the *DSM* specifically excludes bereavement from the criteria for adjustment disorder. This decision was made because, theoretically, symptoms associated with bereavement are not considered to be a disorder and therefore should not be diagnosed as such. The *DSM* includes bereavement within a category of "Other Conditions That May Be a Focus of Clinical Attention," and the diagnostic code is one of "V-Codes," that is, conditions that represent normal experiences commonly encountered in day-to-day life. Clinicians, however, must be aware that a diagnostic code that starts with a V is not covered by most insurance plans, and clients (and/or their parents) must be aware of this limitation. Of course, if bereavement reaction becomes unusually severe or prolonged, a mental disorder may be diagnosed (e.g., depression).

Medical Disorders

When considering disorders that result in ADHD-like impairment, clinicians should also consider medical factors. Some children with symptoms that resemble ADHD actually suffer from medical conditions, although this is uncommon. As discussed previously, head trauma should always be ruled out, and individuals with a history of head injury should be screened for possible brain damage. Lead poisoning, although a well-documented cause of behavioral and learning problems, is rare nowadays among most Americans. Those who grow up in impoverished backgrounds are at a higher risk, however, and so this possibility should be considered. A referral for an appropriate work-up may be needed, and clinicians may try to locate a social service agency that may be performing screening for lead poisoning within the community.

Other medical problems may also contribute to the formation of ADHD-like symptoms. Respiratory problems, especially severe allergies or uncontrolled asthma, commonly cause children to exhibit motor restlessness and inattentiveness. Similarly, endocrine problems have a significant influence. For example, an overactive thyroid commonly causes motor overactivity, and an underactive thyroid affects the ability to concentrate. These disorders are important to rule out, especially when there is evidence of family history of these problems in close biological relations (such as siblings or parents). A careful and thorough medical examination should always accompany the initiation of any mental health treatment.

SUMMARY

When a client presents with symptoms that appear to resemble those of ADHD, it is necessary to perform methodical differential diagnosis. This process usually starts with clinical interviews with the client and significant others (e.g., parents or the spouse). Gathering information from multiple reporters improves the likelihood that obtained data are accurate and comprehensive. Clinical interviews should review a variety of behaviors across many settings (e.g., including the home, school, work, and social adjustment), and a timeline for the onset of the impairment must also be established. When diagnosing ADHD, clinicians must be aware that the *DSM* requires professionals to meet both inclusion and exclusion criteria, and the information gathered from the interviews must sufficiently cover all *DSM* categories.

When information gathered from clinical interviews suggests that symptoms of ADHD may be present, clinicians may benefit from supplementing interview data with results obtained from various instruments. Psychological and neuropsychological evaluations help identify a broad range of symptoms and are often helpful in diagnosing (or ruling out) comorbid conditions, but they do not provide the sensitivity and specificity required to rate the severity of ADHD symptoms. Instead, clinicians are encouraged to consider the use of behavioral inventories (first) and CPTs (second) to further clarify whether symptom severity is sufficient for the diagnosis of ADHD.

When gathering data, clinicians should also consider whether the symptoms that are evident are secondary to ADHD or to other disorders that may produce similar disturbance. In some cases, symptoms of other disorders may mimic symptoms of ADHD, and a different diagnostic label may be more appropriate. In other cases, ADHD can co-occur with other disorders. Mental health professionals need to review all symptoms and make diagnostic decisions that closely follow *DSM* criteria. The purpose of a diagnosis is to provide guidance about treatment strategies, and effective treatment paradigms have been established for the vast majority of syndromes described in the *DSM*. When an accurate and comprehensive diagnosis is established, the selected treatment is likely to be effective. When the diagnosis is inaccurate or incomplete, at least some treatment needs may not be met.

Counseling and Psychotherapy

CHAPTER

6

Individual Counseling With Boys and Young Teens

As discussed in detail in previous chapters (especially in Chapter 1), boys and male teens with attention deficit/hyperactivity disorder (ADHD) exhibit symptoms that result in significant difficulties at home, in school, and with peers. Symptoms of ADHD fall along two clusters, those of hyperactivity/impulsivity and those of inattentiveness/disorganization, and males with ADHD exhibit problems in either or both of those categories. In fact, as research has shown, males are especially likely to exhibit symptoms from both clusters, whereas females with ADHD are more likely to exhibit inattentiveness and distractibility only (Barkley, 2006).

Hyperactivity creates many difficulties in home, school, and social functioning. Those boys who are overactive tend to annoy everyone around them, including parents, teachers, and peers. At home, they often get yelled at because they have difficulties sitting still at times when it is usually necessary to do so (e.g., during meals). In school, they often fidget or leave their desk, and teachers and other students often find these behaviors disruptive. With peers, they are likely to be annoying, and peer rejection is common. Thus, boys need help with these problems.

Impulsivity is likely to be problematic. Impulsive boys lie frequently and make poor decisions. Limited self-control results in poor frustration tolerance, and boys with ADHD tend to be more explosive than same-age peers, especially when they did not get something they desired or were prevented from doing something they wanted to do at the moment. These behaviors frequently result in conflicts and arguments, and these boys are much more likely to get punished at home and in school.

Impulsivity similarly impairs social adjustment; boys with ADHD tend to have difficulties with peers when play activities are not carried out in the way they would like, and conflicts with peers are common.

Symptoms of inattentiveness and disorganization exacerbate these difficulties. Because boys with ADHD lose track of their possessions and assigned responsibilities, parents and teachers frequently get annoyed or angry at them, and problems are especially common around homework and household chores. In school, completing work and remaining on task can be problematic for boys with ADHD, and teachers often have to redirect them, thus also finding them to be exasperating.

It is important for mental health professionals to recognize that these core symptoms further contribute to the development of many secondary symptoms that boys with ADHD gradually begin to experience. Impulsivity goes hand-in-hand with defiance. The more impulsive the boy, the more likely he is to protest and defy when he is told something he does not like to hear. This reaction is usually evident at home and in school, and it results in a great deal of conflict between the boys and their parents and teachers.

Because boys with ADHD frequently get in trouble, they are likely to view themselves as inferior to others. At home, the boy may notice that he gets yelled at more than his siblings. At school, he may recognize that others seem to be more successful at getting better grades and remembering their work. With peers, he may notice that others are more popular and seem to get along better with each other, whereas he gets teased and rejected more frequently. All of these experiences are likely to result in a negative self-concept.

Problems with affect regulation further contribute to difficulties with self-esteem. When things do not come out as boys with ADHD would like, they get upset more intensely than those without the disorder. All children must accept that parents, teachers, or peers will not always allow them to do what they would like, but boys with ADHD overreact to those situations and are more likely to lose control over their emotions. When such experiences are commonplace, boys begin to recognize that they get upset more than most, and they remember those experiences. Because their episodes are more intense, they tend to remember them more and begin to recognize that they get more upset than their siblings. This leads them to believe that they get treated more poorly than their siblings and that their parents prefer the other kids in the family. Even though all the kids in the family may objectively "get their way" about equally, boys with ADHD may perceive themselves as getting their way less often than others do, because other kids are better able to accept situations that do not come out as they would like them to and are much less likely to exhibit intense reactions when things do not come out as planned.

Low self-concept and the perception of being treated more poorly than others contribute to additional difficulties, such as limited motivation. Boys who conclude to themselves that they are not as successful or able and that others do not seem to like them or care about them very much tend to limit how hard they try to succeed. Because they expect failure, they accept it more readily when they are not doing well in school or with peers. They do not devote as much effort to studying not only because core symptoms (such as distractibility) make it harder to do so but also because they expect that their efforts will not be as fruitful. They do not try as hard to find ways to get along with peers, because they assume that no matter what they do, others will dislike them anyway. They do not try as hard to please their parents, because they feel that parents prefer other siblings anyway, so there is no use in trying to change that.

When clinicians initiate treatment by suggesting medications or training parents, the symptoms may improve, but these approaches may not eliminate all problems, and residual symptoms may remain. In other cases, improvement with medication may be more limited, and some patients do not tolerate medications well, and therefore the symptoms must be addressed through other means. Individual counseling may be beneficial, and specific strategies may be helpful in diminishing symptoms of impulsivity and inattentiveness/disorganization.

Clinicians must keep in mind, however, that regardless of how effective some treatments may be to target core symptoms, many of the secondary symptoms (low self-concept, limited motivation) may not change, especially when the boy has experienced long-standing difficulties in school, at home, and with peers. Although the impulsivity and/or inattentiveness may have diminished, and consequently the frequency and intensity of conflicts with parents, teachers, and peers have reduced, the damage to self-esteem has already taken place and will not improve automatically just because the core symptoms may now be under control. For this reason, mental health professionals need to recognize that even when a boy or teen is placed on medications, not all problems will be resolved, and individual counseling can be very helpful to address the remaining problems.

RESEARCH SUPPORT

Results of research studies have confirmed that not all problems treated with medications are resolved with the use of medications. For example, although stimulants improve classroom performance, long-term achievement gains from the use of medication alone are rather modest (Swanson, McBurnett, Christian, & Wigal, 1995). At home, even though the use of medications improves core symptoms, and therefore decreases conflicts surrounding those problems, families of boys with ADHD often exhibit patterns of instability that do not fully resolve when medications are used (Fisher, 1990), and boys with ADHD may exhibit emotional problems that further trigger dysfunctional patterns of interaction even when core symptoms are under control. In social settings, there is no evidence that the use of medications improves the quality of peer relationships in the long run (Pelham, 2002).

In addition, when some types of medications are used (e.g., psychostimulants), the beneficial effect must wear off before dinner and bedtime, and core symptoms will return for the remainder of the day. Furthermore, even though research has suggested that up to 90% of children respond favorably to the use of appropriate medications (Barkley, 2006), studies have also shown that about a quarter of children with ADHD may not exhibit sufficient response or may experience adverse reactions that limit the efficacy of the medications (Swanson et al., 1995). For those children who respond favorably, only a small percentage of them experiences dramatic improvements where all symptoms are eliminated and the behaviors become "normalized" (Pelham, 2002). Residual symptoms often remain, and individual counseling may be helpful in addressing them.

Individual counseling may be delivered from a variety of theoretical perspectives, including psychodynamic, humanistic, cognitive, and behavioral. Generally, only cognitive-behavioral approaches are considered potentially effective in addressing symptoms of ADHD (Barkley, 2006; Pelham, 2002). Meichenbaum and Goodman (1971) published the first article that outlined cognitive-behavioral strategies to address core symptoms of ADHD. Since that time, many studies have investigated the utility of cognitive-behavioral counseling with children with ADHD. Although a number of studies failed to prove the effectiveness of cognitive-behavioral counseling, those studies often compared the use of individual counseling alone, also known as monotherapy, with other treatments (e.g., parent training or medications). It is apparent that treatment effects derived from individual counseling are not as significant as those obtained from those other approaches (Pelham, 2002).

Clinicians, however, should not interpret those findings as indicative of a lack of utility of cognitive-behavioral counseling in the treatment of ADHD. Instead, it is more appropriate to place the benefits of individual counseling in the context of the other treatments. As Pelham (2002), Barkley (2006), and others convincingly argued, in monotherapy, individual counseling is not as effective as the other treatments. Effective management of ADHD, however, should not involve only one modality, and a multisystemic approach is generally regarded as most beneficial (Barkley, 2006). As such, individual counseling plays a significant supplementary role to other necessary interventions, including medications (discussed in Chapters 13, 14, and 15), parenting approaches (discussed in Chapter 7), and educational interventions (discussed in Chapters 11 and 12).

Indeed, results of research support the important, ancillary role of individual counseling. For example, Hinshaw and Erhardt (1991) reported the benefit of anger management training, and Pelham and Hoza (1996) found that adding social problem-solving training to behavioral interventions (such as parent training) improved overall outcomes. Pelham (2002) concurred that cognitive-behavioral counseling may be effective in enhancing maintenance and generalization effects of other treatments. Thus, cognitive-behavioral counseling may improve medication compliance, and individual sessions may help boys and teens with ADHD generalize treatment gains obtained from other techniques (such as contingency management used by parents or teachers) to other settings and situations.

Although many studies have shown that individual counseling is not as effective as medications, studies often discount real-world concerns, such as situations when parents refuse the medications or when clinicians encounter a boy or teen for whom medications are of limited utility (e.g., the adverse effects outweigh the benefits). For those clients, individual therapy is a reasonable alternative that is likely to produce at least some therapeutic effects (Abikoff, 2002). Indeed, head-to-head comparisons of psychosocial interventions with medications usually reveal that medication is more effective, but the psychosocial interventions also provide benefits, and a statistically significant reduction in symptoms is observed, although the effect sizes are smaller (Ambroggio & Jensen, 2002). Thus, when medications cannot be used, or treatment gains are insufficient, individual counseling is a reasonable option.

Of course, efficacy of individual therapy depends on the severity of the core symptoms and the ability of the client to benefit from treatment. For those clients who exhibit very severe impairment, individual counseling alone may be of limited value. For example, clients who are extremely impulsive or hyperactive may not be able to use some of the treatment suggestions, and they may find it too difficult to identify cognitive patterns and self-statements necessary for clinical improvements. Similarly, clients with whom at least minimal rapport and therapeutic alliance cannot be established are not likely to benefit from treatment.

Very young boys or those with severely limited verbal abilities may present a particular challenge. For cognitive-behavioral intervention to be effective, it is necessary for clients to be able to meaningfully participate in verbal interactions and to understand the concepts being addressed. Those boys who cannot meet those requirements are not likely to benefit from traditional "talking-therapy" forms of counseling. For those clients, expressive therapies (e.g., play or art therapy) may be attempted. Although these approaches have not been found to be effective in addressing core symptoms of ADHD, some studies have found them to be beneficial in improving the outcome of other treatment modalities (e.g., parent training; Johnson, Franklin, Hall, & Prieto, 2000).

Individual counseling from a cognitive-behavioral perspective may have additional benefits. In addition to exhibiting the core symptoms, boys and teens with ADHD commonly exhibit significant secondary symptoms that include low self-esteem and limited motivation, and individual counseling provides opportunities to work on these problems. The cognitive-behavioral approach is known to be effective in addressing various symptoms of depression (such as low self-esteem) and anxiety, and it is considered the psychotherapeutic treatment of choice for these problems in children and adolescents (Kendall, 2005). Because other forms of treatment (e.g., medications) are not likely to address these secondary symptoms, clinicians will need to use individual counseling to address those issues.

INTERVENTIONS

As with all forms of individual psychotherapy, it is necessary for the clinician to build a therapeutic relationship and establish a working alliance with the client for interventions to be effective. The discussion that follows will focus on methods of establishing rapport that specifically take into consideration issues of masculinity that pertain to boys and male teens. Treatment goals will then be discussed that focus on educating the client about ADHD and other treatment modalities (e.g., medications), addressing core symptoms, and working on secondary symptoms commonly exhibited by boys and teens with ADHD.

Rapport Building

When boys and teens with ADHD are brought for mental health treatment, they commonly view it as punishment for the difficulties that they have been exhibiting and the frustration their symptoms have been causing their parents and teachers. It is rare for parents to bring boys into treatment when symptoms first appear. Almost always, by the time the boy or teen is brought for treatment, conflicts have long existed within the home, and arguments over issues such as poor school performance, lack of follow-through with home tasks, and defiance were commonplace for quite some time, usually at least a few years. Along the way, the boy likely internalized a defensive attitude, and he recognizes that he is being blamed for these problems, even though he may not recognize how it is that he contributes to them. This may interfere with the establishment of a therapeutic alliance, because the boy will likely try to prove that there is nothing wrong with him and he is not to blame for the conflicts.

Sometimes parents verbalize to the boy that he is brought to treatment because they do not know what else to do, and they want the therapist to try to change (i.e., "fix") him. Mental health professionals need to be vigilant about such scenarios. As discussed in the previous two chapters, it is usually helpful to initially meet with the parents for a full session during which a detailed description of the problem and extensive history are collected. The boy is then invited for the second session. Such an arrangement allows the therapist to address with the parents the most effective methods of introducing the idea of counseling to their son.

It is important to communicate to the parents that they should not blame their son for all conflicts and should not communicate to him that they are bringing him in because he is exhibiting too many problems. Such an approach will exacerbate the defensiveness and significantly interfere with the establishment of a therapeutic relationship. Instead, it may be more effective to frame the treatment as an attempt to seek assistance from a professional who helps people get along with each other. Even if the boy feels he is not to blame, he is likely to recognize that significant conflicts have been taking place. The treatment should be portrayed as involving various members of the family (which is likely to be accurate, because parenting work is usually necessary) where everyone will work on things they can change to better communicate and get along with each other.

The treatment usually involves a combination of individual sessions with the boy and separate sessions (without the boy) with the parents to address parenting strategies (as discussed in Chapter 7). This combination of sessions can be delivered by dividing the usual sessions in half to provide time for both components or by alternating sessions between individual treatment and parenting work. Although the former approach commonly works well, sometimes parents who are especially stressed may need more time than half of a standard session, and in those situations the latter approach sometimes works better.

When both treatment modalities are delivered simultaneously, it is very important to communicate about confidentiality with the boy as well as his parents. Because the boy will know that the therapist is seeing his parents without him, the therapist must go out of his or her way to assure the boy that what is being discussed between him and the therapist is private and that the only time this privacy may be limited is when the therapist learns that someone has gotten (or is about to get) hurt or that some other behavior is being contemplated that may result in serious harm. In those cases, the parents will need to be consulted because they are responsible for the health and welfare of their children. Otherwise, things discussed between the boy and the therapist remain between them, unless they both agree that something should be addressed with the parents.

It is important for the therapist to also discuss issues of confidentiality with the parents. Everything remains private outside of the standard exceptions to confidentiality (such as the duty to warn of or report child abuse). Parents often wonder what goes on in individual sessions with their son, and they may ask the therapist to disclose the content of those sessions. The therapist must recognize that unless the client is old enough to have confidentiality protection within a given state's guidelines, his parents have the right to request information about what goes on in the sessions with their son. It is helpful, however, to communicate to their parents that although they have the legal right to that information, forcing the therapist to disclose it will destroy the integrity of the treatment, because the boy is not likely to trust the therapist if he knows that whatever he says in private will be disclosed to the parents. Instead, the parents need to trust the therapist that any issues that involve safety or danger will be disclosed, but otherwise the therapist must keep the contents of sessions with their son confidential.

The socialization of males in our society includes powerful codes that define appropriate and inappropriate behaviors. Since early in life, boys are socialized against expressing vulnerable emotions (Robertson & Shepard, 2008). This is done through modeling (e.g., boys do not commonly see their fathers express tender or vulnerable feelings, especially not to them directly) as well as reinforcement (e.g., boys are usually rewarded for suppressing the expression of pain, sadness, or similar feelings). Consequently, many boys do not develop the language that is needed to express a wide range of emotions and are likely to be uncomfortable in a setting that focuses on expressing those emotions (e.g., in a therapist's office).

With this in mind, the therapist may find it helpful during individual sessions with the boy to become involved in some play activity with him. This will make it easier for them to interact and will foster rapport building. Many choices are available, but the therapist will find it most appropriate to select a play activity that does not involve much talking, such as playing with toy cars or building blocks. Some games are also useful, such as checkers or the card game of war. Again, only those games should be used that do not require much verbal exchange for the purpose of playing the game ("go fish," for example, will be more difficult). When the play activity does not require verbal exchange, it allows the therapist and the client to begin chatting about pertinent issues while the game goes on. Initiating such a verbal exchange while playing reduces the extent to which the boy feels "on the spot" and may make the sessions more fun, thus lessening the extent to which he may feel uncomfortable or defensive.

During the first few sessions with the boy, the therapist needs to tread lightly. Rather than confronting the client with the problems disclosed by the parents, the therapist should draw the client to disclose his own perception of the difficulties and/or conflicts that are taking place at home (and/or in school). The therapist may want to ask questions about the behaviors that sometimes result in the client getting yelled at or punished, and when querying is necessary to clarify the situation, the therapist should proceed in a collaborative manner, gently prompting the client to think about possible solutions. At the start of treatment, it is useful to get the client to agree to work on at least one problem, such as figuring out ways to reduce arguments between the client and the parents, reducing problems with homework, or helping him get better grades. If the client is able to identify at least one problem that he wants to work on, his motivation to attend treatment and work on this issue is likely to be more significant.

Because the boy or teen may be limited in his abilities to express emotional content, various techniques may be used to help him develop appropriate language. For example, the therapist can name several feelings and ask the boy which one comes closest to reflecting how he felt in a given situations. Therapists can also use handouts that assist in this task. Many forms of "feeling faces" are widely available, where a number of faces with different feelings are drawn on a page, with the name of the feeling underneath, and the boy may be asked to circle those faces that reflect how he feels about a given situation. Most boys and teens have fun with this activity, because some of the faces are comical. Teens who prefer a more stoic approach may be helped through the use of a handout with a large number of feeling words grouped into several categories. These techniques can help the boy or teen improve his abilities to express his feelings verbally.

Psychoeducation

One of the dilemmas that therapists face is whether to share the diagnosis with the clients. At times, it may be helpful to discuss the diagnosis, but in other situations it may be best to avoid using clinical labels. Either way, the therapist must be careful not to portray the boy as "damaged" or "less than normal" in any way. Instead, the therapist should frame the disorder and/or its symptoms within the context of strengths and weaknesses that boys his age commonly exhibit. The following example illustrates some of these principles:

> An 8-year-old boy with ADHD was brought in for treatment. He was told by his parents that he does not listen to them and is not doing well in school, and therefore he must talk to the therapist. The therapist started treatment by asking the boy to identify some of his strengths, asking what specific sports or hobbies he enjoys, if he is physically strong, if he is a fast runner, and so on. The boy was encouraged to be creative and think about all the different things he seems to do well, including aspects of school performance that he may excel at. The therapist also asked the boy about how many other age peers he knows who seem to possess the same attributes. The goal of this intervention was aimed at helping the boy recognize that he has some strengths that many others his age may not have and may find very desirable.
>
> Next, the therapist asked the boy about skills that are more difficult for him. The boy identified some sports that are harder for him to do and academic tasks that he finds more difficult. The therapist asked the boy about other peers he knows who similarly find these skills difficult. The goal was to help the boy understand that he possesses a mix of strengths and weaknesses and that everyone around him similarly has such a profile, although the specific mix of abilities is likely to be different.
>
> Once it was established that everyone has strengths and weaknesses, the therapist proceeded to frame the presenting problem as indicative of skills that the client may find more difficult. Defiance was reframed as a skill involving listening to parents, and poor frustration tolerance was reframed as a skill involving the ability to control anger. Thus, the treatment was

portrayed as involving work to help the boy strengthen the skills that he finds more difficult, which in turn will improve his life in a specific way (e.g., by helping him get along better with his parents or get better grades in school).

Within such a context, when the boy is able to identify specific ways in which the treatment will help him feel better, his willingness to participate in counseling is likely to improve. As the therapeutic alliance strengthens, the boy is more likely to try some of the techniques suggested in treatment, and progress in treatment will be more apparent.

Disclosing the Diagnosis. When the boy was previously told that he has attention deficit disorder or ADHD, or when the boy is receiving medications and is informed that they help him improve self-control or focusing, it is best to be honest and discuss the disorder along with what it means. It may be beneficial to share the name of the disorder (or, at least, its abbreviation) to give the boy the opportunity to hear the terminology within a setting where he is able to ask questions about what it means and how he is different from others.

When discussing impulsivity or hyperactivity, it is best to refer to this dimension as "self-control" and use descriptors such as "high energy" and "the ability to stop and think before you act." When discussing inattentiveness or disorganization, it is best to address them as "the ability to pay attention" especially in school-related matters (such as in the classroom or during homework). It is helpful to specify that the attentional difficulties are connected to school-related behaviors, because the boy is likely to recognize that he can pay attention without difficulties while he performs some other tasks (such as watching television), and discussing in detail why school-related tasks seem to provoke distractibility may be beyond the boy's ability to comprehend. Disorganization can easily be included within this dimension by referring to it as "forgetfulness." In general, it is important to use terms that normalize the problem as much as possible and do not make the boy feel less capable than those without ADHD.

It is often helpful to characterize "self-control" and "paying attention" as being similar to abilities that involve our senses. Even young boys recognize that we interact with the world through senses, such as vision, hearing, touch, smell, and taste. Portraying "self-control" or "paying attention" as additional senselike skills allows the use of a beneficial analogy.

Boys easily accept that people exhibit varying degrees of strengths and weaknesses within our senses. For example, one person has excellent eyesight, whereas another needs to wear glasses. One boy may have excellent hearing and musical abilities that go along with it, whereas another may need to wear a hearing aid because his hearing is poor. Just because someone is born with poor eyesight or limited hearing does not make that person stupid and less capable than anyone else. In other words, how good our senses are has nothing to do with how smart and capable we are.

When self-control and ability to pay attention are presented to the boy as senselike attributes, he may find it much easier to accept that some individuals may have more problems in these areas without affecting their capabilities or overall likeability. Just like boys who wear glasses are not any less smart than those with good eyesight, boys who have problems paying attention are not any less smart that those who have better attentional skills. Normalizing ADHD symptoms as nothing more than an expression of an individual profile of strengths and weaknesses can help the boy accept some of his symptoms while minimizing adverse effects on his self-concept. In addition, within such a framework the treatment can be established as an attempt to help him strengthen those weaknesses, just like glasses are designed to strengthen one's eyesight, and a hearing aid is designed to strengthen one's hearing.

When the boy asks how those weaknesses came about, it is appropriate to extend this analogy and discuss the inborn nature of the senses and some sensory-like abilities. Just like a person who has poor eyesight was probably born with eyes that work a little differently from the eyes of those with good eyesight, the parts of the brain that are involved in attention (of self-control) work a little differently in boys who have some problems in those areas. It is important to avoid blaming the child for those symptoms or portraying him as inferior because he exhibits these problems.

Of course, some boys (especially teens) may view this explanation as an excuse to ask parents and teachers to have lower expectations. For example, a boy with poor eyesight cannot be expected to do the same things as those who can see very well. This argument can easily be challenged, however. Having poor eyesight is not an excuse to stop doing schoolwork or be excused from house chores, and the person is required to wear glasses so that he can see normally and perform his responsibilities. In the same way, those who have problems with attentional skills or self-control must take steps to improve these problems, and the treatment can be portrayed as an avenue to do so.

Psychoeducation About Medications. Boys who take medications to manage their symptoms often feel bad about the need to do so. To protect them from these feelings, sometimes parents present the medication as a vitamin that is taken to help the boy grow up bigger and stronger. Generally, this is not advisable, and parents should be discouraged from misleading the boy. When it becomes clear that the pill is really a medication rather than a vitamin, the boy is likely to feel deceived, and the negative reaction will be magnified.

It is important for the therapist to encourage the boy to express his feelings about the medications. The boy will usually disclose that it makes him feel like there is something wrong with him, because most kids do not have to take medications. Therapists should not dismiss those feelings, but clinicians need to be careful not to confirm them.

Once again, the analogy described in the previous section can provide a useful framework.

> A 10-year-old boy with ADHD is placed on medications and questions why he needs to take it. His parents tell him that it will help him pay attention in school, but he is upset because none of his friends take medications, and he perceives himself as inferior. The therapist starts by helping the boy think about the different ways that kids may exhibit physical strengths and weaknesses. Does he know any boys who wear glasses? How about someone who wears a hearing aid? These are all ways in which we may exhibit some physical limitations, and everyone who is somehow different usually feels bad about it, even though others do not see the person as inferior. For example, a boy who wears a hearing aid is usually self-conscious about it, and although a few mean-spirited children may sometimes tease him about it, most children do not see him any differently and do not care whether he wears a hearing aid. Similarly, a boy who takes medications is likely to be accepted by others without any second thought, although a small minority may sometimes say something mean. Thus, wearing a hearing aid or using medications is not an indication of inferiority.

To internalize this message, the boy will likely need to hear it many times, not only from the therapist but also from people with central importance in his life, such as his parents, siblings, or teachers. Thus, when parents or teachers are part of the treatment, the therapist should encourage them to approach this issue similarly.

Core Symptoms

Dimensions of ADHD symptoms include hyperactivity/impulsivity and inattentiveness/disorganization. Both dimensions can be viewed as skill deficits: Hyperactivity and impulsivity result from limited control over urges, and inattentiveness and disorganization result from insufficient abilities to maintain mental set (to remain on task) and devote sufficient mental energy to process a sequence of cognitive tasks required to keep track of various aspects of responsibilities. To improve these symptoms, the therapist can use a variety of cognitive-behavioral strategies.

Impulsivity. In the cognitive-behavioral model of self-control, internalization of verbal dialogue underlies voluntary control of behavior (Vygotsky, 1962). As suggested by Meichenbaum and Goodman (1971), an impulsive boy does not comprehend the need to mediate his behaviors, does not identify relevant verbal mediators, and consequently does not verbally mediate his behavior. Treatment must focus on each of those three deficits.

To help the boy recognize the need for verbal mediation, the therapist must help him understand that unmediated behaviors (i.e., impulsivity) usually result in adverse consequences. The boy may review with the therapist examples of situations when he reacted without thinking and what consequences resulted from these behaviors, as shown in the following example:

> An 11-year-old boy with ADHD makes decisions impulsively and some-times exercises poor judgment. Consequently, he frequently argues with his parents. In treatment, the therapist helps him separately identify examples of impulsive behaviors that occur in various settings. At home and with his parents, he previously allowed a friend to come over when no one was home, breaking a house rule. He then told a lie (that his parents allowed him to do so), constructed impulsively in a desperate attempt to cover up the misbehavior. As a result, he was grounded for 1 week, and his parents fur-ther extended the punishment because of the lie. Another time, he broke a curfew because he was having too much fun, and he decided to stay longer, even though he knew his parents told him to come home. In school, he has gotten in trouble because he brought his cell phone and was playing games on it during class, a behavior he knew was not allowed in class. With peers, he often makes fun when someone makes a mistake, acts bossy when mak-ing up rules for play activities (thus ignoring others' input), and overreacts when things do not go his way. In treatment, the therapist encourages the boy to identify as many of these situations as possible, each time making sure that the negative outcome is clearly elucidated. The purpose of this activity is not to make the boy feel bad about his mistakes. Rather, the boy needs to recognize that his way of behaving generally uses little fore-thought, and another way of behaving, attainable to him if he works hard to implement it, is likely to result in better outcomes.

Once the boy is able to recognize and accept that he needs to think before he acts, he is ready to start constructing self-statements that will act as situational mediators. As Meichenbaum and Goodman (1971) pointed out, children gradually internalize self-statements they hear around them, those they encounter from the significant role models in their life. These can be used as initial examples to begin developing meditational strategies.

> In treatment, the boy in the previous example is directed to think about the times he hears his parents talk to each other about how to approach a situation or resolve a problem. While having dinner at home, his parents discuss how to deal with a frustrating coworker or how to address a mistake they recently made. In school, teachers verbalize ways to resolve disputes between students and suggest what each boy should say. Television shows commonly relate situations where characters in the story talk about a deci-sion they have to make about what to do. Day to day, the boy is constantly exposed to examples of such mediation strategies, and the therapist can help him identify what the adults say and help him think about whether the verbalized strategy is likely to be effective. In treatment, it is necessary to be creative and identify as many of these strategies as possible.
> Next, the boy learns to apply the meditational statements used by adults to situations that are relevant to him. Analogies are helpful when making

this connection. One by one, verbalizations heard from adults are applied to specific situations that the boy encounters in his life that are similar. For example, dealing with a difficult coworker is similar to dealing with a frustrating peer on the playground. Dealing with a problem at work is similar to addressing a difficult task in school. This trains the boy to suppress the initial impulse to use the first strategy that comes to mind and recognize that self-statements help him make better decisions.

When using cognitive-behavioral therapy with children, the therapist must remember that some boys, depending on their age and developmental level, may not have progressed far enough to be able to use sufficient internal dialogue. Instead, it is better to ask the boy to begin to talk himself through situations aloud. This can be done quietly, thus minimizing disruption in various settings. The boy should get used to talking himself through situations aloud before he gradually begins able to internalize these meditational statements and produce them covertly.

The efficacy of this approach depends on the severity of the problems with impulsivity that a boy presents. When the problems are of moderate severity, and some self-control is evident, this approach is likely to produce beneficial results. When severe impulsivity is evident, however, using this approach may not be very effective. In those situations, therapists should encourage parents to consider the use of medications to produce at least some improvement, which then can be enhanced by the therapeutic strategies discussed in this section.

Therapists also need to recognize that teaching the cognitions described earlier will be more effective when a behavioral program is also developed that uses contingency-management strategies (e.g., as discussed in Chapters 7 and 12). Effective control and manipulation of consequences is likely to increase the boy's motivation to develop strategies that will help him earn more privileges and rewards. As motivation increases, so does effort, and he will work much harder at learning the techniques described herein when he is able to recognize that these techniques are likely to result in increases in desired privileges, rewards, and other positive consequences.

Hyperactivity. High motor output and limited control over exerted energy are additional examples of impaired impulse control. In this case, the impulses are urges to perform motor behaviors. Boys often have limited control over these symptoms, but those who are able to exert at least some control and do not appear severely hyperactive may benefit from an approach that is similar to the one described previously.

A 6-year-old boy with ADHD often gets in trouble because of his notable hyperactivity. He usually does not understand why he is being yelled at. In treatment, the therapist initially helps the boy recognize that his unusually high energy and overactivity are creating problems for people around him. At home, being too active may annoy his parents and siblings; for example, if he makes too much noise or jumps around during meals, his parents may yell at him, and when he wants to run and jump around too much while playing with his siblings, they may not want to play with him. At school, being very active may result in his getting in trouble with the teacher and getting reprimanded for leaving his desk or being too fidgety. When he is playing with other kids, they often get tired and lose interest in activities that require high energy. The therapist helps him recognize that this is something that needs to be addressed, and there may be things he can do to bring at least some of this under control.

As with impulsivity, developing appropriate mediating cognitions for hyperactivity may be helpful. Hyperactive boys may benefit from learning to repeat certain self-statements, such as "I will stay at my desk." The therapist should not try to teach the boy self-statements that are not realistic, for example, "I will stay still." Such a goal may be unattainable, and the boy will quickly discover that the therapist is asking something of him that is beyond his ability to do. A boy may still be active, however, but exercise enough control to remain in one place. This is a good place to start when trying to bring hyperactivity under control, at least to some extent.

It may be helpful to use reminders about the need to use better self-control, as evident in the following example:

> While working with the boy in the previous example, the therapist helped him make two signs for him to place in situations where it is important for him to try to remain still. One of these signs was placed on his desk in the classroom to remind him to remain in one place and not wander off while the class is in session. Another one was used at home during meals. The signs were small enough to be unobtrusive to others but were placed where the boy could easily see them.
>
> Both signs resulted in a small improvement. After a few days, however, other boys in class noticed the sign on his desk and asked him about it, making him self-conscious about the sign. Thus, the teacher was asked to allow him to place a sticker, instead of the sign, on his desk that helped him remember to use self-control. When the teacher noticed that he was unusually active, she gently reminded him to sit on one hand (not the one he writes with) as a signal to try to remain more still. To improve the effectiveness, the therapist also enlisted the teacher to issue a cue to help the boy become aware that he is too active (methods of cuing students are discussed in detail in Chapter 11). All of these techniques did not eliminate the hyperactivity, but they did make the problem somewhat more manageable in school and at home.

As with techniques aimed at impulsivity, this approach helps the boy become aware of situations that require more effort and think about keeping his behavior under control. Over time, he will gradually learn to produce these self-statements spontaneously.

Inattentiveness. Problems with distractibility affect the boy with ADHD in many ways. In school, he may often daydream and find it difficult to pay attention during lectures and activities. At home, he may spend a long time completing homework and may become side-tracked while performing tasks that he was asked to do by his parents. A procedure called self-monitoring has been shown to be effective in helping to reduce these problems.

> A 9-year-old boy is working with his therapist to improve his ability to remain on task. The therapist initially identifies specific situations when it is most important to remain on task—a specific subject in school (e.g., doing math work), and homework time at home. Next, the therapist teaches the boy to ask himself a question during those specific times, such as "What am I doing?" He then has to answer this question in detail. To do so, he must be aware of what he is looking at, what his hands are doing, what he is thinking about, and so on.
>
> Because breaking a spell of daydreaming to perform such an attention check is difficult, the therapist asks the boy to identify what he usually does when he is in the midst of one of the situations where he has to be on task. When he is at his desk doing math work, where does he usually look? Is it out the window? Or at the clock in the room? At home, during homework, where does he usually look? The therapist helps him identify one or two specific items that seem to draw him when his attention is drifting.
>
> Once these items have been identified, the boy is taught to associate seeing these items with asking himself "What am I doing?" For example, whenever he is in the classroom, he asks himself "What am I doing" whenever he catches himself looking out the window or looking at the clock in the room.
>
> If the initial question reveals that the boy is not paying attention, the therapist teaches him to ask a follow-up question, "What am I supposed to be doing?" or "What is everyone else in class doing?" This helps him refocus on the task at hand.

This procedure takes some time to implement, and depending on the boy's age and level of motivation, he may need a lot of practice to successfully use this approach. It has been shown, however, to increase the amount of time children with ADHD can stay on task.

Parents and children can help the boy implement self-monitoring by using cues that trigger him to think about what he is doing. In the classroom, teachers can use cues to the whole class, such as "Boys and girls, is everyone paying attention?" Because these cues are directed to the whole class, no one will feel singled out, but a boy who is taught that such a cue is meant to help him refocus will likely use it to perform the mental check involved in self-monitoring.

Parents can use similar cues during homework time. While the boy is working on his assignments, they can look in every 5 minutes or so and merely state, "Time to make sure you are working." If the boy was off task, his parents should not reprimand him, because this would gradually help the boy associate the cue with getting in trouble. Rather, the cue should be as innocuous as possible, merely triggering the boy to think about whether he is on task. Over time, he will learn to internalize those cues and perform self-monitoring independently.

Disorganization. Although problems with keeping track of the boy's things may cause difficulties in many areas and across many settings, they are likely to present the greatest problems with academic tasks, especially homework. For this reason, it is more beneficial to teach organizational skills specifically as they relate to homework and academic items (such as books and notebooks).

Homework assignments present a particularly difficult challenge. It is necessary to teach the boy to use a homework journal (as discussed in Chapters 7 and 12). The journal should be presented to the boy in a way that portrays it as a tool that most everyone uses; it is his version of a calendar. The counselor, as well as the boy's parents, should show the boy the way they use their calendars to schedule their tasks, events, work that is due, and so on. If he is able to make the connection that he is asked to do things that most individuals do, he will have an easier time accepting it as a normal tool that people use to keep track of their busy life. Through modeling and direct assistance, he needs to be taught to write both daily and longer duration assignments (e.g., class projects) on the day that they are due, and he needs to be taught to check each day's assignments at homework time. Gradually, he will also learn to check what is due several days ahead.

Enlisting the parents and teachers to implement this approach is necessary. In school, the teacher must ensure that the homework journal is used and that all assignments are accurately written where they belong. Assistance needs to be given to help the boy correct any errors and omissions and to make sure that the homework journal is placed in his book bag.

At home, parents must ask for the homework journal at the beginning of every homework session and assist the boy in planning his study activities. For example, it is helpful to group assignments on the table or desk where the homework is being done and guide the boy to complete one assignment at a time, then show it to his parents, place it in his book bag, and move on to the next assignment. To assist with motivation, parents should restrict a privilege until after the homework has been completed, and it should be available to him only as a reward for successful completion of homework and study assignments. When the journal was forgotten, the boy should be required to complete whatever he brought home, and the homework-contingent privilege should be suspended for that day.

To help the boy organize his book bag, his parents should ask him to empty all contents on the bed once per week (e.g., on Sunday evening, in preparation for the forthcoming week). Each item on the bed must then be examined by the boy (with oversight by his parents, but they should not do it for him), and he must explain what each item is and where it belongs. The parents then ask him to place each item where it belongs and then move on to the next item.

To organize school items, many parents find it very helpful to use trappers. Trappers should be color-coded per subject, and it may be helpful to have two sets of trappers—one in the boy's desk where all assignments and tests already marked and returned to him will be kept (as an archive), and another set that stays in the book bag and is used to hold all homework assignments on their way to and from school. Although tedious, the use of such a procedure will, in time, help him internalize the skills necessary to keep track of his assignments and possessions.

Secondary Symptoms

As discussed in previous chapters, boys who exhibit difficulties in self-control often have problems controlling their anger and frustration. Although improving core symptoms is likely to reduce these difficulties, negative reactions to frustrating situations have likely been evident for a long period of time, and improvement in core symptoms will not eliminate this problem. Consequently, addressing anger management and frustration tolerance in treatment is likely to be beneficial.

In addition, boys who have had symptoms of ADHD for some time have usually experienced a significant amount of conflict and failure. Their relationships with parents, teachers, and peers have adversely been affected, and the boys likely started to internalize negative self-esteem and limited motivation to succeed. When core symptoms diminish, the problems with self-esteem and motivation are likely to persist. Thus, therapists should plan to address these problems in treatment.

Anger Management. As previously discussed, boys with ADHD get into frequent conflicts with their parents, teachers, and peers. These conflicts may occur several times per day. As a result, boys learn to expect that each interaction will result in conflict and negative feelings. Thus, they do not anticipate positive outcomes from interpersonal interactions, and they tend to prepare themselves for a battle when they interact with their parents, teachers, siblings, and peers.

This negative expectation affects the interaction in several important ways. Boys with ADHD learn to address others, from the start, with a negative attitude, which may be communicated by a edge in their voice, a menacing body posture, threatening gestures, and belligerent verbalizations. Because they expect a battle, they subconsciously prepare for one and communicate this both verbally and nonverbally.

Treatment should help the boy identify various feeling states and what behaviors are associated with them, as shown in the following example:

> A 10-year-old boy with ADHD is working on his ability to appropriately express feelings of anger. The treatment begins with helping the boy identify what situations make him happy, curious, frustrated, angry, fearful, and so on. The therapist spends some time identifying those situations, and handouts that prompt the client to think about various feelings (e.g., "feeling

faces" described earlier in the chapter) are used along the way. As the boy becomes more aware of the times he is likely to perform behaviors that may result in troubling consequences, he is ready to begin to prepare himself to be "on watch" for those kinds of situations.

Once these situations are identified, the therapist guides the boy to recognize the bodily reactions that he experiences when these instances occur. How does he know he is happy? Angry? Fearful? What is his heart doing? What about his breathing? Are his fists clenched? Many of these bodily reactions are identified and become potential signals that communicate to him that an emotional reaction has been awakened.

Along with helping the boy identify bodily reactions, the therapist helps him identify the thoughts that accompany those feelings. What is he saying to himself when he is angry? When he is afraid of getting punished by his parents? When his curiosity is awakened, and he can't wait to see what a group of friends is doing at the moment? Because thoughts precipitate behaviors, helping the boy become aware of what he is thinking before he acts is very helpful, because it prepares him to be able to potentially change these cognitions as the treatment continues.

Once these thoughts were identified, development of a proactive self-dialogue began. The boy was taught to replace automatic thoughts with those that are more conducive to good behavior. Instead of thinking, "My brother always gets his way, and I must punish him for it," he was taught to think, "I am angry because he got his way, but if I can control myself, I can talk to my parents about these feelings." With friends, instead of thinking, "Billy always gives me a hard time, and I have to make him scared of me so he leaves me alone," he was taught to think, "Billy is a pain in the neck sometimes, but getting into a fight only makes it worse, so I'll get away from him and start playing with kids I like better." Over time, the therapist reviewed various situations when explosive behaviors were most common and helped the boy develop appropriate cognitions to address each situation. In addition, when developing self-statements, the therapist made sure that each self-statement identified a specific proactive behavior that would be performed as a replacement for previous explosions.

One way to maximize benefit with this approach is to teach the boy certain slogans that he may repeat to himself before he goes into situations that evoke emotions. One slogan can be suggested for each common emotion—fear, anger, and so on. These slogans should be framed as "pep talks," similar to those that coaches usually give members of their team. Boys are especially receptive to this idea—many boys are sports fans and have participated at least in some team sports, and so introducing this concept will help them recognize that they are being asked to do for themselves what the coaches have been doing for them all along. This step will likely take much practice and will require frequent role-playing during therapy sessions. Using these pep talks, however, will help the boy significantly increase the processing time that occurs after he has been exposed to emotion-provoking situations.

Once the pep talks have been used to prevent initial overreaction, more rational processing becomes more likely. The boy is taught to think about the various options for behavioral responses—different things he may do and say to react to the situation that just occurred. Each one needs to be followed with a brief assessment of what is going to happen if this behavior is chosen. This approach must be tailored to the boy's age. Young boys, for example, need suggestions of what they should think or say in various situations and recognize that other things they may do or say will result in negative consequences (e.g., being punished). Grounding these suggestions in examples of real situations that happened recently will make this approach more personal and effective. Older boys should be coached to develop this thought process more independently, prompting them to replay examples of recent episodes and behaviors.

The final step involves the selection of the most appropriate action. Once again, it is necessary to continue to stress to the boy that the consequences of any given behavior must always be considered and must be the primary guide that helps the boy decide what to do in any given situation. The more this approach can be used, the more the action–reaction sequence can be slowed down and more effective processing can be used, thus reducing problems with inappropriate expression of anger and frustration.

Low Self-Esteem. Boys with ADHD often experience conflict and failure. Over time, they often develop a negative self-image. It is necessary to address this in counseling. To do so, counselors should focus on the boy's strengths. Although boys with ADHD often exhibit an academic weakness (e.g., difficulties with written language), they may also exhibit a strength (e.g., being good in math). The counselor can help the boy become aware of his pattern of strengths and weaknesses and help him recognize that most children have a similar pattern. This can normalize his school experience and help him accept that, essentially, he is just like any other boy his age.

Recognition of strengths should extend beyond academics. Every boy has at least one interest or skill where he is more accomplished. It may be a sport, an ability to play a musical instrument, or a knowledge of cars or dinosaurs that is more extensive than that of his peers. Helping him recognize what those skills are, and how accomplished he is in those areas, can help his self-esteem. During sessions, it is beneficial to structure activities in such a way that the boy shows the therapist (and the parent) how good he is at doing something, for example, constructing a nice building with Lego blocks, winning in a game of checkers, and so on. Using these activities while talking with the boy in counseling is often very helpful—it assists in rapport building and provides an opportunity for him to receive recognition for something he did. In the office, the therapist can display an art gallery of drawings or an exhibition of building-block constructions and place the boy's item there to help him experience a feeling of accomplishment.

The cognitive approach to the treatment of low self-esteem is based on the recognition that negative self-statements result in negative feelings.

Although very young boys (younger than age 5) may have difficulties recognizing self-dialogue, boys who are at least school age or older can begin to identify the perception they have of themselves and their self-statements. Beck (1995) identified the cognitive triad that underlies the feelings of depression: a negative view of the world, the future, and oneself. Identifying these negative assumptions and replacing them with more appropriate alternatives is an important component of helping a boy with ADHD develop better self-esteem. Again, activities during sessions can act as triggers to identify the boy's thought patterns and replace negative self-statements with positive ones.

Limited Motivation. In the cognitive-behavioral model, motivation is inseparable from self-efficacy. The concept, as introduced by Bandura (1976, 2000), involves the person's recognition of his strengths and abilities. Those people with high self-efficacy perceive themselves as capable of successfully handling the usual demands that day-to-day functioning requires. For a boy with ADHD, this means perceiving himself as able to get along with his parents, do well in school, and be accepted by his peers. Unfortunately, the actual experience of boys with ADHD is contrary to those beliefs, because these boys frequently argue with their parents, teachers, and peers and generally find it difficult to succeed academically or socially. Over time, these experiences become internalized into negative expectations, and the boys' self-efficacy becomes low. As self-efficacy lowers, so does motivation. In therapy, this issue must be addressed.

As proposed by Bandura, the perception of self-efficacy results from self-statements, which is evident in the following example:

> A therapist is treating a 12-year-old boy with ADHD. As the therapy unfolds, it becomes apparent that the boy frequently experiences conflicts and failure and now expects that most situations will result in negative outcomes. The therapist helps him identify the thoughts that underlie these assumptions. The therapist leads the client to recognize that when he is about to start an interaction with his parents, he is thinking, "Here we go again—I am going to get yelled at." When given a homework assignment, he is thinking, "This is too hard. I will not be able to do this." When entering a social setting, he is thinking, "Here is Mike again. He always picks on me. Why does he hate me?" It becomes clear that the therapist must find ways to diminish such negative cognitions and replace them with self-statements that underlie more positive expectations.

Beck's model of collaborative empiricism (as discussed, for example, by Judith Beck, 1995) provides a useful framework. When this approach is used, the therapist and the client become collaborators as they test out the faulty assumptions that the client is maintaining. In this process, the cognitive distortions that underlie these faulty assumptions are illuminated, and the therapist and client begin to work on developing assumptions that are based on reality rather than the distortions. As more realistic assumptions are internalized, motivation increases. Thus, treatment of the boy in the previous example proceeds as follows:

The therapist begins by prompting the boy to think about the various situations he encounters in his life. When he comes home from school, what does he think his parents will say to him? What will they ask him to do? Will that result in conflict? What about school-related issues? What will happen when he has to sit down and do his homework? Will it be hard? Will he be able to do it? Will his parents be satisfied with his efforts? Because the boy was not aware of his automatic thoughts, much patience and guidance was needed to help him identify them, and the therapist had to cue him to think about the situation, its outcome, and so on before the boy was able to identify the specific cognitions.

As the boy became better able to relate what he was anticipating, the therapist introduced the idea that thoughts affect behaviors and that what he thinks about a situation significantly influences how he feels about its outcome and how he behaves when the situation actually takes place. A significant amount of practice was necessary to help the boy recognize and verbalize those thoughts.

Once the boy was able to identify the negative thought patterns, collaborative empiricism began. The therapist helped the boy explore the implications of his negative assumptions. For example, when he expects that when he comes home, he will probably get yelled at, does this happen always? Are there times when he has come home and conflicts did not ensue? Prompting for recent specific events was needed to help him identify his expectations and recognize that these do not always come true.

Similar events were also reviewed pertaining to school. For example, as the boy sits in the classroom and the teacher is about to give out an assignment, is he expecting that it will be too hard for him to do? Has that always been the case? Recalling examples of assigned work over the past week revealed that some assignments indeed were hard, whereas others were much easier. In this step, it was necessary to help the boy recognize that his assumptions often are not accurate.

Next, the boy examined the effect of his negative assumptions on his feelings and behaviors. If he is expecting to get yelled at when he gets home, how does that make him feel? If he feels defensive, how does that affect the way he speaks to his parents and the way he reacts when they approach him? Similarly, if he expects that all work given to him by his teachers will be too hard for him to do, how will this assumption affect his attitude toward the work and his efforts to try hard and get it done? Ultimately, how will that affect his grades? The therapist reviewed many such examples pertaining to home, school, and social settings.

Finally, once the boy recognized that negative expectations are not productive for him, he became able to start to replace these thoughts with more appropriate expectations. At home, he was taught to say to himself, "I get in trouble when I do something wrong, but otherwise I do not. Today, I did not do anything wrong, and so my parents have no reason to yell at me." In school, he was taught to say, "Some assignments are hard, but others are easy, and I am able to do them with no problems. If I get one that seems hard, I will ask for help." With peers, he was encouraged to expect to get along with them, and if anyone teases him, find a way to tease back. With practice, he gradually began to internalize a set of expectations that were more realistic, and an overall improvement in his attitude was evident.

In some situations, negative expectations might not be based on a limited sense of self-efficacy but be dependent on negative assumptions about the nature of the task. For example, boys with ADHD often assume that schoolwork will be boring, and therefore they are not motivated to complete it. A variety of approaches may be effective to address this problem. First, contingency management is usually necessary to administer in conjunction with any other therapeutic technique. Specific methods of implementing behavioral contracts are discussed in detail in Chapters 7 and 12. When such contracts are in place, individual work with the boy can help him recognize that successful completion of a task, even when it appears boring, results in consequences that are desirable to him, such as an increase in privileges.

Parents and teachers sometimes object to this strategy and protest that this teaches the boy to do what is expected of him for the wrong reasons. This, however, is not a realistic complaint. First, the negative cycle of limited effort followed by negative consequences that result in more limited effort must be stopped, because it is entirely nonproductive. Even if the boy begins to do better "for the wrong reasons," he will start to feel better about the outcomes and expect better interactions with parents and teachers. Over time, as his expectations improve, he will begin to internalize the "right reasons" why tasks must be done— the feelings of accomplishment one gets when a task is accomplished, and the sense of appreciation one experiences when assigned responsibilities are completed.

In some cases, consequences available through contingency management techniques may not be sufficient to significantly improve motivation. This may especially be evident with some teenagers. In those cases, the therapist might adapt an approach typical of reality therapy (e.g., Glasser, 2001). Work with the teen should focus on the recognition, and acceptance, of the fact that everyone's life is filled with some tasks that are enjoyable and some that might not be. Completing a math assignment or loading the dishwasher might not be much fun and might, in fact, truly be boring. Moreover, the teenager has the choice to reject those tasks. Doing so, however, brings consequences that the teenager must also accept. Refusing to do house chores is likely to result in conflicts, groundings, and the loss of other privileges (such as rides he needs to go visit his friends after school). In school, his refusal to do math is likely to result in academic failure, retention, and difficulties completing his education. Without a good education, he is less likely to be able to obtain employment that will allow him to get the things in life that he really wants. Thus, the teenager must learn that he is just like most people in the world: To have the kind of life that we all want, we all have to do some things we may not particularly like, and we must all develop sufficient frustration tolerance to be able to do so. As the reader can see, this leads the therapist to work on frustration tolerance and anger management, described earlier in this chapter.

SUMMARY

Although results of research studies reveal that individual counseling is not as effective as other methods of addressing core symptoms (e.g., parent training or contingency management), boys and teens with ADHD are likely to derive at least some benefit. Medications, parent training, and classroom behavior management programs are often effective in managing core symptoms of ADHD, but residual problems commonly remain. In addition, some clients do not respond well to medications. Therapists must also recognize that boys and teens with ADHD often exhibit significant secondary symptoms that may include defiance, anger management problems, low self-esteem, and limited motivation, and improving core symptoms is not likely to eliminate all of these secondary problems. For all these reasons, mental health professionals should recognize that individual therapy provides opportunities to address these concerns.

Cognitive-behavioral treatment has proved most effective. To address impulsivity and hyperactivity, therapists can help clients develop cognitive mediation strategies that will improve their abilities to think about situations before choices of behaviors are made. Self-monitoring has been shown to effectively address inattentiveness, especially when external cues are used and contingency management is used to reinforce this technique. Organizational skills may be improved through the use of schedulers and color-coding.

Using individual counseling to address secondary symptoms may be especially beneficial. Cognitive-behavioral methods are known to be effective in improving anger management skills, enhancing self-esteem, and increasing a sense of self-efficacy. Because these problems commonly accompany core symptoms of ADHD, most boys and teens will benefit from addressing these problems in individual counseling treatment.

7

Parenting Techniques

Although boys with attention deficit/hyperactivity disorder (ADHD) commonly exhibit a variety of problems in different settings, difficulties within the home are probably the most frequent and intense. In particular, boys with significant symptoms of hyperactivity/impulsivity often anger and annoy parents and caretakers. They act out many of the urges they experience and have difficulties with delay of gratification, which usually result in behaviors that get them in trouble.

Sometimes these behaviors can be dangerous, such as when the boys impulsively run out into the street. Impulsivity, however, is evident in many day-to-day behaviors that do not necessarily reflect danger, for example, suppressing the impulse to continue playing when it is time to start doing homework or accepting that it is time to stop watching television because you have to start getting ready for bed. Boys who are impulsive frequently have difficulties accepting tasks that are not "fun," for example, performing house chores, following a morning routine to get ready for school, and so on. When faced with problems in these situations, parents usually get upset, and a conflict ensues that frequently includes screaming and yelling.

In addition, boys who are impulsive have a limited ability to deal with frustration. For example, when playing with a video game and told to stop playing because it is time to do homework, the boy will have the initial reaction to resist the change and continue with the current activity. Boys with ADHD have difficulties containing that internal urge, and they express their disapproval through protests, arguments, and downright defiance. In fact, they are especially likely to express their frustration through physical means, such as hitting or kicking something near them, throwing an item within their reach, or even hitting their parents. Parents usually do not appreciate these reactions, and the conflict escalates further. Indeed, a majority of the interactions between parents and a boy with ADHD are negative and result in an unwanted outcome, such as the boy getting yelled at or punished (Barkley, 2006).

Boys with ADHD frequently experience anger from their parents, and they usually respond in kind. Because they are often on the receiving end of the anger response, boys with ADHD learn to expect that those around them usually give them a hard time. Consequently, they are more likely to exhibit a negative attitude, thus further affecting the interaction with their parents and increasing the likelihood that their parents will yell at them or punish them.

Many boys who are impulsive are also hyperactive, and those who are hyperactive exhibit additional management difficulties. They have problems sitting still at meals. They tend to use high levels of physical activity during play, and they can be very noisy. They are likely to roughhouse with siblings, which often results in conflicts. All in all, parents often find these behaviors frustrating, and therefore hyperactivity once again makes it more likely that the boy will get reprimanded, scolded, or punished.

Boys with ADHD who are not impulsive or hyperactive also present with problems within the home, although these are often more subtle. Although these boys may not exhibit acting out, they tend to have difficulties keeping track of their things and often misplace toys, clothing, and other items of interest. Because they easily get distracted or sidetracked, they need a lot of supervision to complete their morning routine, homework, and so on. They often do not demonstrate the level of independence that their parents expect, and therefore their parents find these boys frustrating to manage.

Homework presents a particular challenge. Boys who are disorganized often lose books, notebooks, and homework assignments. Even when all that is needed to do the assignments is brought home, assignments may not get completed, and even when the assignments are done, boys often lose track of them on the way back to school or forget to hand them in. Their grades suffer as a result, and their parents become angry and upset. Of course, many boys who are distractible and disorganized are also impulsive and/or hyperactive, and the combination of all these symptoms greatly increases the degree of conflicts with their parents.

Boys with ADHD often exhibit difficulties in outside settings. When they accompany parents during shopping trips (e.g., in the supermarket), boys with ADHD are easily affected by what they see on the shelves, and they commonly place items into the shopping basket that caught their interest, regardless of whether their parents allowed them to do so. When boys with ADHD see an item they want, they expect the parent to get it, and they usually tantrum when they do not get their own way. Hyperactive boys are also known to wander (or run) away from their parents, and the interaction results in a power struggle when parents try to catch up with them and bring them under control.

In restaurants, boys with ADHD often present with similar problems. They find it difficult to sit still, and they impulsively wish to order items from the menu that their parents do not approve of. They tend to wander away from the table and require parents to chase after them. They are often loud during meals, and their parents may feel embarrassed.

Attendance at religious services is particularly difficult. In church, or a similar place of worship, parishioners are usually expected to sit still, remain quiet, and follow the protocol of the services (stand during appropriate times, repeat certain phrases with the entire congregation, etc.). Boys with ADHD find it difficult to sit quietly for long periods of time, particularly during an event that does not hold their interest. Consequently, they typically stand out during religious ceremonies and annoy others with their loud and restless behaviors. Again, parents become embarrassed, and a conflict is likely to ensue.

Because boys with ADHD present difficulties in so many aspects of the parent–child interaction, it is necessary to help parents develop techniques to address these problems while minimizing the conflict with the boy. Indeed, parents must learn strategies to deal with most day-to-day situations, starting with the morning routine necessary to get the boy out to school on time and ending with bedtime. Consequently, mental health professionals working with parents of boys with ADHD must help them develop a comprehensive behavior management program that will address most aspects of the daily routine. In addition, because problems arise in so many settings where the boy and the parent are both present, this behavior management program must be comprehensive enough to address problems in many locations and situations.

RESEARCH SUPPORT

Of all the psychological interventions used to address the symptoms of ADHD, parent training has undergone the most research (Barkley, 2006). Forehand and McMahon (1981), Patterson (1982), and Barkley (1987) are generally credited with developing the earliest systematic models of parent training, and early research on parent training generally investigated the effectiveness of these programs. All have been found effective in several empirical trials (Anastopoulos, Rhoads, & Farley, 2006), but most of these did not specifically investigate the efficacy of the program with children with ADHD. Rather, the programs enrolled children of both sexes and with various diagnoses, and they primarily focused on oppositional and defiant aspects of the behavioral difficulties that the children exhibited.

Barkley (1990, 1998, 2006) has often recommended parent training as the treatment that, along with medication, is most effective in reducing symptoms of ADHD within home settings. Studies that have been performed usually limited the interventions to contingency management (positive reinforcement and response cost) and time-out. More recent reviews of literature confirmed that parent training administered to groups of parents of children with ADHD has been found to be effective (e.g., Chronis, Chacko, Fabiano, Wymbs, & Pelham, 2004). In addition to producing changes in child behavior, parent training contributed to a reduction in parent stress, an increase in parent self-esteem, and improvement in family functioning.

Parent training programs generally use a short-term, structured approach where, during each session, parents complete one component of the program. Each part is a discrete step, and each step teaches parents techniques aimed at addressing a specific misbehavior. The treatment generally lasts for 6 to 12 sessions. As outlined by Anastopoulos et al. (2006), these programs commonly focus on giving commands and dealing with temper tantrums, difficulties with daily routines and household chores, problems with homework, and acting out in out-of-home situations.

Although parent training is regarded as an effective treatment approach for parents of children with ADHD, parent training programs have usually lacked component analysis. As a result, only the efficacy of the overall program has been investigated, and the contribution of each technique to the overall reduction in difficulties was not known.

Recently, a parent training program was published that synthesized the components of many parent training programs and structured the sequencing of the steps to improve the cumulative effectiveness (Kapalka, 2007c). Each step has been researched to investigate its contribution to the overall program, and the efficacy of each technique was specifically researched with parents of boys with ADHD. To date, it remains the only parent training program that has undergone rigorous component analysis. The remainder of this chapter will summarize that program.

INTERVENTIONS

Some programs allow for the sequencing of the steps to be flexible. It makes sense, however, conceptually and practically, to proceed through some of the steps in fixed order, because such an implementation allows the steps to build on one another. In addition, some techniques are more complex, and subsequent interventions become easier to implement when preceding steps have already begun to result in partial progress. Consequently, it is recommended that the first six steps in the program be implemented in sequence. After those are mastered, the remaining three techniques can be completed in any order.

Whenever possible, all parents and caretakers should participate in the parent training program. This expectation is often unrealistic, however. Thus, although progress will not be as rapid, it is possible to administer the program with only one parent or caretaker, with the recommendation that the parent participating in treatment then informs the nonparticipating parent or caretaker (e.g., the husband or a grandparent) of each technique. It is helpful to administer the program with the aid of handouts (e.g., those provided in Kapalka, 2007c), and using such materials makes it easier for the participating parent to enlist the nonparticipating parent's support of the program. Although this is not an optimal manner in which to implement parent training, it is the one that most commonly occurs in the real world, as shown in the following example:

Stevie is a 6-year-old active child. He usually doesn't listen when his mom asks him to pick up his toys, turn off the TV, or wash his hands for dinner. Often, it's a battle that includes refusing to obey, crying, and screaming. Today, it's 3:30 p.m., and Mom is about to go out to run some errands, including a trip to the bank that closes at 4:00 p.m. She's in a hurry. Stevie is playing on the living room floor with his blocks. Mom is already dreading what's about to happen next. She comes into the room and says, "Stevie, it's time to pick up your toys. We have to go out."

"In a minute, Mom!"

Mom leaves the room to go put on her shoes. In 2 or 3 minutes, she comes back into the room. Stevie hasn't moved; he's still playing with the blocks. "Stevie, pick up now because Mommy is in a hurry."

"But I just want to finish building the tower!"

Not even waiting for his response, Mom leaves the room again. She gathers her purse, checkbook, and shopping list. From the kitchen, she yells, "Stevie, are you picking up?"

Stevie gives no response. Mom continues to gather what she needs for the errands. She goes into her bedroom and looks for the car keys. From there, she shouts, "Stevie, what did Mommy tell you to do?"

Stevie, again, gives no response. Mom is already getting very angry. She knows the pattern. Next will come his opposition, screaming, yelling, and perhaps a physical confrontation. She tries again, calling from her bedroom, "Stevie!"

"I'm almost done, Mom!"

Now Mom is getting really mad. She knows that while she and Stevie are out, the blocks can't just sit in the middle of the floor because the dog may start chewing on them, and he might even hurt himself in the process. On the other hand, if she has a battle with Stevie, she'll miss the bank. She's thinking, "Why can't he just listen to what I say? Does he enjoy driving me crazy?" She storms into the room, yelling, "What's the matter with you? Didn't you hear what I said? Pick up those darned things now!"

"No, I don't have to!"

Now she is fuming. She is thinking, "My own flesh and blood is telling me I can't tell him what to do? If I ever did that to my own parents, I would have my head handed to me on the silver platter!" It's now almost 3:45, and she is getting desperate. She tries a scare tactic. "Stevie, if you don't pick them up right now, I am putting them all in the garbage! I mean it! Pick them up now!"

Stevie continues to play, and Mom continues to rush around the house, trying to get ready to leave. She is putting on her coat. Finally, she storms into the room. Stevie is still playing. She sees red and screams in anger, "What the heck is wrong with you? Didn't you hear that I will throw them away? I mean it! Pick them up now!"

"I don't care!"

> Mom comes over and yanks Stevie by the hand, away from the blocks. The blocks he had in his hands go flying all over the room. He starts crying, screaming, and yelling, "You can't make me" and "I hate you." She gives him a hard smack on the behind and tells him to go get dressed. He is just sitting on the floor, screaming and carrying on, throwing blocks at her. She bends down and starts to pick up the blocks herself, all along shouting at Stevie that he is driving her crazy and someday he will have children of his own and she wishes that they treat him like he treats her (Kapalka, 2007c, pp. 1–2).

This example illustrates several difficulties that parents of boys with ADHD encounter every day. Thus, an effective parent training program must help parents prepare to handle these situations and develop techniques to intervene while minimizing conflicts.

Mental Preparation

As previously discussed, boys with ADHD get into very frequent conflicts with their parents, usually several times per day. As a result, not only the boys learn to expect that each interaction will result in conflict and negative feelings but the parents likewise begin to anticipate such an outcome. As evident in the case example, parents prepare themselves for a battle every time they are about to approach the boy with a command or a request.

This negative expectation affects the interaction in several important ways. Parents often address the boy, from the start, with a negative attitude. They communicate this expectation with an edge in their voice, a menacing body posture, threatening gestures, and other attempts at intimidation. Because parents expect a battle, they subconsciously prepare for one and convey this to the boy, both verbally and nonverbally.

Sometimes parents react in the opposite manner. Because they expect the boy to be uncooperative, they attempt coercion and act in a manner that is meek rather than assertive. They hope to talk the boy into compliance, and they portray themselves as hesitant and unsure. It is as though they are asking the boy to agree with what they are asking, hoping that if the boy consents, compliance will be more likely.

The boy's reaction to either of the two approaches in not conducive to compliance. When the parents approach with a negative, intimidating tone, the boy is likely to respond in kind, and conflict usually ensues very quickly. The other approach is equally counterproductive. The boy, perceiving the hesitancy, assumes that compliance is not expected and therefore is less likely to listen to his parents. At the onset of a parent training program, participants must learn that neither approach is appropriate.

Instead, parents should be taught the principles of assertive communication. To start, they must begin to believe that the approach they will be following is likely to produce at least some positive results. Reframing the goals of parenting may be helpful. Many parents expect that effective parenting results in a high degree of compliance from their son. Instead, parenting should be framed as a complex relationship that includes a significant teaching component, where parents teach their child the consequences of his behaviors. Thus, an interaction that did not result in compliance is not an indication of failure. It is an opportunity for parents to help their son learn the outcome of that choice. As long as the parents remain calm and in control and are able to administer a positive consequence after a positive behavior (such as compliance) and a negative consequence (however small it may be) after a negative behavior (such as noncompliance), the teaching component of parenting is successfully taking place. It is an approach that takes time, effort, and perseverance but has a higher probability of a positive outcome.

Often, it is also necessary to help parents reframe some of their son's personality characteristics. Many parents of strong-willed boys see this part of his personality as a liability rather than an asset. Because the boy is not cooperative and overreacts when he does not get his own way, his parents focus on the quarrelsome aspect of these tendencies and overlook the larger picture. Instead, it is helpful for parents to begin to recognize that a strong will is an asset in life, so long as it is tempered with good judgment and self-control. Strong-willed individuals are often high achievers, as long as they are able to choose wisely when to exercise the strong will and when to keep it under control. Thus, the job of the parents of a strong-willed boy is to help him learn judgment and self-control, and this task is accomplished through the consistent administration of appropriate (and usually small) consequences—positive consequence for good choices, and negative consequences for poor ones. In this way, rather than learning to control the boy, parents gradually recognize that they are teaching the boy to improve his self-control, a crucial personality characteristic that is an important component of a successful adult life.

In summary, before a mental health professional proceeds with the implementation of the steps described next, it is important to help parents develop a realistic set of expectations about why their son is having difficulties and what role they can play in improving these problems. Before parents approach each interaction, they should learn to remain calm and in control, expect that what they do will make a difference, and present themselves in a commanding but respectful manner.

Step 1: Command Giving

Boys with ADHD exhibit significant problems with following commands. Some of these problems are due to difficulties attending to and fully processing the command, whereas others are secondary to the impulsivity and poor self-control that these boys commonly exhibit. Consequently, it is sensible to address these problems at the very onset of a parent training program.

To help parents improve their son's ability to process the command, they must gain the boy's full attention. The importance of obtaining eye contact cannot be overstated. Most parenting programs recommend that prior to issuing a command, parents need to obtain eye contact (e.g., Barkley, 1997b). "Long distance" commands, those given from another room without seeing the boy, are rarely effective. Obtaining eye contact not only improves the boy's ability to process and attend to the command but also interrupts an activity in which he may be involved long enough for him to process what was said. Afterward he is more likely to perform the desired behavior. Thus, the very first thing parents should do when they are about to give a command is to call the boy's name and, if necessary to obtain eye contact, tell him, "Please look at me."

The manner in which the command is stated is also important. In a commanding but respectful tone, parents should clearly tell the boy to perform a specific action. The command should not be phrased in the form of a question. Many boys with ADHD also exhibit oppositional and defiant behaviors. Phrasing a command in a manner that requires an answer invites a refusal. Instead, an effective command should be phrased in a form of a statement. It should include a respectful preface, such as "please," then a have statement of the action to be performed, such as "start picking up," and end with a specifier of the time frame, such as "now." Thus, an appropriate command might be "Please start picking up now."

What is a parent to do, however, when the boy is still refusing to perform the stated command? Parents get very upset when their son ignores their commands, delays performing the response, or openly refuses to obey. In these situations, parents feel frustrated and angry, and they yell at their son and/or threaten with some consequences. This precipitates conflict, and as it intensifies, it becomes less likely that what the parents commanded in the first place will actually be done. Instead, it is necessary to help the parents avoid such needless escalations.

Boys with ADHD often refuse to follow a command because they experience a quick surge of a negative reaction, an impulse that is difficult for them to contain. If given further time to process the command, however, they are more likely to think about the situation and choose a better response. Thus, it is necessary to help them perform this processing by creating a situation conducive to the reassessment of the interaction.

Instead of arguing with or confronting a boy who just refused to obey a command, it is best for parents to say nothing and just stand and look at the boy for an additional 15 to 20 seconds. Research has suggested that this approach is indeed effective in reducing the noncompliance that boys with ADHD so commonly exhibit (Kapalka, 2004). The 15- to 20-second period (as long as the parents stay there and do not try to intimidate or argue) allows the boy to recognize that parents mean business, and it usually helps him process the situation (think about the events that just happened) and recognize that noncompliance will not be ignored. In many instances, this helps the boy choose to perform the stated command.

What to do after the 15- to 20-second follow-up look depends on the boy's response. If he did not listen, parents should be advised, for now, to do what they usually do following noncompliance, because Step 2 will further extend the technique described herein. Care should be exercised not to combine Steps 1 and 2 in a single session. Parents should not go on and try Step 2 until they had at least a week to diligently practice Step 1.

If Step 1 was effective and resulted in compliance, it is important for parents to acknowledge this positive behavior. Verbal praise can include phrases such as "Thank you," "I appreciate your cooperation," and "I like it when you do what I ask." Nonverbal methods include a wink, a smile, or a gentle pat on the shoulder. Both verbal and nonverbal methods of praise should be used.

Parents should be cautioned that some boys may not immediately exhibit a positive response to being praised. Boys with ADHD usually become so used to negative interactions that they do not expect to hear nice things from their parents and are caught off guard. It is important for the parents to persevere and continue to use praise, even if the 15- to 20-second follow-up look was needed to obtain compliance. Praise results in an internal sense of accomplishment and satisfaction, however small it may be. Consistent exposure to these positive feelings gradually helps the boy recognize that cooperation leads to positive feelings, whereas defiance leads to conflicts and negative consequences.

In summary, the following is an example of a situation employing the described technique:

Parent: [*approaches the boy to be able to make eye contact*] "Michael!"
Boy: "What?"
Parent: "Please look at me!"
Boy: [*looks at parent*] "What?"
Parent: "Please start picking up these toys right now. We have to start getting ready to go out."
Boy: "In a minute. I am not finished."
Parent: [*without saying anything else, stands close to the boy and continues to look at him for some 15 or 20 seconds*]
Boy: "Why are you looking at me?"
Parent: "Because you did not start to do what I told you."
Boy: "All right now, I'll pick up" [*reluctantly begins to pick up the toys*]
Parent: "Thank you! It really helps me when you do what I ask."

One final point should be clarified. This technique is most effective with single-action commands, that is, those that call for an immediate, specific behavior that is relatively simple and goal directed, for example,

"Pick up your toys," "Go wash your hands," or "Hang up your coat." More complex behaviors—for example, "Go do your homework" or "Go clean your room"—require a different approach and are covered in further steps.

Although many parents report that this technique is helpful, there are times when boys with ADHD still choose not to obey. Thus, after a period of time practicing Step 1, parents must also implement the next step.

Step 2: Warnings

Giving warnings is a well-known technique that parents often use. Usually, however, parents allow a repetition loop to take place before they give the warning. As identified by Barkley (1997b), during this repetition loop, parents repeat the command over and over, and the boy continues to ignore or refuses to obey. In the process, the parents become angry, and as the situation escalates, parents begin to threaten. Unfortunately, because the situation already intensified into a conflict, parents issue threats when they are angry, and the consequence that is threatened is often too severe or unrealistic. The boy recognizes (and has learned from prior experience) that his parents are not likely to follow through on this threat. Thus, the boy continues to refuse, and his parents continue to repeat the threat.

Because the threat is also ineffective, parents subsequently face only two options—escalate the situation further (usually including some form of physical punishment) or acquiesce and give up seeking compliance. Neither of these options has a constructive outcome, and each one has negative long-term consequences for the boy. Physical punishment is not a consequence that most child professionals recommend. It is sometimes effective with very young children, because they learn to fear the physical discomfort and obey to avoid it. "Parenting by fear" of the threat of pain (even if minor), however, produces negative feelings in the recipient. Boys with ADHD are already vulnerable to negative reactions. It is not advisable to create situations that further escalate their anger and negative attitude.

Acquiescence is also nonproductive. It teaches the boy that negative behaviors (protesting, refusing, etc.) result in positive outcomes (parents backing down) and therefore reinforces the oppositional reactions. Parents should strongly be cautioned against giving in to the boy during such an interaction.

Acquiescence is especially likely if, during the escalation, parents begin to threaten with a consequence that they do not intend to implement. Scaring a child into compliance is rarely effective, because the boy expects (usually from prior experience) that his parents do not intend to follow through on the threat. Parents should be cautioned to avoid announcing consequences that they do not intend to use.

Instead, parents must learn to give warnings in a manner that is more effective. To start, parents must learn to avoid the nonproductive repetition loops that result in needless escalation. First, parents should issue a command in a manner consistent with Step 1, including the 15- to 20-second follow-up look. If this action did not result in compliance, the command should be repeated once, prefaced by "I said ..." and followed by another 15- to 20-second follow-up look.

If these two attempts were not successful in obtaining compliance, parents must immediately issue one (and only one) warning of a realistic consequence that they are able to implement as quickly as possible (preferably immediately). After the warning, parents should wait another 15 to 20 seconds, and then implement the stated consequence if the warning was not effective. This technique has been found specifically effective in reducing noncompliance in boys with ADHD (Kapalka, 2001a).

In summary, if the approach described in Step 1 did not produce compliance, the next step may be implemented as follows:

Parent:	[*approaches the boy to be able to make eye contact*] "Michael!"
Boy:	"What?"
Parent:	"Please look at me!"
Boy:	[*looks at parent*] "What?"
Parent:	"Please start picking up these toys right now. We have to start getting ready to go out."
Boy:	"In a minute. I am not finished."
Parent:	[*without saying anything else, stands close to the boy and continues to look at him for some 15 or 20 seconds*]
Boy:	"Why are you looking at me?"
Parent:	"Because you did not start to do what I told you."
Boy:	"I said I was not finished!"
Parent:	[*waits for the 20-second period to elapse*] "Michael, please look at me."
Boy:	"What?"
Parent:	"I said please start picking up these toys right now."
Boy:	"No, I am not ready!"
Parent:	[*waits for the 20-second period to elapse*] "Michael, please look at me."
Boy:	"What?"
Parent:	"If you do not start picking these up right now, I will do it for you, but I will put them away, and you will not be able to play with them for 2 days."
Boy:	"Oh, all right. I'll pick up." [*starts picking up*]
Parent:	[*continues to stand to make sure the boy continues picking up*] "Thank you, Michael. It really helps me when you do what I ask."

As discussed before, if this interaction results in compliance, it is important to praise the boy, regardless of the fact that a warning was necessary to get him to obey.

Consistency is very important. Over time, this approach helps the boy learn that when he is noncompliant, his parents will implement the stated consequence, and when he is compliant, a positive consequence will follow (at the least, praise). This will help him process the consequences of situations before he responds, thus allowing him to begin to diminish his impulsivity.

Step 3: Time-out

Many boys with ADHD exhibit temper outbursts. Because impulsive boys have limited self-control, they find it difficult to contain their emotional reactions, and they lose control when they feel frustrated or angry. Parents need to implement a technique that helps the boy calm down by his being removed to a place that is devoid of stimulation that also isolates him from activities that he likes to perform.

Methods of warning about the time-out depend on the situation that precipitates it. If the boy is beginning to tantrum, and no violence (verbal or physical) has occurred, one warning may be used in a manner similar to that described in Step 2. When the boy already has acted violently or verbally assaulted his parents by cursing or calling them an insulting name, however, it is best to take him to time-out without warning.

As pointed out by Barkley (1997b), time-out has also been found to be effective in addressing noncompliance. When the boy refuses to obey a command (issued in accordance with instructions discussed in prior steps), he can be removed to time-out, and when time-out is over, he may be returned to the same situation where noncompliance first occurred. In that instance, time-out should be used as the consequence that is stated in the warning (as outlined in Step 2). This may result in repetitive use of time-out until the boy makes a choice to comply with the command.

Methods of implementation determine the effectiveness of the time-out technique. It is important for parents to consider the time-out spot, the length of the removal to time-out, the way to keep the boy in time-out while he may be trying to get away, and the manner of release from time-out. All these components need to be decided on beforehand to increase the effectiveness of the intervention.

The time-out spot should be a place that is quiet and devoid of stimulation but near enough for parents to monitor. Placing the boy in a chair in the dining room or facing the wall (but not near enough to it so that he can reach it and kick it) while no one is in the room and the television, radio, and so on are not on has been found to be particularly effective. It is best for parents to be nearby to monitor the boy, but they should not be in the same room, because this will further escalate the conflict.

The length of the "minimum sentence" depends on the age of the boy. Most parenting programs recommend a rule of 1 minute per year of age for more minor infractions and twice that time for more major problems. Some recent research, however, has suggested that even shorter time-out durations are effective (Kapalka & Bryk, 2007), and parents should be advised to retain boys up to age 5 for a minimum of 2 minutes in time-out, whereas boys aged 6 to 10 should remain in time-out for at least 5 minutes. The measured length of the time does not start to count until the boy is reasonably quiet and remains in time-out without being violent or trying to get away. Time-out is generally not effective for children aged 11 and older. For those boys, removal to his room is preferred.

If the boy refuses to remain in the chair and/or becomes violent, a restraint procedure should be implemented. Some programs recommend a "basket" hold, where the boy's arms are crossed and he is held from behind by the wrists, but such a hold sometimes allows a boy who is particularly violent to hurt the parent by flailing his head or kicking. Instead, an effective hold involves placing the boy in a dining-room-style chair, preferably with no arm rests, bending the boy's arms and wrists behind the backrest of the chair, and holding him from behind by the wrists. This technique exposes the parents to the least danger while allowing them to retain the boy in the chair until he is able to calm down. Of course, the time-out minimum sentence does not start until he is calm, and the restraint is no longer needed.

When the minimum sentence is over, it is important for the parents to approach the boy and briefly explain to him why he was placed in time-out and that similar misbehaviors will result in another time-out. If he was placed there for noncompliance, he must now be returned to the same situation that precipitated the time-out.

In summary, an interaction involving time-out (as a consequence for noncompliance) may be implemented as follows:

Parent:	[*approaches the boy to be able to make eye contact*] "Michael!"
Boy:	"What?"
Parent:	"Please look at me!"
Boy:	[*looks at parent*] "What?"
Parent:	"Please start picking up these toys right now."
Boy:	"In a minute. I am not finished."
Parent:	[*without saying anything else, stands close to the boy and continues to look at him for some 15 or 20 seconds*]
Boy:	"Why are you looking at me?"
Parent:	"Because you did not start to do what I told you."
Boy:	"I said I was not finished!"
Parent:	[*waits for the 20-second period to elapse*] "Michael, please look at me."
Boy:	"What?"
Parent:	"I said please start picking up these toys right now."
Boy:	"No, I am not ready!"
Parent:	[*waits for the 20-second period to elapse*] "Michael, please look at me."
Boy:	"What?"

Parent:	"If you do not start picking these up right now, you will have to go to time-out."
Boy:	"No!"
Parent:	[*waits for the 20-second period to elapse*] "OK, it's time-out." [*takes the boy, forcibly if necessary, to the time-out spot, places him on the seat*] "You stay here until I say you can leave. You must be quiet."
Parent:	[*once the time-out is over, approaches the boy*] "Do you know why I placed you in time-out?"
Boy:	"No."
Parent:	"Because you did not listen to what I told you to do. Now, let's go back there again, and you have to clean up the toys."

Step 4: Behavioral Contract, Part 1

Boys with ADHD commonly exhibit significant problems with adhering to daily routines. Starting in the morning, they are often reluctant to get out of bed, get washed and dressed, and leave the house in time to catch the school bus. In the afternoon, they forget to do their room chores, do not pick up their toys, leave things lying about, and are reluctant to perform other house chores. In the evening, they have difficulties with washing and going to bed on time. These situations result in almost constant conflicts with their parents.

Establishing a behavioral contract has been shown to be effective in reducing these problems (Kapalka, 2006b). Essentially, a behavioral contract is an exchange program in which boys can earn tokens (points, stickers, or chips) for performing responsibilities and are then able to exchange these tokens for privileges and rewards. When parents implement a behavioral contract, they are effectively increasing structure within the home, a change that has been associated with significant improvements in problem behaviors. In addition, because parents begin to restrict certain privileges and allow the boy to earn them only after certain responsibilities were performed, parents increase their leverage and are able to use withdrawal of privileges effectively as a consequence. In other words, a boy who has lost a privilege because he did not perform a task and has no tokens has, in effect, punished himself.

There are many aspects that determine the efficacy of a behavioral contract. Discussion of all of these aspects is beyond the confines of this chapter. Professionals interested in more detailed information should refer to Kapalka (2007c) and review the chapters that discuss contract implementation. Some of the major principles are summarized next.

It is important to involve the boy in preparing the lists of responsibilities and the rewards and privileges. The responsibilities should primarily include daily tasks that are specific, detailed, and easily monitored. Complex tasks (such as cleaning his room) need to be broken down into discrete components, and each one has to be clearly stated in a manner that leaves little to interpretation (e.g., "no clothing lying on the floor," "no garbage in the room except in the trash basket," "no dishes or cups in the room," etc.). Each task is assigned a specific value of tokens (points, stickers, or chips), and the tokens are immediately dispensed after the boy completes the stated responsibility.

It is helpful to group together tasks that belong together, for example, components of morning or evening routines. The morning routine should include such items as waking up after no more than two wake-up calls, dressing before the timer goes off, washing his hands and brushing his teeth, and leaving the house in time to catch the school bus. The evening routine can include items such as taking a shower, brushing his teeth, and retiring to his room at a specific time with no more than one subsequent exit from the room (e.g., to ask a question).

A sample list of responsibilities might look like this:

Getting out of bed after no more than two prompts	2 chips
Getting dressed by yourself	1 chip
Staying in your room until you are dressed	1 chip
Coming down for breakfast by 7:15 a.m.	1 chip
Getting out of the house by 7:40 a.m. to meet the school bus	2 chips
Making your bed	2 chips
Washing your hands before each meal without being asked	1 chip each
Brushing teeth in the morning and at night	2 chips each time

The list of rewards and privileges should include, first and foremost, watching television, playing with video games (including the handheld models) and the computer, viewing a movie, and so on. Most should be earned in time increments, for example, one token per each half hour of television or one token per each 15 minutes of video game or computer use. Additional earned privileges can also include sleepovers, trips to a video arcade, and so on. Of course, parents must make sure that all privileges on the list are permitted only when the tokens have previously been earned and when the tokens are exchanged right then and there to earn the privilege.

A sample list of rewards and privileges might look like this:

Watch TV (per 30 minutes)	1 chip
Play video games (per 15 minutes)	1 chip
Go outside to play (per hour)	1 chip
Extend bedtime by 15 minutes	1 chip
Make a trip to the grab bag	6 chips
Rent a movie	10 chips
Earn a $20 video game cartridge	50 chips

It is helpful to establish an exchange rate where the boy earns enough tokens each day to buy back the usual amount of privileges that he enjoyed every day before the contract was implemented and has a few tokens left over to "bank" for future use, for example, to earn some prizes (for larger token values). Parents and children generally respond well to this procedure, and problems with the stated tasks usually diminish. It is helpful to implement the contract in stages, beginning with the most rudimentary tasks and situations and gradually expanding it as the boy and the parents become used to the technique. Methods to further extend the contract are covered in Step 6.

Step 5: Homework

Boys with ADHD often resent homework and present management difficulties when asked to complete it. Because difficulties with focusing make it harder for them to remain on task and exert metal effort, and because problems with impulse control make it hard for them to delay the gratification of engaging in play activity to perform homework instead, conflicts frequently occur when it is time to do homework.

It is helpful to extend the behavioral contract to include the completion of homework. Parents can implement a house rule where a privilege (e.g., watching television or playing with video games) is restricted until after homework is completed. This rule means that the privilege must not be made available to be bought with the tokens at any time prior to homework completion. This practice motivates the boy to complete the work sooner, and he is likely to spend less time procrastinating.

Additional aspects of homework completion are also important. Homework should be performed as soon as possible after school. The longer the delay, the less time the boy has after homework completion to enjoy posthomework privileges, and therefore the motivation will be reduced. In addition, the later the homework is attempted, the more tired the boy will be, thus further diminishing his capacity to pay attention and exercise self-control.

It is sensible to arrange the homework spot in a place that is quiet but close enough for the parent to monitor. Parents should not remain in the room with the boy while he completes homework, but they should check in frequently to monitor his progress. When asked to help, parents should be careful not to do the work for the boy. Instead, they should guide him to try to come up with the right answer and apply the same principle to complete the other items.

Establishing effective home–school communication is a crucial component of success with homework. Boys with ADHD often do not correctly write down homework assignments, or they lose their notes and/ or handouts. When parents ask the boy, "Do you have any homework?" and the boy replies, "No," the parents must be reasonably sure that the response is correct. For this reason, it is necessary to implement a homework journal. Every day, the boy should be given the responsibility to write his assignments in the journal while he completes the school day, but before he departs, it is absolutely crucial that the teacher checks the list of assignments for accuracy. Only then are the parents able to have reliable information about whether the boy was assigned any homework for the day. If he forgets the journal, he should lose the privilege for the day that is connected with homework completion. Consistent implementation of a structured homework routine and daily enforcement of a homework journal (with collaboration with the boy's teacher) are the most effective ways to help solve homework problems.

Step 6: Behavioral Contract, Part 2

Once the basic behavioral contract has been established and practiced (Step 4) and homework has been included (Step 5), it is helpful to extend the program to additional behaviors and situations.

The list of responsibilities may be gradually expanded. In Step 4, only daily expectations should be included. Now parents can include tasks that are expected more infrequently, for example, once per week (such as taking out the recyclables on trash days). Similarly, the list of rewards and privileges can be extended to include items that require a larger amount of tokens, for example, the purchase of a video game cartridge.

Parents of older boys may consider a method called "chunking," where components of the morning or evening routine (or steps to clean his room) are grouped into a functional unit, and the boy earns all tokens when every component has been completed successfully and earns no tokens if any part was not done. This is a method of teaching the boy to internalize components of the daily routine, but it should be attempted carefully, and only after the boy has successfully been able to perform each of the individual components in that portion of the routine for at least a few weeks.

Training the boy to listen to commands "on the first try" is also an option. Before issuing a command, parents announce to the boy that he will be told to do something, and if he complies immediately, he will be given a token, but if he does not comply immediately, he will not get the token but will still have to perform the task. This technique is a common component of compliance-training programs.

The boy can also lose a specified amount of tokens as punishment for a specific misbehavior. For example, raising his voice in anger (yelling at his parents), using foul language, or hitting can have a specified token value, and the corresponding amount will be taken away when these behaviors occur. It is important to use this component advisedly. Only one or two behaviors should be focused on at any one time, and each should be specified to the boy beforehand (not out of the blue, in the midst of a confrontation when the parents do not know what else to do). Parents should also make sure that they do not take so many tokens away that the boy has lost all that he has already earned, because this will likely diminish his motivation to continue with the program. It is also important to initially start the contract without implementing token costs (as was presented in Step 4). Only after the contract has been successful for at least 2 weeks should token costs be considered.

The behavioral contract is a flexible intervention that allows the boy and his parents to be creative in designing ways to earn and spend the tokens. Along the way, the boy earns valuable lessons. Tokens are earned only for positive behaviors (and may be lost for negative behaviors), and so the contract allows the parents to frequently administer consequences. These consequences teach the boy to begin to anticipate the results of his behaviors and to think through situations as they occur. In the process, impulse control and self-control gradually improve.

Step 7: Out-of-Home Situations

Boys with ADHD frequently act out while in stores, restaurants, houses of worship, and so on. Some of these problems are secondary to the additional stimulation that these environments commonly contain or the high degree of self-control that some of these settings require (e.g., remaining quiet and still during religious services). Once an effective behavioral contract has been implemented, it can be extended to include behaviors in these settings. The efficacy of this approach has been established with defiant children (Barkley, 1997b) and boys with ADHD (Kapalka, 2003a).

It is necessary to set one or two simple rules for the boy before he is taken to the target setting. The rules must be attainable, clear, and very specific (e.g., "Remain by me" or "Do not take anything off the shelves without my permission"). After the boy confirms his understanding of these rules, a token reward for following the rule should be set (e.g., "You will earn five chips when we get home"). Sometimes it can also be effective to set a token cost if the rules are not followed (e.g., "If you break the rules, you will lose five chips when we get home"). He should then be taken to the target setting, and the appropriate consequence should be administered immediately afterward. It is important that parents focus on only a few rules at a time.

If the boy did not comply with the rules and lost the tokens, a tantrum may occur. In such a situation, the boy should be removed from the setting, and a version of time-out should be administered. Parents should choose a spot that is relatively free from stimulation, such as a bathroom stall or the car. The procedure from implementing time-out should be the same as discussed in Step 3. After the tantrum subsides, the setting should be reattempted, but this time without the possibility of a reward (so that the boy learns that the tantrum eliminated the possibility of earning tokens in that setting today). On another day, the same setting should be tried again, with the possibility to earn the tokens for successful completion.

Parents must start small and expect a gradual, not instant, improvement. It is advisable to gradually implement this procedure by focusing on one outside setting at a time (e.g., a store) before proceeding to others (e.g., a place of worship) and to implement it first in the settings that result in fewer problems and gradually add settings where more difficulties are apparent.

Step 8: Interruptions

Boys with ADHD commonly interrupt adults while they talk with each other or while they are on the telephone. This problem is secondary to difficulties in suppressing the impulse to get the adult's immediate attention. A technique aimed at gradually teaching the child to suppress that impulse has been found to be effective with defiant children (Barkley, 1997b) and boys with ADHD (Kapalka, 2003b). It is a variant of a shaping procedure, an intervention commonly implemented in programs based on operant conditioning.

The technique involves gradual exposure, with warning, to situations where the impulse is likely to occur and the use of positive and negative consequences that depend on whether impulse control was exercised. Over time, the length of time in the situation is steadily increased, and warnings are eventually discontinued.

Phone calls provide the easiest and most controlled opportunity to initially implement this procedure. At the onset, the parents warn the boy that they are about to place a brief call, and he is not to interrupt while they are on the telephone. If he is able to accomplish this, he will be given a token. If he does interrupt, he will lose a token. It is helpful for parents to prearrange a set of "dummy calls," ones that are placed only for the purpose of providing practice for their son. When this technique is first implemented, at least two or three calls per day should be placed. Over time, the length of the calls should be increased, and incoming calls can be added (where the parent issues a brief reminder to the child while the phone is ringing). After a few weeks, warnings can be discontinued, but the same rule applies—no interruption results in earning a token, and an interruption results in losing a token. When the boy is able to successfully inhibit the impulse to interrupt incoming calls without warning, the token can be phased out, but praise should continue to be given and will help maintain the treatment gains.

This technique can also be used to address interruption in other settings, for example, adult conversations while visiting someone else, when visitors come over, or during a chance encounter with another adult (such as a neighbor).

Step 9: Transitions

When boys with ADHD need to switch from one activity (e.g., watching television) to another (e.g., coming to the dinner table), problems frequently ensue. These are mostly secondary to the boy's limited abilities to suppress the impulse to continue with the activity in which he is currently involved. To address this problem, parents can use a technique that has been found effective and that is similar to the technique described in Step 7 (Kapalka, 2005e). It involves the use of warnings before the transition, rewards after a successful transition, and token costs when the transition did not go smoothly.

First, it is necessary to set an appropriate time frame for the warning. Telling a young boy that dinner is coming in 15 minutes is rarely helpful. Instead, the time frame must be put in a manner that is meaningful considering the boy's age. For example, when a boy is watching television, parents can say that the transition will occur when the show is over or when the next commercial comes on. In keeping with a "three bells" approach commonly used at theaters and events, it is helpful to give two warnings before the actual transition takes place—a longer one that announces that a transition will take place a little later, and a second warning when the transition will occur shortly. When the announcement of the actual transition is issued (i.e., the transition is taking place now), the boy must quickly engage in the new activity to earn the tokens. This teaches the boy to anticipate the transition, use mental preparation to adjust to the transition, and suppress the impulse to continue with the previous activity.

As with all other techniques, progress will be gradual. Parents should begin using this technique in transitions that are least likely to present with difficulties and gradually include other transitions that are more problematic.

Long-Term Management

Consistent use of the techniques described in this chapter requires ongoing effort. Over time, some techniques should continue to be used, whereas others can be phased out.

Steps 1 and 2 should be used on an ongoing basis, without stopping. Using this method of issuing commands should become a new way of life for parents of boys with ADHD. Boys with self-control and impulse-control problems tend to return to old patterns of behavior quickly upon discontinuation of these techniques. The need to continue to use Step 3 (time-out) is likely to diminish as the boy learns better self-control, but it is beneficial to retain this consequence in the repertoire just in case it becomes necessary.

The behavioral contract is the component of the program that parents are most likely to suspend when the boy's problems begin to diminish. More often than not, however, when the contract is discontinued, the boy begins to gradually exhibit more problems. At first, it may be sporadic, but over time, the problems may return to prior levels. With young boys, and those who are very impulsive and exhibit significant problems with self-control, it is best to continue to use the contract indefinitely, although it can be streamlined significantly. Some of the techniques outlined in Step 6—for example, chunking—can help parents make the program more manageable for the long term.

Some boys may improve to a point where maintaining a comprehensive contract is no longer necessary, but there may be one or two aspects that require continuing attention (e.g., homework). In this situation, parents may use a one-to-one exchange by which the boy earns a specific privilege (such as the ability to get on the computer that day) in exchange for completion of homework.

School performance and behavior are areas where boys with ADHD frequently need to continue a behavioral contract. Boys who have difficulties with self-control often exhibit these difficulties in school. Younger boys may present with out-of-seat behaviors, calling out, and difficulties with sharing, whereas older boys may exhibit argumentativeness with teachers and problems following directions. A behavioral contract can be developed with a teacher that tracks the boy's daily progress with regard to a finite and limited number of specific problems. This technique is further discussed in Chapter 12 along with other interventions that teachers can use to manage behaviors in the classroom.

Steps 7 and 8 are meant to be used on an as-needed basis, and few parents administer these techniques long term. These steps help boys gradually develop sufficient self-control to suppress the initial impulse to misbehave. Step 9, however, should be used indefinitely. Continuing to follow this procedure during transitions is likely to help the boy develop a method of preparing himself to stop an activity that he is enjoying when it is necessary to do so.

Program Modifications for Use With Older Children and Adolescents

Most of the techniques discussed in this chapter work well with older boys and teenagers, although some modifications may be necessary. Steps 1 and 2 should continue to be used well into the teenage years, although the follow-up look may be modified to avoid a staring match with the teenager. Instead, parents should obtain eye contact (or, at least, make sure that they have the teenager's attention) and issue one clear, specific command. Then, instead of continuing to look right at the teen, the parents should stay in his vicinity to nonverbally communicate to him that they intend to stick around to obtain compliance. Avoiding repetitions when giving commands (Step 2) is important for boys of all ages, and this step will likely continue to be effective throughout the teenage years.

Instead of using time-out (Step 3), parents should encourage the teenager to use his own room as much as possible to handle those times when he may feel angry or upset. Parents' encouraging the teen's removal to his room helps him become able to get himself under control. If he has not yet acted out sufficiently to require a negative consequence, parents should encourage him to go to his room to calm down, and they should avoid making it sound like a punishment. They should encourage him to come out whenever he feels ready. In this manner, the teenager will not view this intervention as negatively and will be much more likely to cooperate with it.

Using a behavioral contract (Steps 4 and 6) through the teenage years can be very effective, but instead of using points and tokens, most parents find it more practical to maintain a one-to-one exchange where specific privileges (e.g., daily use of a cell phone) are earned by compliance with a specific rule (such as coming in before curfew the night before).

Monitoring the boy's school performance and homework compliance are usually necessary through the teenage years. As discussed in this chapter and in Chapters 11 and 12, parents should implement a monitoring system by which the teenager's teachers regularly (usually at the end of the week) report his grades and homework completion. Parents can then establish minimum performance criteria that will earn the teenager specific privileges over the weekend.

Steps 7 and 8 are usually not appropriate for use with teenagers, but Step 9 can be effective. For example, announcing the time when a parent will pick up a teenager from an outing and setting positive and negative consequences dependent on his reaction can help him use self-control to suppress (or, at least, reduce) a negative reaction. Along the way, he is learning frustration tolerance, an important personal skill that will help him become a better functioning adult.

SUMMARY

Because boys with ADHD commonly exhibit many problem behaviors within the home and related settings (e.g., in stores or restaurants), contingency-management techniques are commonly used and have been shown to be effective in reducing symptoms and improving many aspects of family functioning. Usually parent training is administered in a series of sessions, each of which focuses on techniques needed to address specific problems. One such program, based on research by Kapalka (2007c), was described in this chapter.

The program starts by helping parents develop an appropriate mental preparation and a mind-set conducive to effective behavior management. Techniques are then implemented in sessions that are usually spaced 1 to 2 weeks apart, and parents need to practice each technique and become comfortable with its implementation before additional steps are attempted. The first six steps address giving commands and warnings, addressing temper tantrums, developing a behavioral contract, and incorporating homework into the daily routine. Because these steps build on one another, they should be completed in order. The remaining three steps address difficulties with behaviors in out-of-home settings, interruptions, and transitions and may be completed in any order. These techniques are appropriate for boys and teenagers, and various ways to modify the interventions to improve effectiveness with teenagers were discussed.

8

Individual Counseling With Men and Older Teens

Like boys and male teens, men with attention deficit/hyperactivity disorder (ADHD) exhibit symptoms that result in significant difficulties at home, in the workplace, and with peers. During childhood, symptoms of ADHD fall along two clusters, hyperactivity/impulsivity and inattentiveness/disorganization. Although hyperactivity is likely to diminish with age, impulsivity may remain, and males with ADHD are also likely to exhibit problems with attention and organization abilities. In fact, research has suggested that inattentiveness and disorganization tend to persist (and, in some cases, exacerbate) with age regardless of whether symptoms of impulsivity continue (Barkley, 2006).

Impulsive men make poor decisions. As reviewed in Chapter 1, they tend to have problems maintaining employment, and they often engage in high-risk behaviors. They may spend money frivolously, and they often neglect adult responsibilities, such as paying bills. They may have a record of careless driving and accidents. Because of their limited self-control and poor frustration tolerance, they are often explosive, especially when family members, coworkers, or friends do something that is disappointing or frustrating. These overreactions frequently result in conflicts and arguments, and men with ADHD experience strained personal relations and conflicted family life. With peers, impulsivity similarly impairs social adjustment, and men with ADHD tend to have difficulties maintaining friends.

Symptoms of inattentiveness and disorganization may also cause impairment. Men with ADHD may lose track of bills, assigned responsibilities, work-related items, and personal possessions. Their supervisors, coworkers, and spouse may frequently get annoyed at them because they forget to complete tasks and miss appointments and deadlines.

As is the case with the core symptoms of ADHD in boys, the core symptoms of ADHD in men result in significant secondary symptoms. Impulsive men tend to be strong-willed and have difficulties containing negative reactions when things do not go their way. Others often find them to be controlling and oppositional.

After many years of problems, men with ADHD are likely to internalize a negative self-concept, and they often view themselves as inferior to others. With a history of personal relationships filled with conflict and failure, they may start to expect that they are not able to maintain healthy intimate relationships. At work, they may recognize that others seem to be more successful at getting promotions, raises, and so on. With peers, they may notice that others are more popular and seem to get invited to more outings and events. All of these experiences are likely to result in internalization of low self-esteem. In fact, comorbidity between symptoms of ADHD and depression is much higher in adulthood than it is during childhood, and some research studies reveal that about a third of men with ADHD exhibit symptoms of major depression, and another third exhibit symptoms of dysthymia (Ramsay & Rostain, 2008). With such a high comorbidity between symptoms of ADHD and depression, therapists must be prepared to address these symptoms in treatment along with the core symptoms of ADHD.

Low self-concept and symptoms of (or tendencies toward) depression contribute to additional difficulties, such as limited motivation. Men who do not expect that they can be successful limit how hard they try to succeed. Because they expect failure, they accept it more readily when they are not advancing at work or in school (e.g., in college). They do not devote as much effort to learning their jobs (or studying) not only because the core symptoms (such as distractibility) make it harder to do so but also because they expect that their efforts will not be as fruitful.

When the core symptoms of ADHD begin to improve (e.g., because of the use of medications), all problems may not resolve, and residual symptoms may still remain. In other cases, improvement caused by the use of medications may be limited. Some patients do not tolerate medications, and consequently the symptoms must be addressed through other means. Individual counseling may be beneficial for clients who fit those descriptions, and therapeutic strategies should be used that target specific symptoms associated with ADHD.

In addition, regardless of how much improvement is evident in the core symptoms, the secondary symptoms (low self-concept, limited motivation) may not change much. Because a man with ADHD has experienced long-standing difficulties in school, at home, at work, and with peers, he has internalized negative expectations that will not change simply because the core symptoms may now diminish. The damage to self-esteem has already taken place, and mental health professionals need to recognize that treatment must also focus on these secondary symptoms. Individual counseling can be helpful to address these problems.

RESEARCH SUPPORT

Results of research studies with children (reviewed in Chapter 6) confirm that not all symptoms of ADHD resolve with the use of medications, and residual problems commonly persist at home and in school. In social settings, there is no evidence that the use of medications improves the quality of peer relationships in the long run (Pelham, 2002). In addition, some types of medications (e.g., psychostimulants) do not produce around-the-clock changes, because the medication effect must wear off before dinner and bedtime. Consequently, the core symptoms return for the remainder of the day, and the client and his family must find ways to deal with them during those time periods.

Furthermore, when adults are placed on medications to control symptoms of ADHD, they usually do not exhibit the dramatic improvement that is evident in some children. For example, response rates reported in studies of various medications (including stimulants, atomoxetine, and other medications) have revealed that the vast majority of studies found response rates closer to 50% (Barkley, 2006). Interestingly, although results of research studies have clearly revealed that treating men with ADHD with medications does not resolve all symptoms, there is limited research about the effectiveness of individual counseling for men with ADHD, and guidelines about counseling approaches are often based on collective clinical experience rather than empirical data.

As with individual counseling for boys with ADHD, only cognitive-behavioral approaches are considered potentially effective (Barkley, 2006; Ramsay & Rostain, 2008). McDermott (1999, 2000) published pioneering work in this area, outlining cognitive-behavioral strategies that may be useful when counseling adults with ADHD. Since that time, interest in individual counseling with adults with ADHD has expanded. Wilens et al. (1999) reported benefits of cognitive-behavioral therapy (CBT) with adults with ADHD and found that the treatment was particularly effective when used in combination with medications. Safren et al. (2005) conducted a randomized trial in which CBT was used in addition to medications. The therapy was administered in modules that covered organizational skills, distractibility, and cognitive modification. Patients who received medications with CBT exhibited fourfold improvements in the core and secondary symptoms as compared with patients who received medications alone. Rostain and Ramsay (2006) reported similar improvements in a prospective study involving adult patients on medications for ADHD, and results of additional studies currently in progress seem to confirm the utility of such an approach

(Ramsay & Rostain, 2008). It is clear that evidence is emerging that use of CBT, especially when combined with medications, is beneficial.

Although the benefits of individual counseling have primarily been researched when used in conjunction with medications, studies of counseling treatment alone have also shown promising results. Coaching is an emerging field that has sometimes been criticized because it does not involve sufficient depth and breadth, and coaches do not perform differential diagnosis and thorough treatment planning to address the breadth of clinical needs that clients with ADHD often exhibit. Techniques that reportedly have been found effective for coaches, however, can be used by mental health professionals as part of a comprehensive mental health treatment paradigm.

Research on the effectiveness of coaching is still limited and mostly includes reports of case studies. Allsopp, Minskoff, and Bolt (2005), however, investigated the effectiveness of a coaching approach administered with 46 college students with ADHD. They found that individualized strategy instruction aimed at improving academic skills (which mostly included work on focusing and organizational abilities) was effective in improving academic performance and that these gains were maintained one semester after the coaching stopped. Thus, including such strategies within a broader framework of counseling and psychotherapy may prove to be effective in reducing symptoms of ADHD.

INTERVENTIONS

As always, the therapist must initially build a therapeutic relationship and establish a working alliance with the client for interventions to be effective. Because issues of masculinity may interfere with the motivation to participate in counseling, therapists who work with men with ADHD must be prepared to strive hard to engage the men in treatment. Treatment goals should include providing psychoeducation about ADHD and other treatment modalities (e.g., medications), addressing the core symptoms, and working on the secondary symptoms (e.g., depression, anger management problems, and low self-esteem) commonly exhibited by men with ADHD.

Rapport Building

When men with ADHD enter treatment, they commonly view it as a last resort effort to address the difficulties that they have been exhibiting. Because their existence is filled with conflicts and failures, they often feel that they have hit the lowest point in their life. Coming to treatment means to them that they have to accept that they cannot deal with their difficulties on their own. Men are socialized to be problem solvers, and they often gauge their masculinity by the degree to which they are able to successfully address whatever problems they encounter.

Accepting help may be viewed as a sign of weakness. Thus, they may exhibit a defensive attitude and minimize their problems. This may interfere with the establishment of a therapeutic alliance, because clients may try to prove that there is nothing wrong with them and they really do not need to come to treatment.

Sometimes they may enter counseling because of urges or ultimatums verbalized by their spouse. Mental health professionals need to be vigilant about such scenarios, because the men may feel that they are coming simply to satisfy their wife, not because they accept that they need help. In such situations, it may be helpful to initially meet with the man and his wife together so that a detailed description of the problems is elucidated, and the therapist has an opportunity to collect relevant history (from both spouses), observe the interaction between the spouses, and gauge the reaction of the man to the problems that his wife is disclosing.

When the spouses are seen together, it is important to communicate to both of them that no one person should be blamed for all the difficulties, and each person will need to play a part in the solution. The therapist should be portrayed as a consultant who will help both spouses develop the most appropriate ways to communicate and will help them become better able to fulfill their roles in the relationship. In such a scenario, it may be beneficial to plan for individual sessions with the man and joint sessions with the spouse to address relational issues (as discussed in Chapter 9). This plan can be delivered by dividing the usual sessions in half and providing both components during each session or by alternating sessions between individual treatment and work with the spouse. Work with the couples usually involves strategies that require more time than half of a standard session, and therefore the latter approach may be preferred.

When both treatment modalities are delivered simultaneously, it is very important to communicate about confidentiality with the client and spouse. The therapist must assure the client that he is the primary recipient of treatment and that he controls the release of any information to his spouse. Things discussed between the client and the therapist remain between them, unless they both agree that something should be addressed with the spouse. It is important to portray the spouse as a valuable contributor to the process and that work with her is intended to further the client's progress in treatment. The client is the one, however, who controls the boundaries of confidentiality (with the recognition of usual exceptions pertaining to having the duty to warn or to reporting child abuse). Assuring the man that the therapeutic relationship exists primarily between him and the clinician can further help him develop trust and become more comfortable in treatment.

During the first few sessions, the therapist needs to proceed cautiously. Rather than confronting the client with the problems that may have been disclosed by the spouse, the therapist should draw the client to disclose his own perception of the difficulties and/or conflicts that are taking place at home (and/or in the workplace). The therapist may want to ask questions about the situations that seem to result in arguments or adverse consequences, and when querying is necessary to clarify the situation, the therapist should proceed in a collaborative manner, gently prompting the client to think about possible solutions. At the start of treatment, it is useful to get the client to agree to work on at least one problem, such as figuring out ways to reduce arguments between the client and his spouse or to reduce problems related to the workplace. If the client is able to identify at least one problem that he wants to work on, his motivation to attend treatment is likely to be more significant.

Psychoeducation

When treating an older male teen or an adult male, the therapist will find it is usually beneficial to share the diagnosis with the client. The therapist must be careful not to portray the client as "damaged" or "less than normal" in any way, because this may make the man feel compromised and less masculine.

Although framing the disorder and/or its symptoms within the context of strengths and weaknesses, as is recommended for boys and younger teens (discussed in Chapter 6), may sometimes be beneficial, another approach may be more desirable. Because significant evidence exists that states that ADHD is a disorder with underlying neuropsychiatric etiology, it may be helpful to frame the symptoms as related to changes in brain function, caused by inherited differences and genetic factors. Analogies may be very helpful here, as in the following example:

> A 32-year-old male with ADHD is grappling with accepting his diagnosis of ADHD. Findings of neuropsychiatric studies about brain differences were briefly reviewed, and he continues to struggle with accepting that his symptoms have, at least in part, biological underpinnings. As the conversation unfolds, he recalls that his mother was diagnosed with hypertension, but he says that this was different because hypertension is not a mental disorder.
>
> The therapist inquires about the ways in which his mother dealt with her diagnosis. Apparently, she joined the gym, reduced salt in her diet, and lost weight. The therapist helps the client recognize that hypertension is a medical disorder that for most individuals is caused by inherited changes in the physiological mechanism that regulates blood pressure, and environmental changes (such as improving diet, increasing exercise, and losing weight) help control this biological disorder. The same is true about ADHD, and implementing lifestyle changes will be necessary to manage the symptoms.

Diabetes provides another example of the same principle. Portraying ADHD as a disorder that involves environmental and inherited factors is likely to help the client feel less personally responsible for the symptoms and will reduce his tendency to feel emasculated because he is not able to control the symptoms merely through resolve and determination.

Using hypertension or diabetes as an analogy to ADHD may further help the client understand the relative role of biological and psychological factors in controlling of his symptoms. When someone develops hypertension, he needs to implement certain lifestyle changes that will help bring the disorder under control. In the previous example, the patient's mother lost weight, increased exercise, and limited salt intake. Similarly, a patient diagnosed with diabetes needs to eliminate sugar and refined carbohydrates from his diet and needs to control his weight and increase the amount of exercise he gets. In the same way, a client with ADHD needs to understand that even though biological factors may underlie many of the symptoms, he is still responsible for implementing techniques to help him improve self-control, focusing, and organizational skills.

Psychoeducation About Medications. When the use of medications is suggested, men often find this recommendation hard to accept. As discussed in Chapter 13, men are often reluctant to accept medical treatment. Admitting that they need to take medications to control the symptoms makes them feel powerless and threatens their masculinity. It is important for the therapist to encourage the client to express his feelings about the medications, keeping in mind that men often lack the verbal skills necessary to disclose tender feelings (Robertson & Shepard, 2008). Usually the client will relate that considering the use of medications makes him feel like there is something wrong with him, because most men do not have to take drugs to be "normal." Therapists should not dismiss those feelings, but clinicians need to be careful not to confirm them. These feelings are common, especially when the disorder is a psychological one rather than a condition perceived as mostly medical (such as cardiovascular disease or diabetes). The therapist must work hard to help the man recognize, and accept, that any difference between those disorders and neuropsychiatric ones (such as ADHD) is purely based on the differences in perception we develop as we grow up, as shown in the following example:

A man with ADHD admits that he feels like a failure because despite his efforts to remember things and keep track of his responsibilities, he continues to be forgetful and to lose track of deadlines and meetings. He verbalizes that he must not be trying hard enough, because these are problems he should be able to control with sufficient effort and resolve. The therapist directs the conversation to medical disorders and methods to control their symptoms. For example, how do patients with thyroid dysfunction control their symptoms? What about patients with cardiovascular problems? The patient states that this is different because these are medical disorders. The therapist help the client recognize that the difference between neuropsychological and cardiovascular or endocrine disorders is not nearly as clear-cut as it may appear at first glance. Many so-called medical disorders involve changes in the brain, even if symptoms are not necessarily psychological. Hypertension may involve changes in hypothalamic circuitry, which may be involved in sending the wrong messages to the pituitary, thus dysregulating the various hormones and other chemicals involved in the control of blood pressure. Similarly, thyroid dysfunction may include some of the same brain structures. Although the immediate cause of diabetes is the malfunction of the pancreas, brain involvement in the regulation of hormones that mediate appetite and digestion may play an important role in the disease. The client is led to recognize that the mind–body duality is artificial, and in reality the brain is involved in the vast majority of medical disorders. Thus, ADHD should not be viewed differently—it is a disorder in which symptoms result from a physiological dysregulation that involves the brain.

Once the man is ready to accept that the disorder he is exhibiting is not purely psychological but has underlying biological etiology, he will usually become more ready to accept treatment with medications. It is important to portray medications as providing only partial solutions and to help the client recognize that he will need lifestyle (psychological and behavioral) changes to comprehensively manage his symptoms. A patient with hypertension needs to change his diet and exercise habits to work with the medications to attain maximum improvement. A patient with diabetes needs to make similar changes. In the same way, a client with ADHD, even if he takes medications, needs to implement changes in the way he approaches a variety of situations in order to work with the medications and further increase his progress. Men who are able to develop such a comprehensive view of their treatment needs are much more likely to exhibit significant improvement.

Core Symptoms

Dimensions of ADHD symptoms include hyperactivity/impulsivity, and inattentiveness/disorganization. Both can be viewed as reflective of skill deficits—hyperactivity and impulsivity result from limited control over urges, and inattentiveness and disorganization result from insufficient abilities to devote sufficient mental energy to remain on task and process a sequence of cognitive tasks required to keep track of various aspects of responsibilities. To improve these symptoms, the client can use a variety of cognitive-behavioral strategies.

Impulsivity. The model developed by Meichenbaum and Goodman (1971), discussed in Chapter 6, is equally applicable to boys, male teens, and men. In the CBT conceptualization, an impulsive man does not comprehend the need to mediate his behaviors, does not identify relevant verbal mediators, and consequently does not verbally medicate his behavior. Treatment must address each of those three deficits.

To help the client recognize the need for verbal mediation, the therapist should guide him to process the consequences of unmediated (impulsive) behaviors. The client will undoubtedly be able to recall many situations where he made a decision hastily and regretted it later. Reviewing those situations should be helpful, focusing on the nature of the situation, the manner in which a decision was made, and the consequences that resulted from this decision. It may be best to separately identify examples relevant to various settings, as shown in the following example:

> A therapist is working with a man with ADHD and is attempting to help him recognize the various ways in which he acts impulsively. The therapist directs the man to think about different aspects of his life and how impulsivity is apparent within them. Recalling a recent fight with his wife, the man disclosed that a few weeks ago he decided to go see his friends when his wife was waiting for him to come home, and he did not call her to tell her about it because he was having too much fun. Another time, he went to a local flea market for some garden tools but instead saw some baseball cards and spent all the money saved for garden tools on the baseball cards, charging the remainder on the family's credit card. When he came home, his wife was very angry.
>
> The patient works as a plumber. One day at work, a client called and requested to change the appointment when his house would be serviced, and the patient agreed. When his boss came in, he became furious because the patient did not check the schedule, and the company was already committed elsewhere on that day. Previously, he has gotten in trouble with the boss because he went out to an early lunch right after a job and did not notify the office, and no one knew where he was for about 2 hours, which angered his boss and coworkers.
>
> The client also recalled that he seems to get into frequent squabbles with his buddies. The last time they came over to watch a game on television, he started to make fun of one of his friends, disclosing something that was previously said to him in confidence. The friend became very upset and stormed out, and others gradually followed, and the client was left to finish watching the game alone. As each situation was related, the therapist encouraged the client to identify the nature of the decision-making process (quickly, with little thought) and outline the negative outcomes that resulted from such an approach. The therapist made it clear that the purpose of this activity was not to make the client feel bad about his mistakes but to help him recognize that he makes poor decisions when he acts impulsively and that this skill deficit can be addressed in treatment.

Once the client recognizes and accepts that he needs to develop a method to increase the amount of processing that takes place before making decisions, he is ready to start developing self-statements to use as situational mediators. While in session, the client can identify thoughts that would have been more appropriate. It is beneficial to select situations that have occurred in the past and are likely to occur again in the future. For example, at work he may have made a decision too quickly (such as deciding to take a long lunch without checking with the boss). After reviewing the consequences of that mistake, the client can identify cognitions in session that can be used in such a situation in the future. If he is having lunch with a friend and the friend suggests they stay longer, the client can think about appropriate self-statements that would help him evaluate the nature of this situation and make him aware of various choices available to him before he makes a decision about what to do.

It will be helpful to identify such situations across a variety of settings, pertaining not only to work but also to home and family as well as to peer interactions. When his wife's birthday came around, did he save money for a gift for her or impulsively buy something for himself? What was her reaction? What are the thoughts one can use in such a situation that would help one process it more thoroughly and arrive at a better decision? Similarly, in a social setting, the client may have said something mean about one of his friends because it sounded cool and funny at the time, but he did not think about how it made the other person feel. What are some cognitions that can be used in such a situation? Rehearsing these instances during sessions can help the client identify the thoughts that will be more conducive to good decision making.

Sometimes the client can identify external sources of mediational statements that he encounters in his day-to-day life. At work, he may be involved in conversations and meetings where problems are being thought through and a strategy is employed where each possible outcome is reviewed before a decision is made. He may also recall conversations with his wife about a difficulty she encountered (at work, with regard to child care, etc.) and may be able to identify the strategy she used to arrive at a solution. The more the client is sensitized to recognize the prevalence of this approach, the more these situations can trigger him to remember to use such an approach himself.

The next step involves the application of those mediational statements to rehearse future situations in which this approach will be helpful. Scenarios should be thoroughly reviewed, including the triggers that require a decision to be made, the self-statements necessary to improve decision making, and the selection of a choice that will result in the most appropriate outcome. Once again, to improve the likelihood of a transfer of therapeutic gains into real-life situations, examples likely to occur across a variety of settings—home and family, work, and peers—should be reviewed.

It may be helpful to have the client write appropriate mediational statements in the session. This offers several advantages. It forces the client to think about a specific phrase that can be used in a given situation. By writing down the phrase, the client thinks about the way he may phrase it when he says it to himself. The therapist is able to see the statement and provide feedback and guidance. Finally, writing it down may improve the coding of such statements into memory, thus increasing the likelihood that cognitive mediation will actually be used in a real situation.

When using CBT with men who have limited awareness of their self-dialogue, the therapist may find it helpful for the client to start to talk himself through a situation aloud. Of course, this will not always be appropriate, but when the client is alone and facing a situation that requires a decision, he may quietly verbalize self-statements in a manner that will not disturb anyone else. Once the client gets used to talking himself through situations aloud, he will be more likely to gradually internalize these mediational statements and produce them covertly.

The efficacy of this approach depends on the severity of the problems with impulsivity. When the problems are of moderate severity and some control is evident, this approach is likely to produce beneficial results. When severe impulsivity is evident, however, using this approach may not be very effective. In those situations, the therapist should encourage the client to consider the use of medications to help him improve his self-control at least to some degree, and the approach described herein can be delivered with the use of medications to further maximize his progress in getting impulsivity under control.

Inattentiveness. Problems with distractibility affect the man with ADHD in many ways. At work, he may daydream and find it difficult to pay attention during meetings. At home, he may drift off during conversations and lose track of home-care tasks that he may be required to do. As discussed in Chapter 6, self-monitoring has been shown to be effective in helping to reduce these problems in boys with ADHD. This procedure can also be used with older teens and adult men. Self-monitoring requires the client to develop the ability to ask himself questions about what he is doing at the time. Application of this technique is described in the following example:

A man admits to being distractible while he sits at his desk at work. He frequently daydreams, goes on the computer and surfs Web sites unrelated to work, and calls his friends when he feels bored. He says that often the end of the day rolls around, and he discovers that he is behind on his work but has difficulties maintaining himself on task while he is working.

The therapist helps him recognize that he needs to start self-monitoring. While at work, he needs to periodically ask himself, "What am I doing?" He must then answer this question in detail, thinking about what he is looking at during this moment, what his body is doing, what he is currently thinking about, and so on.

The therapist helps him use a variety of cues to prompt self-monitoring. The man is asked to teach himself to use visual cues around him to prompt self-monitoring. For example, looking at a clock or his watch may be a trigger for him to self-monitor. Over time, he is encouraged to teach himself that every time he sees a clock or a watch, *any* clock or watch, he will ask himself, "What am I doing?" "Am I doing what I am supposed to be doing at this time?" "What should I do next?"

Visual cues are unobtrusive and discreet, but they are difficult to implement. Auditory cues are easier to use, although they may disturb others, so they may not always be practical. One effective auditory cue is available to most men who wear an electronic watch. Most modern watches can be set to go off with a short beep every quarter hour. The client can teach himself to associate this sound with the need to self-monitor. This may be especially effective when the client did not use this feature on his watch prior to this suggestion and therefore has not gotten used to this sound. In that instance, every time he hears the sound, it will be novel, and it will be easy to associate it with a new behavior (self-monitoring).

Once self-monitoring is initiated, appropriate follow-up is usually necessary. If the client caught himself being off task, he needs to ask himself, "What am I supposed to be doing?" or "What is everyone else around me doing?" This may help him refocus on the task at hand. If he is on task, he should ask himself, "When I am finished, what should I do next?" This can help him remain on task through the transition in activities that may be forthcoming. Self-monitoring takes time and effort to implement, and it requires significant motivation from the client. With practice, however, it can be effective in improving focusing, especially during activities where the client needs to independently perform a task and persist until it is completed.

The client's spouse can help him implement self-monitoring by using cues that trigger him to think about what he is doing. This is most effective when it is done discretely, so it does not make the man feel controlled or demeaned. For example, if the client has taught himself to use self-monitoring whenever he encounters a clock or a watch, the spouse can use time-related statements to give her husband a subtle cue—"Oh, look at the time" or "I wonder what time it is." Such an indirect approach is not likely to invoke a negative reaction and should help the client refocus on the task at hand.

To minimize distractions, the client should be guided to organize his environment in a manner conducive to remaining on task. In the workplace, he should consider whether his environment interferes with focusing. If he is close to the window, he may consider drawing the shades so that activities outside do not distract him. If there is music playing, he may consider asking his coworkers to lower the volume or turn the music off. When that is not possible, he may use headphones or earplugs when he performs tasks that require concentration. At home, the place where he attends to bills or checks his planner (discussed next) needs to similarly be free of distractions. The specific approach should be personalized to fit the client's personality and needs.

Disorganization. As boys become men, their need to organize their responsibilities and plan to perform a variety of tasks increases significantly. Adults are expected to independently plan their time and keep track of their duties with minimal reminders. Men who have difficulties with planning and organization present significant difficulties in many areas and across many settings, particularly including the workplace and the home. In fact, some researchers have considered problems with disorganization to be the one symptom of ADHD that causes the greatest impairment in overall functioning (Ramsay & Rostain, 2008).

Consequently, work with the client to develop compensatory skills in this area is indispensible.

There are two distinct aspects of disorganization that must be identified. The first of these is procrastination. It involves a delay in attending to a task that needs to be completed. When procrastinating, the client is putting off a task that is not immediately compelling or seemingly manageable at the time. This problem may be compounded by a learned aversion to perform tasks that the client has previously experienced to be overwhelming or frustrating. These tasks may include certain work tasks, academic assignments, or home duties that are disliked or difficult. When a male with ADHD procrastinates, he further exacerbates the second problem commonly associated with disorganization: the ability to manage time and resources. Both of these problems must be addressed separately in treatment.

Behavioral activation strategies may be effective to reduce procrastination (Ramsay & Rostain, 2008). Cognitive interventions generally must precede action, as evident in the following example:

> A college student admits that he procrastinates and has difficulties completing school assignments, especially term papers. He usually waits until the last minute, then feels overwhelmed, and tries to rush through the assignment, which usually results in poor grades. The therapist helps the client identify the self-statements he is making about the assignment whenever he thinks about it. These self-statements include thoughts that magnify the perceived dislike of the task, such as "I can't face this now," "This is too much for me to think about," and "This will take too long, and I don't have the time right now." The therapist intervenes and helps the client develop self-statements that are more appropriate, such as "It has to be done, and putting it off only makes it more difficult and stressful" or "I will do a little at a time so it gradually gets done." The therapist is particularly watchful to make sure that automatic thoughts are refocused from avoidance of the task to approach to the task.
>
> Once self-statements change, the client is encouraged to approach the task. To minimize feeling overwhelmed, however, the client breaks the task down into smaller components and decides that he will work for 15 minutes at a time and then take a break. If he so desires, he can work longer than 15 minutes, but he can make that decision when the 15-minute segment is up. In this way, he avoids feeling overwhelmed. The client is encouraged to make sure that he devotes at least two 15-minute segments per day for the next 7 days, after which his progress is reviewed.

Ramsay and Rostain (2003) found that developing a rule about how long sustained effort will be maintained is beneficial. Depending on the client, a 10-minute rule, a 15-minute rule, or a similar variant may be helpful. When such an approach is adapted, the client tells himself that he will work on a task for the specified amount of time, after which he will be able to take a break. If he wants to work longer, he will have the choice to continue, but he will not have to if the task seems too overwhelming at the time. After a short break, he will then return to the task for the same amount of time, again taking another break afterward. This procedure works especially well if the client is using auditory cues for self-monitoring (described previously) in which his watch beeps every 15 minutes. This provides a natural interval during which activation to task can occur. Because the segments are relatively short, most clients find that the task seems less overwhelming. Even though the first few 15-minute periods may not produce much progress, they are likely to help the client recognize that the task at hand is not as difficult as was originally perceived, and the more progress is being made, the easier it becomes to come back to the task and complete it.

Once procrastination is overcome, at least to some degree, other organizational skills can be addressed. Generally, work on time and resource management will be necessary. To start, the client should begin to use an organizer to help him keep track of his schedule. This organizer can take various forms: a calendar, a personal digital assistant (PDA) that he carries with him through the day, a cell phone with a calendar feature (such as the popular BlackBerry), or a computer program on the client's desktop or laptop computer. The last three choices may be particularly useful. As discussed in Chapter 11, individuals with ADHD find it easier to attend to tasks that involve color, sound, and movement. Because the use of electronic organizers involves three modalities (vision, hearing, and touch), men with ADHD are more likely to enjoy using such devices and will find it easier to sustain attention while using them.

The client will usually require initial assistance in programming the device (or learning how to record tasks in a calendar planner). The therapist can provide guidance, and the spouse can be enlisted to further help at home. The client needs to learn to record each task into the organizer as soon as he learns that it needs to be performed and to indicate the date when it has to be finished. In a calendar planner, the task may be written on the day it is due, and at specified intervals before hand, the client can write reminders to work on parts of the task. Electronic organizers can be set to provide reminders of unfinished tasks, so these may be a particularly good option.

In addition to recording tasks when he learns about them, the client needs to develop a routine for checking the planner at regular intervals. Usually twice per day is the minimum necessary for adaptive functioning. In the morning, while the client is ready to leave for work (or right after arriving at work), he needs to devote about 5 minutes to review what he needs to accomplish that day. This will help him plan his efforts. In fact, if the client is using self-monitoring (described earlier), the two techniques can complement each other, and the client can use the cues to ask himself questions about whether he is accomplishing what is in his planner for that day.

To further maximize the benefit, the client should also use the planner in the evenings, perhaps right before starting the bedtime routine (washing up, brushing teeth, etc.). When reviewing the planner in the evening, the client can check whether everything was accomplished that was designated for that day. If a task was not completed, it can be placed on the agenda for the next day so that efforts to get it done will continue. Devoting a brief period each evening to the review of the planner will also provide an additional benefit. During that time, the client can ask his spouse about any tasks she needs him to complete the next day. This provides an important opportunity to communicate with the spouse about her needs and will improve the client's ability to take part in the family's tasks, plans, and events.

Developing organizational skills involves using additional techniques. Each skill involves small, simple steps that may not seem to contribute much on their own, but when they are taken together, significant progress can be attained. Color-coding is a tried-and-true technique that helps clients with ADHD (Kolberg & Nadeau, 2002). Each component of daily life and responsibilities can be given a separate color, and folders with that color can be used to store items pertaining to those tasks. For example, bills pending payment can be placed in a red folder, items pertaining to home maintenance can be placed in a green folder, and so on. Each client should use colors that somehow help cue him to these items. Color-coding is also effective for tasks that pertain to the workplace. For example, each project may be placed in folders of different colors, and the client can learn to check folders of each color at least once per day to monitor his progress.

All mail should be placed in an in-box, a specific spot designated on the client's desk. Once per day, the client should go through the in-box and place items from the in-box into appropriate folders for further action. The client designates specific days each month during which he will pay all the bills in the red folder. Because bills often have various due dates, at least 2 days per month may be necessary. These days should be written into the daily planner so that the client does not forget. If the client is not able to attend to the bills that day, the evening review of the planner will identify this task as incomplete, and the client will be able to designate another day to attend to this responsibility.

Spouses can provide valuable assistance when developing these techniques. They can place the mail into the designated in-box and use this spot to write messages and lists for the client about what needs to be accomplished. For example, instead of merely telling the client that the bathroom faucet is leaking and the gasket needs to be changed, the spouse can write this on a piece of paper and place it in the client's in-box. Then, when he reviews the in-box each evening, he can place this note into his daily planner on whichever day he feels he will be able to attend to this task.

Becoming organized usually involves learning to make notes and lists, because what is placed into the daily planner is essentially a list of tasks with notes about what needs to be done. There are times, however, when it is not practical to use the planner. For example, while driving or attending a meeting, making notes in the planner is not appropriate.

For this reason, clients with ADHD should have notepads (or small digital recorders) handily available in the workplace, at home, in the car, and so on. When they think of a task that needs to be done, they need to write it there (or dictate it into the recorder) and then take the note (or recording) with them. Then, at the end of the day, they should designate a period during which they empty their pockets and organize the contents—wallet and car keys go on a tray next to the bed, notes get transferred to the planner, dictated notes get listened to and dispensed accordingly, and so on.

Learning organizational skills is a work in progress. Men with ADHD often come to accept that being disorganized is simply a part of them, and they feel that learning to be organized is too difficult. When men with ADHD are motivated to address this problem, however, they can be taught to use a wide variety of techniques to become more organized, only some of which were discussed previously. The therapist and client should think creatively about the additional strategies that may be developed to help the client improve his abilities to keep track of his items, tasks, and responsibilities. For example, Ramsay and Rostain (2008) related work with a client who habitually misplaced his car keys and was usually late for work because he had trouble locating them each morning. The client ended up nailing a hook close to the front door that always had a set hanging on it. The client found this solution simple but effective and became better able to get to work on time. Therapists should be prepared to think outside the box to come up with creative solutions to help clients overcome some of their organizational difficulties.

Secondary Symptoms

Men who exhibit difficulties in self-control often have problems controlling their anger and tolerating situations they find frustrating. Improving the core symptoms, especially impulsivity, will reduce these tendencies, but overreacting to frustrating situations is likely to remain problematic even after medications have been introduced. Therefore, addressing anger management and frustration tolerance in treatment is likely to be beneficial.

In addition, men with ADHD usually have lived a life filled with conflict and failure. Over many years, they have internalized negative self-esteem and limited motivation to succeed. When the core symptoms diminish, problems with self-esteem and motivation will nevertheless persist, and therapists must plan to attend to these remaining symptoms in treatment.

Anger Management. As previously discussed, men with ADHD present a long history of conflicts with family members, teachers, coworkers, and peers. As a result, they have learned to expect that interactions with those around them are likely to result in arguments and negative feelings. They anticipate negative outcomes from most social interactions, and they tend to prepare themselves for problems when they come in contact with those around them.

This negative expectation affects their relationships in many ways. Because men with ADHD expect a battle, they often address others with a negative attitude. They might communicate this attitude with an edge in their voice, a menacing body posture, threatening gestures, and belligerent verbalizations. They subconsciously prepare themselves for conflict and communicate this both verbally and nonverbally.

The therapist should help the client identify what situations make him happy, curious, frustrated, angry, fearful, and so on. It is helpful to spend some time on this topic. Because men with ADHD are likely to experience more negative interactions than positive ones, identifying positive interactions may require effort.

Once a variety of situations have been identified, the therapist should guide the man to recognize the range of bodily reactions that he experiences when these situations occur. How does he know he is happy? Angry? Fearful? What is his heart doing? What about his breathing? Are his fists clenched? Is his body tense? When these physical reactions are identified, they become available as potential signals to communicate to the client that an emotional reaction has been awakened. Depending on the physiological reaction, he can learn to identify the specific feeling that is associated with each physical state.

Along with identifying bodily reactions, it is helpful to identify the thoughts that accompany the feelings. What is the self-dialogue when the man is angry? What are the thoughts that accompany frustration? What about anticipation? How about anxiety? Men often have difficulties identifying feelings. They have been socialized to believe that expressing feelings is a sign of weakness and that a "true man" keeps his feelings under control. Therapists need to recognize that identifying feelings (and thoughts that go along with these feelings) is likely to be a new experience for the adult male, and much guidance will be necessary to accomplish this step.

In accordance with the tenets of cognitive-behavioral counseling, thoughts precipitate behaviors, and therefore helping the man become aware of what he is thinking before he acts is necessary. This is likely to be difficult. The more impulsive the client is, the less cognitive processing he is using. At least some cognitive processing occurs in every situation, however. Men are usually unaware of how their thoughts affect their behaviors. Helping them become aware of this connection is a crucial step in treatment.

When these thoughts are identified, the client is ready to begin to develop a proactive self-dialogue. Once he realizes that he uses at least some (albeit very brief) self-talk about a situation before he acts on it, he can be taught to extend the processing time and include thoughts that are more conducive to self-control. He can learn to repeat these self-statements to himself in situations that evoke emotions. As described in Chapter 6, men can be taught to view these self-statements as pep talks, similar to those that coaches usually give members of their team. Because many men are sports fans, they can relate to this analogy. The therapist can guide the client to think through the ways that a football team maintains control even when the players feel angry at a team that is an archrival. The team learns to recognize that the best strategy to win is to stay in control, play within the rules of the game, and take time to come up with creative moves to combat the other team. The client can identify the statements that the coach is likely to say to his team. He can then be guided to use similar self-statements to help him stay focused and in control when he faces situations, or people, that he finds frustrating.

Once pep talks have been used to prevent initial overreaction, more rational processing can take place. The client can think about different things he might do and say in a situation that makes him feel angry or frustrated. Each behavior needs to be followed by an assessment of consequences that are likely to occur if this option is chosen. Grounding these suggestions in examples of real situations that happened recently will make this approach more personal and effective, and therefore men should be encouraged to relate examples of recent episodes and behaviors and rethink those situations to come up with constructive alternatives.

The final step involves the selection of the most appropriate action. Once again, it is necessary to continue to stress that the consequences of any given behavior must always be considered and must be the primary guide that helps the client decide what to do in any given situation. The more this approach can be used, the more the action–reaction sequence can be slowed down and more effective processing can be used, thus improving frustration tolerance and anger management skills.

This approach is evident in the following example:

A 23-year-old adult male is working at a chemical lab. During a midday break, all the coworkers in the section sit in a small break room and talk while they consume lunch. The client stays to himself, but it is apparent that a few coworkers seek to engage him in some playful verbal sparring. One woman starts to tease him about his clothing, commenting on his funny shoes. The others start to chuckle. The man nervously shifts in his seat, and the others continue to rib him about his T-shirt and the image on it that, to them, looks strange and may have something to do with the occult. The man gets up to leave, and while doing so, the others start to laugh and call him a baby for not being able to take a joke. The man turns around, storms toward the table where the group is sitting, comes very close to the woman he feels is the primary offender, points a finger at her face, and screams at the top of his lungs, warning her that she has not yet seen him angry, and she is better off leaving him alone if she knows what is good for her. He storms out, and the coworkers report him to his supervisor. He receives a reprimand and is warned that another outburst will get him fired.

In treatment, the man worked on all steps of the anger response and rehearsed better ways of responding to such triggers. Before going into the lunchroom, he gives himself the pep talk he was taught to remain calm and in control of his emotions. He also rehearses a number of verbal responses he can use if he is being approached or teased. When in the situation, he self-monitors his body and is vigilant to his reactions to triggers, for example, when someone makes fun of him. When he feels his body tighten and his heart begin to pound, he uses a couple of deep breaths to keep himself under control. Then he responds to a verbal challenge with a verbal comeback, making sure that he does not escalate the conflict. If teased, he teases back. In addition, the therapist helped him reframe the intentions of his coworkers—in all likelihood, they were attempting to befriend him rather than insult him. This approach proved effective, and the client started to socialize with some of those coworkers who previously teased him. He continued to dislike the woman who initially precipitated the incident, but he was able to tolerate her presence without feeling the need to intimidate or scare her.

Low Self-Esteem. Over a lifetime of conflict and failure, men with ADHD often develop a negative self-image. This perception affects their motivation and effort and predisposes them to negative feelings, such as depression. Indeed, research has shown that as boys with ADHD become men with ADHD, symptoms of depression are likely to increase (Barkley, 2006). Consequently, it is necessary to address their self-image in counseling.

To do so, counselors should initially focus on reframing the failures of men with ADHD as related to the symptoms of ADHD. When men begin to recognize that their limited impulse control, poor organization skills, and/or limited ability to remain on task underlie many of the failures they have encountered, they begin to be able to separate their self-identify from those symptoms and recognize that their failures are not due to their limited abilities or limited intelligence. Once again, the therapist will find it useful to portray the difficulties as secondary to a lack of skills that can be remedied in treatment.

As with boys, it may be helpful to ground the limitations within a broader profile of overall abilities, including many strengths. By now, the difficulties may have overshadowed the strengths, but most men can be prompted to think about things they do well and attributes they possess that others may admire. Once a more comprehensive pattern of strengths and weaknesses has been identified, the client can recognize that he exhibits a pattern that is not unlike that of most people, although his specific strengths and differences may be unique. This realization can normalize his experience and help him recognize that in many ways he is just like any other person.

The CBT approach to the treatment of low self-esteem is based on the recognition that negative self-statements result in negative feelings. Although men may have difficulties identifying some of the self-dialogue, therapists can guide them to identify the perception they have of themselves and the negative self-statements they use in various situations. Beck (1995) identified the cognitive triad that underlies the feelings of depression: a negative view of the world, the future, and oneself. Identifying these negative assumptions and replacing them with more appropriate alternatives are important components of helping a man with ADHD develop better self-esteem. Again, activities during sessions can act as triggers to identify pessimistic thought patterns and replace negative self-statements with positive ones.

Limited Motivation. As discussed in Chapter 6, motivation is inseparable from self-efficacy and involves the person's recognition of his strengths and abilities. Those people with high self-efficacy perceive themselves as capable of successfully handling the usual demands that day-to-day functioning requires. Unfortunately the actual experience of men with ADHD is contrary to those beliefs, because they frequently argue with their family members, coworkers, and peers, and they generally find it difficult to succeed personally, academically, occupationally, or socially. Over time, these experiences become internalized into negative expectations, and self-efficacy becomes low. As self-efficacy lowers, so does motivation. In therapy, this pattern must be reversed.

In the CBT model, the perception of self-efficacy results from self-statements. This is evident in the following example:

> A man with ADHD relates to his therapist a series of personal events that are characterized by conflicts and failures. He often argues with his spouse, he feels overwhelmed at work, and he gets along poorly with his coworkers. The therapist helps him identify the thoughts that accompany most of the situations he encounters. When he is about to start an interaction with his spouse, he is thinking, "Here we go again—we are going to have another fight, and she will give me a hard time." At work, when he is given a task, he thinks, "How am I going to do this? It seems too hard." When he is entering the cafeteria, he is thinking, "Why don't they like me?" The therapist helps the client recognize that he usually expects a negative outcome, and he then behaves accordingly, fulfilling those negative expectations.

In treatment, mental health professionals must find ways to diminish such negative cognitions and replace them with self-statements that underlie positive expectations. Collaborative empiricism provides a useful framework. In this approach, the therapist and the client jointly test out the faulty assumptions that the client has internalized. As the cognitive distortions that underlie these faulty assumptions are illuminated, the therapist and the client begin to work on developing assumptions that are based on reality rather than these distortions. As more realistic assumptions are internalized, motivation increases. In the previous example, the therapist intervened as follows:

> To challenge these negative assumptions, the therapist started by prompting the man to think about the various situations he encounters in his life. When he comes home from work, what does he think his wife will say to him? Will she give him a hard time? What about at work—are all tasks he is given too hard for him to accomplish? Has he ever been praised by his boss? Because

the client was not aware of many of his automatic thoughts, he needed much guidance to identify them in treatment. Role-plays were used to help the client re-create the situations and identify the thoughts that went along with each sequence of events.

As the client became better able to relate his negative expectations, the therapist introduced the idea that thoughts go along with behaviors and that what the client thinks about a situation significantly affects how he feels about its outcome and how he behaves when the situation actually takes place. A significant amount of practice followed to help him recognize and verbalize those thoughts.

Once the client was able to identify the thought patterns, the therapist helped him explore the implications of his negative assumptions. When he expects that when he comes home he will probably get into a fight with his wife, does this happen always? Are there times when he has come home and conflicts did not ensue? To help make this process more relevant to the client's life, the therapist replayed specific sequences of events over the past day or two to help the client recognize that his assumptions are not always true.

Similar events were reviewed pertaining to the workplace. When his boss approaches him, is the client expecting that the boss will give him a hard time? Has that always been the case? Reviewing examples that are not consistent with these faulty assumptions helped the client recognize that although there are times when he has conflicts with his supervisor and spouse, there are also times when they get along much better. In this step, it was necessary to help the client recognize that his assumptions often are not accurate.

Next, the client examines the effect of his negative assumptions on his feelings and behaviors. When he is expecting to get into an altercation with his wife, how does that make him feel? If he feels defensive, how does that affect the way he speaks to her and the way he reacts when she approaches him? Similarly, if he expects that his boss will always reprimand him, how does this assumption affect his attitude toward the work and his job? The therapist reviewed many examples of similar situations occurring at home, at work, and in social settings.

Finally, once the client recognized that negative expectations are not productive, he became able to replace negative self-statements with more appropriate expectations. At home, he was able to say to himself, "Today, my wife and I will get along fine, and she has no reason to give me a hard time." At work, he said, "I am doing the best I can, and the boss likely recognizes that. As long as I work hard to do my best, the boss is likely to appreciate my efforts." With practice, he began to internalize a set of expectations that was more realistic, and his sense of self-efficacy improved.

In some situations, negative expectations may not be based on a limited sense of self-efficacy but be dependent on negative assumptions about the nature of the task. For example, men with ADHD often find work-related tasks to be boring or otherwise unpleasant, and therefore they are not motivated to complete them. In those cases, the therapist should focus on the recognition, and acceptance, of the fact that everyone's life is filled with some tasks that are enjoyable and some that may not be. Completing work tasks may not be much fun, and the client may choose to reject those tasks. Doing so, however, brings consequences that he must also accept. Refusal to do what is expected of him is likely to result in a demotion or loss of his job. Without a good job, he is not likely to be able to afford the things in life that he really wants. Thus, he must learn that he is just like most people in the world—to have the kind of life he wants, he must do some things he may not like and must develop sufficient frustration tolerance to be able to do so. This is a life skill that every human being needs to use, because few people are able to do only the things they want. Work on this issue will bring the therapist back to work on frustration tolerance, a topic described earlier in this chapter.

SUMMARY

Although research studies are just beginning to investigate the effectiveness of individual counseling with men with ADHD, early results are promising, and men with ADHD are likely to derive at least some benefit from this form of treatment. Although medications may be effective in managing some of the core symptoms, residual problems commonly remain, and some clients do not respond well to medications. In addition, men with ADHD often exhibit significant secondary symptoms that may include poor frustration tolerance, anger management problems, low self-esteem, and limited motivation, and improving the core symptoms is not likely to eliminate all of those symptoms. For all these reasons, mental health professionals should recognize that individual therapy provides an avenue to address these problems.

CBT has proved most effective. To address impulsivity, therapists can help clients develop cognitive mediation strategies that will improve their abilities to think about situations before they make choices of behaviors. To address inattentiveness, self-monitoring has been shown to be effective, especially when external cues are used, and contingency management is used to reinforce this technique. Organizational skills may be improved through the use of schedulers and planners.

Using individual counseling to address secondary symptoms may be especially beneficial. Cognitive-behavioral methods are known to be effective in improving anger management skills, enhancing self-esteem, and increasing a sense of self-efficacy. Because these problems commonly accompany the core symptoms of ADHD, most men will benefit from addressing these problems in individual counseling treatment.

9

Working With Spouses and Partners of Men With ADHD

Men with attention deficit/hyperactivity disorder (ADHD) frequently have conflicts with their spouse, girlfriend, or partner, and sharing an intimate relationship with a man with ADHD can be a frustrating experience. Whether the men exhibit symptoms of significant impulsivity or distractability/disorganization, their abilities to be an effective partner and father are adversely affected.

Impulsive men have problems with delay of gratification, and they frequently perform behaviors that get them in trouble. They may have difficulties suppressing the impulse to engage in activities that are fun and may make poor choices, neglecting work duties and spending inappropriate amounts of time being involved in hobbies or leisure. These actions may have an adverse impact on their abilities to hold a job or advance within the workplace. Because work may not seem as important to them, they may not exert the amount of effort necessary to secure and cultivate a stable and profitable career. When at work, they may have limited abilities to tolerate frustration and may overreact to being told what to do by their bosses and supervisors. Indeed, men with ADHD are much more likely to have problems maintaining a job (Barkley, 2006) than men without ADHD, which is likely to strain the relationship between a man with ADHD and his spouse or partner.

Many of these men crave stimulation and often pursue high-risk hobbies, such as racing or extreme sports. Their spouse may find those activities nerve-racking. Issues of masculinity complicate this tendency. Many men feel that they prove their masculinity by behaving like a "real man," for instance, by facing danger and refusing to show fear. This attitude drives them toward occupations and professions where they face danger and need to demonstrate abilities to handle the risk. Although socialization factors are likely to play a major role in the development of such expectations, biological factors also play a contributing role. Men with ADHD, whose frontal lobes tend to be underactive, tend to crave stimulation, perhaps in an effort to increase activity in their brain to help them feel more "normal." When such a man was also socialized to express his masculinity by staring down danger, he will be especially likely to be drawn toward high-risk activities. Spouses of men with ADHD must become aware of this dynamic to help them better understand why their partners do some of the things they do.

Men with ADHD often have difficulty handling frustration. This difficulty may reveal itself at home by their lack of attention to house chores and home-maintenance duties. Because they are drawn toward stimulation, rather than the mundane tasks of day-to-day life, they may neglect their responsibilities, which is likely to further aggravate their spouse. As the partner begins to feel more and more dissatisfied, a power struggle may unfold within the home, where the spouse attempts to get the man to do what is needed at home, and the man resists those efforts and feels that the spouse is attempting to control him and tell him what to do. This contest of wills further strains the relationship and adds to tension and conflicts.

Men who have difficulties dealing with frustration tend to make explosive fathers. When they issue a command and do not get immediate compliance (or, even worse, encounter resistance from the child), fathers with ADHD have difficulties containing their urge to react and tend to yell and punish their children too severely. In fact, fathers with ADHD are especially likely to use physical means of parenting, such as spanking (Barkley, 2006), perhaps because they may have experienced this form of punishment as children and are now repeating this pattern.

A mother who witnesses her children being severely punished (or yelled at) by the father tends to act protectively toward her children and confront the father about the inappropriateness of his behaviors. Often, these conflicts occur in front of the children. When this conflict takes place, many fathers feel that their authority and masculinity is being challenged, and conflict between the parents ensues. This conflict is counterproductive and tends to damage the relationship between the parents and strain the bond between the father and the child. Even if such conflict takes place away from the children, the father usually thinks that the mother is dictating to him how to parent, and he feels controlled by his spouse.

Impulsive men tend to react explosively not only with their children but also with their spouse. When they are told something they do not like to hear, they tend to overreact. Sometimes their reaction takes the form of a short, snippy response. Sometimes it may be more intense. Either way, spouses often feel that they need to walk on eggshells to prevent conflicts, which tends to strain the relationship and negatively affect intimacy and closeness.

Men with ADHD who are not impulsive also present with difficulties in relationships with their spouse. Because they find it hard to keep track of their things, they often misplace tools, clothing, and other items they need. This carelessness may result in additional expenses when items (such as tools) need to be replaced. In addition, men with ADHD easily get distracted or sidetracked, and they need reminders to complete the tasks they are responsible for, such as doing home maintenance, paying bills, renewing the car registration or a driver's license, and so on. Not tending to these tasks can result in adverse consequences for the men and additional costs for the family.

Disorganized men also tend to have problems at work. They may forget about meetings or tasks that were assigned to them and may misplace items they need to perform their job duties. Once again, these difficulties result in problems maintaining employment and advancing within their career. Spouses find these problems very difficult and often feel that the men do not sufficiently carry their load and that they contribute an insufficient income. These feelings, in turn, make men feel that their masculinity is being challenged, and conflicts in the relationships are likely to intensify.

Because men with ADHD present difficulties in so many aspects of the spousal and father–child relationships, it is helpful to invite the spouse into treatment to help her understand the nature of the difficulties the man is exhibiting and aid her in developing techniques she will need to address the frictions that occur within the home. She must learn strategies to deal with common day-to-day situations, and she needs to consider what role she will play in helping her spouse gain control of his symptoms. Mental health professionals working with men with ADHD should be prepared to invite the spouse into treatment to comprehensively intervene in various aspects of the client's life that are affected by symptoms of ADHD.

RESEARCH SUPPORT

Because the recognition that, in many cases, symptoms of ADHD continue into adulthood is recent, research on the impact of ADHD on marital relationships has not been extensively studied. Murphy and Barkley (1996a) reported that severe marital dissatisfaction is common in couples where one partner has been diagnosed with ADHD. The spouses often felt confused, angry, and frustrated, and they complained that their partner was a poor listener, messy, forgetful, unreliable, self-centered, insensitive, and irresponsible. Barkley (2006) suggested that because so many of these behaviors may be directly related to symptoms of ADHD, spouses need to learn that many of these problems may not be secondary to "willful misconduct" (p. 699). Instead, partners of men with ADHD need to understand the world from their spouse's perspective, stop blaming him, and align together to fight a common enemy (symptoms of ADHD). If both spouses develop a mutual understanding of how symptoms of ADHD affect the relationship, what each partner needs from the other, and how working together greatly improves the relationship, the chances of a positive outcome are enhanced (Dixon, 1995).

Other studies have also confirmed that marital or couple counseling improves the core symptoms of ADHD in the "identified patient" and reduces stress on the entire family. Nadeau (1995) recommended the inclusion of couple treatment in the comprehensive management of ADHD, and Hallowell (1995) found that including the spouse improved the overall outcome in treatment of adults with ADHD. In fact, Ratey, Hallowell, and Miller (1995) reported that couple counseling contributed to symptom reduction, stress reduction, and increased closeness in families where one of the partners was diagnosed with ADHD.

The coaching model can be especially helpful when working with spouses and partners of men with ADHD. As discussed by Ratey (2002), individuals with ADHD benefit from support and assistance. In the coaching model, one person (the coach) guides the other (the client) to develop strategies that address common life difficulties, such as problems with disorganization, forgetfulness, or maintaining consistent goal orientation. Although there is no standard methodology, spouses of men with ADHD can be taught to act as coaches and help the men manage their life, set realistic goals, and stay on track to accomplish those goals. Of course, this coaching must be done in an atmosphere of mutual respect, and spouses of men with ADHD must be able to manage their own frustration before they can effectively act as coaches.

Working with both parents is especially important in a family where one parent and at least one child have ADHD (Barkley, 2006). This situation contributes additional challenges and adds a level of complexity that must be addressed. In such a situation, each family member diagnosed with ADHD should have his or her own treatment, but in addition, marital or couple treatment becomes indispensible. Both parents must not only find ways to work together and reduce conflict but also participate in parent training (as described in Chapter 7) to help them develop appropriate behavior management strategies and increase consistency in the manner in which they parent the children.

INTERVENTIONS

When working with spouses and partners of men with ADHD, mental health professionals must maintain a clear focus on the goals that need to be addressed in treatment. Although the spouse can not be expected to manage her husband's or partner's symptoms, she must understand that some skills are legitimately difficult for a man with ADHD, and she must develop necessary frustration tolerance to avoid overreacting to her partner's shortcomings. In addition, she can learn ways in which she can help her husband or partner become more organized and responsible.

Treatment Modalities

The first decision that mental health professionals must make is how to include the spouse in treatment. Three methods are most common: marital or couple counseling, collateral counseling (in which the spouse without the identified patient is being seen separately in treatment), and family counseling (in which children are also part of the sessions). Each of these methods has benefits and drawbacks, and each may be appropriate with different clients.

Marital or Couple Counseling. When both members of a couple are seen together, the therapist has opportunities to observe the patterns of interaction and communication that commonly take place between both partners. These meetings can be very beneficial, because the therapist will be able to identify the specific manner in which conflicts escalate, which will greatly improve the therapist's ability to intervene and will help redirect some of these conflicts. In such an arrangement, both partners work to improve communication skills and strive to alter the ways in which they react to each other.

This approach can be especially helpful when a husband and father with ADHD is participating in treatment with his wife or partner to develop effective parenting skills (as discussed in Chapter 7). In joint treatment, both spouses can learn to provide support for each other, help each other use appropriate parenting strategies, and call on each other when a situation seems to be getting out of hand. The spouses' learning to parent consistently is likely to result in significant improvement in the behavior of their children, and delivering parent training to both parents simultaneously is considered to be the most effective.

On the other hand, seeing both partners together may also pose some challenges. In most cases, the spouse is likely to be frustrated with some of the difficulties that the client with ADHD is exhibiting, and she must learn to become more tolerant of her partner's shortcomings. This sometimes requires gentle confrontation and psychoeducation about the disorder and its symptoms. When these efforts are done in front of the man with ADHD, problems may emerge. Sometimes, the man may feel that the therapist and the spouse are ganging up on him and blaming him for all the problems within the family. In other cases, the man may feel that the symptoms of ADHD, because they legitimately make some skills more difficult, become an excuse why he should not be required to do the things expected of him. Teaching the spouse to be more understanding and supportive, and at the same time setting appropriate limits and expectations of the client, may be more difficult when the man is there in the session.

Collateral Counseling. Working with the spouse or partner separately, without the presence of the patient with ADHD, poses benefits and challenges that are exactly opposite of those described for couple counseling. Being able to work individually with the spouse allows the therapist to address difficulties and symptoms of the disorder with less concern that the primary patient will view them as an excuse for bad behaviors. When the spouse needs gentle confrontation to help her develop more realistic expectations, the counselor may be more comfortable doing so without the patient in the room, which is likely to make the spouse less defensive and may make her more receptive to the therapist's goals.

Working with the spouse separately may be particularly beneficial when the therapist needs to work with her to help her develop better frustration tolerance skills. Being able to do so without the patient in the room at the same time will prevent the spouse from losing face in front of her husband, and she will be less likely to perceive the therapist as taking sides. The counselor can help her develop abilities to keep her emotional reactions under control, stay calm, and find ways to compose herself when she feels angry and frustrated. The therapist can do this work while empathizing with the spouse's situation and validating her concerns. Again, this work becomes more difficult when the patient with ADHD is in the room at the same time.

On the other hand, working with the spouse without the patient requires the therapist to obtain accurate descriptions of conflict and maladaptive communication patterns without being able to observe them directly. When mental heath professionals see patients and spouses separately, they obtain partial descriptions of the problem, each skewed by the reporter's perceptions. Sometimes it becomes difficult to construct a balanced and accurate viewpoint, especially when both sides significantly exaggerate the degree of the problems (as may be the case with a couple in the midst of an intense conflict). In addition, working with each partner separately may not be sufficient to address maladaptive patterns of communication, because the therapist is not able to witness the exact reactions of both spouses.

Seeing spouses of identified patients separately presents additional challenges. Because the adult patient controls the release of confidential information contained in his records, therapists who see family members without the patient present must address the limits of confidentiality and clarify what information the patient allows the therapist to release during the session with his wife or partner. Mental health professionals need to proactively address this issue before any contact with the spouse or partner takes place, and it is usually a good idea to obtained a written, signed release that specifies that the patient gives permission to release information and what information is specifically allowed to be released.

Because working with spouses or partners jointly or separately provides various benefits and drawbacks, some therapists use a combination approach, where some contact occurs with the identified patient individually, some sessions take place with the spouse alone, and others sessions are held jointly with the patient and his spouse. This approach may be beneficial, but the therapist must be clear about the goals and limits inherent with each of those therapeutic modalities.

Family Counseling. Family counseling is generally provided when all members of the family that reside together are seen at the same time. Family counseling usually includes the parents and the children but may also include members of the extended family (e.g., a grandparent) who live in the home. As with marital counseling, seeing the whole family together allows the therapist to observe patterns of communication and the manner in which conflicts develop. This information tells the counselor about the family's needs and allows the clinician to intervene while the family is interacting.

Seeing the whole family together allows the therapist to observe the relational patterns between all family members. In families locked in complex struggles, therapists may be able to identify coalitions, triangulations (when a conflict between two family members is redirected through the third, usually a child), and various roles that family members take on. For example, in a family with four children, it may be apparent that major conflicts occur between the father (the identified patient with ADHD) and the mother, and each child may side with one parent. When the father forgets to attend to a responsibility, one child may try to rescue and protect him, whereas the other may look for ways to "tell on him" to the mother, standing up for her in the process. In such a family, it is common to see intense conflict between the children. Issues such as these can rarely be addressed effectively unless the whole family is seen together.

One additional benefit of sessions where the whole family is present is that they allow the therapist to observe the parenting techniques used by each parent. Because men with ADHD often exhibit poor frustration tolerance and tendencies toward being explosive, the therapist will be able to see examples of these problems when the father interacts with his children. This information may be very beneficial, because actual examples of the father's behaviors may be addressed when parenting techniques are being developed. To prevent both parents from feeling that their authority is being challenged, however, the therapist should do the actual parent training without the children present in the room.

Family counseling has some additional drawbacks. When parents need to be confronted about their behaviors, it is more difficult for the therapist to do so when everyone is in the room, especially the children. When parents need to work on changing their behaviors, they may find it difficult to do so in front of the children. Men with ADHD may find that especially uncomfortable. Their perception of masculinity may partially be based on the respect they expect from family members, especially the children. When asked to change their behaviors, those men may feel that their authority is being challenged, and they may respond defensively to these attempts. Therapists must weigh the benefits and drawbacks of family counseling before it is attempted. If the family exhibits complex patterns of maladaptive behaviors, coalitions, and conflicts between various family members, family counseling may be beneficial. When the family's difficulties are limited to poor parenting or conflicts between the spouses, however, addressing these difficulties without the children around may be more beneficial.

Goals and Techniques

When working with spouses and partners of men with ADHD, clinicians need to keep several overlapping goals in mind. It is necessary to help the spouse understand the disorder and the specific pattern of symptoms that her husband exhibits. This will help her recognize which problems within the home may be related to the symptoms of the disorder and realize that managing the symptoms can improve some of those difficulties. In addition, the spouse needs to develop the ability to manage her own frustration and anger when she is faced with some of the behaviors she finds difficult to handle. Developing nonescalating methods of managing those situations will be an important component of improving the relationship. Finally, the spouse may be able to assist her partner in developing ways to overcome some of the symptoms by learning specific coping mechanisms. Here, the spouse can act as a coach, assisting her husband and providing support to him as he works to learn new skills. Those goals are described next, with suggestions about how they can be implemented in treatment.

Psychoeducation. The spouse is likely to come into treatment after prolonged conflicts that may have been precipitated by the husband's explosiveness, lack of reliability, and poor decision making. She may have developed the perception that he does not care enough about her to make better decisions, and she may blame his motivation and "willful malice" for his actions. Although it is important for the clinician to provide empathy and connect with the spouse, the spouse also needs to recognize that men with ADHD exhibit legitimate symptoms that underlie many of the problems evident in the relationship. Reviewing symptom clusters and the underlying etiology may prove helpful. For each symptom, it is beneficial for the clinicians to help the spouse connect the symptom with examples of the specific problems evident in the relationship.

Impulsive men often make poor decisions and find it difficult to contain their reactions when they are faced with situations that provoke frustration or anger. Consider the following scenario:

> A spouse discloses that her husband came home and was visibly angry about something that happened at work. He stormed into the den, turned on the computer, and started to write an angry e-mail message. As the wife asked him what happened, he was barely able to get the words out but stated that he got passed over for a promotion. He was going to let his boss have a piece of his mind and let him know exactly what he thinks of him. The wife, anticipating the likely consequences, attempted to stop him, and

the two got into a heated argument during which he told her, in a verbally abusive manner, that he is tired of her controlling behavior, and he wants her to leave him alone. As this unfolded, their two children went to their rooms and were crying. Despite the wife's protests, the husband sent the e-mail. The next day, the wife found out that his hours at work got cut, and his salary was reduced.

When such a situation is related, the spouse should think about the emotions that precipitated the husband's behavior. When she recognizes that the decision was made in the midst of a rush, when her husband's self-control was diminished, this understanding will help guide her about a strategy that may improve this problem—find ways to delay decision making, when possible, until a time when emotions and excitement are not running high, both spouses can discuss the pros and cons, and a rational decision can be made. For example, in the previous vignette, the spouse could have attempted to pull her husband away by asking him to come to the kitchen, sit down, and tell her all the details about what went on. Along the way, she should offer support and try to gently delay any action until the situation is fully processed. When such an approach is used, the husband is usually able to gradually calm down and, once better self-control returns, consider more appropriate ways of responding.

Similarly, the spouse may think about times when her husband acted irresponsibly by not following through on responsibilities, such as keeping appointments or paying bills. Spouses often attribute these problems to immaturity and the unwillingness of the male to grow up and accept adult responsibilities. Although this may be true in some cases, the spouse should also realize that keeping track of things is particularly difficult for a male who exhibits symptoms of distractibility and disorganization. Consider the following example:

A spouse complains that her husband is very irresponsible. He loses track of bills and deadlines, and the family must often pay late fees. In addition, his credit rating is poor, and consequently the family must now pay higher interest rates on credit cards and an automobile loan. When relating this problem, she describes her husband as immature and states that he never seems to forget about watching his football games and that these games are probably more important to him than anything that has to do with the family. She feels overwhelmed because she must constantly monitor all bills and other deadlines (such as when it is necessary to pay property and income taxes) and feels that he probably does not care about those things.

A few moments later, however, the spouse relates an incident when the husband was looking for his tools to change a broken lamp shade in the hallway. He became angry when he discovered that the tools were left outside in the driveway and had started to rust from the moisture. He blamed his son, but the wife was able to help the husband realize that he left those tools there himself after he changed the oil in the family car a few days ago. Connecting those two incidents, the therapist was able to help the spouse recognize that forgetfulness and disorganization are a pattern in the husband's life that is apparent even in those aspects about which he obviously cares, and therefore those behaviors are not reflective of ill will but may be, to a significant extent, related to his symptoms of inattentiveness and disorganization. Thus, the therapy needs to focus on how to help him overcome those problems rather than helping him increase his caring about family matters.

When teaching the spouse about the disorder, the clinician might find it helpful to use psychoeducational materials, such as books, brochures, and handouts generated by credible sources. Organizations such as Children and Adults With Attention-Deficit/Hyperactivity Disorder (CHADD; chadd.org) and Attention Deficit Disorder Resources (ADD Resources; addresources.org) maintain a large library of resources for patients, parents, and spouses of individuals with ADHD. Clinicians should maintain a library of these aids and use them as adjuncts when working with spouses of men with ADHD.

Mental Preparation. Spouses of men with ADHD frequently argue with their partners. As a result, they learn to expect that most interactions result in negative outcomes and feelings. Over time, they begin to anticipate conflict when they approach their spouse to address an issue or make a request. As a result, from the start, the spouses begin the interaction with a negative attitude. This attitude may be communicated with an edge in the voice, a defensive body posture, and a choice of words that precipitates a conflict. Because they expect a battle, they subconsciously prepare for one and communicate this to their husband both verbally and nonverbally.

Sometimes spouses may react in the opposite manner—they may attempt coercion by acting in a manner that is overly sweet and meek. Instead of acting assertively, they hope to lure the man into agreement and may even use sex as means of coercion. By acting dependent and deferring, they may feel that they are more likely to get their way.

The husband's reaction to either of these two approaches is not likely to be positive. When he is approached with a negative, condescending, or hostile tone, he may respond in kind, and conflict will escalate very quickly. The other approach is equally counterproductive, because the male may feel manipulated and demeaned. Spouses must recognize that neither approach is likely to be healthy for the marriage.

Instead, spouses must learn to contain their own frustration and accept that staying calm and using principles of assertive communication (discussed in the next section) are most likely to produce positive results. To start, they must recognize the emotional reaction they experience when they face their husband. When people anticipate conflict, they use automatic thoughts that escalate the conflict. Spouses should work to identify this cognitive pattern, as shown in the following example:

> A spouse describes an interaction with her husband when she approached him about a bill that is past due and remains unpaid. The therapist cues her

to try to go through the situation, as if it was unfolding at the moment, and identify the thoughts she is having. As she re-creates the situation, she thinks to herself, "Here we go again," "He disappointed me again," and "I guess I can never count on him." The therapist asks her to identify the feelings that go along with these thoughts. The spouse relates that she is getting more angry and is ready to "let him have it" when she sees him. Her heart is racing, her breathing has become more shallow, and she feels physically tense. As the therapist encourages her to role-play the scenario, he asks her to speak to him exactly as she would if he were her husband. She starts yelling at him about how irresponsible he is and that once again he screwed up, and now the family has to pay extra because of his carelessness.

Women need to understand how these thoughts contribute to the escalation of their feelings, and, following the tenets of cognitive-behavioral therapy, they need to replace these negative automatic thoughts with healthier ones, such as "I will stay calm," "We'll try to reach a solution," "If we work together, perhaps the problem will improve," and so on. Although turning off the negative thoughts is difficult, spouses must recognize that unless they do so, their reaction to their husband is not likely to change.

As evident in the previous example, spouses must also learn to recognize what signs their body sends them about being frustrated or angry. When they think about their husband, their body may become tense, their muscles may start twitching, their hands may become clenched, and their breathing patterns may change. Becoming more aware of these signs of physiological arousal may help them recognize that they are in the middle of a self-escalation that will likely result in a conflict. Instead, spouses and partners need to learn that before they approach their husband, they need to find ways of calming down. Various techniques can be helpful—taking a few deep breaths, lying down for a minute or two with their eyes closed and imagining a relaxing scenario, or using a progressive muscle relaxation procedure. When women become able to recognize their emotional state and use effective techniques to calm down before the interaction begins, they find that the conversation with their husband is more productive.

Women can learn to use these techniques not only prior to the start of the interaction but also if the interaction is beginning to turn into a conflict. Becoming more self-aware can help the woman keep track of her own reactions while she is talking with her husband. When she is able to catch herself becoming angry and tense, she may pause the conversation and remove herself so that she is able to calm down and bring her emotions under control. When people argue, they sometimes make the erroneous assumption that the argument must end in the resolution of the conflict. This expectation is counterproductive and only contributes to more intense negative emotions, especially when an argument does not seem to lead to the solution of the problem. Instead, it is helpful for spouses and partners to recognize that an issue can be placed on hold and returned to when everyone feels calmer.

In summary, after helping the spouse learn to identify the symptoms, causes, and treatment of ADHD, the therapist will find it is beneficial to help her recognize how being a partner of a male with this disorder is affecting her and how her negative reaction is contributing to the marital discord. Once she becomes better able to control her reactions, she then becomes better able to work to improve the patterns of communication between her husband and her. She will also become better able to help him develop coping techniques that will further diminish the impact of the symptoms of ADHD on the whole family.

Communication Skills. When spouses argue, maladaptive patterns of communication are responsible for many of the negative outcomes associated with marital conflicts. As many marriage counselors are fond of saying, rather than teaching couples *not* to argue, it is important to teach spouses *how* to argue. This old dictum is very relevant to relational patterns evident between men with ADHD and their partners. Because living with a man with ADHD can be a trying experience, many couples fall into dysfunctional patterns of communication where each argument serves to express each spouse's frustrations rather than being a vehicle for problem solving. Thus, after spouses learn about ADHD, develop appropriate expectations of their husband, and learn to control their anger, they are ready to learn how to resolve conflicts.

Effective communication exists when the following stages occur:

1. The sender is in a mental state conducive to communication.
2. The sender sends a clear and unambiguous message aimed at resolving a problem.
3. The recipient is in a mental state receptive to the exchange.

When communication breaks down, problems in at least one of these stages have occurred.

Helping the sender maintain a mental state conducive to effective communication was covered earlier in this chapter. When spouses understand the impact of the symptoms of ADHD and control their emotions so that they remain calm, they are more likely to be in a state of mind where they are able to communicate constructively. While in that state, they are less apt to formulate their communications as an attack.

When interacting with their husband, spouses need to make sure that they formulate their thoughts clearly. If a topic is being raised that previously has resulted in conflicts, it may be helpful for the spouse to make some written notes about the points that need to be communicated. Because the notes will usually be made while a person is calm, greater clarity of mind will be present, and the notes will be oriented toward constructive solutions. Making notes before the actual exchange has another major advantage—it allows the spouse to rehearse the interaction and prepare herself for possible outcomes. When anger escalates, it is often in situations where an unexpected response takes place that causes the person to scramble in an attempt to find a response. Rehearsing an exchange beforehand allows a careful examination of all possible responses, and the additional preparation will help the spouse remain calm and in control, because she is less likely to be caught off guard by what takes place during the exchange.

When communicating with their spouse, partners of men with ADHD should attempt to place themselves into the men's shoes and try to understand the conversation from the male point of view. Although this may be difficult, it will provide spouses the opportunity to understand the men's reactions. Here, the therapist can offer invaluable assistance. Understanding how issues of gender affect the men's response can help the women comprehend the reasons why their spouse says and does the things he does.

As with other topics covered in this chapter (and elsewhere in this book), resources can be helpful. For example, women can be asked to read books that outline, in approachable ways, the differences in communication patterns between men and women. Men are socialized to be problem solvers, and they communicate to come up with solutions. When engaged in a communication about a problem, men tend to suggest solutions in an attempt to resolve the issue. On the other hand, women often communicate in an attempt to gain support and to contemplate the problem. While expressing their thoughts, they are attempting to come up with their own solutions, and they hope that their spouse will provide support and encouragement. Gray's (1992) popular volume discusses the different expectations that men and women have when they communicate. Although somewhat gimmicky and simplistic, it makes these important points easy to understand, and therapists can expand on the ideas in the book to help spouses appreciate how issues of masculinity affect the ways in which men receive and express messages.

When sending messages to their spouse, women need to make sure that they do not sound controlling or condescending, because this will likely make the man feel emasculated. Both verbal and nonverbal messages should convey a level of respect usually expected in exchanges between two partners who are equals. Women need to make sure that they do not assume that the husband knows what they mean, and communications should not be condescending or sarcastic. Such exchanges will only anger the man, who will feel insulted. Similarly, women should be careful not to come off as though they know all the answers and their partner is clueless. Again, such an attitude will likely be met with a defensive reaction from the man.

Instead, it is helpful to communicate clearly and directly, while maintaining eye contact, in a setting where distractions are minimized (e.g., the television is turned off for the duration of the discussion). Because men with ADHD may have difficulties thinking about several issues at one time, it is important to address one matter at a time and try to bring it to a conclusion before moving on to another topic. When addressing an issue, spouses should remember that one discussion may not be sufficient to fully resolve a problem. If emotions run high, it may be sufficient to raise an issue, explain why it poses a problem, and postpone seeking final resolution until another time. Sometimes it can be very effective to say, "Let's both think about a solution and discuss it another time."

When bringing up a problem, spouses should avoid attacking their partner. It is not usually helpful to point out that the man is to blame, even if it truly is his mistake that created a problem. Wives should keep in mind that their husband usually means well, even though his effort may come up short. When the man makes a mistake, spouses should view it as just that—a mistake—and not willful misconduct. True, men with ADHD are likely to make more mistakes than most men, but pointing this out to them is not likely to be constructive. Instead, it is helpful to frame all problems as joint problems that do not belong to only one spouse or the other. In this way, neither spouse feels attacked, even if it becomes clear that one spouse is responsible for the mistake. When the problem is laid out as a joint issue that affects both spouses, it is more likely that both partners will collaborate in the solution, even if it is the behavior of one spouse that needs to change.

When communicating with men with ADHD, spouses may want to use an effective technique of expressing their feelings. By using "I messages," the spouse expresses her feelings and lays out a problem, but does not attack, and allows the problem to be defined as a joint issue that needs resolution. For example, in the previous vignette about a wife who becomes angry because the husband forgot to pay a bill, a constructive way to approach the husband may unfold in the following way:

> When the spouse discovers a past-due bill, she is vigilant about her feelings and recognizes that she is getting angry. She waits to approach her husband until she feels calmer and is able to speak with him rather than yell at him. When ready, she asks her husband to talk with her about something, and she makes sure that the conversation does not occur while he is watching a sports game or is in the presence of their children. She tells him that she just came across this unpaid bill and says, "Mike, when late charges are incurred, it causes additional stress on our finances. So, what can we do to address this problem?" In this way, a problem is identified, but the husband is not overtly blamed, even though both spouses know who is responsible for the missed payment. If the husband says, "I forgot again," the wife asks, "What can I do to help?" Because the man is not attacked, he is much more likely to be receptive to developing ways of addressing such problems (as further discussed next).

In sum, when working with spouses of men with ADHD, it is important to help the partner realize that she may sometimes communicate her feelings in ways that may exacerbate the problem. Instead, if the spouse understands why some of these problems take place and is able to control her negative feelings, she may be able to communicate with her husband more constructively. When such exchanges take place, it is more likely that effective solutions will be identified and implemented.

Role Definitions. In a marital (or similar) relationship, both partners usually gravitate toward certain tasks and roles expected of each person. Often these roles are unspoken but clearly understood. For example, the wife may attend to cleaning the house and cooking most meals, whereas the husband may attend to the repairs of the home, upkeep of the vehicles, and maintenance of the yard. When it comes to the kids, it is common for one parent to prepare them for school in the morning and the other to attend to homework. In relationships that work well, the division of roles is equitable, and the tasks necessary to run a home are divided in such a way that both partners have about an equal share, and both are comfortable with what is expected of them.

In relationships where the man has ADHD, the division of roles may become problematic. For example, the husband may neglect some of his house duties and may forget about deadlines, things he was supposed to do during a specific day, and so on. In such marriages, wives tend to become frustrated and may argue and complain about the tasks that are not being done. This complaining often makes the man feel inferior, and the wife risks the husband perceiving her as someone who always keeps tabs on him and gives him a hard time, which tends to create conflicts in the relationship, and the closeness between the spouses is likely to diminish.

The woman may also attempt to take on the duties that the husband is neglecting, which results in role strain, a phenomenon that takes place in a home where the woman is expected to attend to the usual duties expected of a wife and mother (e.g., attending to meals, shopping, and doing laundry) while also working and attending to the duties that her husband is neglecting (such as helping with homework, providing rides for the children, paying bills, etc.). When women take on more roles than they can comfortably handle, they become tired and frustrated and often distance themselves from their spouse. This distancing may take many forms, including a lack of interest in sex and intimacy, which men often find difficult to accept.

When a therapist is working with a couple where the man has been diagnosed with ADHD, the clinician should take stock of the roles that both partners play in performing all different tasks associated with running the home and attending to the children. When it is apparent that the wife is overwhelmed because she has taken on too many tasks, the therapist needs to intervene to help the couple restore a healthy balance of tasks and expectations.

One obstacle to this goal often becomes apparent when the wife of a man with ADHD decides that he is unable to perform a task effectively, and rather than argue about it, she prefers to just do it herself. The wife must come to understand how this decision affects the way she feels and what impact these feelings have on important aspects of the marital relationship (such as communication, closeness, and intimacy). The counselor should work with the spouse to help her understand that instead of taking on too much, she needs to let her husband carry his own load, even though some of the tasks may not be done as well as they would be if she decided to do them. When the wife becomes able to approach her husband and the marital roles with such an attitude, an equitable division of responsibilities between both partners will become possible, and her frustration will diminish.

Sometimes when a fair division of roles is overtly established, it becomes evident that the man truly is having difficulties attending to some of his responsibilities. For example, perhaps he is having problems organizing bills, keeping track of deadlines, and so on. It will be more effective for the therapist to work with the spouse and help her become a coach who can assist her husband in developing the skills he needs to be able to successfully perform the tasks expected of him in the marriage rather than to revert to old patterns where the wife simply takes over these tasks herself.

Coaching Techniques. Coaching is a new movement within the field of counseling. It is sometimes viewed as an alternative to formal mental health treatment, although coaching proponents are quick to point out that coaching is not a substitute for real psychotherapy (Buckley & Buckley, 2006). Essentially, a coach is a layperson (not a professional) who understands the nature of the needs of the client (e.g., the person with ADHD) and works collaboratively with the client to help him learn valuable skills. Thus, the coach is sort of a teacher and a support system, and the client voluntarily seeks the coach's expertise to learn new ways of doing things.

Coaching adults with ADHD is becoming more popular, and resources have been published for aspiring coaches (e.g., Ratey, 2008). Although Barkley (2006) succinctly pointed out that coaching clients with ADHD is not a substitute for competent mental health treatment and that therapeutic benefits of coaching have rarely been researched and remain unproven, providing coaching services in addition to mental health treatment may be beneficial. Because coaching is a relationship between peers, where one agrees to assist the other, it is not unlike peer tutoring offered in school, a technique that has been found to be very effective (as discussed in Chapter 11). Conceptually, it makes sense that some tenets of coaching may be useful in a marital (or similar) relationship where both partners regard each other as peers, and yet one may help the other with tasks and skills that need to be learned and implemented.

As a prerequisite of a coaching relationship, a contract must be established between the coach (in this case, the spouse) and the client (the man with ADHD). This contract must be voluntary for both parties, and both spouses must understand the terms and agree to them. The client with ADHD agrees to seek the coach's assistance to address a specific situation that he finds difficult. It must be noted that the contract must specifically state what goals will be worked on. It is not meant to be a general agreement authorizing the coach to intervene every time she encounters a deficiency in her mate. Such an arrangement is surely to fail, because the man will feel inferior and controlled. Instead, the client agrees to seek the coach's advice with specific situations in which he recognizes that he is missing certain skills that the coach (his spouse) can help him develop.

The manner in which the coach delivers the assistance is very important. The coach must be careful not to project a sense of superiority. If the husband feels that the wife feels she is always right and has all the answers, he is not likely to be receptive to the arrangement. The coach must understand that the client must ask her for assistance, and unsolicited advice likely will not be welcome. Thus, at the onset of the arrangement, the coach and her husband must understand and agree on what situations and skills the contract pertains to, when the man will seek advice (and that it is his choice to do so), and what attitude both must maintain for the arrangement to be successful.

There are many situations in which the wife can act as a coach. It is best when the man identifies the ways in which he would like his wife to assist. The need for this may become evident when a division of roles was established in the relationship (as discussed previously), and the man is having some difficulties keeping track of his duties, as shown in the following example:

> The husband is responsible for paying bills in the family, but he often forgets the deadline. He admits that he has difficulties remembering and asks his wife for suggestions about how she can help him keep track of the deadline. They mutually agree to designate two specific days per month to review all outstanding bills. As bills arrive in the mail, his wife places them in an in-basket on the desk to be reviewed and paid on the designated days. He also asks his wife to place all receipts for purchases in another box so that when he pays bills on the designated days, he can balance the accounts and know how much money is available for payments. When this is done, he asks his wife to sit with him while he writes the checks so that she can help him organize all items. He also requests her assistance in developing a filing system at home where all bills, credit card statements, and so on are kept. As these solutions are arrived at, the impetus for all assistance comes from the client, and the wife remains open to provide needed assistance when such is requested by the husband.

Coaching relationships may be established in many ways and are limited only by the comfort and creativity of both parties. It is common for men with ADHD to forget about appointments and work tasks expected of them. Although keeping a daily organizer (such as a calendar) can be helpful, men often forget to look in it each day. If the man desires such an arrangement, the wife can help him remember to look in his calendar, for example:

> The husband and wife agree that the wife will gently remind the husband every morning before he leaves for work to look in his planner. Although it is up to the husband to follow through on this reminder, the reminder is gentle and respectful, and the man does not feel controlled or bossed around

and knows that he is benefitting from this added structure. The husband may also ask his wife to remind him every evening (or at lunchtime, if she is available and willing to call him) to look in the calendar and make sure that he remains on top of things. She also agrees to help in other ways. During a conversation, when she hears her husband mention a forthcoming meeting or a deadline, she gently asks him whether he wrote this in his calendar. If he says he does not need to, she says that she will write it down on a piece of paper, just in case. She then gives it to her husband and lets him handle it in whatever way he feels is appropriate. Because the idea of the reminders came from the man in the first place, he is receptive to this approach, and her assistance and support help him improve his organizational skills.

If it seems too difficult for the man to remember to use a daily planner, the solution is redefined as a joint effort, and an aggregate family planer is established. A calendar is posted that becomes a master planner for house-hold activities and deadlines, including work-related tasks. Each day, the wife takes the lead and asks her husband what deadlines are coming up (including any work-related appointments and tasks), and all are written in the planner. Both spouses review the planner at various points through the day, and the planner then helps both partners remember about their duties. In such an arrangement, the husband gradually internalizes the use of the planner, and over time he goes on to establish and follow his own planner or calendar.

Although these examples focus on organizational skills, the coaching approach can be beneficial in situations that call for impulse control. For example, if the man admits that at times he has difficulties resisting temptation to spend more money than he planned, he can ask his wife to help him develop ways to limit his spending habits. He can leave all credits cards at home with the exception of the one he will need the most. He can discuss with his wife a reasonable limit on discretionary spending that he agrees to abide by, and he will call his wife when he is in a store and sees an item that he finds hard to resist (essentially asking his wife to help him process whether he really wants to buy the item). If he finds it hard to exercise enough control to call her, maybe he can agree to have his wife call him midway through the shopping trip to check on him. Although some of these suggestions may seem controlling, the therapist must keep in mind that perception of control is in the eye of the beholder. If the man *asks* for his wife to do so, in recognition that his own self-control is sometimes limited, he is much more likely to be receptive and will not view her behavior as an attempt to control him. This underscores the prerequisites of an effective coaching relationship: The man is the one who asks for help, both spouses discuss possible solutions, and both agree to a course of action, even though it will be the wife who will do the coaching. When successfully implemented, coaching can offer the husband or partner with ADHD the necessary assistance he needs to develop important skills to improve his self-control and organizational abilities.

SUMMARY

Sharing an intimate relationship with a man with ADHD can be a frustrating experience, and men with ADHD frequently experience conflicts with their spouse, girlfriend, or partner. To improve the marriage, and further reduce symptoms of this disorder, engaging spouses in treatment can be very beneficial. Although research in this area is only beginning to emerge, results of research studies have confirmed that men with ADHD exhibit further improvement when their spouse participates in counseling. The treatment can be delivered jointly with the man and the spouse, through family therapy (including the children), or by working separately with the man and the spouse. Each approach offers benefits and drawbacks, and any of these options may be appropriate with various clients.

When working with spouses of men with ADHD, therapists need to help them develop abilities to manage their own frustration and gain an understanding of how symptoms of this disorder affect many aspects of the man's contribution to the family. Both spouses may benefit from clarifying the definitions of their marital roles, and treatment can help them improve their ability to communicate and resolve problems. The spouse can also learn how to become a coach for her partner and through this approach provide needed assistance and support to him as he strives to control his symptoms.

10

Group Techniques

As described in the previous four chapters, individual counseling, parent training, and family therapy can be helpful to address many of the common core and secondary problems associated with attention deficit/hyperactivity disorder (ADHD). Common skills that are deficient in boys, male teens, and men with ADHD can be taught using psychoeducational and cognitive-behavioral methods, and those skills can be instrumental in improving functioning at home, in school, and in the workplace.

Some symptoms, however, are hard to address effectively in individual or family counseling. For example, problems with social skills are especially difficult to teach, and it has been known for some time that social skills taught away from peer settings generally do not transfer into actual social situations, and patients tend to revert to old patterns of behaviors when around peers (Bellack & Hersen, 1979). This phenomenon occurs primarily because cues and triggers that provoke reactions are not possible to fully re-create in individual or family counseling settings, and therefore there is no way to actually practice newly acquired skills in situations that resemble the actual interactions that take place among peers. For this reason, the acquisition of social skills is much more likely to occur in situations that involve peers, where vignettes that resemble social situations can be created and rehearsed. Peers provide many aspects that enhance the transfer effect, including the opportunity to re-create cues and triggers that lead to behavioral reactions.

In addition to social skills training, group counseling also allows development of other important skills. The ability to resolve conflicts among peers is an important component of adaptive social functioning. Boys, teens, and men with ADHD frequently experience conflicts with friends, classmates, and coworkers. Much of this is secondary to poor social skills, but some of it is also due to limited self-control, poor frustration tolerance, and excessive impulsivity. When these problems become evident among other members of a therapeutic group, the peers have the opportunity to express how they feel about the incident, something that rarely occurs in real life. This opportunity allows the patient to experience his behaviors from the vantage point of the recipients, offering him a unique opportunity to build insight and consider the impact of his behaviors on others. This increases motivation to change some of the problematic behaviors and contributes to greater therapeutic gains.

Group counseling offers additional advantages. Group settings, as described by Yalom (Yalom & Leszcz, 2005), after decades of practice and research with groups, allow various therapeutic factors to flourish. Of the 11 factors he identified, several have specific relevance to boys, teens, and men with ADHD. Individuals with this disorder often feel isolated and think that no one understands them. Within a group setting, especially when other clients with ADHD are members of the group, patients can experience a sense of empathy and universality—a feeling that their problems are common and often shared by others and that others understand and support them in their quest to feel better. Receiving this empathy helps clients with ADHD feel similar feelings toward others, increasing connectedness with peers and helping clients become able to express empathy outside of the therapeutic setting. As members support each other and develop positive feelings toward one another, group cohesion increases, and members develop a sense of ownership of the group and begin to work together to develop solutions for each other's problems. This cohesion can be very powerful, and it instills hope in the group members that the problems one experiences can be solved when everyone works together toward a common goal.

By observing behaviors of others, group members also learn about what works and what does not. Those behaviors that result in a positive outcome are more likely to be imitated, and those that result in conflict and undesired consequences are more likely to be extinguished. This imitative behavior contributes to learning new skills, especially those that involve interpersonal communication. In addition, as members share their successes and failures, this imparting of valuable information further promotes the learning of what works and what does not. All in all, the group setting provides many benefits, and group counseling can be a useful supplement to other therapeutic intervention used to help boys, teens, and men with ADHD.

RESEARCH SUPPORT

Although much anecdotal evidence exists that clinicians commonly use group counseling techniques to work with boys, teens, and men with ADHD, surprisingly little research has been performed on this topic. Most of the research has focused on social skills training attempted within group settings, and the initial results were mixed (Barkley,

2006). It was hypothesized that social deficits within boys with ADHD were very heterogeneous, and consequently social skills training helped some clients but not others. As Hinshaw (1992) pointed out, treatment that was limited to social skills training was too narrowly focused to help all boys with ADHD, although some made notable progress. Some males with ADHD may lack the knowledge of how to act when with peers, but others may know what to do and can verbalize the appropriate course of action, but they do not perform these behaviors in actual social situations because of impulsivity and poor frustration tolerance. Consequently, subsequent attempts at researching this approach expanded the focus of the groups beyond social skills training and included problem solving, conflict resolution, anger management, and communication skills.

Group counseling for boys with ADHD has been found to be effective as an adjunct to other treatment approaches (Pelham & Hoza, 1996). Frankel, Myatt, and Cantwell (1995) obtained similar results and replicated them with another group of children with ADHD (Frankel, Myatt, Cantwell, & Feinberg, 1997). Although their approach primarily focused on social skills training, other components were included, such as anger management.

Although formal group counseling with children and teens with ADHD has rarely been studied, peer-assisted interventions for specific problems and settings have received research support. For example, a student-mediated program has been found to be effective in reducing behavior problems on the playground (Cunningham et al., 1998), and the intervention was effective in improving behaviors not only of target students but also of those students who acted as peer monitors. In addition, student-mediated conflict resolution programs have been effective in reducing acting out within school settings (Cunningham & Cunningham, 1995). Although typically older students act as mediators, methods employing same-age peers have also been found to be effective, and schoolwide mediation programs where all students within a school are trained in the principles and techniques of peer mediation have successfully been used by some school districts (Johnson, Johnson, Dudley, & Burnett, 1992). Clinicians performing group counseling can use some of the skills and methods that have successfully been employed by these programs.

With adults, group counseling is widely considered to be an effective therapeutic method, but research on group counseling with adults with ADHD is very limited. In one study, Solanto and colleagues found that a manualized, group-based treatment for adults with ADHD was effective in helping participants improve their abilities to organize, manage time, and plan their daily activities (Ramsay & Rostain, 2008). Although impulsivity had not improved, the other therapeutic gains had a positive impact on the clients' overall functioning. Although more research is needed, the results obtained thus far are promising, and the use of group counseling is likely to offer benefits when it is delivered to supplement other treatment modalities for boys, teens, and men with ADHD.

GROUP INTERVENTIONS FOR BOYS
AND YOUNG TEENS WITH ADHD

Group counseling sessions for boys and young teens (up to age 14 or so) with ADHD are generally skill oriented and time limited. The therapist uses structured exercises to create a play situation during which the boys acquire and practice a given skill. The groups generally include four to eight participants. Smaller and larger groups can be difficult to work with, and boys in those groups are likely to derive less benefit.

Groups are usually implemented in 12- to 16-session, closed-ended cycles, maintaining the group membership constant and not allowing boys to join midway. Afterward, the cycle can be repeated after the addition or departure of some group members. Each cycle is usually divided into modules of 3 to 4 weeks in length. One model of such an approach is summarized next. Because it is focused on specific skills, it is assumed that boys who participate in this type of a group also receive other services—individual counseling, parent training, and so on—so that other needs not addressed in the group are being attended to. The group described next focuses on social skills training (and related aspects, such as problem solving and anger management), because teaching those skills in a nongroup environment is rarely useful. Other needs (psychoeducation, development of behavior management techniques for parents, etc.) can effectively be addressed in other treatment modalities.

Preparation for Group

When selecting group members, several factors should be considered. The groups should be homogeneous with regard to sex. A boys-only group will eliminate some of the gender dynamics that are present when children of both sexes interact with each other. Although those dynamics may be helpful to observe and address, they generally interfere with the specific goals of this group, particularly with older boys and young teens, when issues related to puberty may begin to alter group interaction.

Because boys of varying ages generally have different interests, limiting the age variation between the boys is usually necessary. This author has found it useful to conduct groups where all the boys are within a 2-year age difference. In addition, it is important to consider age-related play patterns. For example, boys aged 6, 7, and 8 may share similar concerns, as will boys aged 9, 10, and 11. Preteens and teens (aged 12, 13, and 14) will also likely relate to each other better if younger boys are excluded from the group. To maximize effectiveness, the therapist must create a social environment where all boys are peers and can relate to each other as members of a similar group to which they belong in real life.

Whether the group should be homogeneous with regard to diagnosis is an open question, but it may be helpful to include boys in the group who share some of the same problems. For example, boys who are impulsive and have difficulties getting along with peers may relate better to each other when they are in a group with other boys who have similar experiences. Practical considerations, however, must also be reviewed. If several members of the group are very hyperactive, managing the group may be too difficult. If all of the boys exhibit significant problems relating to each other, maintaining interests in activities may be a major challenge. Generally, it is helpful to have boys who present with similar concerns but vary somewhat in levels of severity and are able to at least minimally relate to each other. In addition, having some boys in the group who can model better behaviors may also be beneficial.

Other factors should also be considered when selecting group members. It is disruptive to the group when members leave, because the closed-ended nature of the group means others cannot be accepted until a new cycle begins. Thus, if several members leave, it may be difficult to continue when only two or three boys are left. Such a small group will not re-create a real social setting and will likely produce social interactions that do not closely resemble those evident in larger peer groups. For this reason, clinicians should take time to educate parents about the nature, length, and focus of the groups, so that parents are aware of these factors and commit to have their son complete the cycle.

The room where the group meetings will be held should be large enough to comfortably accommodate the group and should allow enough space to carry out the group activities. The place should include a table that will allow all members to fit around for those activities where this will be useful. In addition, some activities require the use of a stage-audience setup, and chairs for all the boys must be able to be arranged accordingly. Clinicians who plan to administer these groups need to ensure that the physical space will appropriately accommodate the activities.

Weeks 1 Through 4: Social Entry Skills

In the first session, the group should be described to the boys so that appropriate expectations are set. The boys should be told that various skills will be rehearsed to help them get along with each other. They will be expected to participate in play activities, and each member will be asked to take part in role-plays. The boys should expect that the therapist will have an agenda about what will have to be done in group, but the members will contribute their ideas. It is important that the group members recognize the structured nature of the group but also expect that they will be able to influence how the group activities take place.

Group rules must be set. These rules include basic safety rules (no running or hitting), sensible rules of conduct (hold voice levels at a comfortable pitch and volume—no yelling), and observance of appropriate language (no cursing or name calling). The need for privacy must also be explained so that group members recognize that any disclosure of personal information that takes place in the group, as well as the names of group members, must be kept confidential. It is helpful to begin the group by addressing these concerns and rules.

Some boys, especially those with high levels of impulsivity and hyperactivity, may have difficulties with some of these rules. Establishing a behavioral contact may be helpful. As described in detail in Step 4 of the parent training program (Chapter 7), one or two specific behaviors should be selected, and boys who are able to follow those rules during the group time should receive a small prize (a sheet of stickers or a small toy) at the end of the group. Of course, the clinician must be prepared with those items before such a program is initiated. If the boy's parents have also established a behavioral contract within the home, the boy's ability to observe group rules can further be reinforced by the parents by giving him an additional reward (points or chips or a specific extra privilege) at home. The more salient the rewards are that the boys will earn, the harder they will try to observe the rules while in the group. Clinicians should also note that when the boys strive hard to observe the group rules of conduct, they use self-control much in the same manner that they have to in other settings (in school, at home, etc.). Thus, learning to exercise better self-control in the group also helps them learn to use the same skills wherever else they are needed.

The first few sessions in the life of a group allow opportunities to observe how the boys play together and to teach them how to join play activity in a constructive and respectful way. In the first two groups, therapists can allow children to play with some toys that are given to the group by the therapist—building blocks, toy cars, and so on—and observe the patterns of their interactions. Consider the following example:

> Two groups of boys, each with two or three members, are sitting a few feet apart. One group is playing with toy cars, and another is playing with building blocks. After a few moments, one of the boys playing with building blocks becomes bored, looks around, and sees that a boy in the other group is playing with a toy truck. Immediately, he drops the building blocks on the floor, runs toward the other group, barges in on the boys' activity, and grabs the truck from the other boy's hand. That boy screams, "Give it back, I had it first!" while the other turns his back and starts playing with the truck. An argument starts, and the boys start hitting, pushing, screaming, and crying. The therapist intervenes, asking the boy who took the truck to give it back. He slams it to the floor and storms off to another corner, where he sits on the floor and cries.

This example illustrates a common difficulty that boys with ADHD exhibit when entering a social group. If such behavior is not observed spontaneously, the therapist can select a boy and ask him to go join boys in another subgroup and observe the manner in which this is done. It is helpful to allow the boys to continue with the play activity until a few such scenarios take place, before stopping play to help the boys process what went on.

During the part of the group when the therapist and members discuss what went on while playing, the therapist has an opportunity to ask the boys how they felt about being interrupted when others barged in on their activities. This opportunity allows the boys to talk to each other about methods of joining an existing group in a respectful manner. The therapist can then create an exercise and have the boys take turns practicing this scenario, as in the following example:

> A group of four boys is situated in the corner of the office. They are sitting on the floor and are playing with toy cars and building blocks. Another boy is with the therapist a few feet away. The therapist engages the boy just long enough to allow the others to begin playing. He then asks the boy to go join the others and observes whether he did so in a respectful manner. If so, he praises him and asks the others to express how they liked the behavior. If not, the therapist intervenes and pulls the boy aside, reviews the appropriate way to join a group, and allows him another chance to try.

One by one, each remaining member should have the opportunity to join the others, and others observe and comment on whether the manner was collaborative and respectful. At the end of this activity, to increase the saliency of the motivation and effort, the therapist can give the boy who improved the most a certificate or a small prize.

As the sessions continue, the therapist should monitor whether the boys begin to spontaneously use this new skill. As they do so, the therapist should use a "caught you being good" technique by pointing out each instance when social entry was performed proactively. Again, to further increase encouragement, the therapist can give a boy a "good behavior slip" (or another form of a token) every time he is observed to enter a peer group appropriately, and those with the most slips or tokens may exchange them for a small prize at the end of the session.

Weeks 5 Through 8: Communication and Listening Skills

The next phase of the group teaches the boys to play cooperatively while they are in a peer group. This set of interventions is aimed at increasing the attention span of the participants and helping them suppress the impulse to interrupt and take over an activity or a conversation. To create a situation that feels real, the therapist must arrange for the group to participate in an interaction where collaboration is required, such as play activities or games where the boys must take turns and respond to each other's input.

Various board games can be useful. A number of games provided by vendors such as the Creative Therapy Store offer opportunities to create such interactions. For example, a therapeutic activity can be built around the Self-Control Game (Berg, 1990):

> Boys sit in a circle around the game board. As each boy rolls the dice, he moves around the board. As he lands on squares that require him to solve problem vignettes where self-control must be used, he reads a question (or the therapist can read it for him) and tries to answer it, and if he becomes stumped (or does not give an appropriate answer), the other boys may provide additional suggestions, but only those who raise their hand before speaking will be asked to contribute (to teach impulse control). Those who did not call out and had the right answer (meaning they listened) may receive a token, and the boy with the highest number of tokens at the end of the session receives a prize.

This scenario teaches several skills—impulse control, listening (so that each boy can think about an appropriate answer), and problem solving. There are many similar games on the market that allow the clinician to use themes most relevant to the particular members of the group—impulse control, anger management, behavior skills, conduct management, social skills, and so on. Each of these games would be appropriate to use in the activity just described.

Exercises that focus on building these skills can be created without using board games. For example, one technique involves the creation of a simulated television interview.

> Two boys volunteer (or are selected) to perform the interview. One boy is designated as the interviewer, and the other is the interviewee. The two boys should sit at a table in the front of the room, and the others should sit a small distance away and act as the audience. The interviewer asks the interviewee questions about what he likes, what he does in school, what sports he participates in, whether he recently got a new toy or game, and so on, and the audience must listen. After the interview is over, the therapist asks the boys some questions about what was said during the interview. Boys in the audience receive points for each correct response. The activity is brief and repeated during the session enough times so that each boy is a member of the audience for the same number of times. At the end of the session, the boy with the most points receives a prize.

These examples are just two of many activities that can be used to focus on listening and communication skills. The goal of each exercise is to create a situation that requires group participants to listen. As they suppress the impulse to call out or barge in, they are learning important self-control skills that are valuable not only in social situations but also in school and within the home.

Weeks 9 Through 12: Problem-Solving Skills

Boys with ADHD, especially those with symptoms of impulsivity, are very reactive and often cannot suppress the urge to act immediately. Thus, they find it difficult to use the steps involved in effective problem solving, because they tend to implement the first thought that comes to mind, without thinking through the situation more completely. Group activities can be used to teach them to slow down and implement a sequence of steps that improves effective problem solving:

1. They need to learn that the problem first needs to be elucidated and defined accurately so that it becomes evident what the true nature of the difficulty really is.
2. Once the problem has been accurately defined, it is necessary to brainstorm possible behaviors that can be performed to fix the problem and list them without making a decision about which option will be selected.
3. When the list is complete, the consequences of each alternative should be anticipated and identified, and a cost–benefit analysis should be performed.
4. After each possibility has been analyzed, the one behavior most likely to be effective in solving the initial problem should be selected.

Clinicians should look for activities that necessitate and promote this sequence of steps.

As with other examples discussed in this chapter, the therapist can use naturally occurring situations that require the use of these skills and/or create situations within the group that will call for the use of problem-solving strategies, as in the following example:

> The therapist can prearrange a play situation where one or two members of the group will not have enough toys to participate. This will pose a problem, because the boys will have to figure out who will be able to play. Rather than allowing the group to select a student who will be rejected, the therapist should help the group implement the sequence of steps for effective problem solving. Possible solutions may include taking turns playing while one boy at a time sits out and plays with the therapist, and all take turns doing so, or asking for two volunteers to play with a different item while the rest of the group plays with the main toys and then switching activities so everyone has a turn.

Promoting the sequence of steps to resolve this problem will help the boys think about ways of being able to resolve similar problems that occur in their daily life, especially with peers.

Board games can also be used. For example, the Circle of Friends Game (Childswork/Childsplay, 1999) can be very helpful.

> The game requires boys to take turns throwing dice and moving the specified number of spaces on the board. As they do so, they encounter squares that ask them to turn over various cards, and each card presents a common

vignette about social situations that require a solution. The boy who turned the card should then be assisted to follow the steps to define the problem, come up with alternatives, evaluate each one, and select the best one for implementation. If he is able to successfully do so, he receives points. If he becomes stuck along the way, however, others can help and will receive points for each helpful suggestion, so long as they were first called on to contribute (to reduce their calling out and to help them control impulsive reactions). The board is circular, and the game continues until the therapist indicates the last go-around. At the end of the game, the boy with the most tokens receives a prize.

Similar games are also available online and can be accessed during group. One example is Out on a Limb (University of Illinois at Urbana–Champaign, n.d.). This game works like an online book, where viewers click on one page at a time and follow a child who has gotten angry at friends and must find a solution to the problem. As each subsequent card is revealed, group participants can anticipate what the next screen will say, and those who get the right answers can be rewarded with points.

These examples are just some of the many methods that therapists can use to encourage members to implement an effective problem-solving strategy. It is important to teach the boys what the steps are, but situations should then be created that allow group members to practice those skills. The more real and natural the situation, the more likely the skills will be internalized, and the transfer of learning outside the group setting will be more probable.

Weeks 13 Through 16: Anger Management and Peer Conflict Resolution

Anger management is arguably the most important of the modules, and sometimes it is effective to extend the group cycle a week or two if this component requires additional work. As with problem-solving skills, it is necessary to identify and teach an effective sequence of steps, and practice opportunities must be created to help each boy internalize these skills. Because the skills used in effective anger management are similar to those used in effective problem solving, it is helpful to address problem solving first (as described previously) and then proceed to anger management. Anger management is more difficult than problem solving. After boys have practiced problem-solving strategies in situations that do not promote frustration or anger to a significant degree, they will find it easier to use a similar approach when learning to control their anger.

Once again, it is important to remember why effective anger management is so difficult for boys who are impulsive. When they experience a rush of emotion, they have difficulties containing this reaction, and consequently they say or do the very first thing that comes to mind. Often they do so before they are consciously aware that they are angry.

As described by Nay (2004), it is important to catch the escalation of the emotion as early as possible, because the threshold of control can quickly be exceeded, and then an outburst is difficult to contain. The following sequence of steps can be useful:

1. Recognize the physiological signs and signals that an emotion is being evoked.
2. Reduce the physiological arousal.
3. Identify whether the emotion is really anger—it is possible that anger is a secondary emotion (e.g., originally evoked by fear or hurt feelings).
4. Depending on the feeling, generate alternatives available for expressing it.
5. Evaluate each alternative.
6. Select the one that is most appropriate.

As with other activities discussed in this chapter, the therapist should select activities that will allow group members to exercise these skills. Again, board games can be helpful, for example, the Anger Control Game (Berg, 2000).

As the boys roll the dice and travel around the board, they turn over cards that provide a common social scenario and contain questions about events and feelings. For each vignette, the boys are asked to describe the pre-cipitating event, how the event made them feel, what bodily sensations and thoughts went along with each feeling, what possible solutions may be implemented, and which choice is likely to be the best. Depending on the completeness and accuracy of the answer, the boys earn points. As one boy answers, others are also asked to think of (and share) examples of similar situations, and they may receive additional points, especially if the boy with the card becomes stumped for a response.

Identifying bodily sensations involved in the anger response is partic-ularly important. Impulsive children react so quickly that their catching themselves being frustrated or angry is very difficult. Their becoming more aware of their bodies and how their bodies signal feelings to them can be helpful to slow down the speed of the initial reaction. Boys can be taught to quickly go through a body checklist—"What are my arms and hands doing?" ("Am I clenching my fists?"), "Do I feel really warm?" "Do my legs feel like I want to kick?" and so on. A variety of handouts can be helpful, and boys should be encouraged to carry these with them to con-sult as needed. Once the boys identify the arousal, they must be taught techniques to prevent its escalation, for example, leaving the situation to go to a quiet place and counting to 10 while taking a few deep breaths.

The cognitive component is equally important. Each time an event awakens feelings, the boy is taught to recognize not just how he feels but also what he thinks about the event. Following the tenets of cognitive-behavioral approaches, it is not the event but the perception and interpretation of the event that determines the feelings, and teaching the boy to recognize how he thinks about frustrating events is important.

While playing, the boys identify their bodily sensations, thoughts, and resulting feelings. As each situation is portrayed, the boys in the group are asked for alternative thoughts and perceptions that will result in feelings other than anger. As each boy provides such examples, he earns points. The game is played through the session until everyone has had a chance to make several contributions, and at the end of the session, the boy with the most points receives a prize.

In a manner that resembles inoculation training, it is helpful to create opportunities for boys to practice the newly acquired anger management skills in actual social interactions. The therapist may look for natural events where frustration and anger come up between members, for example, when two boys have to learn to share the same toy they wish to play with, or the boys must jointly decide on a play activity, and the one whose idea was not chosen has to deal with it constructively. The therapist may also create situations where anger may be provoked by asking a boy to perform a behavior that may anger others or by modeling a behavior that may evoke anger. For example, while the boys are playing, the therapist can barge into an activity and start taking away the toys. As this happens, the therapist can ask each boy to identify his feelings and how his body is signaling to him that he is getting angry. Then the ways of responding to this situation can be reviewed, asking the boys to respond to the therapist as if he or she were a peer. Along the way, the boys are reminded of the lessons they learned while playing the anger game and are asked to talk about their body sensations, thoughts, and feelings. When they become frustrated but react in a positive, constructive way, they are rewarded with points that can be exchanged for a prize at the end of the session.

As the group progresses, especially if the group life is extended to allow more time to work on anger management skills, it is helpful to teach the boys to take on various roles in resolving conflicts that involve anger. As described by Cunningham, Cunningham, and Martorelli (2001), teaching mediation skills may be helpful. The mediator is trained to remain objective and act only as an intermediary to help both sides resolve their own problems, as in the following example:

> When two boys in the group begin to argue about a toy, the therapist can model the behavior used by a mediator. The therapist asks the boys to stop arguing and take turns telling their story. As the first boy describes his side, the other boy is reminded to stay quiet (even if he disagrees) and listen. When the first boy is finished, the therapist summarizes what was said (without agreeing or disagreeing) and then asks the second boy to tell his side, after which time his position is summarized by the mediator. The therapist then asks both boys to suggest solutions, and the disputants review the pros

and cons of each suggestion. The disputants then choose a solution and agree to abide by it. As this unfolds, other boys are watching. At the end, the group reviews what happened and whether this approach was effective.

It is helpful to extend the group life long enough to allow each member at least one opportunity to be a disputant and one opportunity to be a mediator.

GROUP INTERVENTIONS FOR OLDER MALE TEENS AND MEN WITH ADHD

Group counseling sessions with younger clients usually are highly structured and oriented toward the development of specific skills. Thus, they generally follow a closed-ended format divided into modules aimed at specific goals accomplished through structured activities. Because the therapist must remain in charge, especially with boys who are impulsive and/or hyperactive, group dynamics do not generally receive much attention, and process-oriented factors are not used (at least overtly) to significantly augment the therapeutic effects.

Groups with adults and older teens do not have to be quite as structured and regimented, and process-oriented therapeutic factors can be harnessed. Groups can be open-ended, with new members joining as seats in the group become available. Although the group can still include modules, they can be flexibly scheduled, and their length can vary, depending on the needs of the members. It is still helpful to focus on the development of skills, but a variety of methods can be used to promote skill building, including interactional factors, modeling, didactic presentations, practice exercises, and so on. The group may address not only social skills training (and related factors) but also psychoeducation about the disorder, development of skills that improve performance-oriented settings (such as school or work), and work on issues that affect relationships with spouses and significant others. Because of its broader focus and longer duration, this type of group may be used as monotherapy (perhaps in addition to treatment with medications) or as an adjunct to individual and/or couple counseling.

Preparation for Group

When selecting group members, therapists should think about whether prospective members will be able to communicate with each other and work together. For teens and young adults, it may be helpful to keep the group homogeneous with regard to sex, because young men may still be affected by gender dynamics and may either feel awkward and self-conscious in front of young women or try to impress them. Although those dynamics may be helpful to address, they generally do not closely relate to the specific skills that male teens and men with ADHD need to develop to manage the symptoms of this disorder. When the group is made up of older adults, however, a heterogeneous makeup may be beneficial in some cases. If women are present in the group, they may provide an alternate viewpoint that may be beneficial for the male group members. For example, when talking about relational issues, women may help the men understand the reactions and feelings of their girlfriend or spouse, which may help the men develop more effective ways of communicating with the women in their life.

Although strictly limiting the age variation is not necessary, the therapist should think about the group composition and make sure that the members will have similar life concerns. For this reason, it may be helpful to limit age variation in groups with teens and men in their early 20s. For groups composed of older adults, age variation usually does not matter.

As with younger boys, it may be helpful to limit the diagnostic heterogeneity of the group members. To help them relate to others who have similar experiences, the therapist should ensure that the participants exhibit similar problems. Because older teens and young men are rarely hyperactive, the group leader will not have difficulties managing a group where all members exhibit impulsivity or other symptoms of ADHD. As with boys, it is helpful to vary members somewhat with regard to the level of the severity of symptoms. In this way, those with fewer problems with impulsivity may help those who are more impulsive, and those with fewer problems with inattentiveness or disorganization may help others who have more problems in these areas.

Because exercises that involve physical activity and require rearrangement of the group room are rarely employed, space considerations are not usually an issue. The room must be large enough to accommodate the members, and a table may be useful so that some activities that involve writing can be carried out comfortably.

At the beginning of the group, and each time a new member joins the group, the group should be described to the participants so that appropriate expectations are set. Clients should be informed that group sessions will focus on building skills to reduce impulsivity and distractibility/disorganization, especially focusing on how these problems impact personal relationships and success at school or in work settings. The group will involve sharing personal experiences and participating in activities. The therapist will have an agenda about what will be covered in the sessions, but each session will be tailored to the needs of all members.

Group rules must be set. As with younger boys, these rules should include basic safety rules (no physical contact), sensible rules of conduct (hold voice levels at a comfortable pitch and volume—no yelling), and observance of appropriate language (no name calling). The therapist should be more flexible about the use of strong language and recognize that older male teens and adult men often use strong language (e.g., curse words) when they talk, and prohibiting this language all together will make the group seem very artificial. It is important, however, to communicate to the members that they must be respectful of each other.

The need for privacy must also be stressed. Group members have to agree that any disclosure of personal information that takes place in the group, and the names of group members, must be kept confidential. In addition, it is generally helpful to limit outside contact between group members. It is common for group therapists to discourage contact between group members outside of the group setting and to require any group contact that occurred on the outside to be brought into the group so it can be discussed (Yalom & Leszcz, 2005). Discouraging contact is needed to prevent outside relationships between group members, for example, developing close friendships or starting a sexual relationship (which can be a particular concern if the group involves members of both sexes). A strong relationship between group members outside of the group setting will usually have an adverse impact on the group. When the relationship is positive, those involved in it tend to form a strong coalition within the group, primarily supporting each other. When the relationship deteriorates or becomes conflicted, the tension significantly affects the group and may take over the agenda, thus preventing the group from addressing issues that are important to other members. For this reason, many group therapists advise participants that those who become personally involved with each other outside the group setting will be asked to leave the group.

Process-Oriented Therapeutic Factors

Groups with older teens and adult men allow the therapist to balance leader-induced structure with member-directed focus. Although structured activities play an important part in the group (as discussed in the next section), members also get to know each other as people and begin to develop relationships (within the group setting) with each other. As the group continues, group members slowly begin to form connections with other members, and patterns of interactions emerge that allow the development of various therapeutic factors (Yalom & Leszcz, 2005). Group members begin to recognize that they all share certain experiences and struggles, and they get some comfort from knowing that others also experience similar difficulties (universality). By hearing other members' stories, participants learn that they can find ways of coping with their problems and improving their life. This, in turn, instills hope and a motivation to try. As the group members share their stories, the empathy and support they experience from others helps them feel cared about and respected, improving their sense of self-worth.

This experience can especially be helpful for teens and men with ADHD. Sharing experiences with each other can help them recognize the various ways in which symptoms of this disorder have affected people's lives. They can begin to relate to each other with regard not only to the ways in which they display impulsivity, restlessness, distractibility, or disorganization but also to the ways in which having some of those symptoms has affected their masculinity and ability to relate to others as a male. Sharing those stories and learning to recognize the effects of those symptoms on their life may truly help connect members to each other, thus enhancing group cohesion and fostering the development of a working alliance.

As members interact, especially after they have gotten to know each other for some time, they begin to act toward each other in ways that are similar to those they act toward other people in their life, for example, their peers, coworkers, or significant others. This allows the therapist (and other members of the group) to experience the behavior in a more natural setting, because the person is no longer on his best behavior and acts in a way that is real and natural for him. As a result, interventions that will target those behaviors, especially when coming from members with whom the client has already connected personally, will be more likely to hit home and transfer outside of the group into the client's real life.

When group members have gotten to know each other, they create a social setting each time they interact. Within such a setting, they are able to observe the behaviors of others and learn about what works and what does not. Those behaviors that result in a positive outcome are more likely to be imitated, and those that result in conflict and undesired consequences are more likely to be extinguished. This contributes to the members learning new social skills. Because these new skills will be learned in a social setting, especially one in which the person has become an active member, the transfer of therapeutic gains into other settings will be more likely.

Development of Skills

In addition to teaching process-oriented factors, it is necessary for the therapist to help men with ADHD learn skills to control the symptoms of this disorder and/or to build compensatory strategies to address any residual symptoms.

The therapist should consider what the most appropriate goals for the group experience are. Some men may manage symptoms of ADHD through medications and attend the group as the only psychotherapeutic modality in which they participate. For them, the group experience should include a broader focus, because some of the issues commonly addressed in other forms of counseling (e.g., psychoeducation about the disorder) are not being addressed elsewhere. The therapist should also keep in mind, however, what goals are best suited for the group setting and spend most of the time addressing that component. As discussed with groups for boys, the one aspect of therapeutic interventions where groups provide a unique opportunity is the building of social skills. Consequently, therapists should make sure that they maximize this component of therapy groups, because the learning of social skills is not as effective when done in other therapeutic modalities. Members who have significant treatment needs in other areas may be referred to individual or family treatment to address those issues.

Although the development of social skills should be the central focus, other areas can nevertheless be addressed as the group sessions continue. Although these areas may be addressed in other treatment modalities in which members may participate (e.g., individual counseling), the additional support that the group provides will likely reinforce the therapeutic gains attained elsewhere in treatment. Thus, the following discussion will focus on a number of skills that can successfully be addressed in group settings.

Psychoeducation. Men with ADHD may have learned about the disorder when they first entered treatment, and they may have read books, articles, or handouts about ADHD, but they probably have not met many other men with the disorder. Allowing men with ADHD to share their knowledge of the disorder with each other can be very beneficial, because it allows the group members to hear a variety of information about the etiology, symptoms, and treatment. The therapist can act as a filter to challenge any information that does not appear to be credible.

This sharing of information may be particularly effective when men with ADHD who are on medications share their stories. Many men are reluctant to use medications and feel that accepting the need for medications is a sign of failure and personal weakness. Hearing how other men struggle with, and perhaps overcome, some of these perceptions and yet retain their masculinity may be very helpful for men who still grapple with this issue. Although therapists often make great strides in addressing this issue in individual counseling, and medical professionals similarly address it when they see their patients during office visits, nothing seems to hit home as much as when the information comes from a peer—another man.

Social Skills. Two sets of factors will simultaneously contribute to the improvement of social skills among group members—the process-oriented factors (described earlier in this chapter) and skill-oriented training initiated by the therapist. It is important to recognize that both of these components are synergistic and magnify each other's effects. The use of exercises not only provides opportunities for building new skills and practicing some situations but also triggers the members to interact, thus helping them get to know each other and form a therapeutic alliance. As the bond between group members strengthens, and they begin to act naturally with each other, their reaction to exercises that the therapist brings into the session will be more reflective of how they act in real life. At that point, interventions implemented by the group leader, and further reinforced by other group members, will become much more effective. Thus, group leaders should allow a developing group time for members to talk to each other and share how they are doing, but leaders should also include some exercises that will further stimulate the members to interact with each other.

Group therapists who work with adults with ADHD should develop a library of resources from which group exercises can be selected. For example, a three-volume series of *Creative Therapy* workbooks (Dossick, 1988, 1990, 1995) provides 52 exercises in each volume that may be used to generate discussion in groups. A wide variety of stimuli are available that allow group leaders to select those that are appropriate for the focus and level of longevity of a given group. Many other books are available that also provide exercises to promote group activities.

In the early stages of the formation of a group, or when an existing group has undergone a membership change, the exercises should focus on developing comfort with disclosure rather than concrete cognitive skills. The group therapist may ask the members to draw a likeness of an important person in their life or make a drawing that represents something they would like to accomplish in their life. To stimulate conversation members pass around these drawings and query each other about the content.

As group members become more comfortable with each other, exercises can focus more directly on social skills. Members can draw on a recent social interaction that resulted in their feeling happy or upset. This exercise can propel members to start talking to each other about what happened and how the situation unfolded. As the scenario is related, the therapist has the opportunity to use cognitive-behavioral interventions to illustrate some reasons why the situation did not unfold as planned. For example, a dialogue can be role-played by a client and another group member. As the client relates what was said to him, the therapist can ask him what he thought the other person meant when he said various things to the client. Each member may reveal underlying faulty assumptions and negative automatic thoughts. The therapist can use a variety of cognitive-behavioral techniques to dispute these misattributions, including Beck's collaborative empiricism or Ellis's methods of disputing (both discussed in Chapter 8). The therapist should enlist the participation of other group members in this process so that it is apparent that the group as a whole is helping the client.

This approach can be implemented not only by using concrete stimuli, such as drawings, but also by recreating vignettes from the client's life, in a manner similar to some principles of psychodrama. Consider the following example:

> A client wants to work on an argument that occurred between his wife and him while his children were watching. The situation can be re-created in the group by asking other members of the group to play the roles of the client's spouse and his children. The client (the protagonist) describes to each participant the attributes of the person that he or she will be recreating. Of course, as this is taking place, the therapist and the group become exposed to the assumptions that the protagonist is making about the people in the scenario, and the therapist should begin to plan to address these assumptions during the processing portion of the group.

As the scenario unfolds, the group members play the roles assigned to them and verify with the protagonist that they are accurately (in the protagonist's perception) portraying the characters. After the scenario concludes, the processing portion begins, during which the protagonist, as well as other group members, take turns expressing how they felt during the exercise. If the group feels that the protagonist overreacted or likely misinterpreted the intentions of some of the people in the actual situation, the group can help the protagonist construct a different perception, and the exercise is again performed to help the protagonist exercise a different way of behaving.

This exercise can have a powerful impact on the client, because it allows him to become exposed to others' perceptions of him and his behaviors. In addition, other group members also benefit, because scenarios re-created in groups are common and occur in the life of many people. Repeated participation in these forms of exercises can help group members develop and practice social skills that can improve their relationships with the peers, coworkers, and significant others in their life.

Problem-Solving Skills. As discussed earlier, the development of appropriate problem-solving skills is likely to contribute to an improvement in self-control and a decrease in impulsivity. Because men who are impulsive find it difficult to suppress the urge to act immediately, they do not use the steps involved in effective problem solving, because they tend to act on the first thought that comes to mind, without thinking through the situation more completely. Group activities can be used to teach them to slow down and implement the sequence of steps (outlined previously in this chapter) that improves effective problem solving.

The therapist can use naturally occurring situations to illustrate these skills. As group members discuss events in their life, many times the situations will involve a problem that needs to be thought through to arrive at the best solution, as shown in the following example:

> The client relates that a boss at work asked him to perform a job that is not part of his regular work duties. Employing the steps discussed earlier, the group is encouraged to help the member define the problem appropriately, for instance, is it that the job really is not part of his regular work duties, or perhaps do his work duties involve that job, but the client does not know how to do it or dislikes the nature of the task? The potential solutions will have to be different for each of those possibilities.
>
> Next, the group helps the client generate alternative reactions to this situation. For example, if the job really is not within his expected duties, the client may refuse to do it, do the job anyway, or complain to the supervisor's boss. Each of those options should then be thought through so that the pros and cons of each potential solution become evident. In the end, the client selects which option seems best for his particular situation.

In this process, the client and all other members of the group have an opportunity to learn problem-solving skills. Along the way, additional skills must also be used—stopping the urge to react right away and controlling the negative emotional reaction that may accompany the situation (more about this in the next section). The therapist should make sure that gradually, as group sessions continue, all members of the group have the opportunity to present similar problems and receive assistance from other group members in building impulse control and problem-solving skills.

Anger Management. Many of the vignettes that clients relate in groups commonly include negative affect, especially anger. When anger is provoked, impulsive men experience a quick rush of emotions that is often difficult for them to control. It is helpful to devote group time to help members develop more effective anger management skills.

As previously described in this chapter, effective anger management requires recognition of physiological signals that were evoked, proper identification of the emotion (e.g., does anger reflect underlying fear or hurt feelings?), generation of alternatives available to express it, evaluation of each alternative, and selection of the most appropriate course of action. As described in other portions of this chapter, the therapist should use opportunities presented by group members to illustrate the steps needed to control anger outbursts. Consider the following example:

> A group member talks about a fight he recently had with his spouse when she told him that she did not want him to go over to a friend's house to watch a football game. Following the sequence of steps, the group members help the client identify the specific emotion (likely, disappointment) and the signals his body was sending him that he was getting angry (his body got stiffer, heart started racing, breathing became more shallow). Group members then help the client think about ways to calm himself down before he reacts—perhaps by walking away for a moment, taking a few deep breaths, sitting or lying down, and relaxing his body. The group helps the client recognize that once he is calmer, he is better able to think clearly and come up with effective strategies to address the situation. Perhaps he can talk with his wife and find out why she did not want him to go. Perhaps she was looking forward to something both of them can do. Group members can relate to the client examples of similar situations they experienced in their life and how these situations were resolved.

Once again, when using this approach, all members of the group have an opportunity to learn anger management, along with additional skills, such as relaxation, identification of feelings, and impulse control. The therapist should make sure that gradually, as group sessions continue, all members of the group have the opportunity to discuss similar situations and receive assistance from other group members in building anger control skills.

Organizational Skills. Group members may also need help improving their organizational skills and developing ways to keep track of their responsibilities. Once again, the therapist can promote group members to help each other and share various techniques that may be used to improve their life.

As group members relate their own experiences, it may become apparent that a client is disclosing difficulties with remembering his responsibilities. A coaching model, further described in Chapter 9, is a good approach that allows group members to help each other. The basic principle revolves around skill building in a peerlike relationship, where the client is in charge of whether he wants the help, and others provide assistance, but only when they are asked, as shown in the following example:

> A client discloses an argument he had with his wife because he forgot to pay a bill on time and now has to pay late charges. Other group members relate similar experiences and ask the client whether he has difficulties keeping track of any other deadlines, appointments, and so on. If this is revealed, the therapist can facilitate group members to act as coaches to help the client develop organizational strategies.
>
> Group members ask the client whether he would like them to help identify strategies that may improve organization. If he agrees, the group suggests to the client to keep a calendar, record reminders in his PDA, or set his computer to issue daily notes about what he needs to accomplish during any given day. Group members who have used some of these approaches give him tips about what worked and what proved a little more difficult. As the group continues, all members rally around the client with the problem and help him benefit from their past experiences. The therapist can further assist with this process by having materials ready about common techniques that can be used to provide daily reminders (instructions how to use calendar software, etc.).

As with the other examples, this approach allows all group members to learn from each other and share experiences, tips, and strategies. Because the advice comes from peers, the client may be more receptive, especially when the other group members also have ADHD and disclose how the symptoms have affected their life. In addition, all group members benefit by participating in the discussion and hearing others' experiences with similar problems and solutions. Along the way, as group members reach out to help each other, group cohesion further improves, and the therapeutic alliance within the group strengthens.

SUMMARY

Although individual counseling, parent training, and couple counseling can be effective in addressing many symptoms of ADHD, the development of social skills is rarely effective unless the new skills are learned among peers. For this reason, group counseling can be helpful as an adjunct to other treatments, and results of research studies have confirmed that teaching social skills and related abilities (e.g., anger management) in group settings is effective.

With boys and young teens, the groups should be focused and structured. It is helpful to adopt a closed-ended format and administer a modular program that focuses on specific goals, including the improvement of social entry skills, communication and listening skills, problem-solving skills, and anger management skills. Each component should be addressed through exercises, and ample practice opportunities should be provided to help participants rehearse their newly acquired skills.

With older teens and adult men, groups can be more open-ended, and therapists have the opportunity to harness the benefits of process-oriented factors, not just focused skill training. When relating within the group, members connect to each other, and group cohesion increases. When members experience empathy and support and come to recognize the universality of their experience, they find it easier to strive hard to manage their symptoms and develop necessary compensatory strategies. In addition, when members get to know each other, the therapeutic group becomes a peer group, and members begin to act toward each other in ways that are similar to those they use with their peers, coworkers, and significant others. As this occurs, all interventions used in the group become more effective, because they are, in effect, administered within the clients' peer group. Consequently, the transfer of therapeutic gains into other settings is much more likely.

Educational Interventions

Educational Modifications

Boys, male teens, and men with attention deficit/hyperactivity disorder (ADHD) exhibit difficulties in educational settings so commonly that school-related problems are considered to be a central feature of the disorder. For a clinician to diagnose ADHD, the *Diagnostic and Statistical Manual of Mental Disorders* (*DSM-IV*; American Psychiatric Association, 1994) requires the presence of impairment in school, work, or social functioning, and the vast majority of boys and teens with ADHD exhibit difficulties in school (Hinshaw, 2002). Areas of impairment include difficulties completing work, poor homework compliance, low test grades, and a variety of behavioral difficulties that frequently results in conflicts with teachers and peers. For this reason, the most effective treatment strategies are considered to be multisystemic, usually including three loci of intervention: domestic (individual counseling, parent training, etc.), educational (instructional modifications, classroom behavior management), and medical (use of medications). Home-related interventions were discussed in the preceding chapters, medical approaches are discussed in the last section of this volume, and educational approaches are discussed in this and next chapters.

The two symptom clusters of ADHD are likely to present with different problems in the classroom. Boys who are impulsive and hyperactive commonly have difficulties remaining in their seat, appear excessively fidgety, call out answers, disrupt the work of others, and so on. Although hyperactivity tends to diminish with age, teenagers with ADHD (combined, or predominantly hyperactive-impulsive type) generally continue to exhibit impulsive behaviors—they intrude on others and have difficulties controlling the urge to say or do things unrelated to the academic tasks at hand. These problems commonly persist into adulthood, and college students with ADHD exhibit similar problem behaviors (Johnston, 2002).

In addition, boys and teens who are impulsive tend to present with oppositional and defiant behaviors that commonly persist well into the adolescent and adult years. In the classroom, they commonly refuse to do work and argue with teachers and other classmates. Because they also present with difficulties regulating emotional discharges, they are prone to outbursts and tantrums. Classroom teachers need to be able to use interventions that will minimize the impact of all of these problems on other students and help the boys or teens with ADHD learn better self-control.

Although boys, teens, and men with ADHD, predominantly inattentive type generally present with fewer management problems, they exhibit other problem behaviors that are apparent in the classroom: daydreaming, remaining off task, forgetting work-related items and assignments, not completing their work, and so on. These problems, even more than those from the hyperactive/impulsive cluster of symptoms, tend to persist into adulthood. Consequently, teachers need to be prepared to address these problems within the classroom.

As discussed previously, boys, teens, and men with ADHD are at a higher risk for learning disorders. In addition, they are also at a higher risk for other emotional disorders (e.g., depression). To select the appropriate strategy to use in educational settings, the clinician must assess whether the symptoms of ADHD are accompanied by another disorder (such as a learning, emotional, or developmental problem) or whether the impact on learning and behavior that is observed in school is solely secondary to documented ADHD symptoms. This determination is the starting point that provides direction about how to intervene.

This chapter reviews methods of helping individuals with ADHD in educational settings. Initially, it is necessary to determine what approach will be necessary and what the appropriate placement within the school system should be. Making this determination requires the knowledge of educational law and the rights that students with ADHD have to receive assistance. Once the issues of classification and placement are resolved, it is necessary to determine what classroom modifications will be helpful. This chapter reviews changes in the physical class space, structure of the school day, and instructional techniques that will help students with ADHD improve their academic performance. The next chapter reviews a behavior management program that teachers can implement in the classroom to address disruptive behaviors.

RESEARCH SUPPORT

Intervening within the school setting has been shown to be the most effective method of improving the academic performance of students with ADHD (Barkley, 2006). For interventions to be effective, teachers must use both proactive and reactive techniques (DuPaul & Stoner, 2003). Proactive techniques (discussed in this chapter) involve changing the classroom environment, modifying academic instruction and tasks, developing strategic ways to improve attention, and establishing home–school collaboration. Reactive techniques involve contingency-management programs (discussed in the next chapter).

Implementing changes in the classroom environment has been suggested by most researchers who develop guidelines for the management of ADHD symptoms in schools. For example, Barkley (2006) recommended that changing the student's seating by moving him closer to the teacher and separating desks further from each other reduces distractibility and increases on-task behaviors. DuPaul and Stoner (2003) suggested rearranging classroom rules and routines to improve structure and manageability of behaviors. Using peers as a support system for instruction, especially in dyads where a student with ADHD is paired with a high-achieving student without ADHD has also received significant support in the literature (Greenwood, Delquadri, & Carta, 2002).

Similarly, instructional and tasks adjustments make a significant difference. Teachers who use methodical strategies have greater success with students, including those who present behavioral and attentional challenges (Berliner, 1987). The use of stimulation, variety, and computers in instruction is helpful for all students but especially for those with ADHD (Clarfield & Stoner, 2005). Increasing participation and helping students seek assistance when needed are similarly associated with greater academic success for students with ADHD.

Reducing distractibility is also well supported. Using "strategic teacher attention" (Barkley, 2006, p. 558) has been shown to improve on-task behaviors, and helping the student to express excessive motor output in more appropriate ways within the classroom has been shown to reduce disruptiveness (DuPaul & Stoner, 2003).

Although, in general, the techniques described in this chapter have not been investigated as frequently and rigorously as contingency-management approaches (covered in the next chapter), there is sufficient evidence from existing research studies that including these techniques in a comprehensive school-based approach will be of significant benefit to students with ADHD.

PATHWAYS TO SCHOOL-BASED INTERVENTIONS

Prior to the 1960s, there were no provisions in public law that mandated education of children with special needs. The first recognition of the need to deliver appropriate education for children with special needs came in 1965 with the passage of Public Law 89-10, and its amendment (Public Law 89-313) created the first federal grant to help states fund programs to educate children and youth with disabilities. Subsequent laws were passed in the late 1960s and early 1970s, including the Rehabilitation Act of 1973, which created programs to teach students with disabilities in local schools and provided federal funding to offset some of the cost.

Most of the provisions were still discretionary, however, allowing states to choose what disabilities would be remediated.

In 1975, Public Law 94-142, the Education of All Handicapped Children Act, was passed and finally mandated "free appropriate public education" to students with a wide range of disabilities, including physical handicaps; mental retardation; speech, vision, and language problems; emotional and behavioral problems; and other learning disorders. It also mandated the delivery of education in the "least restrictive environment." ADHD, which at that time was not yet formally included in the *DSM* diagnostic system, was not a disability protected under the law, however, and therefore there were no provisions that required public schools to modify educational practices specifically to address the needs of children with that disorder. Thus, the majority of children with ADHD attended regular classes and received no special help, and only those who qualified for special education because of a comorbid condition (e.g., a learning disability in reading) received special education.

In 1991, the Education of All Handicapped Children Act amendments were passed, and the law, since reauthorized, became known as Public Law 101-476, the Individuals With Disabilities Education Act (IDEA). During the debate preceding the passage of the bill, amendments were introduced to specifically include ADHD as a qualifying disability but were then dropped (Aleman, 1991). In September 1991, however, the U.S. Department of Education released a memorandum that specified that children with ADHD are eligible for special education under IDEA if they meet the criteria under one of the 13 categories officially recognized by IDEA, including other health impairments (OHI). The memorandum further clarified that those students with ADHD are also eligible for services under Section 504 of the Rehabilitation Act of 1973, which independently requires school districts to deliver specialized educational services to children who have a physical or mental impairment. In summary, students with ADHD, providing the condition is clearly documented to impair their academic functioning, are eligible for accommodations under the main provisions of IDEA or special provisions within Section 504. In most school districts across the country, this means that a student with ADHD is eligible for either special education or regular education with modifications that are implemented through a "504 Plan." Each of these approaches has benefits and drawbacks that must be carefully considered.

Special Education

Special education services are managed by the school district's child study team (CST). To be eligible, a student has to be evaluated by members of the CST. The evaluations commonly include psychological, learning, and social assessments, and additional evaluations (e.g., by a neurologist or a psychiatrist) may also be requested. The results of the evaluations are reviewed with the parent or guardian, who is allowed input into every step of the process. At the end of the evaluation, which generally must be completed within 90 days, eligibility for special education services is determined. If the child or adolescent is eligible for special education, appropriate classification will be identified, and an individualized education plan (IEP) will be developed. The placement will follow the "least restrictive environment" provisions, meaning that the student will be placed in an educational setting that will resemble regular education as closely as it is possible, given the severity of the identified disability. The placement needs to be reviewed at least annually, with a new IEP developed for every academic year (or sooner, if a change in academic needs becomes evident).

Once classified, a student will generally be placed into a mainstream or special education classroom. Mainstream placements involve education within a regular education classroom, and often some form of academic support is provided, for example, by placing a special education teacher or a teacher's aide (in addition to the regular education teacher) in the classroom to provide academic support for the student(s) who needs additional help. In cases where minimal academic assistance is required, the student is usually placed in such a classroom. When this placement is not sufficient, the next level is usually implemented by placing the student in a regular education classroom for those subjects where minimal (if any) problems are evident and having the student attend a resource room for subjects where more significant help is needed. There the student is taught by a special education teacher(s) and receives much one-on-one instruction. When this middle-ground level is not sufficient, students are placed in a self-contained program, which means that all classes (perhaps with the exception of "specials," such as art, computers, or gymnastics) are being taught within special education classes staffed by special education teachers.

Which of those choices is appropriate in any one case depends on a number of factors, and clinicians should use a decision tree to advise their clients and their families. When a student, in addition to having attentional and/or behavior difficulties, appears to exhibit evidence of overall academic struggle and apparent deficits in at least one academic area (such as reading, writing, or arithmetic), a CST evaluation should be sought. If a specific learning problem is revealed, the student should receive special education placement in a least restrictive environment in accordance with the choices outlined earlier.

If the student does not exhibit deficits in one specific academic area (or a CST evaluation failed to identify a specific learning disorder), but ADHD results in an impairment in academic functioning that is characterized by significant struggles and high severity of problems, a CST classification can still be sought under the OHI category, and the student can similarly receive special education placement in a least restrictive setting, in accordance with the choices discussed earlier.

Either of these two options is appropriate when the level of severity and academic struggles is significant. As with all approaches, there are both benefits and drawbacks. On the one hand, classification by the CST allows the student to be eligible for a significant amount of assistance, and if notable academic impairment is apparent, special education placements are likely to make the most difference. Teachers in those classrooms are able to devote much individualized attention to the student and use intensive instruction (including a one-on-one approach) if needed. Some parents object to their child being labeled, however, and students in special education may be excluded from at least some regular education settings, thus isolating them from nonclassified peers.

504 Plan

If the student's impairment is not severe enough to qualify him for special education, but he nevertheless exhibits evidence of significant problems that clearly stem from symptoms of ADHD (he struggles with keeping track of homework, has problems remaining on task, etc.), the student is still eligible to receive special accommodations under IDEA Section 504. In those cases, the student remains in a regular education placement, and a 504 Plan will be developed during a meeting between the student's parents and the school district representatives responsible for developing such educational plans.

When the meeting takes place, it is often helpful for parents to be accompanied by a mental health professional who can help them communicate with school professionals and make sure that the student's academic and behavioral needs are appropriately met. In addition, during the meeting, the clinician can also educate the school professionals about the nature of ADHD, specifically as it is reflected in the symptoms that the student is displaying in school. Teachers and administrators often welcome this input, and Barkley (2006) argued that such psychoeducation of school professionals helps them understand the disorder and conceptualize the approach that will be used to help the student.

During the meeting, it is expected that a list of classroom accommodations will be developed. Some schools have templates that are used to check off those interventions that are applicable to the specific student, whereas others develop a list from scratch at the meeting. Generally, the following categories of accommodations are available:

- Changes in physical arrangement of the classroom (e.g., seating the student near the teacher, seating him near a positive role model, or increasing the distance between desks);
- Instructional modifications (e.g., pairing the student with a peer who will provide assistance when needed, asking the student to repeat directions back to the teacher to ensure comprehension, breaking longer classes into shorter segments, and allowing the student to review key points orally);

- Changes in assignments (e.g., giving extra time to complete tasks and tests, shortening assignments or breaking them into segments, allowing computer-printed assignments, and relaxing rules about the neatness of handwriting);
- Assistance with organization (e.g., assigning a homework buddy, sending daily or weekly progress reports home, and assisting the student in the use of a homework journal);
- Behavior management (e.g., praising appropriate behaviors, using privileges and rewards, using appropriate negative consequences, increasing the immediacy of consequences, and using time-out procedures).

This list is not exhaustive, and clinicians, parents, and school professionals are encouraged to think about other creative ways to address the student's needs.

A 504 Plan provides the least significant accommodations and is appropriate in cases where some impairment is apparent, but the student, with limited assistance, is likely to be able to return to relatively normal academic functioning. On the one hand, it minimizes the labeling associated with special education, and the student continues to attend classes with his peers. On the other hand, the accommodations usually available under a 504 Plan are limited and include only those that will not cost the district any additional monetary costs. The cost of educating students who are classified is offset by state and federal funds, whereas the cost of educating students under a 504 Plan does not allow the district to recuperate any expenses. Thus, under a 504 Plan, most districts will not place a student in any special education placement and will not provide an educational aide.

Although students with ADHD are generally educated in accordance with one of the two options discussed previously, any teacher in any setting can perform most educational modifications. Thus, the interventions discussed in this chapter can be implemented in special education or regular education classes, regardless of whether a student with ADHD is educated in a mainstream classroom without support (e.g., under a 504 Plan), a mainstream classroom with special education support, a mainstream classroom with resource room support, or a self-contained special education placement. The main difference between all of those placement options involves the amount of academic modifications that the teacher will also implement. In regular education placements (with a 504 Plan), it is likely that only the techniques discussed in this chapter can be implemented. In a special education placement, the interventions recommended herein will be supplemented by changes in the method of instruction (e.g., more one-on-one instruction) and changes in the level of academic performance expected of the student (e.g., not requiring grade-level work).

INTERVENTIONS

There are many changes that teachers can implement within their class-room. Some involve arranging the classroom space so that the environment becomes conducive to better attention and on-task behavior, whereas others require changes in the teaching style to further improve student engagement. This chapter reviews various aspects of physical space, teaching methods, and daily classroom routines that affect ADHD symptoms in school. It is likely that most teachers will not be able to implement all of the suggestions in this chapter. The more of these suggestions that are put into practice, however, the more improvement in academic performance can be expected. Consequently, clinicians consulting with teachers should encourage them to implement as many of the following suggestions as possible in light of the dynamics of the specific classroom, district policies, and other limitations that must be observed.

Structure of the Classroom

To maximize student learning, teachers should structure classrooms to minimize problem behaviors and improve on-task performance. There are some classrooms that seem to invite more difficulties, especially from impulsive students who have poor self-control. Understanding these issues and properly structuring the physical space, scheduling, and classroom rules and regulations help teachers improve educational outcomes of all students, not just those with ADHD.

Classroom Space. Consider the following example:

> Some time ago, I was asked to assist a teacher address problems with a first-grade student who was frequently off task, looked around the classroom, left his desk and started to walk around, started conversations with other students while the class was going on, and so on. I made an appointment to meet with the teacher on her lunch hour, in her classroom.
>
> Walking into her classroom, I discover that the desks are arranged in groups of four, facing each other at 90-degree angles. This means that no matter where the teacher stands, one student will always have his back toward her, and two others will have the teacher at their side. Only one student in the group of four, at any given point in time, directly faces the teacher. To make matters worse, there are planters with tall plants in the classroom in the vicinity of each group of four desks, essentially further separating each group from the others (and from the teacher).
>
> But, it gets even worse. It is a midsize room that houses about 30 students. There are so many posters on the wall that I am unable to tell the color of the walls in the room. Even the windows have all kinds of stickers on them. Of course, all those wall posters and stickers are brightly colored, so the room has the appearance of an artist's studio with blotches of bright color scattered abundantly all around the room. And, for good measure, there are things hanging from the ceiling—mobile-type decorations,

a model of the solar system, and so on, again all brightly colored. As I sat down to meet with the teacher, I found myself being distracted and needing to refocus myself to pay attention to her during our meeting, even though I am a middle-aged adult, and the meeting was held one-on-one. I can only imagine what this poor first grader, especially an impulsive one with poor self-control, must be going through each day in this class (Kapalka, 2009, p. 163).

This example exemplifies all the *wrong* things that a teacher can do to affect distractibility and impulsivity. Classrooms that encourage good on-task behaviors have physical setups directly opposite of the classroom in the example. Instead of seating students in groups, teachers should have the students sit in traditional rows, facing the teacher. There should be sufficient space between the desks to allow the teacher to walk in between them, and increasing spacing makes it more difficult for students to become distracted by what their neighbors are doing at their desks at any point in time. Although this desk arrangement makes it less convenient during group activities, it greatly enhances on-task behaviors at all other times in the classroom. Thus, the teacher has to pick the lesser of the two evils—go through the minor inconvenience of rearranging the desks during small-group portions of the class or deal with the negative consequences of a desk arrangement that makes all other times throughout the day much more difficult.

In addition, the distractible student should be placed in a seat that is close to the teacher. Proxemics affect attention—the closer the student is to the teacher, the less likely he will be to become distracted during the teacher's instruction. If possible, the student should be seated away from sources of external stimulation, such as a window or a doorway. Additional sounds and images coming from those areas will frequently divert his attention away from classroom activities during a typical day. And to further discourage distractibility, the teacher should ensure that the student is surrounded by students who do not like to be distracted and therefore will not go along with his attempts to start talking to them in the middle of class. Although at first those neighbors may get a little annoyed that he is sitting next to them, most of the time this arrangement works well because the student learns that his neighbors do not like to be interrupted, and therefore he starts to use more self-control to suppress his impulse to bother them.

If the student is not seated in the first row, he should still sit close enough so that the teacher can walk toward his desk easily and effortlessly during instruction. There should be few obstacles between the teacher and the student, so that walking toward him and using physical cues (discussed later) will be easy.

Teachers should be careful not to place additional distracters in the room. Posters should be kept to a minimum, and if some are there, a boy or teen with ADHD should not face them and preferably should sit so that the posters are behind him. In the classroom, things should not hang from the ceiling, and there should be no additional items on the floor between desks.

Clinicians may find that some teachers may not like these recommendations. They may complain that these recommendations seem old fashioned. After all, the "new" approach to education is to make it more fun. Once again, however, a teacher has to choose the option that ultimately will produce the greatest benefits with the fewest drawbacks. Although a more sterile learning environment may, in fact, be less fun for some students, this can be compensated for by making some of the activities more enjoyable, such as playing educational games in the classroom or using hands-on projects. In the end, it becomes a choice of which is better—having a more boring physical environment in the classroom or having to deal with the constant need to redirect a student with ADHD when he becomes disengaged and distracted and then interferes with *everyone's* ability to learn.

Student Grouping. Teachers can take steps to have classroom peers help the boy or teen who is impulsive or distractible or has poor self-control. This is best accomplished by arranging study groups where teachers assign students to work with each other based on how they can help each other. Small groups of two, three, or four usually work best. Larger groups are not as effective. Generally, the younger the students, the smaller the groups should be, so in early grades, pairing works best.

When selecting peers for the work groups, the teacher should group the distractible, impulsive student with peers who are especially well organized and motivated to learn. In this way, they will set limits on his tendencies to be off task and will further help him during crucial points in the academic day, such as when he needs to get his homework assignments organized. In other words, pairing students who have academic needs with those who exhibit academic strengths is an effective approach.

When clinicians suggest this arrangement, some teachers may exhibit a negative reaction. Teachers are often concerned that this is not fair to the student who is stronger academically and has to help the weaker student. These concerns are unfounded, however. Students who are motivated to learn, have academic strengths, and are less distractible derive a significant benefit from rendering assistance. They benefit academically, because they use their existing knowledge to help another student, and their academic skills are further reinforced. They benefit emotionally, because they experience how good it feels to help someone else, and they also enhance their self-esteem by being able to recognize that they have academic strengths that not every student exhibits. The student being helped also benefits. He is assisted by a peer, and most students are receptive to peer assistance. It helps him build social skills (which is so crucial for students with ADHD) as he experiences the limits that others place on him when he begins to act inappropriately. It makes assistance easily available to him at various times throughout the school day, such as when he needs to organize his homework assignments. This truly is a win–win scenario.

Classroom Routines

Effective classroom routines have been shown to reduce the amount of problems within the classroom. Classes with minimal structure and poorly (or overly) elucidated rules generally experience the greatest difficulties, whereas classrooms with a moderate amount of rules and high amount of structure generally help distractible and impulsive students remain on task. To minimize problems, teachers should consider both aspects.

Classroom Rules and Regulations. Students with ADHD, especially those who are impulsive, frequently break rules. Some of the time, they do so even when they know what the rules are. The behavior management program described in the next chapter targets those situations. Teachers, however, must also recognize that students with ADHD sometimes break rules because they do not know them, or they legitimately forget those rules at the moment. Consequently, teachers need to go out of their way to help students learn what the rules are and regularly remind them of these rules to help students internalize the teacher's expectations.

It is a good idea to post a set of rules and expectations in the front of the classroom, written in large letters so students can easily see it. Teachers should incorporate into the classroom routine a short time, a few times per week, to review the rules and ask the students how, in their opinion, the class as a whole is doing in following these rules and what may need to be addressed or changed. When students as a group take ownership of the rules and expectations, they start to help each other abide by them. In such a setup, the whole class sets limits on the impulsive student and helps control his behaviors. As pointed out before, the boy or teen with ADHD will be more receptive because the limit setting will come from his peers.

Teachers should be judicious when they consider what rules and regulations need to be established. Some are obvious—students should remain at their desk while class activities are going on, students should raise their hand before giving answers, and so on. The list should not be too long and should not include behaviors not relevant to daily routines. The list should, first and foremost, reflect expectations that every student has to follow every day.

It is helpful to develop the list with the input of the class. It should be a group activity, lead by the teacher, to make students feel that they have significant input. As pointed out before, the more ownership the class takes for these rules, the more likely the students are to help each other observe them. When writing down the rules, teachers should phrase each rule as a positive behavior, not one to avoid. In other words, they should write "Students remain in their seat during class" rather than "Don't leave your desk while the class is going on."

The next chapter describes the implementation of a contingency-management program. In classrooms with several difficult students, it may be good to establish a classroomwide system of dispensing rewards and privileges to all students based on how well they follow the rules. In other classrooms, where only one student with ADHD needs such a system, contingency management can be implemented individually, and the whole class does not necessarily have to earn specific privileges and prizes for following the rules. At regular, frequent intervals, however, teachers should openly review how the class is doing with regard to these rules and be very forthcoming with giving praise to the students for every rule that is successfully observed.

Consistency. Just as important as having clear and consistent rules is establishing daily routines that promote good behavior. A few principles, applied consistently, can be very helpful. Routines make the student's day more predictable, because he gradually learns what to expect. As he becomes better able to anticipate what is about to happen next, he is able to prepare himself for it, and as a result, he will exhibit fewer problems. An impulsive student exhibits most difficulties when he is being told to do something that, at least from his point of view, comes out of the blue. On the other hand, expecting that something will happen prepares the brain, and even if what is being asked is not to the student's liking, his reaction will be more controlled.

The easiest way to teach students what to expect is to try to follow a consistent routine every day. If possible, the academic subjects should be covered in the same order every day. Thus, the impulsive and disorganized student will learn to expect what happens next, and each transition will gradually become less problematic. For each subject, the teacher should develop a consistent method of covering the material. For example, homework may be reviewed at the start of class, followed by a brief review of what was covered yesterday, then the introduction of new material, and then the assignment of homework (written on the blackboard) at the end of class. It is necessary to help the student anticipate what comes next. This technique works well at all levels of education, including in middle schools and high schools.

Structure. Students who are impulsive or distractible exhibit the greatest difficulties in situations with little structure. For example, the lunchroom, playground, or gym class is usually the first place where they begin to act out. When structure is limited, the students' mind becomes occupied with everything around them, and the attention is diverted away from the current setting, rules, and so on. In addition, activities with less structure usually involve more stimulation. For example, there is more movement as students walk around or run around (as is the case on the playground), and there is more noise as students talk to each other. There usually is also more visual stimulation. All this activity is more likely to stimulate the brain and divert it away from any task at hand.

Teachers should keep some things in mind with regard to structure. Activities that involve group interaction, movement, and so forth will usually precipitate more problems. These activities should not be avoided—to the contrary, they can be very effective in engaging and motivating an impulsive or disconnected student. Teachers, however, must accept that low-structured activities will precipitate more difficult behaviors, and therefore teachers must adjust their expectations about how the impulsive student will act. Teachers need to be careful not to set rules that are unrealistic and virtually guarantee that the student will get in trouble. In other words, some tolerance of minor misbehaviors will become necessary. In the end, this compromise is more than worth the benefits that come from using these teaching methods.

Conversely, activities that involve students' remaining at their desk should be very structured. Teachers must provide clear, detailed instructions about what needs to be done. A time limit should be set for any portion of class where students work on their own. For older students, the classroom clock can be used to announce when they are expected to complete the task. Teachers should cue students once about midway through the task to remind them about the time limit. For younger students, teachers may want to set a timer in plain view of all students and cue them once to look at the timer and see how much time they have left. There are large timers on the market with big dials that are suitable for that purpose. Generally, teachers find that the more structure they are able to implement during desk work, the fewer difficulties they experience with those portions of the school day.

Increasing structure can significantly improve organizational abilities. One way to help a disorganized student is to color-code his assignments, books, notebooks, and handouts. The most logical way to do so is to assign a color to a subject and ask the student to use a folder or a trapper of that color to keep all assignments and handouts within it. To further engage the student, the teacher may ask him to select the color he would like to use for each subject. When work is assigned, the student learns to place the assignment within the appropriately colored folder. When work needs to be handed in, the student has an easier job finding where the work is, because he simply locates the folder with a specific color. To further help the student associate colors with subjects, the teacher should use covers of the same color for each subject's textbook, notebook, and workbook. This system will make it much easier for the student to learn that all red items pertain to math, all green items have to do with social studies, and so on. When it is time to pack for the day, the matching folders and books will help the student remember what needs to be brought home. The same technique will similarly assist the student in remembering to bring completed homework assignments to school the next day.

When students reach middle school or high school, they often find that they need to carry a large number of books, assignments, notebooks, and handouts back and forth between home and school, which may present a particular problem for a disorganized student, who easily forgets to bring items home from school that are needed for homework or forgets to bring books back to school the next day. One way to remedy that problem is to give the student a second set of books to keep at home so that he does not have to carry the books back and forth each day. This system usually helps with homework compliance because the textbooks are always with the student at home and in school. To further reinforce the color-coding system described previously, the student should cover the books that remain at home with the same color of book covers as selected for each subject so that the colors remain consistent.

Instructional Modifications

Even if a student does not present with a bona fide learning disorder, some instructional techniques are more likely to stimulate interest and active participation. When a student participates, he is less likely to become distracted, and therefore selecting instructional methods that hold the student's interest is an important way for teachers to control ADHD symptoms.

Sensory Stimulation. When teachers use instructional methods that primarily focus on learning through one modality, the stimulation of this modality should be increased as much as possible. Many of the most common teaching methods primarily involve the visual modality. This is true, for example, when students are asked to read. In addition, the visual modality is often involved in conjunction with another modality. For example, when students are asked to write, they must use graphomotor skills (to move the hand and form the letters) as well as the visual modality (to look at the task). Thus, increasing the stimulation of the visual modality is often helpful, even if the academic task is not purely a visual one.

There are many ways of increasing visual stimulation, but to understand these, the reader will find it helpful to review some of the principles of vision. A system of rods and cones is responsible for sight. Processing achromatic stimuli, such as black letters on white paper, involves just one relatively small portion, because without color only the rods become stimulated, and the subsequent amount of perceptual (brain) activation is relatively small. When color is employed, the cone cells become stimulated, and the subsequent activation of the brain is more significant. In fact, the cones are prewired to respond proportionally to the intensity of the color—the more intense the color, the faster the cones fire, and the amount of cortical activation is greater. The greater the amount of brain stimulation, the more difficult it becomes to divert attention away from that task.

Teachers can use this information to help stimulate the student's visual processing. Rather than using achromatic handouts and assignments, teachers should use as much color as possible; the more intense the better. Content printed on colored paper, especially bright red, purple, or mustard yellow, draws the eye to it, and the amount of time spent attending to that task will increase.

This tip can be helpful when applied to other learning modalities as well. For example, when using auditory stimulation (for instance, when students take turns reading), teachers can make it more fun by having students act out what they read in some way or having them take turns in a group scenario in front of the class. These activities increase the intensity of the auditory stimulation and also involve another modality (motor), thus using multiple learning modalities.

Multiple Modalities. Teaching techniques commonly involve one or more of the most common pedagogical modalities—visual, auditory, or graphomotor. Most techniques exhibit a preference for processing the environment through one dominant modality while another modality is much weaker. Unfortunately, most instructional methods involve one main modality, for example, visual (when reading), auditory (when listening to the teacher lecture), or graphomotor (when writing). If one of those modalities happens to be weaker for a student, he will more likely disengage during (and have difficulties following) the activity that primarily involves that modality. Thus, identifying the student's weakest modality may help the teacher predict what types of academic tasks are most likely to be problematic.

Although identifying the weakest modality may be helpful, avoiding that modality during daily instruction may not be possible. For that reason, it is beneficial to use instructional methods that involve multiple modalities. For example, the verbal or expressive modality may be combined with the visual modality when students read a passage and then complete in small groups an assignment that is based on what they just read. Or the class can be divided into two halves, and students can compete in a game that involves a physical task (such as being the first student to get to the back of the room) and a cognitive one (such as giving the correct answer to randomly selected questions that reinforce the academic content), and points are awarded for both components. Many teachers find that adding a tactile component to common academic tasks, such as playing a game that involves movement or putting together a project, reinforces the other learning modalities and further engages students.

An excellent way of using multiple modalities during teaching is to use educational games on the computer. Because the task is a game, most students, even teenagers, usually engage quickly in it. In addition, computer programs and games commonly involve tactile, visual, and auditory modalities. So much of the brain becomes involved in processing the activity that little is left over for anything else (such as daydreaming). In addition, time on the computer can become an effective classroom privilege that a student can earn through good behavior (as discussed in the next chapter).

Academic Assistance. As discussed earlier, students who are impulsive and oppositional commonly exhibit a weaker learning modality. Because teachers cannot use multiple-modality instruction all the time, there will be times when an assignment or classroom activity targets that weak modality. Teachers should make sure that the student knows how he can obtain assistance and that he will encounter a receptive response when he seeks help. When appropriate, teachers need to encourage the student to directly seek help by raising his hand or approaching the teacher's desk. At times, when the student needs more frequent assistance than the teacher can deliver or when the teacher is busy attending to other students, it may be helpful to make an "assistance buddy" available to the student. This can be accomplished by asking another student, beforehand, to agree to be helpful to someone in class. If that student is reluctant, extra credit for such assistance can be offered. Then the teacher can instruct the boy with ADHD to seek out that peer for assistance, especially when the teacher is busy at the moment. Of course, if pairing is already being used (as discussed earlier in this chapter), a structure that easily provides peer assistance is already being implemented.

One method of increasing the availability of assistance is to provide sufficient learning aides. These aides can take many forms. Some may be classroom resources that the student can use while working in the classroom (such as a dictionary or spell-checker), and some may involve after-school resources that a student may consult (with the help of his parents, if needed) while doing homework (such as a useful Web site that relates to the homework assignment). Generally, the more the teacher does to make assistance available to the student, the more motivated he will be to learn, and his attitude in class will improve as well.

Novelty and Stimulation. Repetitive, rote-oriented tasks cause the brain of a student with ADHD to habituate very quickly, and he becomes bored with the activity. Consequently, it is helpful to come up with novel activities and assignments. Teachers should be creative. For example, knowledge of current events and/or interests of students within that age group may suggest topics that will be particularly relevant. Teachers should allow the student some input into customizing an assignment in a way that will meet academic objectives on the one hand but stimulate some of his interest (and a sense of fun) on the other. It is helpful to think outside the box. For example, if rap music was around at the time of the Civil War, what would a rap song sound like (reflecting a preassigned theme)? With some effort, teachers can come up with ideas that have a current feel but contain the academic content that needs to be covered.

Variety also is very important. Teachers should not overrely on one type of assignment or one learning modality. Unfortunately, many of the cookbook curricula do not contain sufficient variety and easily bore students who are impulsive and distractible. Those students crave stimulation and novelty. Teachers need to think about how they can tap into those themes when preparing lesson plans and assignments. Success in this area will greatly improve the student's engagement in the classroom, and in turn he will spend much more time on task.

Opportunities for Success. Impulsive and distractible students commonly develop a negative expectation of their academic abilities. Their poor frustration tolerance and a weak learning modality (such as problems with writing) affect their motivation because they recognize that they have to work hard to produce a product that is at least of acceptable quality. In addition, because those students frequently argue with their teachers, they usually conclude to themselves that the teachers do not like them, and consequently they do not want to work hard to satisfy the standards those teachers impose on them.

Teachers should try to reverse this negative pattern. The way to do so is to stack the deck and think about classroom activities that the student with ADHD may be good at. If the student plays an instrument, the teacher can have him play a piece of music that relates to the theme being studied. If he likes sports, he can construct a game that all students will play that will reflect a certain theme. It is necessary for teachers to go out of the way to do an activity where he can succeed, even if the academic benefit is more indirect. If he succeeds, he will start to feel better about himself and about being in class. With repeated experiences of success, he will be motivated to try harder. As his motivation improves, his academic performance will as well.

Techniques to Reduce Distractibility

When students are off task, they are more likely to disconnect from academic activities and miss significant portions of instruction. They are likely to fall behind and, over time, begin to exhibit deficits in academic skills. Distractible students, especially when they are also impulsive, are also more likely to exhibit problem behaviors. Students who become distracted often get involved in behaviors that disrupt the class and interfere with effective teaching and learning. For example, students may start a conversation with their neighbors and may disrupt others in the class. Or students may lose their place in the class activity and feel reprimanded when the teacher makes them realize that they are not following the classroom routine. They may be embarrassed in front of their peers and exhibit an oppositional reaction. Thus, addressing distractibility is an important component of helping students with ADHD.

Signals and Cues. Developing "attention-getters" and teaching students to recognize them is an effective way to reduce distractibility. Essentially, students learn that certain words, phrases, or behaviors performed by the teacher signal the students to stop what they are doing, look at the teacher, and await instructions. There are many ways of accomplishing this, and cues can be issued to a whole class or only a specific student.

Most teachers find it helpful to teach the whole class that certain behaviors performed by the teacher (group cues) signal that students need to stop whatever they are doing, stay where they are, look at the teacher, and await further instructions. Common ways of doing so include flashing the lights quickly two or three times or using a sound (such as a bell or a buzzer). At times, especially if the class seems very involved in an activity that involves movement and/or a significant amount of noise, it is helpful for the teacher to freeze and stand in place, perhaps raising one or two hands in the air. Although only a few students may recognize this at first, a few will, and they will begin to pass down a chain message to other students, telling them to similarly stop whatever they are doing. Students one-by-one respond to this cue like a domino effect and cease current activity, and the student with ADHD will also likely stop, under pressure from peers. Although it may take a short while, the whole class will quiet down and look at the teacher.

Although group cues are very effective when it is necessary to summon the attention of the entire classroom, there are many times when a teacher needs to issue a cue specifically to the student with ADHD and not the rest of the class. Individual cues fall into two broad categories, covert and overt, and each has its advantages and disadvantages.

Covert cues do not interrupt the flow of the class activity, and with practice the teacher can weave these cues seamlessly into the teaching activities. These cues can be performed during most any activity, even during a lecture to the class. The most effective covert cues involve the use of subtle body language to signal the student that he needs to think about what he is doing and check whether he is doing what is expected of him (as opposed to daydreaming, talking to others, etc.). For example, during a reading activity when students take turns reading a passage, if one student seems to be looking around, getting involved in another's business, and so on, a subtle but effective way to bring him back on task is to simply start walking toward him. If he is positioned so he is looking away, the teacher should enter the student's field of vision and gradually approach him (without saying anything to him directly) while other students simply continue to carry on with the reading activity. When the teacher walks near, most students perform an automatic mental check about what they are doing and whether their behavior is appropriate at the moment, and the teacher's proximity is often enough to redirect them.

It is best not to turn this cue into a challenge or confrontation. The teacher may want to start by looking elsewhere (e.g., at the student reading aloud at the moment) while walking toward the off-task student. If the teacher is very near, and the student is still not picking up on the cue, then the teacher should look at him but try not to say anything. The teacher should try to avoid embarrassing him or singling him out. If this is still not enough, the teacher can casually touch his hand or his shoulder (again, without looking at him directly). If that is not enough, and the student seems puzzled by the cue, the teacher can gently point at what is lying on his desk (such as his reading book) to nonverbally indicate to him to get back on task. Because the class flow will not be interrupted, the student will feel less embarrassed, and the whole interaction will be subtle but effective. In fact, techniques that use subtle body language are effective across all ages, even with teenagers.

One problem with these techniques, however, especially when teachers have to use them many times per day, is that students over time habituate to them and begin to ignore those cues. This is when developing overt cues may be helpful.

Overt cues are those that are clear, but because these are *individual* cues, they should be known only to the recipient. In other words, teachers need to develop a set of signals that will subtly be issued while the class is in session, and no one but the target student will know that an attention-getter was just issued. These cues are more difficult to get off the ground, and they require some trial and error, but they can be an effective supplement to covert cues, especially when a student needs to be cued frequently.

To start, the teacher should gently point out to the student (in private) that there are times in the classroom when he is not paying attention, and the teacher does not want to embarrass him in front of others, but a method must be agreed on to give him a reminder that will be known only to him, and thus no one else will know, but it will help him refocus and get back on task. For example, a teacher can say something to the whole class that will seem general enough that no one will be the obvious target, but the student with ADHD will know that it was said to help him refocus, such as, "It is so nice when all students pay attention, because it helps everyone learn."

Teachers will have to be creative when using overt individual cues. Sometimes, instead of giving a verbal cue, a teacher can approach the student's desk, without saying anything, and hold an item that seems out of place at the moment, such as a stapler. Other students will not know why, all of a sudden, the teacher picked up a stapler and started walking around with it. A student with ADHD, however, can be taught that when he sees the teacher holding a stapler, especially when he or she is walking in his direction, it means that the teacher is trying to (nicely and privately) tell him that he is not paying attention.

These techniques take time to get off the ground and are not a quick fix. The student will appreciate that the teacher goes out of the way to help him save face in front of others, however, and because of that he will be more motivated to respond to those cues. Of course, it is most effective to use a combination of covert and overt cues, and it is best to establish only one overt cue that will be used repeatedly. By using an individual overt cue intermittently with the covert cues discussed previously, many teachers find that the mix of the two types of attention-getters begins to reduce the frequency of off-task behaviors.

Self-Monitoring. Self-monitoring is a technique that involves teaching a student to use a cue to perform his own mental check to become aware of what he is doing at the moment and whether his behavior is, in fact, the expected one at the time. It also involves the use of a cue, but less teacher intervention is necessary, because the teacher does not necessarily need to issue the prompt.

The easiest way to teach the student to self-monitor is to use items around the room that signal him to perform a mental check about whether he is paying attention. Barkley (2006) recommended smiley faces, but other items are at least as likely to work—signs that encourage attention, drawings of hands with a finger pointing toward the teacher, and so on. It is important to place these all around the room so that students who start to look around encounter these cues as their eyes wander about the room.

Sometimes students can be trained to use a single item in the classroom, such as the clock, to remind them to check whether they are on task. At first, the teacher can encourage this by pointing to the clock regularly and encouraging all students to keep an eye on the time and make sure they remain on task. The more frequently this is done, the more likely the student is to associate that item with the need to self-monitor. Gradually, that association will strengthen to the point that he will begin to think about what he is doing whenever he spontaneously looks at the clock, even though it was not precipitated by a cue.

Although self-monitoring is potentially a beneficial technique, it is often difficult to implement. First, students must be old enough to be able to self-monitor. This technique is usually effective with students in fifth grade or higher. In addition, the student's personality must be taken into consideration. Because this is a technique that requires the student to perform a mental check on his own, a student who is very oppositional or exhibits minimal effort to comply with classroom rules and routines usually will not want to bother trying this approach. A student who seems motivated to do well but is distractible, however, may appreciate an opportunity to bring himself under control. In addition, self-monitoring can be made more effective when it is combined with a contingency-management program described in the next chapter.

Transitions. Students who are distractible and impulsive often exhibit difficult behaviors at specific points in their school day. One of these moments commonly occurs when students are required to terminate an activity that they currently perform and get started on another, for example, when playtime is over and they have to return to their desk or when a group activity is finished and another academic task must begin. During those times, a version of a "three bells" technique (commonly done at concerts and sporting events) may be helpful. Combining this technique with one of the group cues discussed earlier in this section works especially well.

For example, when students are performing a play activity, the teacher can flash the classroom lights one time about 3 or 4 minutes before it is time for them to return to their desk. If students were previously taught that this is a cue that means that they need to pay attention to the teacher, they will look and await further instructions. The teacher can simply announce that students should start finishing up whatever they are doing because shortly it will be time to put the items away and return to their desk. About 2 minutes later, the teacher can flash the lights two times and announce that now is the time students have to start putting the items away. About a minute later, the teacher can flash the lights three times and announce that the time to return to their desk is right now. Because students with ADHD commonly exhibit difficulties with these situations, using both group approaches (such as the three bells technique) and contingency management (described in the next chapter) is more likely to produce significant improvement.

SUMMARY

Because school-related problems are a central feature of ADHD, intervening within the school setting is paramount. Students with ADHD can be assisted through CST classification or regular instruction with modifications summarized in a 504 Plan. Special education instruction is necessary if problems are severe or ADHD is comorbid with learning disabilities, but mainstream placement is effective in less severe cases.

To assist students with ADHD, teachers in regular and special education classrooms can use modifications in the many aspects in which they deliver instruction in the classroom. Physical space should be structured to reduce distractibility, and appropriate grouping will encourage students to help each other and monitor each other's behaviors. Classroom rules, routines, and structure should be implemented that encourage on-task performance. The use of novelty, increased sensory stimulation, and multiple learning modalities are similarly helpful, as are techniques that teach students to respond to signals and cues. These changes take time to implement, and none may produce a significant change in isolation, but together they help teachers create a learning environment that reduces classroom problems. Although the interventions described in this chapter are likely to produce at least some positive change, they are more effective when combined with the contingency-management techniques described in the next chapter.

CHAPTER

12

Student Behavior Management

Although boys with attention deficit/hyperactivity disorder (ADHD) exhibit a variety of school-related problems, disruptive behaviors in the classroom, especially seen in boys and teens who are impulsive and hyperactive, are among the most frustrating. Because these students exhibit poor self-control, they frequently perform behaviors that get them in trouble.

In early grades, boys with ADHD tend to call out answers without raising their hand and blurt things out during the course of a normal school day. When they experience an urge, they perform behaviors that take them off task, such as leaving their seat or approaching a neighboring student. If they are also hyperactive, their constant fidgeting may disrupt other students. As they get older, some of these tendencies may diminish, but impulsivity, in one form or another, often persists into the teen years and beyond.

Students who are impulsive generally exhibit poor frustration tolerance. When directed to do work, they are likely to resist if the task requires effort. When being directed from an activity they currently enjoy to one that is less fun (such as academic work), they often exhibit a negative reaction. When prevented from doing what they like, they have difficulties containing the urge to resist, and they express their disapproval through protests, arguments, and defiance. As a result, a majority of the interactions between a teacher and a boy with ADHD result in a negative outcome, such as the boy getting yelled at or punished.

Teachers quickly learn which students in the class are difficult to manage, and they often approach those students with anger and frustration. As a result, students with ADHD perceive this negative attitude

229

and similarly respond with an edge. In turn, teachers are even more likely to learn that a student is "trouble." This spiral affects how students and teachers feel about each other and further minimizes the likelihood of positive interactions between them.

Students with ADHD who are not impulsive or hyperactive also present with challenges in the classroom. Often, they are off task and do not complete their work. They easily get distracted and need much encouragement to attend to classroom routines. Homework is often a major challenge, and boys who are disorganized often lose assignments and other items they need to do their work (books, notebooks, etc.). Their grades usually suffer as a result.

RESEARCH SUPPORT

As was the case with parent training, contingency management is the nonmedical treatment approach with the most research support in school settings (Barkley, 2006). Generally, research findings have suggested that rules and instructions must be clear and brief and need to be provided through a variety of modalities (e.g., explained verbally and posted visually). Positive behaviors should be reinforced, and negative behaviors should be followed by appropriate and swift costs. Students must experience these consequences (positive and negative) frequently, and recurrent repetition has been associated with faster learning. Behavior tracking should be employed to maintain consistency. The types of consequences used must be of high salience to the student, especially regarding incentives—the higher the salience, the more learning will take place. In addition, the contingency-management program should be based primarily on reinforcement of appropriate behaviors, and response costs should be employed to a more minor degree, mostly when other methods did not produce extinction of the unwanted behaviors.

A variety of classroom behavior management programs have been developed (e.g., DuPaul & Stoner, 2003). Generally, these programs include a number of techniques that are covered in a program of steps, administered in 1- to 2-week intervals, and each step is designed to present a specific technique that teachers can use within the classroom. Most of these programs focus on methods of giving instructions, addressing misbehaviors, and developing long-term behavioral contracts that operate by setting (and adjusting, as needed) a series of point-based rewards given in exchange for target behaviors. These programs have become a mainstay of teacher-administered interventions for students with special needs, and some teacher educators suggest that teachers should use these techniques year-round and make them a part of their daily academic routine (Pfiffner, 1996).

Kapalka (2009) developed one such program. It is divided into eight steps, each of which helps teachers implement a technique to address a discrete problem behavior. It is designed to address difficulties most commonly associated with students with ADHD—problems with following commands and instructions, arguing, temper tantrums, problems remaining on task, problems during transitions, and acting out in out-of-class situations (e.g., on the playground or in the lunchroom). Teachers are generally encouraged to complete one step every 1 to 2 weeks to become comfortable with each technique. In addition, because some of the steps build on one another, teachers are encouraged to complete the first half of the program in order. Although the program resembles a similar program developed for parents (Kapalka, 2007c), described in Chapter 7 of this volume, the interventions and techniques discussed in this chapter were specifically adjusted to be relevant for students and teachers.

Although contingency-management programs are generally researched by investigating the overall effectiveness of the whole program, Kapalka (2009) designed the program by researching each technique separately in a series of sequential studies with two different samples of teachers (Kapalka, 2001b, 2002, 2005a, 2005b, 2005c, 2005d, 2006b, 2007a, 2007b, 2007d, 2008a, 2008b; Kapalka & Bryk, 2007). The remainder of this chapter will describe this program.

INTERVENTIONS

To engage teacher participation in the program, clinicians should reach out and offer assistance. Research results have revealed that single-session training and consultation are not nearly as effective as a continuing program where the school psychologist (or another clinician) develops an ongoing consulting relationship with the teacher and maintains contact at regular intervals to provide assistance and personalize the program (Barkley, 2006). With this in mind, the clinician must establish a working relationship with the teacher that will include periodic contact and will allow the teacher to reach out to the professional when problems arise for which he or she needs assistance.

When intervening, clinicians need to follow a structured plan. First and foremost, teachers should be educated about ADHD, which will help them establish realistic expectations and develop an understanding of the approach that they will need to employ to help the student. Then, systematically and methodically, clinicians should gradually implement interventions, allowing teachers practice opportunities to become comfortable with each technique.

Mental Preparation

Although teachers may have some knowledge about ADHD, it is likely that they do not have an accurate perception of why the boy or teenager is performing the problem behaviors. They often attribute a much greater portion to willful disobedience and purposeful breaking of rules rather than to problems with self-control. This belief causes a negative mind-set that predisposes many teachers to view the student negatively and expect the worst when they are about to interact with him.

This negative expectation affects the interaction, and teachers often address the problem student with an edge in their voice and a defensive stance. This negativity is communicated through both nonverbal and often verbal means, and the student reacts in kind. This pattern makes it much more likely that conflicts will ensue.

Instead, teachers need to be educated about the nature of ADHD and its symptoms and the way in which the core deficits affect self-control. If the boy or teen presents with a lot of argumentativeness or defiance, it is important for teachers to also place these behaviors in the context of the impulsivity that underlies those problems. Clinicians need to accept that "job one" is to help teachers develop a more positive reaction to the student and break the cycle of negative expectations.

Like parents, teachers should be taught the principles of assertive communication. They must believe that the approach they will be following is likely to produce at least some positive results. Teaching should be framed as involving both academic and life skills, and an important life skill is to learn to recognize (and accurately predict) consequences of one's behavior. Interactions with a boy or teen with ADHD present opportunities to help him learn those lessons, and this can be accomplished whether the outcome of any one situation was positive (e.g., good behavior or successful completion work) or negative (such as his being defiant or off task). As long as teachers are able to remain calm and in control and will administer an appropriate positive or negative consequence, the "teaching moment" can be successful. Thus, before teachers implement the steps described next, they need to develop a realistic set of expectations about why the student is behaving that way and what role teachers can play in changing those behaviors. Before teachers approach each interaction, they need to learn to remain calm and in control, expect that their approach will make at least some difference in the student's behavior, and present themselves in a commanding but respectful manner.

Step 1: Giving Instructions and Commands

Consider the following example:

> Mrs. Smith is a second-grade teacher. She teaches a group of 25 children, including Barry, an active youngster who frequently gets into conflicts with other children. The class is just finishing spelling, and it is time for a short recess. Today, the children will stay in the classroom and play with games available to them in the back of the room. There are five computers in the classroom, so five students will have an opportunity to play games on them while the rest of the students break into small groups and play with the board games.

As the children begin to break into groups, the teacher is gathering the materials she just used to teach the preceding subject. Barry runs to the back of the classroom. He approaches a child who has selected a computer to play with and attempts to commandeer it. The other boy does not give up, and an argument between the two boys ensues, including some pushing.

The teacher yells across the room, "What's going on there?"

Barry yells, "I want to play!"

The other boy chimes in, "But I got here first!"

"Barry, he got there first, so please let him stay on," says the teacher.

Barry yells, "Nooo, I really want to play!"

The teacher approaches Barry and leads him away from the computer. He yells even louder, "Nooo, you can't make me!"

The teacher places Barry in the corner by the building blocks. In anger, he starts to throw the blocks around the room.

The teacher yells, "Stop that!" She returns to her desk to finish what she was doing.

After a moment, Barry goes over to a group of children who just started to play with a board game. He wants to join them, but they already assigned all available spots for the game and tell him he can't play. He goes over to one girl sitting on the side and gets in front of her.

The other children start to yell at him, "No, get away from here!"

Barry swipes his hand across the board, knocking all the pieces to the floor.

The teacher goes over and says, "I told you to stop! Now you have to behave! Go over there, sit down, and read a book!"

Barry protests, "Nooo! It's not fair! I want to play!"

The teacher asks the class whether any group will accept Barry. No one responds. The teacher goes over to one group of children and asks that they let Barry join them. They protest but agree.

As Barry and the group play with the game, Barry attempts to take over the game in the manner in which he likes (not in accordance with the stated rules). Every few moments, when things do not go his way, Barry acts up again. The other children try to shush him, to no avail. Throughout the 25-minute recess, the teacher must frequently go back and intervene with Barry, proclaiming "I said knock it off!"

As the recess comes to an end, the teacher asks the children to return to their assigned seats. Barry is the last one in the back of the room. While the children return to their desks, Barry starts to build a tower with the building blocks.

The teacher addresses Barry from across the classroom, "Barry, put those away and return to your seat."

Barry replies, "In a minute."

The teacher starts giving out a handout with a math assignment. Barry is still playing with the blocks. The teacher says, "Barry, I said put those away and come back to your desk."

"But I just want to finish building the tower!"

The other children start working, and the teacher starts to circulate around the room to see if anyone needs help. Barry is still playing.

She raises her voice, "Barry, your work is waiting here for you." He responds, "I'm not finished!"

The teacher answers a question from another student and realizes that Barry is still in the back of the room. She tells Barry, "Come to your desk now, or I'll have to tell your mother you're not listening."

Barry does not respond. The teacher, still in the front of the room, answers another student's question and then yells, "Barry, did you hear me? I am calling your mother!"

Barry does not respond and continues to build.

The teacher, now visibly angry, marches toward Barry, starts to take the blocks out of his hands, and pulls him toward his desk. Barry starts yelling and crying, "But I was not finished! It's not fair!" He throws across the room the blocks he still had in his hand.

He gets to his desk, still crying, and his noise is disrupting the other students in the classroom.

After a minute or two, he calms down and turns around to ask the neighbor behind him a question. Other students become distracted and say, "Barry, be quiet!"

The teacher walks over to Barry, who turns toward her. The teacher directs him to do his work. He engages for the moment, but as soon as the teacher walks away, he starts to ask a neighbor to his right for a pencil. The neighbor says, "Barry, stop!" The teacher walks over to Barry.

"What do you need?"

"I don't have anything to write with."

"Where is your pencil?"

"I don't know."

The teacher gives Barry a pencil, directs him to work, and walks away. After a moment, Barry gets up from his desk and walks to the back of the classroom. "Where are you going?" asks the teacher. He replies, "To sharpen my pencil."

Barry gets to the pencil sharpener and sharpens his pencil loudly and repeatedly. He then starts to walk back. Passing the first desk, he starts to ask his friend a question. The two start talking. The neighbor in the front turns around and says, "Be quiet!"

The teacher walks back toward Barry and his friend. She asks, "What are you talking about?"

He replies, "I had to ask him whether he will come over later to play."

"Now?"

"But I won't see him later!" replies Barry. The teacher, exasperated, directs Barry to get back to his desk. He complies and starts to work on the sheet, but 2 minutes later, he again starts bothering his neighbor. The teacher walks over toward Barry. "What are you doing?"

"I did not know how to do this one."

"Then ask *me*, and I'll help you." The teacher shows him, and he again begins to work. A moment later, he again turns to the neighbor and starts whispering. Both boys start giggling. The girl next to them says, "Why don't you knock it off?"

The teacher walks over, but Barry saw her coming and returned to his work. Another few minutes go by.

Barry gets attention of the teacher, "Psst, I want to ask you a question."

The teacher, thinking Barry needs help, walks over and says, "What is it?"

Barry says, "Tomorrow, can I be the first one to play on the computer?"

"We'll see," says the teacher. "Now get back to work."

He does, for a few moments, after which he again loses focus and becomes distracted. This pattern continues through the whole day (Kapalka, 2009).

It is clear in this example that Barry is an impulsive student who exhibits poor self-control. When attending to the multitude of problems that students like him present, the teacher needs a starting place. Research findings have revealed that the most logical place to start is with developing a more effective way to issue commands and instructions.

As discussed in Chapter 7, boys and teens with ADHD do not follow commands because they either have not processed them or have difficulties suppressing the urge to resist what is being asked. To help with a student with these problems, the teacher must start by getting his full attention. Rather than yelling a command from across the room (as in the previous example), the teacher needs to approach the student and seek eye contact before the command is given. The easiest way to do so is by calling his name and, if necessary, saying, "Please look at me." The teacher should speak with a commanding but respectful tone.

Next, the teacher should clearly and briefly tell the student to perform a specific action. The command should not be phrased in the form of a question, because it may make it easier for him to refuse. Instead, a command should be stated in a form of a statement. The teacher should say "please," continue with a statement of the action to be performed, such as "open your math book," and end with a specifier of the time frame, such as "now." Thus, an appropriate command may be "Please open your math book now."

The student may delay responding or refuse altogether. In these situations, teachers often begin to repeat themselves, and an escalation ensues (more about that in the next step). Instead, if the command has not resulted in compliance, the teacher should say nothing but remain in the student's vicinity for an additional 15 to 20 seconds. Research findings have suggested that this approach is effective in reducing the noncompliance that students with ADHD commonly exhibit in the classroom (Kapalka, 2001b, 2005b). This follow-up look allows the student to process the situation and recognize that noncompliance will not be ignored. In many instances, this helps the student make the choice to perform the stated command.

If the student did not listen, the teacher should be advised that for now, the teacher should do what he or she usually does following noncompliance, because Step 2 will further extend the technique described herein. Because most teachers need much practice suppressing the urge to start repeating the command when immediate compliance is not evident, it is usually not a good idea to combine Steps 1 and 2 and attempt to learn both at once. Many teachers need time to get used to practicing Step 1 before they can further continue with the program.

If Step 1 resulted in compliance, it is important to acknowledge this positive behavior. Verbal praise can include phrases such as "Thank you," "I appreciate your cooperation," and "I like it when you do what I ask." Nonverbal methods include a wink, a smile, or a gentle pat on the shoulder. Both verbal and nonverbal methods of praise should be used.

The interaction described earlier may go as follows if the teacher uses the techniques described in Step 1:

As the recess comes to an end, the teacher asks the children to return to their assigned seats. Barry is the last one in the back of the room. While the children return to their desks, Barry starts to build a tower with the building blocks.

The teacher approaches Barry. She stands close enough so they can see each other clearly, and she says, "Barry, please look at me."

Barry does not reply.

The teacher walks a little closer and repeats, "Barry, please look at me."

Barry looks at the teacher and says, "What?"

The teacher, looking at Barry, says, "Recess is over. Please pick these up right now."

Barry says, "But I just want to finish building the tower!"

The teacher does not respond and merely starts to walk toward Barry so she is standing right next to him, and she continues to silently look right at him while he is still playing.

Barry says, "Why are you looking at me?"

The teacher responds, "Because you did not do what I asked you to do."

Reluctantly, Barry starts to pick up the blocks, all along protesting that it is not fair because he was not finished.

As he does so, the teacher says, "Thanks, Barry. I appreciate your help. It makes my day so much easier" and smiles at him.

The teacher waits until he is finished picking up the blocks; she walks away only after he is finished, and she attends to her other tasks in the classroom.

If Barry is picking up the blocks too slowly or tries to continue building while he is picking up, the teacher says, "Here, let's do it together. You have to do it with me." She assists in the cleanup and still offers praise when it is done (Kapalka, 2009, p. 38–39).

With a teenager, this technique should be implemented with minor modifications. The best way to get the student's attention is to call his name, but the teacher should be careful not to get into a conflict over getting eye contact. Generally, as long as the teacher gets the impression that the student heard the cue, the goal of the attentional cue was accomplished. As with younger students, the teacher should issue a command or instruction that calls for a single, specific behavior. Even though teenagers exhibit more sophisticated reasoning skills than younger children, adolescents with ADHD are still more likely to exhibit problems following complex, multistep commands, so asking them one thing at a time is generally preferred. The follow-up look is similarly effective with teens, but some older students may exhibit a negative response when the teacher continues to look at them. A teenager may feel that the look is a form of a stare and may then try to prove to the teacher that he will not be intimidated. Such a contest of stares is not productive. Instead, teachers should be sensitive to the student's reaction to the follow-up look. If he seems to respond by initiating a staring match, the teacher should look away but remain in his vicinity. By continuing to be close, the teacher will accomplish nearly the same effect as with giving the look—the student will still feel the teacher's presence and therefore will find it more difficult to merely continue with his current activity.

Step 2: Giving Warnings

Like parents, teachers are also at risk for becoming involved in the counterproductive repetition loops described by Barkley (1997b), where a command is repeated many times, and the student continues to ignore or refuse to obey it. In the process, teachers become frustrated and angry and may threaten with unrealistic consequences. The student recognizes that the consequences are not likely to be administered, and therefore the threats become ineffective. In the end, teachers face two counterproductive options—escalate the situation further or acquiesce and give up seeking compliance. To avoid this predicament, teachers must learn to give effective warnings.

When giving a command or instruction, teachers should initially issue it in a manner consistent with Step 1 (discussed previously), including the attentional cue and the 15- to 20-second follow-up look. If this attempt did not result in compliance, the command should be repeated once, prefaced by "I said" and again followed by another 15- to 20-second waiting period. If these two attempts were not successful, teachers should immediately issue one (and only one) warning of a realistic consequence that they are able to implement as quickly as possible (preferably immediately). After the warning, teachers should wait another 15 to 20 seconds and then implement the stated consequence if the warning was not effective. This technique has been found effective in reducing classroom noncompliance in boys with ADHD (Kapalka, 2005a, 2007a).

In summary, if the approach described in Step 1 did not produce compliance, the next step may be implemented as follows:

> As the recess comes to an end, the teacher asks the children to return to their assigned seats. Barry is the last one in the back of the room. While the children return to their desks, Barry starts to build a tower with the building blocks.
>
> The teacher approaches Barry. She stands close enough so they can see each other clearly, and she says, "Barry, please look at me."
>
> Barry does not reply.
>
> The teacher walks a little closer and repeats, "Barry, please look at me."
>
> Barry looks at the teacher and says, "What?"
>
> The teacher, looking at Barry, says, "Recess is over. Please pick these up right now."
>
> Barry says, "But I just want to finish building the tower!"
>
> The teacher does not respond and merely starts to walk toward Barry so she is standing right next to him, and she continues to silently look right at him while he is still playing.

> Barry does not respond and continues to build.
> The teacher says, "Barry, please look at me."
> "What?!"
> While looking right at Barry, the teacher says, "If you do not start picking up these blocks right now, I will do it for you, but you will lose your computer time today."
> Barry continues to build, and the teacher continues to look at him. After approximately 15 seconds elapse, the teacher says, "Barry, please look at me."
> Barry ignores her.
> She bends down and starts picking up the blocks, saying, "OK, I see that you have made your choice. I will pick these up, and you will miss your computer time later."
> Barry, hurrying, starts to pick up now. The teacher stops Barry and says, "No, it's OK. I'll do it this time. Next time, please do it when I ask."
> If Barry starts crying, she escorts him to his desk. (Kapalka, 2009, p. 54)

With teenagers, a similar procedure should be used. A command should start with Step 1, and Step 1 may be repeated (one time only) if necessary. If the command or instruction is not being followed, a warning should be issued, making sure that the teacher follows all of the necessary components (attentional cue, then a clear and firm statement announcing a consequence that will occur as immediately as possible, and then a follow-up look). If the student did not comply, a consequence should be announced, but care should be taken to do so in a manner that is matter-of-fact and does not sound vengeful. If the student becomes defensive, the teacher should walk away and avoid becoming engaged in an argument but should remain firm about the consequence. Teachers should keep in mind that it does not really matter who speaks the last word. It is the consequence that will determine the final outcome of the interaction.

Step 3: Time-out

Boys and teens with ADHD commonly exhibit temper tantrums, and these tantrums are often evident in the classroom. Because these boys have limited self-control, they find it difficult to contain frustration or anger. When an outburst takes place, teachers need to intervene to minimize the disruption to other students, avoid escalation, and eliminate the negative attention that often accompanies a flare-up. The most effective method of intervening involves the implementation of a technique that removes the student from the situation and minimizes further stimulation.

It is important to recognize that some outbursts are mild and may not require much action to attend to them. For example, if a student yells out "That's not fair," the mild outburst is best left alone. If a student doesn't act out while angry but calls the teacher a name, this behavior should not be addressed through a removal technique but be addressed through a behavioral contract discussed in the next step. Only those tantrums where a student continuously screams, yells, wails, and carries on long enough to disrupt teaching the class should result in some form of a time-out. For example, if physical aggression is evident, a time-out is not needed when the student simply throws a pencil to the floor or knocks into a desk while walking away from it, but it becomes necessary when he throws an object across the room (or at the teacher), turns over a desk, breaks an object, or thrashes about in a fit of anger.

Before using time-out, teachers must review some important considerations. There are important state-to-state differences in the definition of corporal punishment. Some states define this term very broadly, not only restricting teachers from placing their hands on the students but also restricting teachers from using certain removal techniques such as placing a student in a corner, facing the wall. In those instances, the teacher can still attain removal by separating the student from others and placing him in a quiet spot, perhaps a corner, but not requiring him to face the wall. It is crucial that teachers check state and local district regulations before selecting an intended time-out procedure.

The most effective method of administering time-out is often seen in schools that specialize in teaching students with emotional and behavioral difficulties. These schools often designate special rooms as time-out rooms. These time-out rooms are devoid of stimulation, are often locked (with a teacher or an aide standing outside and looking in to make sure the student is not in danger), and essentially isolate the student for the duration of the time-out. It is clear that this form of time-out requires special circumstances (and, often, special permission). It is by far, however, the most effective form of time-out. Although teachers in less restrictive settings do not have the option to use such a time-out procedure, this benchmark should be remembered when a time-out procedure within the proper limits of all regulations is established. In other words, teachers should strive to come as close as possible to this ideal use of time-out while remaining within the limits imposed by the educational setting and all pertinent laws and regulations.

Before using this technique, teachers need to prepare a removal spot that will be practical to arrange and will have as little stimulation as possible. Some possibilities include a corner in the classroom, brief removal into the hallway (with supervision), or removal to the front office (not necessarily to see the principal). Teachers should experiment with various settings to come up with the one that will be most effective.

If a student acted out and requires time-out but does not continue to be disruptive (e.g., he continues to cry but does not act out physically), such situations are probably best handled by retaining the student in the classroom but separating him from the rest of the students. For example, the student can be placed in the corner of the classroom that is the furthest away from the other students and not near a computer, toys, or other items that can attract his attention. Some rearrangement of the classroom may be required to establish such a spot. This effort will improve the effectiveness of the time-out, however, and therefore will be rewarded in the long term.

If the student is acting out verbally, it is usually helpful to issue one warning, in accordance with the procedure described in Steps 1 and 2. The teacher should issue the attentional cue, then tell the student to stop, and then administer the follow-up look (if possible) by standing in his vicinity and looking at him for about 15 seconds.

If the warning was not effective, or if the transgression included any form of physical violence, the student should be escorted to the time-out spot and told, "You have to stay here until I say you can leave." If the student continues to act out while in the time-out spot, the teacher should say, "If you don't stop, you'll have to stay here longer."

Once the student begins to calm down, the teacher should start timing. The amount of time the student spends in time-out depends on his age and the seriousness of the offense. Generally, 1 minute per year of age is the rule. Some research has suggested, however, that shorter time-outs are also effective (Kapalka & Bryk, 2007). Thus, teachers may choose a 2-minute time-out for students aged 5 or younger, and older students may require a time-out that follows the rule of 1 minute per year of age.

Once the student has served the time-out sentence, the teacher should approach him and ask, "Do you know why I put you here?" The teacher should try to get the student to recognize why he was placed in time-out. When released, he should be warned, "If you do this again, I'll put you in time-out." If possible and practical, the student should then be returned to the same activity that made him act out in the first place in order for him to have the opportunity to make a better choice of behaviors and experience a different consequence if he makes that better choice.

This technique is often effective with teenagers, but modifications are necessary to make it more practical. With teenagers, time-out cannot be framed as a punishment. Therefore, no warning should be administered, or a power struggle is likely to ensue. Instead, a student who is escalating his anger should be asked to accompany the teacher to a quiet spot in back of the classroom (while others are assigned a task to work on) and told that it is very difficult to teach while he is getting louder and that the teacher is asking him to sit in the back for a few minutes so that he can calm down. When he is calmer, he can return to his desk.

When time-out within the classroom is inappropriate (e.g., the student is violent or continues to be disruptive) or when time-out within the classroom is attempted but the student refuses to comply, a removal-type time-out has to be administered. Teachers should be very careful when approaching teenagers who seem agitated. Although assaults on teachers are relatively rare, it is sensible to be cautious and recognize that many teenagers possess the strength of adults, especially when angry. It is very important to avoid performing behaviors that may agitate him further (e.g., blaming him, questioning him, or violating his space). Instead, it is crucial to remain calm and address him without appearing frantic. If he is behaving in a manner that seems physically intimidating, it is OK to say to the student, "Please stop. You are scaring me, and I do not want to get hurt." Most students, when agitated, do not recognize how threatening they may appear at the time, and when this is pointed out to them in a manner that is calm and nonconfrontational, they begin to bring themselves under control.

Once again, the time-out should be portrayed as a way to help the student rather than as a punishment. The teacher should politely point out to the student that his behaviors are preventing the class from working, and therefore he should go somewhere so he can calm down. A good place to try is the hallway (with supervision) while other students are working on an assignment. If the student continues to be agitated and does not allow removal without incident, the teacher needs to call for help. Although it will be very disruptive to the class to have the student removed from the classroom, it is nevertheless crucial to communicate to the student that if he continues to be disruptive and does not respond to reasonable attempts to get him to stop and/or leave the classroom, the teacher is willing to do whatever is necessary to remain in control of the class.

Most students attending regular education settings will not require such a drastic measure. Some situations, however, may occasionally escalate beyond control. If these episodes become commonplace, the student's placement may need to be changed as quickly as possible, because he may require a setting that is prepared to handle such problems. Students in special education, especially those who attend programs designed to address emotional and behavioral problems, are more likely to exhibit behaviors that require regular removal from class. Teachers in any educational setting, however, should not shy away from removing a student when he is behaving inappropriately and is not responding to less restrictive interventions. It is important to set limits and send a clear message to students regarding which behaviors are (and are not) permitted and what the consequences are for remaining disruptive.

Step 4: Behavioral Contract

The myriad difficulties that boys and teens with ADHD commonly exhibit in the classroom require a comprehensive approach, one that allows the teacher to simultaneously address a variety of problems. A behavioral contract allows teachers to accomplish that goal by providing a method that can be used to encourage appropriate behaviors and discourage problems. This approach has been shown to be effective in reducing classroom problems (Kapalka, 2007b, 2008a). Essentially, a behavioral contract is an exchange program where students earn points or tokens for successfully performing assigned responsibilities, and they are then able to exchange these tokens for privileges and rewards. By implementing a behavioral contract, teachers increase structure within the class. In addition, because certain privileges are now restricted and available only when earned, students learn that the reward or privilege is available only after appropriate behaviors have been performed. This helps them internalize the connection between their behaviors and the resulting consequences, a lesson that is especially valuable for boys and teens with ADHD, because their impulsivity and limited processing of situations make it harder for them to learn these connections.

Developing an effective behavioral contract is a complex task that involves the consideration of many factors. Discussion of all these factors is beyond the confines of this chapter, and professionals interested in a more detailed discussion should consult resources that discuss contingency management more comprehensively (e.g., Kapalka, 2009). This section summarizes some of the most basic principles of behavioral contracting in schools.

First, the teacher needs to list the duties and responsibilities that the student is expected to perform every day (or nearly every day). It is best to start small, with a maximum of about five or six items, and include only things that are part of the student's daily routine, such as handing in a completed assignment at the end of work time in the class, handing in homework, raising his hand before giving an answer, or remaining in his seat throughout a specific period of time. Each task must call for a single, specific behavior that has to be defined precisely. For each item, point values need to be assigned that are commensurate with the amount of effort that a task requires as well as the degree of difficulty evident in the student's ability (or willingness) to perform the behavior.

Next, a list of rewards needs to be developed collaboratively with the student. The rewards should primarily include classroom privileges. Examples include earning recess time, selecting an activity (from a predetermined list) during recess, earning a homework pass for 1 day (which can be specified for a specific subject only), being first in line when going to the playground or lunch, and being allowed to leave the classroom to run an errand to the front office. Some privileges that are used regularly throughout the day (e.g., time on the computer) may be best given out in shorter chunks of time, for example, time on the computer before and after lunch may be used as two separate privileges.

A sample behavioral contract may look like the following (Kapalka, 2009, p. 85):

Responsibilities	Number of chips
Completing assigned class work	1 chip per subject
Remaining on task during class work	1 chip per subject
Raising hand before giving an answer	1 chip per subject matter or per hour

Responsibilities	Number of chips
Remaining quiet during class lecture	1 chip per subject matter or per hour
Remaining seated during class lecture	1 chip per subject matter or per hour

Rewards or privileges	Number of chips
Time on the computer (separately before and after lunch)	2 chips each
Being first in line for recess	4 chips
Being first in line for lunch	4 chips
Homework pass (limit of one per day)	10 chips
Trip to the grab bag	8 chips

After each target behavior is performed, the teacher must immediately give the earned chips or points. Likewise, the teacher needs to require the chips to be cashed in before any item is dispensed from the Rewards or Privileges list. The teacher needs to be consistent and ready to restrict the availability of the items on that list, unless the appropriate number of chips is given beforehand.

The behavioral contract is a tool that is flexible and practical. It can be a skeletal, limited agreement that contains only one target behavior and a single, specific reward or privilege. On the other hand, it can include a comprehensive list of behaviors—some of which occur daily, and some of which are sporadic—and an equally complex system of rewards and privileges. Once the initial contract has successfully been in place for several weeks, various methods can be used to extend it to address a variety of additional problems. These methods can include sporadic tasks and "on the first try" commands (Barkley, 1997b), where the teacher dispenses a small reward (such as a chip) to a student only if he performed a task right after it was assigned, with no repetition or reminder needed. This technique is especially helpful for impulsive and defiant students, as it teaches them to suppress the initial urge to oppose a command or instruction. The boundaries of a successful contract are limited only by the teacher's and student's effort and creativity.

It is also important to start a contract by including only positive behaviors that result in earning points or tokens. Token costs should not be introduced until a few weeks after the contract is running smoothly, and the teacher should designate only one or two behaviors that will result in a small loss of chips. Care should be taken not to take so many chips that the student will lose all that he has earned thus far.

With minor modifications, this technique is very effective with teen-agers. It is best to use points instead of stickers or use point slips that operate in a system of exchange similar to money. Students in middle school and high school commonly attend several classes in a school day. This structure lends itself well to including items pertinent to specific periods, and these items may be different from class to class or remain the same through the whole day (depending on the student's needs and the nature of the problems). This affords his teachers much flexibility with selecting the target behaviors and specific classroom settings that will be included in the contract.

For adolescents, teachers should use age-appropriate rewards, such as increased time using the computer, the privilege to listen to an iPod (with headphones) at the end of a class, or a homework pass. For older adolescents, it may not be necessary to use points. Rather, teachers can use a one-to-one exchange for a privilege if a task is completed, for example, a teenager will be able to use the iPod only after he completed the assigned work for the day (and is at least 75% correct).

Step 5: Transitions

Readers who reviewed the discussion in Chapter 7 of a similar pro-gram for parents may notice that this step was completed as the last portion of the program. Teachers, however, frequently need to direct students to switch from one activity (e.g., free time) to another (e.g., desk work). Because boys and teens with ADHD commonly experi-ence problems with transitions, the frequency of these situations in the classroom requires the completion of this step earlier in the program. This technique has been found effective in reducing transition-related problems in students with ADHD (Kapalka, 2006b). It involves the use of warnings before the transition, rewards after successful transitions, and token costs when the transition did not go smoothly.

Depending on the age of the student, the teacher needs to consider the manner in which the warning will be issued. Teenagers generally have the ability to track time lapse, so announcing that a transition will take place in 5 minutes is meaningful, because teenagers can gauge about how long of a time span that is. Boys in elementary school, especially in lower grades, have not yet developed a sufficient concept of time lapse, so issuing a statement that announces a transition in 5 minutes is rarely helpful. Instead, the time frame must be expressed in a manner that is meaningful considering the student's age. For example, when the student is playing a game, the teacher can warn that the transition will occur when the current level (or portion of the game) is completed. In keeping with the "three bells" approach described in Chapter 11, it is helpful to give two warnings before the actual transition takes place—a longer one that announces that a transition will take place a little later, and a second warning when the transition will occur shortly. When the announcement of the actual transition is issued (i.e., the transition is to take place now), the student must quickly engage in the new situation in order to earn the tokens. This technique teaches the student to anticipate the transition, use mental preparation to adjust to the transition, and suppress the impulse to continue with the previous activity. As with all other techniques, extensive practice enhances learning, and teachers should look for opportunities to use this technique frequently through the school day. After problems have diminished for a sufficient amount of time (at least 2 weeks, with good transitions evident), teachers may gradually fade the use of the reward, for example, issue a token reward after several successful transitions in a portion of the school day.

Step 6: Interruptions

Students with ADHD commonly interrupt others because they have difficulties suppressing the impulse to say something or get someone's attention. Young students are especially likely to exhibit calling out within the classroom, a behavior that is troubling to many teachers. A technique aimed at gradually teaching the child to suppress that impulse has been found effective with defiant children (Barkley, 1997b) and with students with ADHD (Kapalka, 2005c, 2005d). It is based on operant conditioning and involves gradual exposure to situations where the impulse is likely to occur, while warning the student that the situation is about to occur. Because good impulse control is rewarded, the behavior is gradually shaped, and eventually the warnings are discontinued.

Class lectures provide the best opportunities for teachers to implement this procedure. At the onset, the teacher warns the student, in private, that a portion of a lecture is about to take place, and he is not to call out answers without first raising his hand and waiting to be called on. When he exhibits good self-control, a token will be set aside to be given to him right after the portion of the lecture is over. Every time he calls out without waiting to be asked, he will lose a token. When the technique is first implemented, teachers should use it during at least two or three distinct segments per day, making sure that each segment is not longer than a half hour. Over time, the length of the segments may be increased. After a few weeks, the warnings can be discontinued, but the same rule applies—no interruption results in earning a token, and an interruption results in losing a token. When the student becomes able to successfully inhibit the impulse to interrupt, the tokens can be phased out, but praise should continue to be given and will help maintain the treatment gains.

Step 7: Out-of-Class Settings

Boys with ADHD frequently act out while in the lunchroom, in a gym class, on the playground, and so on. Some of these problems are secondary to the additional stimulation that these environments commonly contain. Once an effective behavioral contract has been implemented, it can be extended to include behaviors in these settings, and the efficacy of this approach has been established with defiant children (Barkley, 1997b) and students with ADHD (Kapalka, 2002, 2008b).

It is necessary to set one or two simple rules for the student before he goes to the target setting. The rules must be attainable, clear, and very specific (e.g., "Remain at your seat during lunch" or "Do not run while on the playground"). After the student confirms his understanding of these rules, a token reward for following the rule should be set (e.g., "You will earn five chips when you get back to the classroom"). Sometimes, it can also be effective to set a token cost if the rules are not followed (e.g., "If you break the rules, you will lose five chips"). It is important to focus only on a few rules at a time.

Because someone other than the classroom teacher will usually monitor the student's behavior in those settings, it becomes important to review with that teacher or staff member the major principles of the techniques used thus far, including the importance of eye contact and the avoidance of repetitions. The person who will monitor the student has to establish appropriate expectations and determine the point at which the student is considered to have broken the rules.

Teachers should start small and expect a gradual improvement. It is advisable to initially implement this procedure by focusing on one outside setting (e.g., the lunchroom) before proceeding to others (e.g., the library) and to implement it first in the settings that result in fewer difficulties and gradually add settings in accordance with a hierarchy of the degree of the severity of the problems.

Step 8: Homework

Boys and teens with ADHD often forget to write down homework assignments or fail to bring home necessary books, notebooks, and so on. In addition to being disorganized, students with ADHD often do not like doing homework because their problems with impulse control make it hard to delay the gratification of engaging in play activity and perform homework instead.

To address problems with homework, the teacher must develop an effective homework routine in the classroom. First, the teacher must implement a homework journal. When homework is assigned, the specifics must be written on the board to help the student with ADHD know exactly what needs to be written in the homework journal. Before students are dismissed, it is necessary for the teacher to check whether the student with ADHD wrote everything accurately in the journal. Before the student leaves school for the day, the teacher must also help him make sure that everything needed for homework will be brought home. For younger students, teachers should offer assistance at the end of the day. For older students, a homework buddy may be assigned (as discussed in the previous chapter).

Although maintaining this routine has been shown to be among the most effective changes that teachers can implement (Barkley, 2006; DuPaul & Stoner, 2003), teachers often resist these interventions. Teachers of students in upper elementary school grades or those in middle school often feel that they are fostering dependence and instead must force students, through a "sink-or-swim" approach, to learn to be more independent. Clinicians must help teachers recognize that boys and teens with ADHD are generally unable to exhibit the same level of academic independence as their age and grade peers, especially when it comes to homework, and an approach that attempts to place too much responsibility on the student, without appropriate assistance and oversight, is likely to be very counterproductive.

Teachers usually find it helpful to extend the behavioral contract to include the completion of homework. They can do this by designating an amount of tokens or points for every assignment handed in the next day. Alternately, teachers may use a similar approach but give the points or tokens only when all assignments have been handed in for the day, with none of them missing. This motivates the student to complete all of the work to earn the reward.

Establishing effective home–school communication is a crucial component of success with homework. Teachers should reach out to parents and offer to develop a collaborative approach to help the student. When a homework journal is established, it provides a convenient way for teachers and parents to communicate. Boys with ADHD often do not write down homework assignments correctly, or they lose their notes and/or assignments. When parents ask the boy, "Do you have any homework?" and the boy replies, "No," the parents must be reasonably sure that the response is correct. A homework journal provides the means to help parents receive accurate information about homework that is verified by the teacher. To back up the school contract, parents may want to connect a privilege to full completion of all homework assignments (as discussed in Chapter 7). If the student forgets the journal or any materials necessary to complete all assignments, he will lose that privilege for the day. Consistent implementation of a constructive homework procedure and an effective homework journal (in collaboration with the student's parents) is the most effective way of improving homework problems.

Long-Term Management

Consistent use of the techniques described in this chapter requires teacher perseverance and ongoing effort. Over time, some of these steps should continue to be used indefinitely, whereas others can be phased out.

Teachers should continue to use Steps 1 and 2 without stopping. Students with ADHD have impulsive tendencies and self-control problems, and they return to old patterns of behavior quickly upon discontinuation of these techniques. The need for Step 3 (time-out) is likely to diminish as students learn better self-control, but it is beneficial to retain this option just in case it becomes necessary.

Teachers often stop using the behavioral contract when problems begin to diminish. When the contract is discontinued, however, many students with ADHD gradually begin to exhibit more problems. It is usually desirable to continue the contract indefinitely, although it can be streamlined significantly, for example, by focusing on only one or two aspects that still require attention (e.g., homework). A one-to-one exchange may be used where the student earns a specific privilege (such as the ability to use the computer that day) in exchange for completion of homework.

SUMMARY

Results of research studies have revealed that contingency-management programs are the most effective pedagogical methods of addressing problem behaviors in school. To maximize the effectiveness of these programs, mental health professionals should establish a consulting relationship with the student's teacher and offer assistance on an ongoing basis. A variety of behavior management programs have been developed to help teachers address problems commonly associated with symptoms of ADHD, including disruptive behaviors and noncompletion of work. Typically, teachers are guided to gradually implement a set of techniques that target common classroom problems. One such program was reviewed in this chapter.

When implementing a comprehensive behavior management program, teachers need to start by learning about ADHD and developing an understanding of how symptoms of this disorder become expressed in school settings. This will help teachers establish appropriate expectations. Next, teachers should methodically implement techniques aimed at giving commands, avoiding repetitions, giving warnings, addressing temper tantrums, and implementing a behavioral contract. When contingency management is established, the system can be used to address remaining problems with classroom routines, work completion, disruptive behaviors (such as interrupting), transitions, and behavior control in out-of-class settings. Collaboration between the student's teachers and parents is an important component of school success, and the contingency-management program can also assist teachers and parents in improving the student's homework completion.

Medical Approaches

13

Stimulant Medications

As reviewed in Chapter 3 of this volume, extensive data are now available that suggest that individuals with attention deficit/hyperactivity disorder (ADHD) exhibit differences in transporter gene markers that strongly suggest a genetic predisposition for functional brain differences. Neuroanatomical and neurophysiological scans consistently reveal that individuals with ADHD exhibit abnormalities in the size and level of activity on the frontal and prefrontal lobes, basal ganglia, and cerebellum. These differences are associated with underactivation of dopaminergic and noradrenergic neurotransmission that underlies the difficulties in self-control, impulse control, and sustained attention that individuals with ADHD exhibit.

Effective treatment of boys, male teens, and men with ADHD is generally accomplished through a multisystemic approach. The components usually include psychotherapeutic work with the client and immediate family members and education interventions. In many cases, these components are supplemented by the use of medications that aim to address the neurophysiological deficits associated with this disorder.

Clinicians, clients, and family members often ask when it is necessary to consider medications. The medical literature does not address this question. Indeed, the presumption in medical research is that medications are the treatment of choice and should be implemented regardless of what other approaches are used (Greenhill, 2002). Most nonmedical professionals, however, do not regard the use of medications as mandatory in all cases. Thus, clinicians must first consider which clients should be referred for medications.

WHEN TO CONSIDER MEDICATIONS

Determining who should be referred for treatment with medications requires a review of several factors, not the least of which is the client's and/or family members' receptivity to such a recommendation. Many clients are not comfortable with the use of medications, especially to treat psychological disorders. In fact, there is a significant antimedication movement, lead by well-known figures such as Peter Breggin, who considers himself a crusader against psychiatric interventions (Gorman & Park, 1994). Although most individuals do not hold such extreme views, many are still reluctant to try psychotropics.

Of all psychotropic medications, stimulants have received perhaps the most attention in the popular media. In the past two decades, there have been hundreds, if not thousands, of television programs, magazine articles, and newspaper stories that portray these medications as dangerous drugs. Clinicians need to develop a more objective view about medications, based on data rather than on irrational fear and conjecture. True, no medications are 100% safe, and all medications cause side effects, at least in some people. Mental health professionals, however, must also be aware that psychostimulants, as a group, have the least likelihood of adverse effects of any group of psychotropic medications and have been studied for over 50 years. Media-induced paranoia notwithstanding, psychostimulants really are safe and effective overall.

Regardless of objective evidence, however, many clients may still reject the idea of medications. In fact, males are especially likely to reject medical and mental health treatment, and members of ethnic minorities exhibit this trend even more strongly (Cuffe, Waller, Cuccaro, Pumariega, & Garrison, 1995). Clinicians must think about these factors when considering a referral for medications. Clearly, there are some cases where treatment with medications should be attempted. Professionals should review two factors when deciding which clients are likely to exhibit minimal improvement without medications.

Severity of Symptoms

Boys, teens, and men who exhibit symptoms of severe intensity and very significant impairment are not likely to exhibit much improvement when medications are not used. For example, young boys with major deficits in self-control that produce considerable impulsivity and hyperactivity will generally continue to exhibit unmanageable behaviors, and attempts at working with them to improve self-control will be of minimal value. Although parents need to use appropriate behavior management strategies regardless of whether medications are used, severe conflicts are likely to continue. Although no one likes to use medications with children, professionals (and parents) need to consider which is the worst alternative—continue the conflicts and expose the child and the family to the additional negative effects on self-esteem that these problems gradually produce or help the boy begin to bring himself under control by trying some medications. Of course, when medications are used, counseling and behavior management techniques should be used in conjunction.

The issue of symptom severity is similarly relevant to older boys, teens, and men. Those who struggle with self-control and exhibit severe impulsivity, hyperactivity, and/or distractibility are not likely to make much progress without medications. Clinicians can gauge the level of severity of symptoms from interview data, but sometimes self-report and observer-report accounts are not accurate and may exaggerate severity. When clinicians have reasons to question the accuracy of information received during the interviews, use of the standardized instruments discussed in Chapter 4 may prove very valuable. The higher the severity scores evident on those measures, the more likely it is that the use of medications will be unavoidable.

Settings With Significant Problems

Most clients, as well as nonmedical mental health professionals, prefer to try to address symptoms without medications. In some settings, nonmedical interventions usually produce significant changes. Although the use of medications may also be helpful, especially when symptoms are severe, boys and teens who present with behavioral problems within the home can be helped through individual treatment (Chapter 6) and parent training (Chapter 7). Similarly, personal and family problems that men with ADHD exhibit are good candidates for individual (Chapter 8) and family (Chapter 9) interventions. In some cases, group interventions (Chapter 10) may also be very helpful, particularly to help boys, teens, and men develop social skills.

In some settings, however, nonmedical approaches may produce some changes, but these changes may not be enough to sufficiently address present impairment. For boys and teens, school-related problems fall into this category. Although educational modifications (Chapter 11) and behavioral management programs (Chapter 12) are necessary and usually produce results, when symptoms are severe, the improvement seen with those strategies will not be sufficient.

Clinicians must keep in mind that the school setting particularly predisposes boys and teens with ADHD to difficulties, because the skills and behaviors needed to succeed within that setting are directly impaired by the symptoms of ADHD. In school, students are required to remain still and quiet much more so than within most other settings. For example, an impulsive boy who often interrupts at home may be somewhat difficult to deal with, but the same level of symptoms at school will result in a significant disruption of the classroom. When the boy is fidgety or hyperactive, the disruption is even more severe. When the boy is stimulated by the presence (and behaviors) of other students, his self-control will diminish even further.

Inattention also presents with the same pattern. Although at home it may be a moderate problem that causes difficulties completing assigned tasks and chores, the same symptoms cause more significant impairment in school. Students who are distractible and disorganized miss significant portions of classroom instruction, fail to complete assignments, and generally fall behind academically. Some older students who present primarily inattentive symptoms, especially when they are motivated to improve and are receptive to psychotherapy, may be successfully treated with the interventions discussed in Chapter 6. Students who are very young, are not very receptive to suggestions, and exhibit more severe symptoms, however, usually will need to be treated with medications in addition to counseling.

The same holds true for men with ADHD. When they exhibit significant impairment in the workplace, medications may need to be considered. Some men who have problems organizing their work and keeping track of tasks and responsibilities respond well to counseling treatment, especially when they are very motivated to improve. Those men who may be ambivalent about psychotherapy, however, have a low sense of self-efficacy, and those who present with severe impairment are also likely to require medications in addition to the interventions discussed in Chapter 7.

When clinicians are discussing the topic of medication with clients, it is helpful to use an analogy to illustrate the principles that must be considered when making a decision. As an example, as previously discussed in Chapters 6 and 7, clinicians may discuss a patient who comes into the physician's office and is found to have high blood pressure. Whether the physician will recommend medications is based on several factors. If the patient is overweight and does not exercise or watch his diet and if the blood pressure level is not at an alarming level, the physician may recommend delaying the use of medications and trying to control the blood pressure through weight loss, an increase of exercise, and a proper diet (e.g., limiting the intake of sodium). When the blood pressure is alarmingly high and/or the patient is not overweight, eats right, and exercises daily and still presents with blood pressure problems, however, medications will usually be needed.

RATIONALE

Symptoms of ADHD are produced, at least in part, by underlying structural and functional differences in the brain. As reviewed in Chapter 3, children with ADHD exhibit smaller basal ganglia, a smaller inferior posterior lobe of the cerebellum, and a smaller size in three regions of the frontal lobes—the anterior cingulate gyrus (linked to the control of executive functions), the left dorsolateral region (involved in working memory and cognitive functions), and the right frontal region (linked to alertness and focusing). Changes in the size of the corpus callosum were also revealed.

According to the current understanding of neurophysiology, these identified brain regions are regulated by catecholamine neurotransmitters, especially dopamine and norepinephrine. More specifically, symptoms of ADHD are presumed to be produced by functional deficits in three of the brain's four dopaminergic pathways (mesocortical, mesolimbic, and nigrostriatal) as well as the prefrontal norepinephrine pathway. In essence, those pathways are underactivated, and functional deficits result that present as symptoms of ADHD. To correct these deficits, medications that target the action of dopamine (primarily) and norepinephrine (as a secondary mechanism) are used and increase the activity of those neurotransmitters. The medications that accomplish this increase most directly, and to the greatest degree, are known as psychostimulants.

The amount of neurotransmitter that is available to traverse the synapse and activate the postsynaptic neuron is regulated by a complex mechanism that includes many components. The most direct manner of increasing the action of a neurotransmitter is to introduce a compound that will mimic the endogenous chemical and directly bind to the postsynaptic receptors. More indirect ways involve increasing the availability of the neurotransmitter to perform its own action, which can be accomplished by increasing the production of the neurotransmitter in presynaptic cells, so it more becomes available for release into the synapse when the neuron fires. Another method involves interfering with any mechanism involved in removing the neurotransmitter from the synapse. For example, one way in which catecholamines are regulated is through a process of reuptake, where the neuron that just released the neurotransmitter into the synapse takes the chemical back in. Blocking or diminishing that reuptake results in more neurotransmitters remaining in the synapse, and therefore the chance of stimulating the postsynaptic neuron increases. Psychostimulants use a variety of these mechanisms to increase dopaminergic action. Although the primary mechanism is that of reuptake inhibition, various stimulants also use these other mechanisms, at least to some degree. The net effect of stimulants is a significant increase in dopaminergic activity and a lesser (but still important) increase in noradrenergic activity. As a result, the brain structures identified previously, particularly including the basal ganglia and the frontal lobes, become more active.

Sometimes clients, and some clinicians, refer to the effect of stimulants on symptoms of ADHD as "paradoxical," because the medication (a stimulant) seems to have a calming effect. This term is a misnomer, however, and clinicians are discouraged from thinking about psychostimulants in that way. It is more accurate to conceptualize the impulsivity and motor overactivity as failures of self-control because parts of the brain are less active than they should be. Thus, a stimulant stimulates the brain to improve its ability to control motor (and other) impulses because areas in the brain responsible for self-control become more active.

RESEARCH SUPPORT

Of all the treatment approaches to address the symptoms of ADHD, the use of psychostimulants has been researched the longest. Since Bradley's (1937) seminal paper, child professionals have noted that the use of stimulants has a positive effect on the reduction of disruptive behaviors and the improvement of attention to task. In the 1960s double-blind, placebo-controlled trials began, and to date over 200 have been performed (Connor & Steingard, 2004). In fact, the use of stimulants to treat symptoms of ADHD is considered to be the best-supported approach, with the most research evidence documenting its effectiveness (Greenhill, 2002). The results of these studies reveal that 50% to 90% of children with ADHD exhibit significant improvement in the core symptoms of ADHD and subsequent improvement in behavioral, social, and academic functioning (Barkley, 2006).

The degree of improvement in the symptoms is directly relevant to whether comorbid conditions are present. It is apparent that psychostimulants are most effective in individuals who present with pure symptoms of ADHD, with no comorbid disorders. For example, 95% of children with ADHD hyperactive-impulsive type or ADHD combined type and 76% of children with ADHD inattentive type have been shown to exhibit significant improvement on stimulant medications (Carlson & Mann, 2000). The response rates for patients with ADHD comorbid with other disorders are not as high. Thus, clinicians should be aware that a careful and comprehensive diagnosis is necessary to administer effective treatment. Those boys and teens with ADHD who present with no comorbidities and a high severity of symptoms are probably the best candidates for medications, whereas those who exhibit symptoms of comorbid disorders may need be treated with other medications (as discussed in the next chapter).

In adults, stimulant medications are also the best-studied approach (Barkley, 2006), but only about 20 trials have been published, and not all of them were placebo controlled (Wilens, Spencer, & Biederman, 2002). In addition, the results are not as unequivocal, and 25% to 78% of adults with ADHD have been shown to exhibit significant symptom reduction (Barkley, 2006). As with boys and teens, comorbidities are important to consider. Men who present with symptoms of ADHD without comorbid disorders are expected to exhibit the best response to stimulants, whereas those who also exhibit symptoms of other disorders may need different medications. Once again, an accurate and comprehensive differential diagnosis is crucial.

For a variety of reasons, including the influence of the media, clients are often reluctant to try stimulant medications. Nonstimulant medications have been developed, one of which (Atomoxetine) is specifically approved to treat symptoms of ADHD in children, teens, and adults. Thus, the question of whether to use a stimulant as the first-line drug must be considered. Although some research has shown that Atomoxetine is as effective as stimulants (Spencer et al., 2002), other research findings have suggested that the response to Atomoxetine is not as good as it is to stimulants (Gibson, Bettinger, Patel, & Crimson, 2006). In addition, as discussed in the next chapter, Atomoxetine presents with a greater risk of side effects than stimulants. Consequently, stimulants are still considered the first-line medications to address symptoms of ADHD, and other drugs are generally used when stimulants are not effective or not appropriate.

Because the brain action of psychostimulants is similar to that of methamphetamine and cocaine, some clients and clinicians are concerned about the risk of abuse and dependence on psychostimulants. When used in high doses, and in ways in which stimulants are quickly introduced into the blood stream (e.g., by snorting or smoking), these medications indeed produce euphoric feelings that are similar to those produced by methamphetamine and cocaine, and when they are abused repeatedly over a significant period of time, physiological and psychological dependence is likely, and withdrawal symptoms will be evident upon discontinuation. Clients and mental health professionals contemplating the use of stimulant medications, however, need to recognize that the dosage used to treat symptoms of ADHD is far from sufficient to produce any of the effects associated with substance abuse and dependence. That said, teenagers and men who are given prescriptions for psychostimulants should be monitored to make sure they are taking only the appropriate dose and administering the medication in the manner in which it is prescribed. Those clients who have a history of significant use of drugs or alcohol will need to be watched carefully to make sure they do not begin to abuse the stimulants or sell them to others.

A related concern is often expressed regarding the risk of subsequent drug abuse or dependence problems that may develop in individuals who previously have been treated with psychostimulants. Research findings have not supported this hypothesis. It has been shown that teenagers and adults who were previously diagnosed with ADHD exhibit greater rates of smoking (Lambert, 2002) and illegal drug use (Manuzza, Klein, Bessler, Malloy, & LaPadulla, 1993), especially when comorbid psychological conditions are present (Biederman et al., 1995), but the vast majority of studies do not differentiate individuals who have been treated with stimulants from those who received other treatment or no treatment at all. Some studies have specifically investigated whether the use of stimulants in childhood sensitizes individuals for subsequent substance abuse, and only one study out of 14 found a link. It is notable that the one study that suggested the connection (Lambert & Harsough, 1998) did not control for comorbidities, for example, conduct disorder, which has been shown to be a better predictor of substance abuse problems. Thus, it is likely that the severity of the symptoms of ADHD, rather than prior treatment with stimulants, is a factor that affects the risk for future substance abuse.

In fact, some evidence has suggested that individuals with ADHD who have previously been treated with stimulants exhibit lower risks of substance abuse problems (Biederman et al., 1997). A recent meta-analysis of six studies that compared individuals with ADHD treated with stimulants to those treated with other means found that studies seem to consistently reveal that individuals treated with stimulants actually exhibit a lower risk of future substance abuse problems (Wilens, Faraone, Biederman, & Gunawardene, 2003). This finding is not surprising. Individuals with ADHD who have been untreated, especially when the onset of symptoms was very early and the severity was high, are at the greatest risk for developing substance abuse problems (Wilens, 2002). With treatment, the risk diminishes, and because studies have shown that treatment with stimulants seems to result in greater symptom reduction than other treatments (Ambroggio & Jensen, 2002), it is logical to conclude that treatment with stimulants reduces future risk of substance abuse difficulties.

Stimulants offer one additional advantage over all other medications used to treat symptoms of ADHD. Stimulant medications do not have to be given every day. So-called drug holidays have been studied over many years (Barkley, 2006). Some time ago, doctors recommended drug holidays—for example, not taking medications on weekends or during the summer—because it was expected that those periods without medications would compensate for the reduction in caloric intake that many children experience on stimulant medications. Since then, studies have shown that this approach has not been effective, and doctors now recommend taking the medications daily (Janicak et al., 2006). Drug holidays have not been found to be harmful, however, and do not appear to limit efficacy of stimulants on the days when medications are used. Many parents prefer to use medications only on those days when boys and teens need them most, for example, on school days or on weekends when there is an event during which poor self-control is especially problematic. With stimulants, parents have that choice, whereas that choice is not available when other medications are used.

Clinicians should consider one final point about the use of stimulants, as well as any other medications. When drug trials are performed, efficacy of a medication is defined by a statistically significant reduction in symptoms. In most cases, this does not mean that symptoms were eliminated, but it indicates that symptoms significantly diminished from the baseline only with the use of medications. In fact, Stahl (2000) suggested that, on average, medical studies consider a medication to be effective when only a 50% improvement in symptoms is noted. Clearly, the remaining symptoms still need clinical attention. Mental health professionals should not expect that individuals treated with stimulant (or other) medications will exhibit total symptom remission. Rather, a significant improvement can be expected, but other methods of treatment will still be necessary to address the remaining symptoms.

AVAILABLE MEDICATIONS

Although stimulants are rather similar to each other with regard to their pharmacodynamics (the neurophysiologic action), they differ in many other aspects, for example, with regard to pharmacokinetics (routes of administration, onset, and duration of effect, etc.). Clinicians should be aware of the various stimulant medications available on the market and the practical differences that separate them.

Methylphenidate and Derivatives

Methylphenidate is among the oldest stimulants on the market. It was introduced in 1957 and continues to be marketed in the United States as Ritalin in its original, immediate-release preparation. It is also available in sustained release form as Ritalin SR, and both of these are available as generics. This information is especially important for clients who have limited health care coverage and must pay for medications out of pocket.

Other preparations of methylphenidate have also been developed, primarily to extend its duration of action or provide another method of taking the medication. Various forms of extended release methylphenidate are being marketed, including Ritalin LA, Concerta, Metadate ER, Metadate CD, and Methylin ER. Differences in their duration of action are discussed next. Methylin is a chewable form of immediate-release methylphenidate. It is appropriate for those clients who have difficulties swallowing tablets or capsules. It is also available in an oral solution. Daytrana is a methylphenidate patch that allows administration of the medication through parenteral (not involving the digestive tract) means. Unfortunately, none of these are available as generics.

Another form of methylphenidate is also being marketed. Dexmethylphenidate is a selected isomer of methylphenidate, meaning that it is only a portion of the entire chemical chain of the methylphenidate molecule. It is available in immediate-release form as Focalin and in extended-release form as Focalin XR. These are not available as generics.

Pharmacodynamics. All psychostimulants increase catecholamine activity, and most stimulants are generally selective for dopamine and affect norepinephrine to a minor degree. Thus, the use of stimulants results in enhanced brain function in all dopaminergic regions, including the nigrostriatal, mesolimbic, and mesocortical pathways that are primarily involved in the symptoms of ADHD. Methylphenidate increases the amount of dopamine in the synapse primarily by blocking the reuptake process, and therefore the dopamine that is released into the synapse remains there in higher amounts, thus increasing the likelihood of postsynaptic stimulation.

Some research has tried to identify which portion of the amphetamine chain seems to have the greatest result in affecting the specific subtypes of dopaminergic receptors involved in symptoms of ADHD. For example, Challman and Lipsky (2000) suggested that the dextro isomer is more involved in the mediation of symptoms of ADHD (especially, attention) and that the levo isomer, when isolated, seems to have little effect. As a result, the dextro isomer has been marketed as dexmethylphenidate (Focalin and Focalin XR). Head-to-head studies comparing dexmethylphenidate with methylphenidate, however, have not revealed significant differences in efficacy. This may be because of the significant individual differences in the distribution of dopaminergic receptor subtypes (Ballas, Evans, & Dinges, 2004). Thus, the choice of which stimulant to prescribe is primarily made by considering differences in pharmacokinetics and by tracking individual response patterns.

Pharmacokinetics. The first issue that is usually considered when a prescription for a stimulant is contemplated is whether the patient will tolerate swallowing a tablet or a capsule. Those who are expected to have difficulties with pills are good candidates for chewable tablets or the oral solution, although only immediate-release methylphenidate is available in these forms (Methylin). Another option has been explored by using Metadate CD and Ritalin LA capsules and sprinkling the contents into food (apple sauce or a similar food works especially well as a base). Although drug manufacturers claim that this method of using the medication does not change its effectiveness, some have suggested that it decreases the duration of the clinical effect.

Recently, a patch has become available (Daytrana). It is used by placing a square of medicated adhesive pad onto an inconspicuous part of the skin. This patch offers numerous advantages—the digestive tract is bypassed, and the duration of action can be controlled by removing the patch when the effect is no longer needed. Some children who are very active, however, may have difficulties keeping the patch applied to their skin, and others may find it annoying to have the patch present on their skin. Skin irritation in some patients has also been reported.

When administered, methylphenidate starts to act quickly. Generally, improvement in symptoms is seen in less than an hour, although consuming the medication after a heavy breakfast may delay the onset of effect to some extent. Most doctors recommend taking the medication right before breakfast. This allows the medication to start working quickly, but if breakfast is consumed before the medication takes full effect, suppression of appetite (discussed later) will not yet be evident.

The duration of effect of immediate-release stimulants is rather short. Ritalin is marketed as acting for about 4 hours, but clinical data have shown that in many children the effect lasts for only 2 or 3 hours. Ritalin SR lasts about an hour or 2 longer than immediate-release Ritalin. The duration of effect of Methylin (chewable tablets or liquid) varies widely, with a range of 3 to 8 hours reported (Bezchlibnyk-Butler & Jeffries, 2007). Most individuals taking immediate-release methylphenidate will need multiple dosing, usually every 4 hours or so. This may present practical difficulties, for example, boys and teens will have to take a dose in school, and men will need to take divided doses during work hours. Because of that inconvenience, extended-release forms are usually preferred.

Because it is desirable to attain immediate relief of symptoms, extended-release preparations must generally include a dual-release mechanism, where some portion of the medication is released immediately after administration, to begin to work quickly, whereas the remaining portion is released more slowly, to provide an extended duration of effect. Concerta releases 22% of its content immediately and 78% through delayed release and has been shown to last for up to 12 hours. Metadate CD has a similar ratio, but the effect lasts for only about 8 hours. Focalin XR releases 50% immediately and the remaining 50% through delayed release and lasts up to 12 hours. Ritalin LA has a similar ratio, but the effect lasts for about 8 hours. Rather than being engineered with dual-release, both Methylin ER and Metadate ER provide a slow, continual release of the active compound and last between 4 and 8 hours (Bezchlibnyk-Butler & Jeffries, 2007). Such a wide option of choices allows doctors to select the medication based on how much immediate release is necessary to quickly result in improvement of symptoms and how long the effect will last. Ideally, a stimulant begins to work quickly and lasts through late afternoon (e.g., through homework time), but its effects wear off well before dinner so that there is no suppression of appetite.

Dosing. Methylphenidate is generally dosed by body weight. In children, efficacy is expected at the dose of 1 mg of total daily intake for every 1 kg of body weight. Thus, a child weighing about 70 pounds (approximately 32 kg) would generally be expected to respond to a dose between 30 mg and 35 mg of the medication per day. Immediate-release preparations are generally given in two or three divided doses. Extended-release products are administered in the morning with a single dose approximately equal to the 1 mg/kg ratio. Sometimes lower doses are effective, and some children with fast metabolisms require daily doses up to 3 mg/kg (Bezchlibnyk-Butler & Jeffries, 2007). Dexmethylphenidate is usually dosed at lower levels—usually about 50% to 75% of the dose of methylphenidate.

Immediate-release methylphenidate is usually started with a 2.5 mg dose twice a day (BID), and medication is increased weekly by 2.5 mg per day until the desired response is observed (providing no serious adverse effects are evident). The maximum dose is generally 60 mg per day, although higher doses are sometimes used if they are needed and if the medication is well tolerated. If the medication is used three times a day (TID), it is common for the last dose to be the lowest. For example, a child who takes 20 mg in the morning and 20 mg at lunchtime might be given only 5 mg or 10 mg after school. The last dose must be taken well in advance of bedtime so that the duration of effect will cease before dinner or, at the latest, before bedtime.

Adults are not generally dosed by body weight. Immediate-release medication is usually started with a dose of 10 mg to 20 mg BID or TID and gradually increased until sufficient clinical effect is observed (and adverse effects are minimal). Extended-release formulations are taken at full dose once per day, in the morning. Adults generally receive up to 120 mg of total dose per day, although most respond at a much lower level (Bezchlibnyk-Butler & Jeffries, 2007).

Adverse Effects. Methylphenidate is generally well tolerated. The most common side effect is the suppression of appetite. During the duration of the clinical effect, patients generally eat little, although this varies from person to person. Some research studies have revealed that because of the suppression of appetite, those individuals who were treated with stimulants as children generally attain somewhat lower height as adults (Barkley, 2006). For this reason, it is recommended that the medication be taken close to breakfast so that the clinical effect does not yet begin when breakfast is consumed, thus ensuring the intake of adequate food at the first meal. During lunch, medication is generally in the system, and many patients eat little or may skip lunch all together. If the medication is timed appropriately so that the clinical effect wears off in advance of dinner, however, most patients make up during dinner the intake of food they missed during lunch. Still, some who take stimulants exhibit significant suppression of appetite later in the day as well. Stimulants may not be appropriate for those clients.

Methylphenidate interferes with sleep. Although this is a desirable effect in some situations (accordingly the compound is approved to treat narcolepsy), those who take this medication to treat symptoms of ADHD must make sure that the clinical effect wears off well before bedtime. With immediate-release preparations, this is usually not a major concern, because the medication can easily be timed so that the last dose is taken at least 4 to 6 hours before bedtime. With extended-release forms, this may be more difficult. Dose-response curves for methylphenidate reveal that when the clinical effect begins to wear off, there is still enough medication in the system to interfere with sleep. For this reason, extended-release preparations are always dosed once per day, in the morning. If more medication is needed in the afternoon, for example, if the clinical effect begins to wear off while homework must still be done, a small dose of immediate-release methylphenidate to take after school may be prescribed.

Some adverse effects are transient and may be seen in some patients at the onset of treatment. These effects generally resolve after a week or two and may include abdominal pain, nausea, and headaches. These effects are relatively uncommon and are seen in 23% of patients or less. In addition, these effects are usually mild and do not cause patients to discontinue the medication. Of course, if these effects persist and the patient is uncomfortable, another medication should be considered.

Other side effects are less common but can nevertheless be encountered, especially in individuals who present with additional disorders comorbid with ADHD. Some patients exhibit symptoms of agitation when administered methylphenidate. This effect may be evident through increased anger, explosive behaviors, flattening of affect, and withdrawal. Sometimes this is accompanied by a dazed quality where motor output is decreased, and the individual appears more lethargic. This reaction is more likely in individuals who present with symptoms of depression or agitation, but sometimes those who do not present these tendencies exhibit these symptoms after they take the medication. Those patients are best treated with nonstimulant medications.

Methylphenidate, as all stimulants, belongs to a broader category of medications called sympathomimetics. This category includes medications that have the effect of mimicking the activation of the sympathetic branch of the autonomic nervous system. Part of this action includes activation of the fight–flight mechanism involved in anxiety reactions. Thus, some patients who take methylphenidate begin to exhibit symptoms of anxiety. This anxiety is especially likely in individuals who initially present with comorbid anxiety. Patient response varies widely, however. Although some children with ADHD and comorbid anxiety disorders tend to become more anxious on methylphenidate, others exhibit positive response in both symptom clusters, and anxiety diminishes along with symptoms of ADHD (Barkley, 2006). For this reason, the presence of anxiety is not necessarily a counterindication for the use of methylphenidate, and individual response must be carefully monitored.

Much has been written about the risk of patients developing motor tics while on stimulant medications. Some time ago, it was feared that the use of methylphenidate may somehow sensitize children to tics, and those who began to exhibit tics on the medication were presumed to be at risk for developing permanent motor tics and twitches. This fear has been largely dispelled. It is now understood that ADHD and tic disorders share some of the same neurophysiological etiology, and those patients who begin to tic on the medications are likely to have genetic tendencies toward tic disorders. More important, it is now recognized that when the stimulant is discontinued, the tics go away. The presence of a diagnosed tic disorder comorbid with ADHD may be expected to be a counterindication for the use of methylphenidate. Studies have revealed, however, that some patients who are diagnosed with comorbid Tourette's disorder and ADHD exhibit a reduction in symptoms of both disorders when given methylphenidate (Barkley, 2006). For this reason, even when comorbid tics are evident, doctors may still try a prescription for methylphenidate, and individual response will be carefully monitored.

It has recently become clear that about 13% of patients who take methylphenidate exhibit cardiovascular side effects, including increased heart rate and blood pressure (Bezchlibnyk-Butler & Jeffries, 2007). Although these changes are generally seen upon the start of therapy, and most patients return to normal cardiovascular function after about 2 weeks of treatment, some continue to exhibit problems. In fact, a small number of deaths have been reported. In all cases, however, it was revealed that the child had a congenital heart defect that was asymptomatic and therefore was not discovered before the medication was started. For this reason, doctors will sometimes require an electrocardiogram (EKG) before methylphenidate is prescribed, particularly when patients have a history of cardiovascular problems or present with a family history that suggests a high risk of cardiac problems.

Finally, one more adverse effect must be discussed. When the clinical effect of methylphenidate wears off toward the end of the day, some patients exhibit a rebound of ADHD symptoms where the impulsivity and/or hyperactivity becomes much more pronounced for a short period of time (generally about 30 minutes). This rebound is caused by the brain's reaction to the compound. When any medication is introduced into the body, the disruption in endogenous equilibrium caused by the compound's pharmacodynamic effects creates an opposing action. For example, when methylphenidate causes levels of dopamine to increase, the brain attempts to counteract this action by downregulating its production and release of dopamine. Because a clinical effect is still seen, this downregulation is not very significant and becomes overwhelmed by the action of the compound. When the medication wears off, however, for a short period of time, the brain is still in this downregulated mode and needs some time to restore prior equilibrium. During this time, rebound symptoms are evident.

Downregulation is most pronounced when the slope of the elimination of the compound is very steep, that is, when the medication is eliminated rapidly. This rapid elimination is the case with regular-release methylphenidate preparations, and those forms are most susceptible to rebound effects. When significant rebound is evident, a small dose of the stimulant may be administered about an hour before the rebound is generally seen, and this additional dose tends to smooth the elimination curve and reduce the slope of the elimination time. Trial and error is often needed to determine what dose will be sufficient to counteract the rebound and is still small enough so that no interference with meals or sleep is evident. The rebound effect is not generally seen with extended-release forms of methylphenidate, because the elimination curve is gradual, and the brain is able to slowly upregulate to its preprogrammed equilibrium while the compound is being eliminated.

Amphetamine and Derivatives

Amphetamine has been around for over a century and is primarily known as a drug of abuse through one of its variants, methamphetamine. Although methamphetamine is also available by prescription (Desoxyn), it is rarely prescribed because of its potent euphoric effects when taken at higher doses. Instead, amphetamine-based medications used to treat ADHD include a dextro isomer, dextroamphetamine, available as Dexedrine in immediate-release and extended-release forms, and lisdexamfetamine, marketed as Vyvanse, an inactive pro-drug that is converted in the body into l-lysine and dextroamphetamine. Dextroamphetamine is also available as a generic.

Another available version is a mixture of two forms of dextroam-phetamine and two forms of amphetamine, marketed as Adderall. It is a racemic blend in which the dextro and levo isomers are present in a ratio of 3:1. It was originally approved in the 1970s for the treat-ment of obesity and was then withdrawn. In 1994 it was reintroduced as Adderall and approved by the U.S. Food and Drug Administration (FDA) to treat symptoms of ADHD. It is available in immediate-release tablets and extended-release spansules.

Pharmacodynamics. Amphetamine and its various forms increase cate-cholamine activity and do so with more broad effects. Amphetamine not only blocks the reuptake, causing catecholamines to remain in the synapse in higher amounts, but also causes greater release of catecholamines into the synapse by partially reversing the direction of the reuptake mecha-nism (Stahl, 2000). In addition, amphetamine closely resembles endog-enous catecholamines. As a result, whatever reuptake still exists takes up amphetamine along with endogenous catecholamines into the presynap-tic neuron, thus making more neurotransmitters available within the cell and consequently causing an even greater amount to be released.

Like methylphenidate, the dextro isomer of amphetamine is highly selective for dopamine and precipitates an increase in dopaminergic brain function in the nigrostriatal, mesolimbic, and mesocortical path-ways. The levo isomer of amphetamine is less selective for dopamine and increases dopaminergic and noradrenergic activity more equally (Stahl, 2000). Thus, in addition to the dopaminergic pathways affected by dextroamphetamine, noradrenergic activity in the frontal, limbic, and cerebellar pathways is also increased. Adderall, however, is the only version of amphetamine that includes the levo isomers, and they are outnumbered by the dextro isomers by a ratio of 3:1. Thus, all forms of amphetamine used to treat symptoms of ADHD primarily rely on the action of the dextro isomers and mostly target the dopaminergic pathways in the brain.

The vast majority of stimulants can be abused when taken in high doses, especially when the patient alters the route of administration by crushing the medication and snorting or smoking it. This way of taking the medication generates a rapid onset of effect that produces feelings of euphoria, similar to those experienced with the abuse of cocaine or methamphetamine. For this reason, almost all stimulants are catego-rized in Schedule II of the Controlled Substance Act. Vyvanse provides an alternative because the medication includes only a precursor (called a prodrug) that is not active until the body converts it into the active compound. For this reason, the abuse potential for Vyvanse is signifi-cantly diminished.

Pharmacokinetics. Amphetamine-related stimulants are meant for oral administration. Those patients who have difficulties swallowing pills may use Dexedrine spansules or Adderall XR and open the capsule to sprinkle the contents into food. As with methylphenidate, drug manufacturers claim that this method of administration does not change the drugs' effectiveness, but the duration of effect may be somewhat shorter. A similar approach is available with Vyvanse. The capsule can be opened and the contents dissolved in water and then swallowed.

Like methylphenidate, amphetamine-related stimulants act quickly, and onset of the clinical effect is usually seen in less than an hour. Consuming the medication after a heavy breakfast may delay the onset of effect to some extent. It is best for the patient to take the medication right before breakfast to allow the drug to start working quickly and avoid the suppression of appetite that would occur if the medication was taken well before breakfast.

The duration of effect of immediate-release amphetamine derivatives is short, but it may be a little longer than it is for methylphenidate, and the clinical effect generally lasts about 4 hours (perhaps even longer for Adderall). Most individuals taking immediate-release preparations need multiple dosing about every 4 to 6 hours. This requires a dose in school during lunchtime and divided doses for adults during work hours. Once again, extended-release forms are usually preferred.

As with methylphenidate, extended-release preparations generally include a dual-release mechanism to allow fast onset of clinical effect and to extend the action into the later part of the day. Dexedrine spansules contain both immediate- and slow-release beads, and the action of effect generally lasts up to about 9 hours, but that varies significantly from patient to patient, and some patients exhibit improvement for only about 4 hours. Adderall XR releases 50% immediately, and the remaining 50% works through delayed release and lasts up to 12 hours (Bezchlibnyk-Butler & Jeffries, 2007). Vyvanse is the longest acting stimulant on the market, and its clinical effects have been reported to last for about 12 to 14 hours.

Dosing. Amphetamine derivatives are generally dosed by body weight, and the expected effective dose is about 0.8 mg/kg of body weight. Unlike methylphenidate, doses higher than this ratio are rarely used, and most patients respond at a dose that is somewhat lower than comparable doses of methylphenidate. Immediate-release preparations are usually given in two to three divided doses. Extended-release products are administered in the morning with a single dose (Bezchlibnyk-Butler & Jeffries, 2007).

Immediate-release Dexedrine and Adderall are usually started with a 2.5 mg dose bid, and the medication is gradually increased weekly by 2.5 mg per day until the desired response is observed (providing no serious adverse effects are evident). The maximum dose is generally 40 mg per day. If the medication is used TID, it is common for the last dose to be the lowest. Because immediate-release amphetamine derivatives exhibit somewhat longer action than immediate-release methylphenidate, it is especially important to make sure that the last dose is taken well in advance of dinner and bedtime. Extended-release preparations are generally given once per day with the full dose administered in the morning.

Adults are not generally dosed by body weight. Immediate-release medication is usually started with a dose of 10 mg BID or TID and gradually increased until sufficient clinical effect is observed (and adverse effects are minimal). Extended-release preparations are given in the morning. Adults generally receive up to 40 mg of total dose per day (Bezchlibnyk-Butler & Jeffries, 2007), and higher doses are occasionally used.

Vyvanse is usually dosed starting at 20 mg and gradually titrated upward until sufficient clinical response is evident with minimal adverse effects. The maximum dose is 70 mg/day for children. The maximum dose for adults has not been established.

Adverse Effects. Amphetamine derivatives are generally well tolerated. As with methylphenidate, the most common side effect is the suppression of appetite. It is recommended that the medication be taken close to breakfast so that the clinical effect does not yet begin when breakfast is consumed, thus ensuring the intake of adequate food at the first meal. If the medication is timed appropriately so that the clinical effect wears off in advance of dinner, most patients consume a sufficient amount of food to offset the loss of calories during lunch. Still, some who take stimulants exhibit significant suppression of appetite later in the day as well. For those patients, amphetamine derivatives may not be a good choice.

Amphetamines interfere with sleep, and those who take this medication must make sure that the clinical effect wears off well before bedtime. Immediate-release preparations must be administered so that the last dose is taken at least 6 or 7 hours before bedtime. Extended-release preparations are always dosed once per day, in the morning. If more medication is needed in the afternoon, a small dose of immediate-release preparation may be prescribed.

Transient adverse effects evident at the onset of treatment may include headaches, insomnia, and stomach discomfort. These effects are usually mild and generally do not cause patients to discontinue the medications.

Other side effects can be encountered in individuals who present with additional disorders comorbid with ADHD. These effects include agitation, irritability, and dysphoria, especially in individuals predisposed to symptoms of depression or agitation. Other patients, especially if they are susceptible to symptoms of anxiety, may exhibit nervousness and anxiety. Because individual response varies widely, a trial of amphetamines may still be attempted, and individual response should be carefully monitored.

The risk of developing motor tics is about the same as it is for methylphenidate, especially at higher doses. When comorbid tics are evident, a trial of amphetamines may still be attempted. If a patient did not exhibit tics until placed on the medication, the compound should be discontinued, and nonstimulant medications should be considered.

The risk of cardiovascular side effects is at least as significant as it is for methylphenidate, and deaths have been reported in children and adults susceptible to stroke and cardiac difficulties. For this reason, family history should be carefully reviewed, and an EKG should be performed when patients present with any risk factors for cardiovascular problems.

The rebound effect associated with the use of methylphenidate is similar to that associated with the use of amphetamines. When the immediate-release preparation of Dexedrine or Adderall wears off, an exacerbation of symptoms is common for about the next 30 minutes. As with methylphenidate, this effect is caused by the rapid clearance of the medication that does not allow a downregulated brain to upregulate back to its state of equilibrium. When significant rebound is evident, a small dose of immediate-release formulation may be administered about an hour before the rebound is generally seen, and this additional dose tends to smooth the elimination curve and reduce the slope of the elimination time. The rebound effect is not generally seen with extended-release forms of amphetamines, particularly with Adderall XR or Vyvanse.

Modafinil and Armodafinil

Modafinil is an atypical stimulant that increases brain activity through mechanisms that are different from the psychostimulants described earlier. It is marketed as Provigil. Although the FDA has not approved modafinil to treat symptoms of ADHD, it is commonly used off label for this purpose when individuals exhibit a good response to stimulants but present some adverse effects, such as motor tics. In 2007, an isomer of modafinil, armodafinil (marketed as Nuvigil), was also released in the United States. Both versions are FDA approved to treat various forms of sleep disorders, such as narcolepsy. Neither is available as a generic.

In December 2004, the manufacturer of modafinil submitted an application to the FDA to approve it (under the brand name Sparlon) to treat symptoms of ADHD. At least eight randomized clinical trials were performed (Lindsay, Gudelsky, & Heaton, 2006), but the FDA did not approve Sparlon because although modafinil's efficacy was established, it was no more effective than currently available treatments and overall did not present fewer adverse effects than available stimulants. In addition, a possible risk of Stevens-Johnson syndrome, a potentially fatal disorder, was also identified (but not confirmed) in one patient. Further studies are reportedly ongoing.

Pharmacodynamics. Modafinil works primarily by altering the balance between two key neurotransmitters, gamma-aminobutyric acid (GABA) and glutamate. Both are present in the entire brain and regulate the overall level of neuronal activity. Glutamate is an excitatory neurotransmitter that increases brain activity, and GABA is an inhibitory one that opposes glutamate and reduces neuronal firing. Modafinil alters the balance between these two by increasing the release of glutamate and decreasing the release of GABA. As a result, the brain exhibits higher levels of activity in most areas, including those that are responsible for producing symptoms of ADHD.

Modafinil is also suspected to exert its effect through additional action that reduces dopamine reuptake, resulting in a direct increase in dopaminergic brain function. It may also increase the release of all catecholamines into the synapse, including dopamine, norepinephrine, and serotonin (Bezchlibnyk-Butler & Jeffries, 2007). These mechanisms of action are likely supplemental to the overall stimulatory effect resulting from the alteration of the balance between glutamate and GABA.

Stimulants that directly work on increasing the release of dopamine, such as methylphenidate or amphetamine, can be abused when taken in high doses or are crushed and snorted or smoked. Because modafinil exerts action on dopaminergic pathways more indirectly, however, abuse of the medication generally does not result in significant euphoria. For this reason, modafinil is not associated with the same risk of abuse or dependence as methylphenidate or amphetamines and is classified in Schedule IV of the Controlled Substance Act. Still, some increase in physical performance has been associated with this substance, and modafinil is sometimes abused by athletes.

Pharmacokinetics. Modafinil is available in tablets that should be administered during the portions of the day when greater vigilance is desired. Onset of clinical effect is usually within 1 hour. Consuming the medication after a heavy meal may delay the onset of effect. Modafinil is generally taken right before breakfast.

Although modafinil is an immediate-release compound, the duration of effect is much longer than that of immediate-release methylphenidate or amphetamines. Clinical effect usually lasts for 10 to 12 hours, and therefore a single dose usually lasts all day. If an additional dose of medication is needed after school, it should not be modafinil, because its long duration of effect is likely to interfere with sleep.

Modafinil presents with an additional consideration that differentiates it from the other stimulants discussed previously. Modafinil has a significant effect on the liver functions involved in the metabolism of nutrients and other drugs. It induces cytochrome P450 enzymes 1A2, 2B6, and 3A4. These enzymes metabolize many medications currently on the market. For this reason, when modafinil is administered together with other medications, blood levels of medications metabolized by these enzymes will decrease. For example, use of modafinil has been shown to interfere with the effectiveness of hormonal contraceptives, and the effect continued for 1 month after discontinuation of modafinil. Conversely, modafinil also inhibits the liver enzymes 2C9 and 2C19, causing the levels of any drugs metabolized by these enzymes to increase. Overall, using modafinil with other medications may be difficult, and dosage adjustments of various medications may be necessary (Bezchlibnyk-Butler & Jeffries, 2007).

Dosing. To treat symptoms of narcolepsy, modafinil is generally used at doses of 200 mg to 300 mg per day. Research studies have shown, however, that this dose is inadequate to address symptoms of ADHD, and doses of 400 mg per day or higher are necessary. Armodafinil is dosed somewhat lower, but individual response varies. The effective dosage for armodafinil to treat symptoms of ADHD has not yet been established. With both medications, the full daily dose is taken once per day in the morning.

Adults' response varies, and the effective dose may be similar or somewhat higher than those used with children and adolescents. The use of modafinil or armodafinil to treat symptoms of ADHD in adults has not been studied, so dosing guidelines for this population do not yet exist.

Adverse Effects. As with other stimulants, suppression of appetite is common, although individual response is much more varied, and some patients experience fewer appetite effects with modafinil than with other stimulants. Still, it is recommended that the medication be taken close to breakfast so that the clinical effect does not interfere with the intake of food at the first meal. If the medication is taken in the morning, the clinical effect usually wears off in advance of dinner, so the intake of food in the evening is not affected.

Modafinil interferes with sleep, and those who take this medication must make sure that the clinical effect wears off well before bedtime. The medication is taken early in the day, at least 10 to 12 hours before bedtime. If an additional dose seems necessary in the afternoon, it should not be modafinil. Patients for whom the medication does not seem to work long enough may have to consider other medications.

Headache is the most common transient adverse effect evident at the onset of treatment and has been reported for up to a third of all patients placed on this medication (Bezchlibnyk-Butler & Jeffries, 2007). Generally, it resolves within a week or two of treatment, but for some patients it may persist. Nausea and stomach discomfort have also been reported in about 10% of patients.

Other side effects are more rare. Agitation and irritability are less likely than they are for other stimulants, although patients susceptible to symptoms of anxiety may exhibit nervousness. These effects are evident in only about 5% of the patients, and individual response varies widely.

The risk of developing motor tics is much lower for modafinil than it is for methylphenidate or amphetamines. For this reason, modafinil is sometimes prescribed for patients who exhibited a good symptomatic response to a traditional stimulant, but tics became evident. When ADHD and comorbid tics are evident at the onset, and a stimulant medication is sought, modafinil may be a good choice.

The risk of cardiovascular side effects is less significant for modafinil than it is for methylphenidate or amphetamines, and deaths have not been reported. Thus far, only a single case of modafinil-related cardiac difficulties has been identified in research literature (Oskooilar, 2005).

The rebound effect is less commonly seen with modafinil than it is with methylphenidate or amphetamines. The duration of effect is longer than it is for immediate-release stimulants, and consequently the clearance of medication is slower, allowing the brain to gradually upregulate. When a patient exhibits a good symptomatic response to a stimulant, but significant rebound is evident, switching the patient to modafinil may be a good option.

SUMMARY

Deciding whether to try medications is a difficult choice. Although results of research studies have suggested that the use of stimulant medications is the treatment modality most likely to produce significant improvement in symptoms, some patients remain skeptical about medications, especially when prescribed to children. Making the decision about whether to use medications should be based on the severity of the patient's symptoms and the degree of problems evident in settings where the symptoms cause particularly serious impairment, for example, at school or at work. The more severe the symptoms and the more serious the impairment in academic or vocational settings, the more likely it is that the use of medications will be unavoidable.

Of all the medications available to treat symptoms of ADHD, stimulants have been around the longest and are still associated with the greatest degree of improvement in the symptoms. For that reason, even though nonstimulant medications are available, stimulants are still the first-line treatment of choice. A large number of stimulants are available, including various preparations of methylphenidate, amphetamine, and modafinil. These medications work primarily by stimulating the dopaminergic pathways of the brain thus directly targeting the brain functions likely responsible for the symptoms. Immediate-release and extended-release formulations are available for most compounds, and these offer benefits and drawbacks that must be considered on a case-by-case basis. As a group, stimulants generally present the most favorable side effect profile of all psychotropic medications, but some patients still exhibit problems with gastrointestinal and cardiovascular symptoms, and these medications must be administered carefully so that adverse effects on appetite and sleep are minimized.

14

Nonstimulant Medications

According to our current understanding, symptoms of attention deficit/ hyperactivity disorder (ADHD) are produced by functional deficits in three of the brain's dopaminergic pathways and possibly the prefrontal norepinephrine pathway. To correct these deficits, stimulants are effective because they target the action of dopamine (primary action) and norepinephrine (secondary action) and increase the activity associated with those neurotransmitters.

There are some patients, however, who do not respond well to stimulants or who exhibit side effects that preclude the use of stimulant medications. For example, a client may develop tics or a suppression of appetite that results in an inadequate intake of food. Those with symptoms of comorbid disorders also may not respond well to stimulants. Clients with tendencies toward depression or agitation may exhibit a worsening of those symptoms while on a stimulant medication. Those who present with anxiety may exhibit an increase in nervousness. For those reasons, other medications are also used to address the symptoms of ADHD.

ANTIDEPRESSANT MEDICATIONS

Antidepressants have been used to treat symptoms of ADHD since the 1960s, and many studies have shown adequate efficacy, sometimes equal to stimulants (Biederman & Spencer, 2002). There are classes of antidepressant medications that specifically target noradrenergic and dopaminergic function, and those are the antidepressants used with patients with ADHD. The medications differ in the specific manner in which they increase those catecholamines, and various classes of antidepressants present significantly different adverse effects. This discussion reviews those compounds for which specific efficacy in treating ADHD has been established.

Antidepressants may be considered as first-line medications for ADHD when the symptoms presentation includes comorbid agitation and depression. For patients with such a symptom profile, antidepressants are a better choice than stimulants because their pharmacodynamic effects may be able to simultaneously address both groups of symptoms.

Antidepressants are also an excellent choice when medications are needed to treat symptoms of ADHD in male teenagers or adult males at risk for substance abuse, either directly or by making the drug available to others (e.g., by selling it). The action of antidepressants affects the brain reward center to a minimal degree. For this reason, antidepressants have no known abuse potential and are generally not listed in the schedule of controlled substances.

Atomoxetine

Atomoxetine is not technically an antidepressant. It was developed to be an antidepressant, however, and it is a close cousin to a similar medication, reboxetine, which is a well-known antidepressant (not available in the United States). Because the antidepressant effects of atomoxetine were not superior to other compounds on the market, a decision was made not to seek approval for it as an antidepressant. Because it was previously established that medications that increase norepinephrine tend to improve symptoms of ADHD, however, the manufacturer sought, and received, approval to market atomoxetine (available in the United States as Strattera) to treat symptoms of ADHD. In the United States, no generic version of atomoxetine is available.

Evidence of Efficacy. Several randomized, placebo-controlled trials (RCTs) have been performed to investigate the efficacy of atomoxetine (Janicak et al., 2006). It is apparent that the compound is effective in children with ADHD. The medication has also been found to be effective in adolescents, and a lower mg/kg dose was needed for improvement of symptoms (Michelson et al., 2001). Because anorexic effects are not associated with this medication, some doctors prefer it and use it as first-line treatment. A meta-analysis of five head-to-head comparisons, however, revealed that atomoxetine is not as effective as stimulants (Gibson, Bettinger, Patel, & Crimson, 2006). For this reason, it is best to use this compound when stimulants are not appropriate or patients have not responded well to their use.

The use of atomoxetine in adults has also been researched, although fewer studies have been completed. To date, hundreds of patients have been examined in RCTs, and atomoxetine has been found to be superior to placebo (Barkley, 2006), but no head-to head comparisons (in adults) with stimulants have been performed. In one study, patterns of use were examined to determine when doctors prescribe atomoxetine rather than stimulants (Van Brunt, Johnston, Ye, Pohl, & O'Hara, 2006). The study revealed that atomoxetine is more likely to be prescribed as a first-line medication for adult males rather than females, and especially for those men with comorbid conditions (e.g., agitation or depression) or at risk for substance abuse. For females, and males without these risks, stimulant medications were still the first choice. This result confirms that atomoxetine is probably best used when patients present risks when on stimulants or when the pattern of comorbid symptoms suggests that a medication with some presumed antidepressant effect is preferred.

Atomoxetine has also been studied in patients who exhibit symptoms of oppositional defiant disorder (ODD) and conduct disorder. A recent meta-analysis revealed that atomoxetine was particularly effective in treating children with ADHD who have comorbid ODD and that the reduction of symptoms of ODD was not merely secondary to the reduction of symptoms of ADHD and may have contributed to the reduction of symptoms of ADHD (Biederman et al., 2007). Similar results have also been found when atomoxetine is used to address conduct problems (especially aggression), depression, and anxiety (Cheng, Chen, Ko, & Ng, 2007). This result again confirms that atomoxetine may be a particularly good choice for patients who exhibit symptoms of ADHD comorbid with symptoms of ODD, conduct problems, depression or agitation, or anxiety.

Pharmacodynamics. Atomoxetine is a selective norepinephrine reuptake inhibitor. As such, it primarily targets noradrenergic function and increases activity in norepinephrine pathways, including the frontal, limbic, and cerebral portions involved in producing symptoms of ADHD. Although norepinephrine is thought to play a minor role in ADHD, it seems that increasing noradrenergic function is effective, although, predictably, the effect on the symptoms is not as pronounced as it is when dopaminergic pathways are targeted by the medications (as is the case with stimulants). Because noradrenergic function also includes various brain-stem and sympathetic nervous system functions, increasing noradrenergic function in those pathways is associated with some adverse effects (described later).

Dopamine and norepinephrine are very similar chemically. In fact, norepinephrine is produced when dopamine is converted by the dopamine beta hydroxylase enzyme (Stahl, 2000). Although atomoxetine is highly selective for norepinephrine when it inhibits the reuptake transporter, postsynaptically there may be some cross-talk between the two, involving the cross-binding of dopamine and norepinephrine to each other's receptors. For this reason, atomoxetine has been found to also increase dopaminergic action to some extent, although the effect is most evident in the frontal cortex (Bezchlibnyk-Butler & Jeffries, 2007). If atomoxetine increases dopaminergic activity in the frontal and nigrostriatal pathways, this effect likely contributes to its effectiveness in reducing symptoms of ADHD.

Pharmacokinetics. Atomoxetine is available only in capsules, and sprinkling the formulation has not been studied, so patients must be able to swallow the medication. When administered, atomoxetine starts to act quickly, and blood plasma peak is evident in 1 to 2 hours. Unlike stimulants, however, effects of atomoxetine are not immediate. Atomoxetine has to be given every day, and clinical effects are gradually evident, usually over a course of 1 to 2 weeks. The medication's elimination half-life (the length of time it takes the body to eliminate half of the medication) is long enough that once per day dosing is used. Because the medication is given daily, after about a week of use, a steady state is accomplished, and the plasma level of the medication is consistent and does not significantly change with additional doses. Thus, patients who take atomoxetine do not experience the peaks and valleys associated with stimulants, and the effect is seen through the entire day. This also means that the use of atomoxetine is not subject to the rebound effect seen with psychostimulants.

Dosing. Like stimulants, atomoxetine is generally dosed by body weight. The recommended starting dose for children is 0.5 mg/kg per day, and if sufficient effect was not observed after at least 10 days, the daily dose should be increased to 0.8 mg/kg. The dose can further be increased every 2 weeks or so, and the maximum dose is 1.4 mg/kg or 100 mg per day, whichever is less (Bezchlibnyk-Butler & Jeffries, 2007). Although some anecdotal evidence exists for the efficacy of doses up to 1.8 mg/kg (Michelson et al., 2001), these doses have not been sufficiently studied, and adverse effects may increase. For this reason, the maximums of 1.4 mg/kg or 100 mg per day are generally observed.

Teens and men are not generally dosed by body weight. The medication is usually started at a dose of 40 mg and then increased by 20 mg about every 2 weeks until sufficient response is evident (providing adverse effects are minimal). The maximum dose for adults is 100 mg per day (Bezchlibnyk-Butler & Jeffries, 2007).

Adverse Effects. Atomoxetine is generally well tolerated. Suppression of appetite is less likely than with stimulants, although some patients have reported some weight loss while on the medication (Bezchlibnyk-Butler & Jeffries, 2007). The medication may be taken with or without meals, and because atomoxetine must be taken daily, no peaks and valleys in appetite have been observed, and therefore atomoxetine is not likely to interfere with appetite for any specific meal (such as breakfast or lunch).

Atomoxetine may interfere with sleep, although this effect varies from patient to patient. Most patients experience an increase in vigilance, although the effect is not as pronounced as it is with psychostimulants. Some patients, however, report minor sedation, especially at the onset of treatment, and therefore the medication is sometimes prescribed to be taken at bedtime.

Some transient side effects may be seen in some patients at the onset of treatment. These effects generally resolve after the first 2 weeks and include dizziness, headaches, and fatigue. The severity is usually mild and does not cause patients to discontinue the medication. Of course, if these effects persist, and the patient is uncomfortable, another medication should be considered.

Atomoxetine alters noradrenergic as well as cholinergic activity in the entire nervous system, including not only the brain and spinal cord but the peripheral branches as well. As a result, some clients report adverse effects related to digestive tract function. These effects include nausea, dry mouth, constipation, and abdominal pain. These problems usually resolve on their own. If they persist, a lower dose may be attempted, or a different medication will need to be used.

Changes in noradrenergic function are also associated with cardiovascular side effects. In some patients, atomoxetine has been shown to increase blood pressure and heart rate. Although these changes are usually minor, in a few cases they have been found to be significant, even life threatening (Stahl, 2006). This effect may be especially important to consider with patients who are very active physically, for example, those who participate in sports that involve vigorous exertion. In those patients, atomoxetine may sometimes result in dysregulation of cardiovascular function, and the increase in pulse and blood pressure that accompanies physical activity may not properly resolve after the activity is ceased.

Atomoxetine usually does not stimulate the sympathetic branch of the autonomic nervous system. Thus, increase of anxiety is much less likely, and the medication is often used with patients who exhibit comorbid symptoms of ADHD and anxiety. A minority of patients, however, may experience an increase in nervousness and anxiety. When this occurs, it is recommended to wait and see whether these symptoms resolve. If not, a lower dose may be attempted, or a different medication will need to be administered.

Atomoxetine presents much less risk of motor tics and sometimes is used with patients who developed tics while on stimulants. In fact, atomoxetine is sometimes used with patients who present with comorbid symptoms of ADHD and motor tics, and both symptom clusters appear to improve (Lewis et al., 2003). Case reports of patients who developed tics on atomoxetine, however, have been identified (Bezchlibnyk-Butler & Jeffries, 2007). When the development of tics is encountered, atomoxetine should be discontinued, and another medication should be tried.

Atomoxetine is metabolized by the cytochrome P450 system of liver enzymes. Specifically, the enzyme 2D6 is the primary metabolizer, and the enzyme 2C19 contributes to this metabolism to a minor degree. For this reason, any medications that change the activity of CYP2D6 will likely change the level of atomoxetine in the system. Medications that induce this enzyme will decrease the effectiveness of atomoxetine, and medications that inhibit the enzyme will increase atomoxetine's effect and may increase the risk of toxicity. The dose of atomoxetine needs to be carefully monitored when other medications are also used.

In addition, atomoxetine has been shown to result in dangerous liver problems in a small minority of patients. Two cases of severe liver damage have been reported (Bezchlibnyk-Butler & Jeffries, 2007). In all cases, the damage was reversed when the medications were discontinued, and no deaths have been reported. Patients who take this medication, however, should receive baseline liver function screening at the onset of treatment and periodic liver function checks throughout the period that atomoxetine is prescribed.

One additional adverse effect must be discussed. Like all antidepressants currently on the market, atomoxetine has been associated with a small increase in suicidal tendencies in those patients who take this medication and present with symptoms of depression. For this reason, atomoxetine, like every antidepressant, has a "black box" warning issued by the U.S. Food and Drug Administration (FDA) that appears on the packaging insert. This topic is rather controversial. It is true that a small portion of teenagers and young adults exhibits a transient increase in suicidality after antidepressant medications are first started. The risk of these tendencies appears greatest in the first 2 weeks of use (Bezchlibnyk-Butler & Jeffries, 2007). No actual suicides have been reported, however, and the "suicidality" refers to greater thoughts about suicide. The mechanism of this effect has not been specifically identified, but mental health professionals generally believe that the increased suicidality is not an exacerbation of depression but secondary to behavioral activation that some patients may experience at a time when depression is still significant and has not yet started to respond to treatment. The black box warning was not intended to sway potential patients away from using the medications, but some have suggested that the warning has resulted in underuse of antidepressants in those who need them, because patients and their families are afraid to start the medications. Indeed, an increase in suicide rates has been reported since the black box warning was introduced, and rates of prescribing antidepressants has dropped (Lineberry, Bostwick, Beebe, & Decker, 2007).

Finally, because of atomoxetine's relationship to antidepressants, it is associated with a small risk of inducing hypomanic or manic symptoms (Stahl, 2006). Patients who have tendencies toward symptoms of bipolar disorder have been known to exhibit switching from depressive to manic symptoms while on an antidepressant medication. Atomoxetine is also associated with this risk, but the incidence of such problems is very rare.

Buproprion

Buproprion is an antidepressant that is classified as a norepinephrine and dopamine reuptake inhibitor. It has been on the market since the 1980s and is FDA approved for the treatment of depression and seasonal affective disorder. It is marketed as immediate-release Wellbutrin, and sustained-release (Wellbutrin SR) and extended-release (Wellbutrin XL) versions are also available, and all three are available as generics.

In 1997, the FDA further approved buproprion as a smoking cessation treatment, and for this purpose it is marketed as Zyban.

Nomifensine (Merital) is an antidepressant similar to buproprion. It is not marketed in the United States but is available in other parts of the world.

Evidence of Efficacy. Buproprion's efficacy as an antidepressant has been well established in adults, and the medication has similarly been found effective in treating depression in children (Wagner, 2004). Several studies have shown that buproprion is also effective in treating symptoms of ADHD in children (Biederman & Spencer, 2002). One small study compared buproprion head-to-head with stimulants and found similar efficacy (Manshadi, Lippman, O'Daniel, & Blackman, 1983), but generally there are few direct comparisons. Results of research studies, however, also reveal that buproprion is effective in treating comorbid symptoms of ADHD and depression in children (Daviss, Bentivoglio, & Racusin, 2001). In addition, because of some risks (discussed later), buproprion has a relatively low dosage ceiling. For this reason, buproprion is not usually regarded as a first-line treatment for symptoms of ADHD, but for those who present comorbid depression or agitation, it may be a good choice.

The use of buproprion to treat symptoms of ADHD in adults has also been researched, and some evidence exists that supports its efficacy (Mattes, 1986). Although most studies have been open-label trials, an RCT has also confirmed buproprion's efficacy (Wilens et al., 2001). Similarly, nomifensine has also been found effective in adults with ADHD (Shekim, Masterson, Cantwell, Hanna, & McCracken, 1989). No head-to head comparisons (in adults) have been performed with stimulants. As is the case with children, the use of buproprion to treat symptoms of ADHD in men is probably best considered when comorbid symptoms of depression are present. The overlap between depression and ADHD is especially high in adults, however, and sometimes has been reported to be as high as 75% (Ramsay & Rostain, 2008). Thus, it is more rare to encounter a male with pure ADHD, and the presentation of ADHD comorbid with depression is the most common. For this reason, buproprion may be a particularly good choice for men with ADHD.

Pharmacodynamics. Buproprion is a norepinephrine and dopamine reuptake inhibitor. It primarily targets noradrenergic function and increases activity in the frontal, limbic, and cerebral norepinephrine pathways that are involved in producing symptoms of ADHD. As with atomoxetine, increasing noradrenergic function is effective in decreasing symptoms of ADHD, although to a lesser extent. Because these same noradrenergic pathways are also involved in some of the symptoms of depression, buproprion is an effective antidepressant. Although noradrenergic function also includes various brain-stem and sympathetic nervous system functions, it seems that buproprion's action on these functions is not as significant as that of atomoxetine, and therefore noradrenergic side effects are less pronounced (as described later).

Although buproprion is more selective for norepinephrine when it inhibits the reuptake transporter, it also inhibits the dopamine reuptake transporter to a lesser, but significant, degree. Consequently, buproprion increases action in the frontal and nigrostriatal dopaminergic pathways, thus targeting symptoms of ADHD more directly. This action is likely responsible for most of the reduction of symptoms of ADHD, including both inattentiveness and hyperactivity/impulsivity, with the increase of norepinephrine function contributing a minor (but nevertheless important) role.

Pharmacokinetics. Buproprion is available only in tablets, and sprinkling is not possible. Patients must be able to swallow the medication. When administered, buproprion starts to act quickly, and blood plasma peak is evident in 1 to 2 hours. As with atomoxetine, however, effects are not immediate. Buproprion has to be given every day, and clinical effects are gradually evident usually over a course of 1 to 4 weeks. The elimination half-life of the immediate-release formulation is about 12 hours, but the body converts the medication into an active metabolite that lasts longer (Bezchlibnyk-Butler & Jeffries, 2007). Still, the immediate-release and sustained-release formulations usually require twice a day (BID) dosing, and the extended-release formulation can be taken once per day, although divided doses are generally recommended (see discussion of adverse effects).

As with all nonstimulant medications, buproprion has to be taken daily, and a steady state is accomplished when the plasma level of the medication is consistent and does not significantly change with additional doses. Thus, those who take buproprion do not experience the peaks and valleys associated with stimulants, and the effect is seen through the entire day, which also means that the use of buproprion is not subject to the rebound effect seen with psychostimulants.

Dosing. Buproprion is not usually dosed by body weight. In children, the recommended starting dose is 75 mg (immediate-release), 100 mg (sustained-release) divided into BID doses, or 150 mg (extended-release) taken once per day. If a sufficient effect was not observed, it is recommended that after 4 weeks the daily dose can gradually be increased up to a maximum of 450 mg per day, with no single dose greater than 150 mg (Stahl, 2006). This means that at least BID dosing is required, and some patients may need to take the medication three times a day (TID).

Teens and men are dosed similarly. The medication is usually started at a dose of 75 mg to 100 mg BID, and if a sufficient response is not observed in 4 weeks, dosing can gradually be increased to 450 mg per day in divided doses. Extended-release formulation can be dosed once a day with a maximum single dose of 300 mg, although if 450 mg is desired, the medication will have to be taken at least BID—a dose of 300 mg and another of 150 mg (Bezchlibnyk-Butler & Jeffries, 2007).

Adverse Effects. Buproprion is generally well tolerated. Suppression of appetite generally is not observed, although some patients have reported a small weight loss while on the medication (Stahl, 2006). The

medication may be taken with or without meals, and because buproprion must be taken daily, no peaks and valleys in appetite have been
observed, and therefore buproprion is not likely to interfere with appetite for any specific meal (such as breakfast or lunch). Mild stomach
discomfort and nausea are sometimes observed when the medication is
started, and they usually resolve after a week or two.

Buproprion generally does not interfere with sleep, and divided doses
can be taken in the morning and at bedtime, although some patients
(about 10%) have reported insomnia. On the other hand, about 2%
of patients also reported drowsiness and sedation, so this effect varies from patient to patient. Most patients experience no immediate
increase in vigilance, and a gradual decrease in distractibility is apparent. Some other transient side effects include headaches and dry mouth
(Bezchlibnyk-Butler & Jeffries, 2007). These effects are usually mild
and do not cause patients to discontinue the medication. Of course if
these effects persist, and the patient is uncomfortable, another medication should be considered.

Although changes in noradrenergic function are often associated
with cardiovascular side effects, buproprion does not usually increase
blood pressure and heart rate (Bezchlibnyk-Butler & Jeffries, 2007).
Patients who participate in sports that involve vigorous exertion generally tolerate the medication well, and no dysregulation of cardiovascular
function is usually observed.

Buproprion does not stimulate the sympathetic branch of the autonomic nervous system to a significant degree. Thus, anxiety is much
less likely but rarely has been reported (Stahl, 2006). When this effect
occurs, it is recommended to wait and see whether these symptoms
resolve. If not, a different medication will need to be administered.

Buproprion's risk of motor tics is very limited, although case reports
exist of tic exacerbation (Bezchlibnyk-Butler & Jeffries, 2007). For this
reason, buproprion is sometimes used with patients who develop tics
while on stimulants, although the effectiveness of buproprion has not
been studied with patients who present with comorbid symptoms of
ADHD and motor tics. In cases where buproprion seems to precipitate
tics, the medication should be discontinued, and another medication
should be tried.

Buproprion is metabolized by multiple cytochrome P450 liver
enzymes, which means that when buproprion is used with other medications, its plasma levels are not likely to change. Buproprion inhibits
the enzyme 2D6 to a minor degree, however, so plasma levels of medications that rely on this enzyme for metabolism may increase to some
degree. As always, when multiple medications are used, all doses need
to be carefully monitored.

Like all antidepressants, buproprion is associated with a small
increase in suicidal tendencies in those patients who take this medication and present with symptoms of depression. For this reason, buproprion, like every antidepressant, has a black box warning issued by the

FDA. Although a small portion of teenagers and young adults may exhibit a transient increase in suicidality after the medication is first started, no actual suicides have been reported. Clinicians should carefully monitor patient response and intervene if an increase in suicidal thoughts or plans becomes evident. In addition, like all antidepressants, buproprion is also associated with a small risk of inducing hypomanic or manic symptoms (Stahl, 2006), and some patients who have tendencies toward symptoms of bipolar disorder may exhibit switching from depressive to manic symptoms while on the medication. Although this risk is reported, it appears that the incidence of such problems with buproprion is more rare than with other antidepressants (Bezchlibnyk-Butler & Jeffries, 2007).

Finally, clinicians need to be aware of one additional potential side effect. Buproprion lowers the seizure threshold and presents somewhat greater risk of seizures than some other antidepressants (Stahl, 2006). For this reason, after buproprion was initially introduced in the 1980s, it was withdrawn from the market and needed further study. It was reintroduced in 1989 when it became apparent that the risk is dose dependent, and seizures in patients on doses of 450 mg/day or less are extremely rare. It is also apparent that the immediate-release formulation presents somewhat greater risk (Stahl, 2006), although the overall risk of seizures is less than 2% (Bezchlibnyk-Butler & Jeffries, 2007). Still, for this reason, the maximum daily dose of 450 mg/day has been established, and limits on single doses are being observed (as discussed previously).

This effect has two implications for clinicians. First, those patients who present particular risks of seizures may not be good candidates for buproprion. These patients include those with a history of epilepsy (personal or in close biological family), those who are on other medications that decrease seizure threshold, or those who present additional risks because of head trauma, a history of purging behaviors (e.g., as seen in bulimia), and other medical factors. In addition, because limits on dosage are strictly imposed, the therapeutic range for buproprion is smaller than it is for most other medications. The effective dose is usually about 300 mg/day, and because the maximum dose is 450 mg/day, there is limited room for increasing the dose when only partial response is evident. For this reason, those patients who do not exhibit a sufficient response are usually switched to other medications.

Tricyclic Antidepressants

Tricyclic antidepressants include amitriptyline (Elavil), protriptyline (Vivactil), imipramine (Tofranil), nortriptyline (Pamelor), desipramine (Norpramin), trimipramine (Surmontil), clomipramine (Anafranil), and doxepin (Sinequan). Although not technically tricyclics, amoxapine (Asendin) and maprotiline (Ludiomil) are usually categorized with tricyclics, because of their similarities in mechanism of action and adverse effects. Tricyclic antidepressants have been on the market for many decades, and all are available in generic formulations. Because they present with greater side effects than other antidepressants, nowadays they are not used as frequently. Evidence of efficacy is well established, however. There are patients for whom antidepressant treatment of ADHD may be indicated because of comorbid symptoms of depression. If those patients have not responded to (or tolerated) buproprion or atomoxetine, they may be good candidates for a trial of a tricyclic.

Evidence of Efficacy. Imipramine, desipramine, and nortriptyline are the tricyclics most studied in addressing symptoms of ADHD, and evidence of their efficacy has been known for decades (Biederman & Spencer, 2002). More than 30 studies have been performed, most of which were RCTs, and efficacy has been established with more than 1,000 children. Thirteen studies specifically compared tricyclics to stimulants. Although most found that stimulants had better efficacy, several found equal improvement, and a few showed greater improvement with tricyclics. As with other antidepressants, improvement was greatest in treating comorbid symptoms of ADHD and depression (Hunt, Minderaa, & Cohen, 1985). In addition, several studies of tricyclic antidepressants have consistently shown robust improvement in children with comorbid tics (Biederman & Spencer, 2002), and recent investigations seem to confirm the efficacy of tricyclics with this population (Lanau, Zenner, Civelli, & Hartman, 1997). Thus, although tricyclics are not regarded as a first-line treatment for symptoms of ADHD, for those patients who present comorbid depression or agitation or tics, tricyclics may be a good choice.

The use of tricyclics in adults to treat symptoms of ADHD has also been researched, and some evidence exists that supports its efficacy (Biederman & Spencer, 2002). Both open-label and RCT trials have been performed, and a response rate greater than two thirds has been observed (Barkley, 2006). No head-to-head comparisons (in adults) have been performed with stimulants. As is the case with children, the use of tricyclics to treat symptoms of ADHD in men is probably best considered when comorbid symptoms of depression are evident. Because the overlap between depression and ADHD is especially high in adults, tricyclics may be a particularly good choice for men with ADHD who do not respond favorably to buproprion or atomoxetine.

Pharmacodynamics. Tricyclics primarily are norepinephrine reuptake inhibitors, and therefore their action is somewhat similar to that of atomoxetine. They increase noradrenergic function and activate the frontal, limbic, and cerebral norepinephrine pathways that are involved in producing symptoms of ADHD. Because norepinephrine plays a minor role in symptoms of ADHD, increasing noradrenergic function produces results that are not as pronounced as those when dopaminergic pathways are targeted by the medications (as is the case for stimulants). Because noradrenergic function also includes various brain-stem and sympathetic nervous system functions, increasing noradrenergic function in those pathways is associated with many adverse effects (described later).

Tricyclics are not particularly selective for norepinephrine, and dopaminergic and serotonergic effects are also evident. Although the increase in serotonin has not been associated with improvement in symptoms of ADHD, those tricyclics that also exert some effect on dopamine seem most effective. In addition, norepinephrine and dopamine are very similar chemically, and cross-binding dopamine and norepinephrine to each other's receptors has been observed. For this reason, tricyclics may also increase dopaminergic action in the frontal, and perhaps nigrostriatal, pathways. This effect likely contributes to tricyclics' effectiveness in reducing symptoms of ADHD.

Pharmacokinetics. Tricyclics are available in a wide variety of products, including tablets, capsules, syrup, oral suspension, and oral solution. This variety provides many options for patients who have difficulties swallowing medications. Tricyclics vary in the time it takes to achieve peak plasma levels—some do so in 1 to 3 hours, whereas others take 4 to 8 hours. As with the other antidepressants discussed before, however, time to peak is not very crucial because effects are not immediate, and tricyclics have to be taken every day for 1 to 4 weeks before clinical effects gradually become evident. The elimination half-life of tricyclics is close to 24 hours, and therefore once per day dosing is generally used.

Because tricyclics have to be taken daily, a steady state is accomplished, and the plasma level of the medication does not significantly change with additional doses. Thus, the peaks and valleys associated with stimulants are not observed, and the effect is seen through the entire day. This also means that the use of tricyclics is not subject to the rebound effect seen with psychostimulants.

Dosing. Tricyclics are often dosed by body weight and sometimes by checking blood plasma levels. Because of significant adverse effects, including sedation, it is recommended that children start with the lowest possible dose once per day (usually at bedtime), and the dose is then gradually increased in small increments every 3 to 5 days (Bezchlibnyk-Butler & Jeffries, 2007). Depending on the specific compound used, the effective dose is generally between 2 and 5 mg/kg per day (Biederman & Spencer, 2002). Higher doses have been studied but did not produce additional benefits. If sufficient efficacy is not evident, blood plasma levels can be drawn to investigate whether a patient is metabolizing the medication more completely than expected. Depending on the compound, target plasma levels should be between 150 and 1,000 nanomoles per liter (nmol/L), or about 40 to 300 nanograms per milliliter (ng/mL). Obviously, this is a wide range, and individual response, particularly in light of adverse effects, must be closely monitored.

Teens and men are dosed similarly. The medication is usually started at the lowest dose, at night, and gradually increased about once per week. A favorable response is usually seen with doses of about 200 mg per day of desipramine, about 100 mg per day of nortriptyline, and about 150 mg per day of desipramine (Barkley, 2006). Of course, individual response varies widely, and close monitoring of response and adverse effects is required.

Adverse Effects. Tricyclics present much more significant side effects than the other antidepressants discussed thus far. Suppression of appetite and weight loss generally are not reported, and weight gain is common with some specific compounds (e.g., about a third of the patients gain weight on amitriptyline). In addition, because tricyclics also block cholinergic transmission, constipation and dry mouth are evident in up to 30% of patients. These effects are sometimes accompanied by blurry vision and increased sweating (Bezchlibnyk-Butler & Jeffries, 2007).

Tricyclics commonly exert a sedating effect and are generally dosed in the evening. Although this effect may be potentially beneficial, especially for those who exhibit sleep problems, it also means that patients who initially start the medication must deal with several days of feeling drowsy while the body gets used to the medication. Gradually, this effect becomes less pronounced, and sedation resolves, but some patients exhibit fatigue for the first week or two and then for a few days every time the dose is increased. Other transient side effects include headaches (Bezchlibnyk-Butler & Jeffries, 2007).

Changes in noradrenergic function are associated with cardiac side effects, and the use of tricyclics may cause significant cardiovascular changes in many patients. These effects include dizziness, orthostatic hypotension, tachycardia, and palpitations, which are evident in up to 30% of patients (Bezchlibnyk-Butler & Jeffries, 2007). In addition, because tricyclics also block sodium channels, additional cardiac effects are seen, including changes in heart rhythm patterns evident on electrocardiograms (EKGs). Some patients exhibit a congenital condition in which the interval between the Q and T portions of the cardiac rhythm is prolonged. Although this condition is benign in most individuals, some medications (such as tricyclics) further increase the length of this interval and produce cardiac arrhythmias. Some of these arrhythmias may be fatal, and sudden deaths have been reported in children treated with tricyclics (Law & Schachar, 1999). For this reason, most doctors recommend a baseline EKG before treatment and then additional EKGs to check heart rhythm patterns after the medication is started.

Although the risk of motor tics is very limited with tricyclics, other motor effects have been reported. Some patients exhibit a fine tremor associated with changes in extrapyramidal function, and some motor changes have been reported in up to 10% of patients (depending on which tricyclic is used). When these changes are encountered, tricyclics should be discontinued, because there is a rare but serious risk of tardive dyskinesia, a permanent change in motor function that is usually associated with older generation antipsychotics (such as Thorazine).

The metabolism of tricyclics varies widely from one compound to another. Most are metabolized by cytochrome P450 liver enzymes, and some rely primarily on one enzyme, whereas others are metabolized by many enzymes. In addition, many tricyclics also exert influence on other liver enzymes, thus changing plasma levels of other medications that may be metabolized by those enzymes. Clinicians should become familiar with the CYP450 profile of the specific compound, and they need to carefully monitor levels of all medications when polypharmacy is being used, especially for those tricyclics that significantly inhibit liver enzymes.

Like all antidepressants, tricyclics are associated with a small increase in suicidal tendencies in those patients who present with symptoms of depression, and all tricyclics carry the same black box warning that applies to all antidepressants. Clinicians should carefully monitor patient response and intervene if an increase in suicidal thoughts or plans becomes evident. In addition, like all antidepressants, tricyclics are also associated with a small risk of inducing hypomanic or manic symptoms (Stahl, 2006), and some patients who have tendencies toward symptoms of bipolar disorder may exhibit switching from depressive to manic symptoms. Once again, careful monitoring of dose and response and adverse effects is necessary.

Other Antidepressants

Antidepressants generally exert their clinical effects by changes in various monoamine neurotransmitters. These neurotransmitters include the catecholamines dopamine and norepinephrine and the indolamine serotonin. As evident from the earlier reviews, antidepressants that primarily increase the activity of dopaminergic and noradrenergic pathways have been found efficacious in the treatment of symptoms of ADHD. Conversely, serotonergic pathways have been presumed to have much less involvement in symptoms of ADHD, and therefore medications that primarily work by increasing serotonergic activity have not been found particularly effective in treating symptoms of ADHD (Milberger, Biederman, Faraone, Chen, & Jones, 1997). Still, others have found some efficacy with serotonergic medications or with those medications that affect serotonin and one or both catecholamines (Barkley, 2006). Especially in adults, where comorbidity with depression is commonly seen, some of these medications may be tried, and clinicians should have at least basic familiarity with other antidepressants and their potential benefits in the treatment of symptoms of ADHD.

Serotonin and Norepinephrine Reuptake Inhibitors (SNRIs). The SNRIs venlafaxine (Effexor) and duloxetine (Cymbalta) are two antidepressants that block the reuptake of both serotonin and norepinephrine. Venlafaxine is available as a generic, but duloxetine is not. Venlafaxine's effect is primarily seen in the increase in serotonergic activity, and the noradrenergic increase is minor. On the other hand, duloxetine affects both neurotransmitters more equally (Stahl, 2006). The benefits of venlafaxine in treating symptoms of ADHD have been examined in several small, open-label studies with children as well as adults (Barkley, 2006). Although beneficial effects were generally seen, dropout rates were high because of adverse effects. The effects of duloxetine on symptoms of ADHD have not yet been studied, although some patients have reported a good response and adverse effects that were less pronounced than those experienced with venlafaxine. Because SNRIs have been shown to be effective in addressing symptoms of both depression and anxiety, they may be an option for patients who present with symptoms from both categories in addition to symptoms of ADHD. In addition, duloxetine is showing promise when used to treat individuals with chronic pain and therefore may also be tried with patients who exhibit symptoms of ADHD and chronic pain. Still, the use of SNRIs to treat symptoms of ADHD, regardless of comorbidity, must be regarded as experimental.

SNRIs are generally taken once per day. Duloxetine may be sedating, and it is usually taken at night, whereas venlafaxine may be somewhat activating, and therefore it is generally taken in the morning. SNRIs are associated with a variety of adverse effects, including dry mouth, constipation, sweating, orthostatic hypotension, and gastrointestinal symptoms (nausea, etc.). Most of these effects are transient and diminish after the first few weeks of use. SNRIs (especially venlafaxine), however, are also associated with sexual side effects for at least 30% of the patients (Bezchlibnyk-Butler & Jeffries, 2007). These effects include delays in the time it takes to reach orgasm and greater difficulties in attaining orgasm. Individual response varies, but this problem has been a major reason why many discontinue the medication.

Monoamine Oxidase Inhibitors (MAOIs). MAOIs are among the oldest antidepressants on the market. Their efficacy in improving symptoms of depression and anxiety is well established, and these medications carry FDA approvals for both indications.

Various subtypes of MAOIs are available. The oldest are the classic MAOIs, isocarboxazid (Marplan), phenelzine (Nardil), and tranylcypromine (Parnate), all of which are available in generic. These medications are considered nonselective because they target both types of the MAO enzyme (Types A and B). They are also irreversible, because they destroy the MAO enzyme so effectively that their effect is reversed only when the medication is discontinued and a new enzyme is produced. These MAOIs are the most effective, because their action is broad based, and the changes in neuronal activity are most pronounced. These MAOIs also have shown some efficacy in reducing symptoms of ADHD (Biederman & Spencer, 2002). The nonselective, irreversible MAOIs are also the most dangerous, however, and have the most severe side effects. As a result, these medications are rarely used.

The MAO enzyme is involved in balancing the amount of monoamine neurotransmitters that remain in the synapse. It destroys all monoamines, including norepinephrine, thus removing excess and the potential for overstimulation. When an increase in the neurotransmitters is desired, this enzyme can be destroyed, and as a result the synaptic availability of all monoamines (including serotonin, dopamine, and norepinephrine) will be greatly increased. Because a major regulatory system has been disabled, however, introduction of additional amounts of precursors for these neurotransmitters can result in a rapid increase in synaptic neurotransmission. In the case of norepinephrine, which is synthesized from tyramine, this increase may result in a hypertensive crisis that can lead to a stroke. Because tyramine is ingested from common foods, such as cheese and other aged food products, patients who take nonselective irreversible MAOIs must observe rigid dietary restrictions. In addition, the older MAOIs also have other side effects that many find very troubling, including weight gain, agitation, headache, dry mouth, gastrointestinal distress, tremors, and orthostatic hypotension.

Medications have been developed that target the MAO enzymes more selectively. For example, selegiline (deprenyl, marketed as Eldepryl tablets and EMSAM transdermal patch) is an MAOI that selectively targets Type B of the enzyme. As a result, hypertensive crisis is not associated with this medication, and adverse effects (with the exception of headache) are much less common. Selegiline, however, has been shown to be effective as a treatment primarily of the symptoms of Parkinson's disease, although adjunctive use for the management of depression and anxiety has also been reported (Stahl, 2006). In addition, deprenyl has shown activating effects and is sometimes used off-label to treat symptoms of narcolepsy. With this in mind, one small, open-label study investigated the use of deprenyl in the treatment of symptoms of ADHD in adults (Wender et al., 1985) and found it to be effective. A more recent, small RCT confirmed its effectiveness when used in the patch formulation. Other research is lacking, however, and therefore the use of this medication to treat symptoms of ADHD is considered experimental.

Another MAOI has also been developed. Moclobemide is a reversible inhibitor of MAO-A (RIMA). Thus far it is the only RIMA available, but it is not marketed in the United States. It is sold elsewhere, for example, as Manerix in Canada, where it is also available as a generic. Because it inhibits Type A of the MAO enzyme, it has significant effects in improving symptoms of depression and anxiety. Because it is a reversible inhibitor, its effects are easily overwhelmed by the additional presence of monoamine precursors (such as tyramine), and therefore moclobemide is not associated with the hypertensive crisis and is generally much better tolerated than irreversible MAOIs. Some research findings have suggested that moclobemide is effective in treating symptoms of ADHD in adults, especially when comorbid conditions are present, and the medication is generally well tolerated (Weiss, Weiss, & Hechtman, 2002). The medication has not been researched on individuals younger than 18 years of age (for ADHD or otherwise). Clinicians who practice in a country where moclobemide is available may consider it to be a viable choice for men who present with comorbid symptoms of ADHD with depression and/or anxiety.

Serotonergic Antidepressants. Although medications that act by increasing serotonin are not generally regarded as effective in treating symptoms of ADHD (Spencer, Biederman, & Wilens, 2004), they nevertheless continue to be prescribed to many adults who exhibit symptoms of ADHD. The rationale for this practice is based on the high comorbidity between ADHD and depression, especially in adults, that sometimes has been reported to be as high as 75% (Ramsay & Rostain, 2008). When boys become teenagers, symptoms of ADHD often change in presentation, and many clients develop compensatory strategies that reduce the apparent severity of the distractibility and hyperactivity/impulsivity. If the client also exhibits tendencies toward depression, however, these symptoms may increase with age because of the cumulative experience of failure and greater stressors that developing young adults must face in life. Thus, it is possible that for adults with ADHD, classic symptoms of this disorder diminish at least to some extent while simultaneously the symptoms of depression become more prominent.

Serotonergic antidepressants belong to several subgroups. Selective serotonin reuptake inhibitors (SSRIs) are the most commonly prescribed and include fluoxetine (Prozac), paroxetine (Paxil), sertraline (Zoloft), fluvoxamine (Luvox), and citalopram/escitalopram (Celexa and Lexapro). Most of these are available as generics. Other serotonergic medications include the serotonin-2 antagonist/reuptake inhibitors (SARIs) nefazodone (once marketed as Serzone but currently only marketed as generic) and trazodone (available as Trazodone or generic), and the noradrenergic/specific serotonergic antidepressant (NaSSA) mirtazapine (marketed as Remeron, also available as generic).

Serotonergic antidepressants are generally dosed once per day. Most are not particularly sedating, but some produce drowsiness at least initially and therefore are dosed at bedtime. Serotonergic antidepressants are generally well tolerated, but some patients experience dry mouth, constipation, sweating, orthostatic hypotension, and gastrointestinal symptoms (nausea etc.). Most of these effects are transient and diminish after the first few weeks of use. Serotonergic antidepressants are also associated with sexual side effects that include delays in the time it takes to reach orgasm and greater difficulties in attaining orgasm. With most SSRIs (e.g., fluoxetine), these problems are experienced by at least 30% of patients (Bezchlibnyk-Butler & Jeffries, 2007), although this problem is somewhat less common with escitalopram. Individual response varies, but sexual side effects are a major reason why many patients discontinue these medications. Other serotonergic medications, such as mirtazapine, nefazodone, and trazodone, have much less potential for sexual side effects but are more sedating.

ANTIHYPERTENSIVE MEDICATIONS

Antihypertensives have been used to treat symptoms of ADHD since the 1970s, and some studies have shown adequate efficacy, although head-to-head comparisons with stimulants have not been performed.

There are classes of hypertensive medications that specifically target noradrenergic function, and those are the antihypertensives that are potentially beneficial in reducing the symptoms of ADHD. The medications differ in the specific manner in which they affect the action of norepinephrine, and all tend to be at least somewhat sedating. This discussion will review those compounds for which specific efficacy in treating ADHD has been established.

Noradrenergic antihypertensives may be considered as first-line medications for ADHD when symptom presentation includes comorbid anxiety or tics. For patients with such a symptom profile, noradrenergic antihypertensives may be a better choice than stimulants, because their pharmacodynamic effects may be able to simultaneously address all symptoms—those of ADHD, anxiety, and tics.

Noradrenergic antihypertensives are also an excellent choice when a medication is needed to treat symptoms of ADHD in a teenager or an adult male who is at risk for substance abuse, either directly or by making the drug available to others (e.g., by selling it). The action of antihypertensives does not affect the brain's reward center. In fact, some of these medications are commonly used in patients who are going through drug withdrawal. For this reason, antihypertensives have no known abuse potential and are not listed in the schedule of controlled substances.

Alpha-2 Adrenergic Agonists

Clonidine and guanfacine are the two alpha-2 agonists that have been used to treat symptoms of ADHD. They are marketed as Catapres and Tenex, respectively, and both are available as generics. Catapres is also available as a transdermal patch (not available as generic). They have been used in the treatment of ADHD for several decades, and research results have revealed that they are sometimes effective. Interestingly, even though this subgroup of medications includes other hypertensive compounds, such as xylazine (an analog of clonidine, sold as Rompun), dexmedetomidine (Precedex), tizanidine (Zanaflex), and lofexidine (BritLofex, not available in the United States), clonidine and guanfacine are the only two that have been considered potentially beneficial in treating ADHD.

Evidence of Efficacy. Clonidine has long been known to reduce at least some symptoms of ADHD. Although several studies have been performed, only two were placebo controlled, and less than 200 children have been studied (Biederman & Spencer, 2002). Results have shown greater benefits in decreasing disinhibition than inattentiveness. Guanfacine has been studied even less than clonidine, and only three small open studies have been performed. Results suggested beneficial effects on both hyperactivity and inattentiveness (Biederman & Spencer, 2002).

In adults, the use of clonidine to treat symptoms of ADHD has not been studied, but one placebo-controlled study investigated the use of guanfacine in 17 participants and found beneficial effects (Taylor & Russo, 2001). Other studies have also reported some benefits in patients with comorbid anxiety or aggression (Bezchlibnyk-Butler & Jeffries, 2007). Clonidine and guanfacine may be beneficial in specialized applications where traditional medications are inappropriate, and the sedating effect of alpha-2 agonists is desired.

Pharmacodynamics. Alpha-2 agonists work presynaptically by blocking autoreceptors for norepinephrine. This action results in a decrease of the release of norepinephrine, thus accounting for the medications' antihypertensive effects. The subjective effects include sedation and a decrease of the hyperkinesis associated with hyperactivity, as well as a decrease in the "sympathetic tone" of the limbic system that is experienced as a reduction in nervousness or anxiety. Thus, it is apparent that clonidine and guanfacine may be more effective in addressing symptoms of impulsivity and hyperactivity than symptoms of distractibility.

Stahl (2006) hypothesized that additional poorly understood effects may be responsible for some of the psychogenic action. Alpha-2 agonists may also work by binding to postsynaptic alpha-2 receptors, thus resulting in some limited amount of postsynaptic stimulation of norepinephrine pathways. This may especially be evident in the brain and less so in pathways involved in cardiovascular regulation.

In addition, clonidine (and possibly guanfacine) may act on imidazoline receptors. By inhibiting the sodium–hydrogen antiporter, catecholamine synthesis may be induced, increasing availability of norepinephrine and dopamine in the brain. This mechanism may be responsible for the effect on symptoms of ADHD, including a decrease in hyperactivity and impulsivity as well as inattentiveness.

Pharmacokinetics. Clonidine and guanfacine are sedating, especially when first administered, and should initially be taken when sedation is not problematic and may be desired, for example, at bedtime. Over time, as the body becomes used to the sedating effects, the medication is usually taken two to three times per day. Clonidine and guanfacine need to be taken daily to produce the desired effect, and the action of the medication is not affected if it is taken with food.

Clonidine and guanfacine are immediate-release compounds, and clinical effect is usually evident within an hour, with blood plasma peak evident in 3 to 5 hours. The clinical effect usually lasts for 6 to 20 hours, and children usually require dosing at least BID for round-the-clock clinical effect. The patch needs to be used for 3 to 5 days before significant clinical effects are observed, and it is meant to be affixed to the skin for 24 hours per day. The effects of guanfacine often last shorter than those of clonidine, and therefore guanfacine may need to be taken TID (Bezchlibnyk-Butler & Jeffries, 2007).

Dosing. To treat symptoms of ADHD, clonidine is usually dosed at 3 to 10 µg/kg per day, or 0.05 to 0.4 mg/day. Transdermal patches are available in dosages of 0.1, 0.2, and 0.3 mg. Guanfacine is dosed higher, and usual doses range from 0.5 to 0.9 mg/day (Bezchlibnyk-Butler &

Jeffries, 2007). With both, the medication is initially taken at bedtime and then gradually increased to BID or TID dosing.

Adults generally exhibit a clinical response at similar doses, although up to 0.6 mg/day may be required (Stahl, 2006). With guanfacine, higher doses may be needed.

Adverse Effects. Clonidine and guanfacine do not cause suppression of appetite or weight loss. In fact, in some cases, weight gain has been reported. Otherwise, no gastrointestinal side effects are associated with these medications.

Headache and dizziness are common transient adverse effects evident at the onset of treatment. These generally resolve after the body becomes tolerant to the antihypertensive effects. Some agitation and increase in depressive symptoms has also been reported (Bezchlibnyk-Butler & Jeffries, 2007).

Clonidine and guanfacine are sedating, especially when treatment is initiated. Because these are antihypertensives, hypotension is a common adverse effect at the onset of treatment, and blood pressure must frequently be monitored. When used to treat symptoms of ADHD, clonidine and guanfacine are dosed lower than they are when used to treat hypertension, and at lower doses, patients develop a tolerance to the hypotensive effects, and blood pressure gradually returns to baseline (Stahl, 2006). When clonidine and guanfacine are used to control symptoms of ADHD, the dosage should be carefully monitored to make sure that no long-term hypotensive effects become evident.

The sedative effects of clonidine and guanfacine can sometimes be beneficial. As discussed in the previous chapter, some patients treated with stimulants exhibit a significant rebound effect during the evening hours, and sometimes this rebound may interfere with sleep. For this reason, many doctors prescribe a low dose of clonidine or guanfacine at bedtime for patients who are treated with stimulants during the day. Unfortunately, this practice has sometimes proved to be dangerous, and some deaths have been reported (Silva, Munoz, & Alpert, 1996). As discussed with regard to tricyclics earlier in this chapter, this effect may be secondary to congenital differences in the length of the Q–T interval, and EKG monitoring is suggested when doctors consider the simultaneous use of stimulants and clonidine or guanfacine (Bezchlibnyk-Butler & Jeffries, 2007).

Clonidine and guanfacine are not associated with the nervousness and anxiety sometimes seen with psychostimulants. Conversely, these medications are often used to treat symptoms of anxiety, for example, the combination of hypervigilance and agitation seen in patients with post-traumatic stress disorder. For this reason, clonidine and guanfacine may be good options to consider for patients with comorbid symptoms of ADHD and anxiety, especially when the anxiety symptoms are very notable and accompanied by agitation and aggression.

Clonidine and guanfacine pose no risks of motor tics. In fact, both medications are commonly used off label to treat vocal and motor tics associated with Tourette's syndrome and other tic disorders, and significant research evidence exists that supports the use of these medications to treat tics (Bezchlibnyk-Butler & Jeffries, 2007). For this reason, clonidine and guanfacine are commonly prescribed for patients who exhibit tics, whether or not comorbid symptoms of ADHD are present.

Because clonidine and guanfacine are antihypertensives, rapid discontinuation of the medication can be dangerous. When these compounds are used in miniscule doses at bedtime to induce sedation, significant changes in blood pressure are not evident. If the medications are used for round-the-clock effect, at multiple doses per day, however, rapid discontinuation is likely to result in rebound hypertension that may be dangerous. For this reason, clonidine and guanfacine must be discontinued very gradually, by small decrements over several weeks.

Beta-Blockers

Although alpha-2 adrenergic agonists are the antihypertensives most closely associated with treatment of ADHD, beta noradrenergic blockers have sometimes also been used. Propranolol (Inderal), pindolol (Visken), and nadolol (once sold as Corgard, now available only as generic) are the only beta-blockers that have thus far been studied. While many other compounds are available in this category of antihypertensives, none have been studied in treating symptoms of ADHD. All beta-blockers are available as generics.

Evidence of Efficacy. Pindolol was studied in one placebo-controlled study in 52 children with ADHD (Spencer, Biederman, Kerman, Steingard, & Wilens, 1993). Improvement of cognitive function (e.g., inattentiveness) was not observed, but improvement in hyperactivity and impulsivity was noted. Nadolol was studied in children with ADHD and comorbid aggression, and improvement in aggression was observed, but symptoms of ADHD did not significantly diminish (Spencer et al., 1996). Propranolol has been studied in ADHD with comorbid aggression and has been found effective in reducing both sets of symptoms (Singer et al., 1994). Another report suggested that beta-blockers may be effective for treatment-resistant patients and are best used in combination with psychostimulants (Biederman & Spencer, 2002).

Pharmacodynamics. Beta-blockers exert their antihypertensive action peripherally, by blocking beta-1 receptors within the cardiovascular and pulmonary systems. The mechanism of effect on psychological symptoms is poorly understood. Beta-blockers may block the release of norepinephrine centrally, thus decreasing action associated with the stimulation of the sympathetic functions. Like alpha-2 agonists, these medications may also work by binding to postsynaptic beta receptors, thus resulting in some limited amount of postsynaptic stimulation of norepinephrine pathways in the brain.

Pharmacokinetics. Beta-blockers are somewhat sedating and should initially be taken when sedation is not problematic and may be desired, for example, at bedtime. Small doses are commonly used when situational anxiety is targeted, for example, to treat symptoms of specific phobias (such as a fear of public speaking). Over time, as the body becomes used to the sedating effects, the medication can be taken anytime and is usually dosed once per day, although metabolism varies from patient to patient, and some need BID dosing.

Dosing. Beta-blockers are dosed differently, depending on the specific compound. Propranolol is generally dosed up to 120 mg/day, but when used to control symptoms of ADHD, much higher doses were required, up to 640 mg/day (Singer et al., 1994). Obviously, the dose–response relationship must be closely monitored, and cardiovascular and other effects need to be examined.

Adverse Effects. Beta-blockers are associated with similar side effects to those seen with clonidine and guanfacine. Headache and dizziness may sometimes be experienced, and these effects usually resolve after a few weeks of treatment. Sedation is common but similarly wears off in time. Hypotension must be closely watched. Interestingly, perhaps because the sedation is not as pronounced as it is with clonidine or guanfacine, beta-blockers are not commonly used to counteract the rebound associated with stimulants. Symptoms of anxiety may improve, and beta-blockers may be a good option for patients with comorbid symptoms of ADHD and anxiety and/or aggression. The effectiveness of beta-blockers to treat motor tics has not been established. Rapid discontinuation can be dangerous. When these compounds are used in miniscule doses to address situational anxiety, significant changes in blood pressure are not evident. If the medications are used regularly, at daily doses that result in reaching the steady state, however, rapid discontinuation is likely to result in rebound hypertension that may be dangerous. For this reason, beta-blockers must be discontinued very gradually, in small decrements over several weeks.

OTHER MEDICATIONS

Psychostimulants, antidepressants, and antihypertensives are the classes of medications that are used in the vast majority of cases. Some patients, however, are treatment resistant and do not respond to these medications. In addition, other mechanisms that may contribute to treating the symptoms of ADHD continue to be discovered. For this reason, the usefulness of other compounds in treating ADHD has been investigated.

Antipsychotic Medications

Antipsychotic medications primarily work through exerting a dopaminergic system blockade. As a result, dopamine activity in the brain is diminished. Older generation "typical" antipsychotics antagonize dopamine activity in all pathways, thus resulting in exacerbation rather than improvement of symptoms of ADHD. They are sedating, however, and for this reason these medications have sometimes been used with individuals who may have been diagnosed with ADHD but also presented with severe aggression (Castellanos et al., 1997). It is likely that the sedation, rather than specific dopaminergic effects, were responsible for the improvement in aggression, and typical antipsychotics are not generally prescribed to treat individuals with ADHD. Because older generation antipsychotics present with very significant adverse effects and pose a risk of permanent damage (known as tardive dyskinesia) to parts of the brain that control the motor system, nowadays they are rarely used for any purpose.

A more recent generation of "atypical" antipsychotics has sometimes been used, primarily in individuals who exhibit symptoms of ADHD with comorbid (or suspected) symptoms of bipolar disorder. These medications work through a selective dopaminergic and serotonergic blockade that result in a decrease of activity in the mesolimbic pathway, but other dopaminergic pathways are unaffected and, because of corresponding serotonergic blockade, may even increase in activity to some extent. Data that support the effectiveness of these medications for symptoms of ADHD are lacking, but atypical antipsychotics are well documented to be effective mood stabilizers that are used with children, teens, and adults, and for this reason, they are sometimes used as adjuncts to other medications when a patient with ADHD exhibits significant mood disturbance (manic, hypomanic, or mixed-manic symptoms).

Mood Stabilizers

As discussed earlier, some patients exhibit comorbid symptoms of ADHD and mania-related mood disturbance. For this reason, the efficacy of mood stabilizers in treating symptoms of ADHD has been examined. Older generation mood stabilizers are antiepileptic medications, some of which have also shown efficacy in controlling symptoms of manic, hypomanic, or mixed-manic symptoms. Of these, carbamazepine (Tegretol) has been investigated, and a meta-analysis of 10 studies suggested that this medication may be effective in controlling some symptoms of ADHD (Spencer, Wilens, & Biederman, 1995; cf. Biederman & Spencer, 2002). Carbamazepine, however, like most older mood stabilizers, has significant adverse effects that make the use of this medication impractical, especially in light of other medications that are at least as effective to treat symptoms of ADHD or mood disturbance. Carbamazepine, therefore, is rarely used in individuals who exhibit symptoms of ADHD, alone or comorbid with other disorders. In addition, atypical antipsychotics also show efficacy as mood stabilizers (and are FDA approved for that use). Consequently, those medications are generally considered better choices to use when a mood stabilizer is needed.

Anxiolytic Medications

The most commonly prescribed anxiolytic medications are benzodiaz-epines and SSRIs. Neither has shown efficacy in treating symptoms of ADHD, but buspirone, a compound similar to the SSRIs, has shown efficacy in one open study with 12 children with ADHD (Biederman & Spencer, 2002). Although buspirone primarily works through a sero-tonergic mechanism, a modest effect on the dopaminergic system and alpha-adrenergic activity has been hypothesized. A subsequent multi-site clinical trial, however, did not reveal efficacy (Biederman & Spencer, 2002). Thus, the use of buspirone to treat symptoms of ADHD is regarded as experimental.

Cholinergic Medications

Recent investigations have examined other factors that may contribute to dopaminergic dysregulation. Acetylcholine is a neurotransmitter that has a complex relationship with dopamine, and both may be respon-sible for regulation of symptoms of ADHD. In general, stimulation of nicotinic-type cholinergic receptors has been shown to improve atten-tion, memory, and executive functions in individuals who do not pres-ent symptoms of ADHD (Biederman & Spencer, 2002). Consequently, the use of nicotine to improve symptoms of ADHD has been investi-gated, and one short study has shown that the use of nicotine patches has resulted in a significant improvement of working memory and symp-toms of ADHD (Wilens et al., 1996).

In addition, studies have investigated the utility of ABT-418, an investigational agent that stimulates nicotinic-type acetylcholine recep-tors in the nervous system, and improvement in ADHD symptoms was apparent (Biederman & Spencer, 2002). Because ABT-418 does not stimulate the reward pathway of the brain in the same way that is seen with nicotine, addictive properties associated with tobacco use may not be evident. This compound holds promise not only for treatment of symptoms of ADHD but also for treatment of dementia.

SUMMARY

Although psychostimulants are considered the first-line medications for patients with ADHD, some do not tolerate these medications or exhibit a limited response. This is especially the case when comorbid symptoms, such as depression, anxiety, agitation, or tics, must also be addressed. For these reasons, many nonstimulant medications have also been used to treat patients with ADHD, and research studies have con-firmed the potential efficacy of several of these compounds.

Atomoxetine and selected antidepressants are best supported as nonstimulants alternatives. These medications have been shown to be effective with boys, teens, and adults and offer advantages when adverse effects preclude the use of stimulants, when there is a risk of stimulant abuse (or distribution), or when comorbid symptoms of depression are present. Antidepressants pose various risks of side effects, including cardiac problems, seizures, weight gain, and sedation, and clinicians must weigh the potential benefits against the risks of adverse effects associated with these medications.

When significant anxiety and/or tics are evident, antihypertensives may prove beneficial. Clonidine and guanfacine have been used in monotherapy or adjunct treatment to manage symptoms of ADHD for several decades, although few studies exist that have investigated their efficacy. Hypotensive effects, cardiac problems, and sedation may be problematic, and the effect on symptoms of ADHD is likely to be less pronounced. In cases where other medications have not produced beneficial effects, and comorbid anxiety and/or tics are evident, however, these medications may be considered.

Attempts at managing symptoms of ADHD with other medications have been carried out, and limited data exist about the efficacy of antipsychotics, mood stabilizers, or anxiolytics. These compounds must be considered investigational and should not be attempted as first-line treatment. More recently, cholinergic compounds have started to show efficacy, but more research is needed before these medications can be recommended.

15

Nutritional and Herbal Interventions

Because functional deficits in the brain's dopaminergic and noradrenergic pathways underlie the behavioral presentation of the symptoms of attention deficit/hyperactivity disorder (ADHD), medications that increase the action of dopamine and norepinephrine have been found to be effective in addressing these symptoms. As reviewed in the previous two chapters, a wide variety of medications is available, including stimulants, antidepressants, and so on. Some clients, however, are opposed to medications, and despite clinicians' best efforts to help them understand why medications may be helpful, they refuse to follow through on recommendations to see a prescriber. These clients often are more receptive to naturopathic alternatives, and clinicians should be aware of the benefits and drawbacks of these compounds.

RATIONALE

Although the use of medications is prevalent, many patients continue to be skeptical about prescription drugs. There are complex reasons for this perception, some of which are more legitimate than others. It is important for mental health professionals to be able to separate truth from fiction when discussing naturopathic interventions with their clients.

One reason for this skepticism is related to the information that continues to become available about the influence that the drug industry has on the studies that investigate the effectiveness of medications. The process of bringing a medication to market is more involved in the United States than in the vast majority of countries around the world.

Overtly, this may imply that medications marketed in the United States are safer than those marketed elsewhere and that a greater amount of safety data are sought by the U.S. Food and Drug Administration (FDA) before the drug is approved. In practice, however, drug manufacturers have a significant amount of influence over various portions of this process. Although the FDA requires three stages of studies to investigate the safety and efficacy of medications, there are no requirements that compel drug manufacturers to report *all* research findings to the FDA, and it is becoming increasingly evident that drug manufacturers perform many studies and choose to release to the FDA only the findings of those studies that support the drug's safety and efficacy. Consequently, the public is losing confidence in widely publicized claims of effectiveness, and drug manufacturers have lost a lot of creditability with the American public.

As a result, many clients are turning to nutritional and herbal supplements. Often, these supplements are perceived as viable alternatives that have been around for thousands of years and have been used for various purposes in many cultures through many centuries. Thus, they must be effective. This assumption, however, is often inaccurate. Although the efficacy of medications *must* be established through empirical studies, no such requirement is placed on nutritional and herbal supplements, unless they are being marketed specifically to treat an existing illness or disorder. Because nutritional and herbal supplements are not usually marketed to treat a specific disorder, they are exempt from this requirement, and a vast majority of supplements have undergone a miniscule amount of research. Thus, the efficacy of a compound is frequently presumed rather than established. The review in this chapter attempts to help readers determine which supplements have been shown to be effective and which are only presumed or expected to be (with little research support).

Moreover, clients and clinicians must be aware of differences in marketing. Medications can be advertised to treat only the specific condition for which they are FDA approved (the so-called on-label use). Although medications are brought to market to treat a specific condition, in subsequent research they are sometimes shown to be effective for another disorder. Because of the staggering cost involved in filing another application with the FDA, most drug manufacturers do not bother, knowing that any prescriber can potentially prescribe any medication to treat any disorder so long as in the prescriber's professional opinion there is good likelihood that the medication will be effective. This off-label use is usually based on the availability of research studies that support the use of the medication for a specific purpose, even though the original FDA approval was for a different disorder. For example, a vast majority of the medications reviewed in the previous chapter are not specifically FDA approved to treat ADHD and cannot be advertised as such, but they are nevertheless used in some cases because there is research evidence that supports their efficacy.

The situation is different with nutritional and herbal supplements. Although these compounds cannot be marketed to treat symptoms of ADHD without submitting evidence of efficacy to treat this disorder, they can be advertised to "improve attention" or provide other similar benefits, as long as no specific claim is being made to treat ADHD. This is exemplified by the marketing practices of Focus Factor, a vitamin compound that lacks any objective efficacy in treating symptoms of ADHD, and yet it is commonly sold to "improve attention." Obviously, this loophole in current regulations is successfully exploited by the manufacturers of nutritional and herbal supplements, and clients must understand that they have to be even more skeptical about claims of efficacy of nutritional compounds than similar claims made about medications, for which advertising practices are more tightly regulated.

The lack of oversight over the manufacture and sale of nutritional and herbal supplements presents additional problems. Because prescription (as well as over-the-counter) medications are regulated, manufacturers are mandated to ensure that the medication being sold contains the exact amount of the compound that is being listed. For example, 20 mg of methylphenidate must contain very close to 20 mg of the compound. Because the supplement market is left to self-regulate, no such oversight exists, and consumers have no way of knowing if a 200 mg capsule of SAMe really contains 200 mg of the compound or, for that matter, *any* amount of that specific compound. In addition, because these supplements usually are not patented, identical doses of the compound from various manufacturers are likely to dissolve differently and have different bioavailability. This difference makes the use of supplements very unpredictable.

Clients often have concerns about the safety of prescription medications. This concern is especially the case with some medications specifically marketed to treat symptoms of ADHD, such as psychostimulants and atomoxetine. Stimulants, in particular, have been portrayed as dangerous drugs in much of the media coverage. They have been likened to cocaine and amphetamines, and exaggerated fears have been propagated about the addictiveness of these compounds. In some media coverage, the levels of side effects seen with the abuse of cocaine and crystal meth have been extrapolated to also be relevant to Ritalin and related medications. This distorted view of the danger of stimulants has resulted in widespread fear of these medications. Makers of other drugs and manufacturers of naturopathic supplements have exploited this apprehension. For example, atomoxetine is marketed to be an alternative to stimulants with the presumption that the "dangerous" side effects associated with stimulants are not a risk with this medication. As is often the case, the truth is different from the presumption, for example, atomoxetine is associated with more significant side effects than any of the psychostimulants, and a careful review of any comprehensive reference (e.g., Bezchlibnyk-Butler & Jeffries, 2007) reveals that psychostimulants, as a group, present with fewer frequent and less dangerous side effects than any other category of psychotropic medications.

Clinicians and clients need to be aware that media coverage is based, at least in part, on the sensationalism of the tale. It does not make an interesting story to say that stimulants are safe and effective and have helped millions of patients with ADHD. It makes for a more interesting story to film a segment on *48 Hours* about the dangers of stimulants ("Out of Control," November 9, 2001), and the viewership for such a show is likely to increase, even if the message within it is greatly distorted.

Because of these exaggerated fears, naturopathic compounds are often expected to be safer. After all, these compounds are usually extracts of plants or other naturally occurring elements, and anything that comes from nature is presumed to be safe. Clinicians must dispel this misperception. Naturopathic compounds, on the whole, are not any safer than medications. In fact, some of the deadliest compounds occur naturally—radon, strychnine, gyromitrin (a deadly toxin commonly found in wild mushrooms), and so on. Mistakenly assuming that something is safe just because it occurs naturally can be lethal. Of course, supplements available for sale generally are not as toxic, but they still sometimes carry risks similar to those of some prescription medications. For example, use of kava kava, a relaxant sometimes taken to treat symptoms of anxiety, may result in liver damage.

Prescription medications are extensively refined, and most contain a single active compound that is carefully isolated and studied. Their pharmacokinetics and pharmacodynamics are established, and patients have a lot of information available about potential adverse reactions, how much they need to take, how long it will take before improvement can be expected, and so on. By contrast, supplements are unrefined and often contain dozens of active compounds, all of which have different pharmacokinetic and pharmacodynamics properties, which makes herbals much more unpredictable and difficult to study, because separate active components are not isolated and individually examined. Generally, clients who take supplements can expect a much broader spectrum of effect, and changes may be observed not only in behaviors targeted by the supplement (such as symptoms of ADHD) but also in many other unrelated reactions.

Because supplements have not undergone much research, pragmatics of their use are often poorly established. For this reason, it is hard to determine the effective dose, the manner in which the dose needs to be titrated, the onset of effect, and the duration of action of the substance. Although some studies have addressed those issues, most have not. In addition, the limited research that has been performed was usually done with adults rather than children or adolescents. Thus, clinicians who plan to use supplements with boys or teens must generally extrapolate from adult data.

The following discussion reviews those compounds for which efficacy in treating symptoms of ADHD has been investigated or presumed. Results of available studies are reviewed, and guidelines about using the supplements with boys, male teens, and men are provided.

Some compounds are also discussed that are widely marketed for treating symptoms of ADHD but lack reasonable evidence of efficacy. The supplements are divided into categories of those with established efficacy, those with likely efficacy, those with possible efficacy, and those for which efficacy should not be expected.

SUPPLEMENTS WITH ESTABLISHED EFFICACY

Although the use of many herbal and nutritional supplements has not been studied, some compounds have undergone at least some research. Moreover, because the treatment of ADHD primarily focuses on addressing symptoms in children, some of these compounds have specifically been researched in children and adolescents.

Medications that work by increasing the amount of activity in the catecholamine pathways are generally effective in addressing symptoms of ADHD. Similarly, supplements that accomplish similar changes in the brain have been shown to be effective.

Caffeine

Caffeine is a psychostimulant classified as a methylxanthine. This category also includes theophylline (commonly found in tea) and theobromine (found in chocolate). Xantine is a purine base found in most tissues and body fluids and is converted to uric acid. Caffeine is found in many beverages. Some naturally contain caffeine in varying amounts. For example, a 5 oz cup of coffee contains 60 mg to 120 mg of caffeine, depending on the method of brewing. The same amount of tea contains only about 40 mg of caffeine (and 1 mg of theophylline). Chocolate contains up to 40 mg of caffeine per 1 oz serving (and about 200 mg of theobromine), with darker chocolate containing much more caffeine than milk chocolate. Chocolate milk contains about 35 mg of caffeine per 8 oz serving, and a cup of hot cocoa contains between 10 mg and 30 mg of caffeine (and about 150 mg of theobromine). Theophylline and theobromine have lesser stimulating effects than caffeine, and therefore most of the mild stimulant properties of tea and chocolate are due to their caffeine content rather than the amount of the other methylxanthines.

Caffeine is also commonly added to soft drinks. Common colas (Coke, Pepsi, etc.) and Mountain Dew contain 355 mg of caffeine per 12 oz serving, and some soft drinks are specifically marketed for their stimulant properties—Jolt contains about 700 mg of caffeine (per 24 oz serving), Red Bull contains about 250 mg (per 8 oz serving), and Wired contains about 475 mg (per 16 oz serving). Soft drinks usually do not list the specific amounts of caffeine, and caffeine sometimes is listed by other names, for example, it is referred as guaranine (in guarana), mateine (in mate), and theine (in tea). Thus, it is difficult for consumers to know the exact amount of caffeine that any soft drink may contain.

Caffeine is also sold in both generic and brand-name pills, including brands such as Vivarin and NoDoz. It usually is available in 100 mg or 200 mg tablets. In addition, small doses of caffeine are commonly added to some over-the-counter medications, including Dristan, Excedrin, Midol, and some prescription drugs commonly used to treat migraines (e.g., Fioricet).

Evidence of Efficacy. Although some studies have found that caffeine was not effective in improving symptoms of ADHD (Klein, 1987), and some noted authorities have recommended against its use (Barkley, 2006), there is significant evidence to the contrary. Leon (2000) reviewed the results of 19 studies that investigated the effects of caffeine on children with ADHD. The review revealed that studies consistently found at least some benefit of caffeine, and using it was better than providing no treatment at all. Positive effects included not only increased attention to task but decreased aggression as well. In fact, in some studies reviewed, combining caffeine with prescription stimulants did not increase adverse effects but enhanced therapeutic response.

The use of caffeine specifically to treat symptoms of ADHD in adults has not been studied. Moderate intake of caffeine, however, has been shown to enhance sustained effort and the ability to remain on task (Ritchie, 1975). Caffeine has also been shown to increase the speed of reaction time and enhance the ability to perform complex, intense tasks, such as performance in a flight simulator (Nehlig, Daval, & Debry, 1992). Other reviews have confirmed these findings but also suggested that enhanced performance is evident only when there is prior evidence of fatigue and boredom (Dews, 1984). Because the subjective experience of boredom is commonly reported by teenagers and adults with ADHD, however, and it commonly is associated with difficulties in remaining on task and maintaining sustained attention, it is reasonable to expect that caffeine has some beneficial effects on reducing these problems.

In addition, caffeine has also been found to increase the ability to perform tasks that require physical exertion, such as cycling or running (Trice & Haymes, 1995). For this reason, it is banned by the International Olympic Committee (Lombardo, 1986). The mechanism by which caffeine increases physical performance is complex but may involve an increase in fatty acids that can be used as fuel by the muscles (Tarnopolsky, 1994) and improvement in respiration. In fact, for over three decades, caffeine has been used to treat apnea of prematurity that is often seen in premature infants (Schmidt, 2005). It is possible that the effects of caffeine ingestion may improve oxygenation of blood, thus further contributing to its impact on vigilance and ability to sustain attention.

Pharmacodynamics. The main psychoactive effect of caffeine is evident through its inhibition of the action of adenosine. Adenosine, a neurotransmitter that is also found throughout most of the body, has an inhibitory function that slows metabolic activity. Its action may contribute to that of gamma-aminobutyric acid (GABA) in opposing the stimulatory effects of glutamate. In fact, adenosine has been found to stabilize the function of the NMDA-type glutaminergic receptors (Fredholm, Ijzerman, Jacobson, Klotz, & Linden, 2001). Caffeine molecules closely resemble adenosine and occupy adenosine receptors without activating them, thus caffeine is an antagonist for adenosine. The net effect is that the inhibitory action associated with adenosine is reduced, thus providing more broad-based neuronal activation. In this manner, the pharmacodynamic action of caffeine is somewhat similar to that of modafinil (discussed in Chapter 13), which exerts its stimulant effect by inhibiting GABA, thus allowing glutamate to have a greater stimulatory effect on the brain.

In addition, adenosine acts presynaptically and inhibits the release of other neurotransmitters, including the catecholamines. This effect is seen on both dopamine and norepinephrine and epinephrine. By blocking adenosine, caffeine seems to increase the activation of dopaminergic receptors (Garrett & Griffiths, 1997) and causes an additional release of norepinephrine and epinephrine (Bolton and Null, 1981). These effects likely contribute to caffeine's stimulant properties. Because epinephrine is also involved in the stimulation of the limbic system's fight–flight reaction, however, use of caffeine sometimes results in an increase of anxiety, especially in individuals susceptible to anxiety and panic.

Pharmacokinetics. Caffeine is rapidly absorbed from the gastrointestinal tract, especially from the small intestine. When caffeine is consumed in food (e.g., chocolate or a beverage), its absorption rate depends on how much food was consumed and what other substances were consumed at the same time (e.g., alcohol slows the absorption of caffeine). When caffeine is used therapeutically, it should be administered in tablets, because the caffeine in tablets is more rapidly absorbed than the caffeine ingested in food. Generally, the effects of caffeine are seen in less than an hour, and the effect lasts about 3 to 4 hours. The pharmacokinetics of caffeine, however, is dose dependent. With repeated dosing, as is often evident in individuals who consume caffeine throughout the day, the elimination half-life is increased. There are also substantial individual differences in the rates of absorption and metabolism of caffeine, and therefore the duration of effect may be somewhat unpredictable. Still, most individuals will require dosing at least twice per day to address symptoms of ADHD in school and at home, and some trial and error may be necessary to maintain the effect of caffeine after school hours (e.g., during homework completion), while making sure that the compound is eliminated by the body well ahead of bedtime.

Although caffeine is a psychostimulant, its effect on the brain is not as pronounced as the effect of prescription stimulants (such as methylphenidate or dextroamphetamine). For this reason, the rebound effect commonly associated with immediate-release prescription stimulants is not generally seen when caffeine is used.

Dosing. Like other stimulants, caffeine is generally dosed by body weight. Because of its anxiety-promoting properties, low ceiling dosages have been established. The recommended dose in children is about

2.5 mg/kg per day, and adverse effects may be seen over 300 mg or 400 mg per day. Because doses lower than 200 mg have usually been found to be clinically ineffective (Hingle, 2007), a narrow therapeutic window is available. Of course, because significant variation in metabolizing and responding to caffeine is widely reported, careful titration must be performed to determine the optimal dose for a specific patient.

Teens and men are not generally dosed by body weight. Caffeine is usually started at a dose of 200 mg every 4 hours or so for as long as the benefit of the compound is required. As with children, teens and men must be carefully monitored for an increase of anxiety or interference with sleep. Generally, adverse effects on sleep are not seen in individuals who take the last dose of caffeine prior to 6:00 p.m. With such wide individual variation, however, each person's response must be carefully monitored.

Most medications require a gradual increase of dose as the brain attempts to counteract the pharmacodynamic effects of the compound, and tolerance is more evident with caffeine than it is with prescription stimulants. When prescription stimulants are used at appropriate therapeutic levels, there is no appreciable tolerance observed with them. Because caffeine affects adenosine, however, the tolerance potential is much more significant. When chronically inhibited, adenosine receptors upregulate by increasing in number, presumably to restore the equilibrium that existed prior to the administration of caffeine. Occasional use of caffeine, especially at lower doses, is not associated with significant tolerance. Doses of 300 mg or higher, however, result in a decrease of the stimulating effect in as little as 4 days (Evans & Griffiths, 1992). This requires careful monitoring of response in individuals who take caffeine at those (or higher) doses.

Tolerance is a sign of gradual dependence on the substance, indicating that the body has changed its function to allow for the presence of a substance in the system. Indeed, caffeine is often associated with dependence and withdrawal. Once again, wide individual differences are evident. Some individuals exhibit withdrawal effects after using as little of 100 mg of caffeine per day over an extended period of time, whereas others will exhibit withdrawal effects after using 600 mg of caffeine for as little as 6 days (Griffiths & Mumford, 1995). Individuals who drink coffee every day for extended periods of time usually begin to exhibit withdrawal effects after 24 to 28 hours, which commonly peak at 20 to 51 hours and last as long as 9 days (Griffiths & Mumford, 1995). The most common withdrawal effects are headaches and irritability. Interestingly, the use of caffeine in pill form is not associated with tolerance and withdrawal nearly as frequently, and a vast majority of withdrawal effects are associated with the use of coffee. It is possible that other compounds in coffee are responsible for the magnification of the dependence and withdrawal. Individuals who use caffeine at doses of 300 mg or higher, however, should be monitored for possible signs of dependence and withdrawal. One possible way to counteract some of these effects is to use caffeine intermittently, for example, only during the week and not on weekends.

Adverse Effects. Caffeine is usually well tolerated. The suppression of appetite commonly seen with psychostimulants is much less evident, although a less dramatic decrease in appetite is sometimes reported. Because the absorption of caffeine can be slowed by food, caffeine is best taken before a meal or in between meals. Those patients who experience some decrease in appetite may take the compound right before breakfast and right before lunch. In this way, the clinical effect will not yet be evident, and no changes in appetite will be observed during the meal.

Caffeine interferes with sleep. Although this is a desirable effect when greater vigilance is sought, those who take caffeine to treat symptoms of ADHD must make sure that the last dose is taken well ahead of bedtime. Because caffeine is available only in immediate-release preparations, patients can easily time the last dose to be taken at least 4 to 6 hours before bedtime. Teens and men who take higher daily doses need to monitor their sleep response very carefully, because chronic use of caffeine in higher doses has been associated with longer half-life. For some individuals, this effect may be subtle. For example, a person may feel drowsy and therefore assume that the caffeine has been eliminated from the system. Smaller amounts of caffeine, however, may still interfere with sleep patterns, even if the ability to go to sleep does not seem to be affected. For example, caffeine may decrease the total amount of time spent sleeping (Brenesova, Oswald, & Loudon, 1975). The sleep patterns of boys, teens, and men who take caffeine should be carefully monitored to make sure that sleep is not interfered with in any way.

Caffeine is metabolized by the cytochrome P450 1A2 liver enzyme. This means that when caffeine is used with other medications, its plasma levels may change. Taking medications that inhibit this enzyme will result in higher levels of caffeine, whereas taking those that induce the enzyme will lower caffeine plasma levels. Not only medications affect this enzyme. For example, nicotine is a potent inducer of 1A2, and smokers tend to metabolize caffeine twice as fast as nonsmokers (James, 1991). Boys, teens, and men who are on other medications and those who smoke must be carefully monitored when given caffeine.

Caffeine users sometimes report some transient adverse effects, most common of which are nausea and relaxation of some gastrointestinal sphincter functions that may results in mild diarrhea. These effects generally resolve after a few doses. Caffeine is also a diuretic. For this reason, urinary urgency is increased when caffeine is used. Individuals will urinate more frequently, and consequently some may experience an increase in dehydration. For this reason, the intake of fluid should generally be increased when caffeine is being administered.

Caffeine, as all stimulants, exhibits sympathomimetic qualities that include the activation of the fight–flight mechanism involved in anxiety reactions. In fact, although caffeine's psychostimulant effects are less pronounced than those seen with prescription stimulants, its effect on anxiety is at least as significant. Thus, some patients who take caffeine begin to exhibit symptoms of anxiety. These symptoms are especially likely in individuals who present a history of anxiety symptoms. Patients with comorbid symptoms of ADHD and anxiety are likely to become more anxious on caffeine. With prescription stimulants, some patients exhibit a positive response in both symptom clusters, and anxiety diminishes along with symptoms of ADHD. This response, however, has not been seen with caffeine, and an increase in anxiety is more likely. For this reason, individuals with ADHD and symptoms of anxiety generally should not use caffeine.

The risk of developing motor tics on stimulant medications is well known. Because caffeine's effect on the brain pathways that control motor functions is less significant, however, the onset (or exacerbation) of tics is rarely reported with caffeine. Studies have not been performed to investigate the response of individuals with ADHD and comorbid tics. Because caffeine is not known to exacerbate tics in the vast majority of individuals, however, a trial of caffeine in this population of patients may be reasonable.

The use of caffeine results in some cardiovascular effects that are similar to those effects of other psychostimulants, including small increases in pulse rate. Caffeine causes vasoconstriction in the brain, and as a result it has been found to be effective in addressing migraine headaches. For this reason, caffeine is sometimes added to migraine medications. Peripherally, however, caffeine generally causes vasodilation, thus increasing blood flow. Because caffeine is not associated with cardiac risks, the use of caffeine does not usually necessitate the kinds of cardiac function tests (e.g., a baseline electrocardiogram) that are sometimes needed when patients at risk for cardiovascular problems are placed on prescription stimulants.

Because the stimulating effects of caffeine are not as significant as they are for prescription stimulants, rebound effects are rarely reported. When the compound is eliminated from the body, it is likely that symptoms of ADHD will return to unmedicated levels, but further exacerbation of the symptoms is not expected, which is one reason why caffeine has sometimes been added to a prescription stimulant instead of augmenting the dose of the prescription medication. With higher doses of immediate-release prescription stimulants, rebound effects are more likely, because the elimination slope is very steep, and the medication is eliminated rapidly. With caffeine, these effects are not commonly seen. Although extended-release stimulants have a much lower risk of rebound effects, some individuals do not respond well to the gradual release of the compound, and clinical effects may not be sufficient. Patients who seem to do best on regular-release compounds but exhibit significant rebound effects may try to take a lower dose of the prescription stimulant augmented with caffeine. Clinical improvement may be similar to that seen on a higher dose of the prescription stimulant, but the rebound effect may be less evident.

SUPPLEMENTS WITH LIKELY EFFICACY

Although caffeine is the only supplement that has undergone significant research and has shown consistent efficacy, some other compounds have also undergone at least some research, although the results are sometimes contradictory. In addition, not all of these supplements have been researched with children, adolescents, and adults. Clinicians must use their judgment when weighing the benefits and drawbacks of these supplements.

Omega-3 Polyunsaturated Fatty Acids

Beneficial effects of omega-3 have been widely touted for about a decade. Indeed, the supplement has been found to stabilize mood, reduce depression, protect the brain against Alzheimer's disease, and reduce the negative effects of low-density lipoproteins, the type of fat responsible for clogging of the arteries. Although much of the research about omega-3's beneficial effects comes from studying cultures where the endogenous diet is rich in the intake of omega-3 in food (e.g., by consuming fish), some evidence now exists about the beneficial effects of omega-3 supplementation.

Omega-3 supplements are generally available as caplets filled with fish oil rich in omega-3. The pills usually contain 1,000 mg, but those containing higher and lower amounts are also available. In addition, because the caplets are usually rather large and may be difficult to swallow for some patients, other forms are also available, for example, a chewable preparation. As is the case with all supplements, there are many manufacturers, and omega-3 supplements are sold in drugstores, supermarkets, and health food stores. Many are also available through the Internet.

Omega-3 is also sold by prescription in 1,000 mg tablets that contain 465 mg of eicosapentaenoic acid (EPA) and 375 mg of docosahexaenoic acid (DHA). These tablets are approved to treat hyperlipidemia and are marketed as Lovaza (formally Omacor). They are manufactured in a process the removes mercury from the fish oil, and therefore these pills are marketed as being superior to other omega-3 supplements (which usually do not remove mercury from the fish oil). The amount of mercury contained in fish oil supplements is considered to be much lower than it is in many types of fish, because the oil is not usually derived from fish known to have high amounts of mercury. In addition, plant-based omega-3 supplements (in flax, soybean, or canola oil), also available on the market, do not contain mercury. One potential benefit of Lovaza, as an FDA-approved compound, is that its sale and manufacture is regulated, and therefore the consumer can be more certain that Lovaza really contains the ingredients that it claims to have, in the specific amount that is advertised. Consumers must balance these benefits against the added cost of this medication and the inconvenience of seeking a prescription.

Although evidence of the effectiveness of omega-3 fatty acids to treat symptoms of ADHD is only now emerging, the supplement is already shown to have benefits in stabilizing mood and possibly improving symptoms of depression. For this reason, boys, teens, and men who present with comorbid symptoms of ADHD and agitation or depression may be especially good candidates for a trial of omega-3 supplementation.

Evidence of Efficacy. Omega-3's efficacy to treat symptoms of ADHD is not well established, and some studies have revealed limited efficacy. For example, Voigt, Llorente, and Jensen (2001) found no benefit in using DHA to address symptoms of ADHD in children, and Hirayama, Hamazaki, and Terasawa (2004) reported similar results. Others have found more promising results, however. Richardson and Puri (2002) reported that children with ADHD who took a mixture of DHA, EPA, and two types of omega-6 fatty acids experienced significant improvement in hyperactivity and impulsivity, and another placebo-controlled trial revealed that children who took a mixture of omega-6 and omega-3 fatty acids experienced decreases in inattention and disruptive behavior (Stevens, Zhang, & Peck, 2003). Another study revealed similar findings but also found that children with ADHD, inattentive type responded better to omega-3 and omega-6 than those with symptoms of hyperactivity and/or impulsivity (Johnson, Ostlund, Fransson, & Kadesjo, in press). Overall, the results of all these studies are inconsistent. At first glance, it may seem that different combinations of DHA and EPA may be responsible for the differential response in studies. Because these fatty acids undergo significant cross-transformation in the body (as described later), however, it is unlikely that taking one form is likely to be better than another.

The use of omega-3 to treat symptoms of ADHD has also been researched with teenagers. In one small study, levels of endogenous DHA were found to be lower in teens with ADHD (Colter, Cutler, & Meckling, in press), but augmentation was not studied to see whether it had beneficial effects. Similarly, it has been hypothesized that low levels of DHA or related fatty acids are also responsible for difficulties with cognitive functioning in adults, including problems remaining on task (Richardson, 2003). As with the study of adolescents, whether supplementation of omega-3 would be beneficial was not studied. Prior research, however, linked low levels of essential fatty acids (omega-3 and omega-6) with low levels of monoamine metabolites in the cerebrospinal fluid (Hibbeln et al., 1998). Although this finding is correlational, some studies with children have revealed that symptoms of ADHD are accompanied by such deficits. Thus, it is plausible that supplementation with essential fatty acids may have some beneficial effects for individuals with ADHD.

Pharmacodynamics. Essential omega-3 fatty acids include alpha-linolenic acid (ALA), EPA, and DHA. These acids cannot be synthesized by the body and must be ingested from food. Following ingestion, DHA inhibits lipogenesis and stimulates oxidation. ALA, EPA, and DHA undergo downconversion and retroconversion (as described later) and contribute to the metabolism of various nutrients and lipids. This is responsible for a broad-based therapeutic effect that includes changes in cardiovascular function, a decrease in triglycerides, and an improvement in pulmonary function. Most of these effects are directly associated with DHA, although related fatty acids may play a contributory role.

The brain takes up DHA at greater rates than it does the other fatty acids. DHA is then incorporated into the phospholipids of cell membranes. DHA contributes to proper formation and elongation of synapses. In addition, DHA-containing phospholipids improve cell function by stabilizing the membrane fluidity and changing firing rates of neurons (Horrocks & Yeo, 1999). Thus, DHA may play a role in the synchronization of neuronal action. It can be hypothesized that poor phosphorization may be partially responsible for decreased neuronal function, and when such deficits are evident in catecholaminergic pathways that control executive functions, focusing, and self-control, symptoms of ADHD are apparent. Consequently, increasing phosphorization of cell membranes in these areas may be responsible for the beneficial effects of DHA (and other fatty acid) supplementation that is sometimes observed in individuals with ADHD.

Eicosanoids contribute to this process. They are localized in cells and serve as catalysts for a large number of processes, including the movement of calcium in and out of the cells (Enig & Fallon, 1999). Because calcium channels are involved in the rates of firing of brain cells, regulation of these channels changes the brain's action potential. It is possible that EPA's regulation of calcium channels may contribute to DHA's influence of cell membrane phosphorization, providing a synergistic effect on the rates of neuronal firing. When this regulation of firing affects catecholaminergic pathways, improvement in symptoms of ADHD may be observed.

Pharmacokinetics. The metabolism of fatty acids following ingestion begins in the small intestine by special digestive enzymes. These lipases break down fatty acids into individual chains, glycerol, and monoglycerides (glycerol with one remaining fatty acid still attached). These are then absorbed through the intestinal wall into the lymph stream. Fat molecules are then carried in the lymph system and slowly metabolized to provide a gradual release of energy (Enig, 2000).

Essential fatty acids go through many conversions. ALA is converted into EPA and DHA, and these are then gradually absorbed into cell membranes. They also undergo complex cross-metabolism, however. Although omega-6, also known as linoleic acid, undergoes a one-way transformation into various fatty chains, culminating in docosapentaenoic acid, ALA undergoes a circular transformation that involves many steps, including the formation of EPA and DHA and then retroconversion of EPA and DHA. It is difficult to determine how the body regulates the amounts of DHA and EPA that remain in the cells. It is likely that these are constantly transformed into each other to provide a balance of essential nutrients necessary for many metabolic processes, including membrane phosphorization.

Because ALA is converted into EPA and DHA, and EPA and DHA are retroconverted into each other, it is not necessary to purchase a specific combination of these fatty acids. Some manufacturers focus on the hypothesized benefits of DHA over EPA or vice versa, and omega-3 pills are available in various combinations of these components. Consumers need to keep in mind that the balance of these components in the pill is probably immaterial, because the complex conversion chains will probably result in the same balance of these nutrients in the body, regardless of the specific ratio included in the caplet.

The optimal ratio of omega-6 to omega-3 in the human body is estimated to be 2:1. It is not uncommon for individuals in westernized countries, however, to consume diets where the two are ingested at a ratio of about 20:1. For this reason, a majority of supplements primarily focus on delivering additional amounts of omega-3 into the body, and any amounts of omega-6 in the tablet may be superfluous, because the common diet already includes so many foods rich in linoleic acid. When purchasing a supplement, consumers should select one that maximizes the amount of omega-3 and minimizes the amount of omega-6 in the preparation.

Manufacturers of omega-3 supplements generally advise consumers to take the supplements with or without food. Researchers, however, have long recognized that omega-3 fatty acids ingested in food are better absorbed than those taken in supplements. Some studies have found that omega-3 taken without a meal is poorly absorbed. For this reason, nutritionists generally recommend taking an omega-3 supplement as part of a meal, so that it is absorbed together with the food that is being consumed (Neville, 2006).

To prevent oxidation of fatty acids before they are taken up into cell membranes, antioxidants must be present. Those whose diets are rich in antioxidant foods probably consume enough of these during a meal to prevent fatty acid oxidation. Those who consume meals low in antioxidants, however, may need to take an antioxidant supplement, for example, tocopherol, a form of vitamin E. For this reason, some formulations of omega-3 supplements include a small amount of tocopherol. Some supplements, however, also include vitamins A and/or D instead of (or in addition to) tocopherol. Because these vitamins do not get cleared from the body, clients should be careful with these supplements, because high intake of these vitamins may lead to toxicity.

Although fatty acids are metabolized and absorbed rapidly, the onset of effect is not evident for a long time. Some clinicians have reported that the onset of clinical effect is not evident for weeks, even months, and that treatment for up to 3 months is necessary to determine the eventual clinical response (Lake, 2007). This makes it difficult to dose the supplements, because clinical effects are not likely to be immediately evident.

Dosing. Omega-3 supplements are not usually dosed by body weight. In children, the recommended starting dose is 500 mg, and doses usually range up to 4,000 mg/day (Bezchlibnyk-Butler & Virani, 2004). Some clinicians have found doses below 1,000 mg/day to be ineffective (Lake, 2007). Because omega-3 is generally well tolerated, gradual titration is recommended. The maximum dose, however, is often determined by how many tablets the boy is willing to take and whether digestive effects (e.g., fish burps or a fishy taste in the mouth) prevent a further increase in dose. Because response will not be immediately evident, it is difficult to determine what dose will eventually be effective.

Teens and men are generally dosed at 1,000 to 4,000 mg/day (Bezchlibnyk-Butler & Jeffries, 2007). Some clinicians have found doses lower than 2,000 mg/day to be ineffective, and some adults require doses in excess of 9,000 mg (Lake, 2007). As with children, dosing should gradually be increased to a maximum level that can be tolerated with minimal gastrointestinal discomfort. Again, it is difficult to determine what dose will be effective because response to the supplement may not be immediately evident.

Cofactors are necessary for metabolism of some of the fatty acids, especially EFA. Carnitine is necessary for the elongating EFA and transporting it across inner cell membranes. It is possible that some of the inconsistent findings about the efficacy of fatty acids may be secondary to carnitine deficits. For this reason, supplementation with l-carnitine has been studied and has shown promising effects in hyperactive girls with fragile X syndrome (Torrioli et al., 1999). Because humans metabolize only a portion of the necessary supply of carnitine, supplementing fatty acid therapy with l-carnitine may be helpful. L-carnitine is supplied in capsules, tablets, solution, and chewable wafer. Children may take about 250 mg of l-carnitine with fatty acids, whereas adults may need to take about 500 mg. These doses are generally well tolerated, although a small incidence of seizures has been reported (Medical Economics, 2001). Individuals with risk factors for seizures should consider l-carnitine supplementation only under supervision of a physician.

Adverse Effects. Omega-3 oils are generally well tolerated. The most common adverse effects involve the gastrointestinal tract, including nausea and diarrhea. Because the majority of omega-3 supplements are sold as fish oils, some individuals experience an unpleasant fishy taste in their mouth, fishy smelling breath after a meal during which the omega-3 supplement was taken, and fishy burps that may last for several hours. For this reason, some manufacturers offer "burpless" formulas manufactured by increasing the thickness of the pill's outer coating. This coating allows the supplement to survive the stomach acids and dissolve when it reaches the small intestine. This coating has been shown to effectively reduce these problems. Omega-3 supplements are also available in nonfish-based formulas that are not associated with burps or an unpleasant taste.

Because omega-3 supplements are oil based, there is a caloric value associated with the caplet. The exact amount varies, but generally a 1,000 mg pill will contain about 20 calories. For individuals who consume a low amount, an extra 20 or 40 calories per day will probably have a minimal amount on weight. Those individuals on higher amounts (e.g., 8,000 mg or 9,000 mg per day), however, must remember that they are consuming an additional 160 or 180 calories. In addition, fatty acids are high-density lipoproteins (HDL) and contribute to the overall HDL levels within the body. Although this is generally beneficial, those individuals on high levels of omega-3 supplements who also consume diets rich in HDL may experience additional increases of HDL and total cholesterol, which may not always be beneficial. Individuals who take high doses of fatty acid supplements should periodically check their cholesterol profile.

Omega-3 fatty acids are associated with an antithrombotic effect. Men who take blood thinners (e.g., Coumadin) must be careful about taking subsequent fatty acid supplements and should consult a physician before initiating omega-3 therapy. In addition, many men regularly take nonprescription blood thinners (e.g., aspirin) or use over-the-counter nonsteroidal anti-inflammatory drugs (NSAIDs, such as Advil or Motrin) to manage headaches, backaches, or similar conditions. Although combining fatty acids with NSAIDs has not been shown to pose a risk, many NSAIDs have some blood-thinning properties, and combining NSAIDs with fatty acids has sometimes been linked to nose bleeds and easy bruising (Medical Economics, 2001). For this reason, those individuals who take NSAIDs daily should probably consult a physician before initiating omega-3 therapy.

Use of fatty acid supplements has sometimes been reported to alter glucose tolerance, especially in patients with type 2 diabetes. The mechanism of this is poorly understood, and some studies have not confirmed this finding. Because there is a risk, however, boys, teens, or men who are diabetic and take insulin should consult their physician before starting omega-3 treatment.

S-Adenosyl-L-Methionine

S-adenosyl-L-methionine (SAMe) is a natural substance present in the body. It was discovered in 1952 by an Italian scientist and became marketed in Europe shortly afterward, where it is considered (and regulated as) a drug. It has been available in the United States since only 1999, and it is classified as a nutritional supplement. It is known by a variety of names, including ademetionine and S-adenosylmethionine, and it is also sometimes referred to as SAM or SAM-e. It is primarily used to treat osteoarthritis, fibromyalgia, and liver disorders. Efficacy for those applications is well established, with many studies published in European journals, and it is considered to be one of the most researched nutritional supplements (Settle, 2007).

More recently, SAMe has also been shown to have potentially beneficial effects in treating symptoms of depression and ADHD. Its impact on depression is recognized in the United States and abroad and is presumed to be secondary to pharmacodynamic effects that resemble the action of some antidepressants. These effects include the increase in catecholaminergic activity throughout the brain, and consequently, benefits in treating symptoms of ADHD have also been reported.

Evidence of Efficacy. The evidence of SAMe's benefits in treating symptoms of ADHD comes primarily from the recognition that SAMe is an effective antidepressant, and studies, as well as meta-analyses, have shown that its efficacy is at least as significant as that of tricyclic antidepressants (Settle, 2007). SAMe regulates the activity of catecholaminergic pathways, including stimulation of the ones that are involved in symptoms of ADHD. Thus, the rationale seems sound, although the evidence at this time is limited.

There are a few studies that have investigated the benefit of SAMe in treating ADHD. A small open-label study with adults found that SAMe was beneficial in reducing symptoms of distractibility and self-control (Wood, Reimherr, & Wender, 1985), although the benefits were possibly secondary to improvements in mood symptoms. Another study reviewed benefits of SAMe (and other supplements) in treating ADHD and found short-term improvement (Nemzer, Arnold, Votolato, & McConnell, 1986), and a large open-trial follow-up with about 6,000 patients has been announced, but its results have not yet been disseminated (Walsh, 2003).

Unfortunately, the benefits of SAMe have been reported to last for only 2 or 3 months. It is apparent that tolerance develops, perhaps because of downregulation effects. For this reason, use of SAMe should probably be reserved for applications with those individuals who present with comorbid symptoms of depression that may be exacerbating symptoms of ADHD. In addition, SAMe has primarily been used with adults. Although no specific counterindications exist for use with children or adolescents, clinicians should be very cautious when using SAMe with boys or teens.

Pharmacodynamics. SAMe is a second messenger. This term refers to substances that act within cells to change some aspects of cell metabolism. In this case, SAMe is a methyl donor that contributes to dozens of reactions throughout the brain, including the synthesis of monoamine transmitters—dopamine, norepinephrine, and serotonin, among others (Settle, 2007). This action is responsible, at least in part, for its antidepressant effect and probably underlies the reduction of symptoms of ADHD. Because functional deficits in ADHD result from the underactivation of key pathways for dopamine and norepinephrine, producing additional amounts of these catecholamines has potential benefits in alleviating the symptoms (as has been shown with many of the medications used to treat ADHD). Indeed, a review of European research has revealed that SAMe may be involved in increasing activity in dopaminergic and serotonergic pathways (Settle, 2007).

SAMe is also involved in methylation and/or phosphorization processes that affect membrane fluidity. As such, its effects may be similar to those of omega-3 fatty acids, where regulation of the membrane fluidity may be involved in stabilization of neurotransmitter release and neuronal firing. SAMe has been found to increase the number of receptors on the cell, increase binding to receptors, and enhance membrane fluidity (Settle, 2007). These effects likely contribute to increases in dopamine and serotonin and further enhance its clinical effect.

Pharmacokinetics. SAMe is available in tablets. Some of these tablets have an enteric coating, and some do not. Those that are coated are a better choice because SAMe is absorbed from the small intestine, and therefore as much compound as possible should survive the stomach acids and get through into the small intestine. In addition, SAMe is unstable at temperatures above freezing (0 degrees Celsius or 32 degrees Fahrenheit). A wide variety of SAMe preparations are available on the market. Forms that have been researched for efficacy are stable at higher temperatures, but other forms are marketed for which efficacy may be questionable. Consumers should seek the form that includes SAMe paratoluene sulfonates (SAMe tosyls) because these salts have been found to be stable at room temperature. In addition, SAMe must be kept very dry because moisture can cause hydrolysis. It is recommended that the best form to purchase is the stable formulation of SAMe tosyls that is also enteric coated (Medical Economics, 2001).

SAMe should be taken on an empty stomach—about 1 hour before or 2 hours after a meal. The peak is usually attained in 3 to 5 hours (Medical Economics, 2001), but onset of clinical effect is not generally evident for at least 1 to 2 weeks (Walsh, 2003).

SAMe is metabolized by the liver but seems to have minimal effects on liver enzymes, and drug–drug interactions have not been reported with SAMe. Most of the substance is incorporated into various cells, and only a small portion is eliminated in urine (15%) and feces (23%). Thus, liver and kidney functions seem to have limited effect on the metabolism and excretion of SAMe (Medical Economics, 2001).

When SAMe is metabolized, cofactors are involved. Metabolism of SAMe to homocysteine requires the presence of vitamin B_6. This pathway probably has minor (if any) effects on symptoms of ADHD, and therefore levels of vitamin B_6 are less important for this specific application. SAMe is also metabolized into methionine, and this pathway has greater relevance to ADHD. To accomplish this metabolism, folic acid, vitamin B_{12}, and betaine are needed (Medical Economics, 2001). Consequently, when minimal effects of SAMe supplementation are seen, folic acid, vitamin B_{12}, or betaine can be taken. Because these compounds are already present in a normal diet, supplementation should be minimal. A multivitamin containing these cofactors may be beneficial, but higher, focused doses of any of these nutrients are not recommended because of a variety of medical risks.

Dosing. The clinical dose of SAMe varies widely. Children should start at about 200 mg once per day (preferably in the morning) and gradually titrate at intervals of 1 to 2 weeks between dose increases. Adults are generally dosed up to 2,400 mg/day (Bezchlibnyk-Butler & Jeffries, 2007), although doses higher than 1,600 mg/day have not been studied for adverse effects (Medical Economics, 2001). Clearly, children should receive lower doses, although no specific guidelines exist for dosing children and adolescents. According to the National Center for Health Statistics (2002), the weight of an average adult male in the United States is about 190 pounds (about 86 kg). Thus, the dose-to-weight ratio for adults is about 18 to 28 mg/kg per day. The effective ratio for children and adolescents may be similar. Clinicians are advised to start low and go slow—begin with a minimal dose and gradually titrate, making sure that the correct mg/kg ratios are not exceeded.

Adverse Effects. SAMe is generally well tolerated. Suppression of appetite and weight change are not reported. Mild gastrointestinal upsets (nausea, diarrhea, and flatulence), however, may be evident at the start of treatment (Medical Economics, 2001). These effects usually resolve after a week or two. Sometimes those individuals at higher doses experience more persistent nausea (Bezchlibnyk-Butler & Jeffries, 2007).

SAMe may interfere with sleep, and some insomnia has been reported (Medical Economics, 2001). For this reason, it is generally recommended that SAMe be taken in the morning. Especially when SAMe is used to treat symptoms of ADHD, the activating effect may be beneficial and may contribute to a reduction in distractibility.

Because SAMe is not a stimulant, it poses little risk of motor tics. Other motor effects have rarely been reported, however, including some hyperactive muscle movement (Medical Economics, 2001). When these effects are encountered, the dose should be lowered for a week or two, following which the patient may gradually be rechallenged with a higher dose, if needed.

Because SAMe does not alter liver enzymes and does not seem to rely on any one CP450 enzyme for metabolism, drug–drug interactions are less likely. SAMe may have some effects on lowering lipids and improving liver function, however. It is also used to treat osteoarthritis and fibromyalgia. Thus, patients who already take medications to lower cholesterol or treat osteoarthritis or fibromyalgia should consult their physician before initiating SAMe therapy.

Although the specific "black box" warning that applies to all antidepressants is not issued for SAMe, it, because of its antidepressant action, may be associated with a small increase in suicidal tendencies in those patients who present with symptoms of depression. As with any antidepressant, clinicians should carefully monitor patient response and intervene if an increase in suicidal thoughts or plans becomes evident. In addition, like all antidepressants, SAMe is also associated with a small risk of inducing hypomanic or manic symptoms (Bezchlibnyk-Butler & Jeffries, 2007), and some patients who have tendencies toward symptoms of bipolar disorder may exhibit switching from depressive to manic symptoms. Once again, careful monitoring of dose and response and adverse effects is necessary.

SUPPLEMENTS WITH POSSIBLE EFFICACY

In addition to the supplements previously discussed, there are some data available that suggest that other compounds may also have some efficacy in treating symptoms of ADHD. Because those data that support the use of the following supplements are extremely limited, however, clinicians should proceed with caution and consider the use of the compounds discussed in this section as experimental.

Inositol

Inositol is an isomer of glucose and is present in high concentrations in the brain. It is part of intracellular processes mediated by second messenger systems and may be involved in regulating the activity of monoamines (especially serotonin, with possible action on dopamine and norepinephrine) as well as other neurotransmitters. It has primarily been shown to treat symptoms of depression (Settle, 2007) and anxiety (Bezchlibnyk-Butler & Jeffries, 2007), including anxiety-spectrum disorders such as obsessive compulsive disorder and trichotillomania. Its use in treating symptoms of ADHD is recent, and scant evidence exists thus far. Although some studies have reported that use of inositol may aggravate symptoms of ADHD (Bezchlibnyk-Butler & Jeffries, 2007), others have found that inositol supplementation, with or without concomitant use with omega-3 fatty acids, improved symptoms of ADHD in children (Alvarado et al., 2004). At this time, inositol is probably best reserved for a cautious trial with individuals who exhibit symptoms of ADHD that are significantly exacerbated by anxiety or depression.

Inositol is available in several forms, and only some of these are appropriate for psychiatric use. These forms include inositol and myo-inositol. Other forms, such as inositol hexaphosphate, inositol nicotinate, and D-chiro-inositol, have not been shown to have mental health effects and are used to treat cancer, vascular diseases, and insulin resistance.

Inositol is dosed at much higher levels than other supplements. Therapeutic doses usually range from 12 to 18 grams per day, taken in divided doses (usually two to three times per day). Inositol is also available as a powder that dissolves easily in water or juice. This may be a good option for those who have difficulties swallowing pills. Dosing usually starts at 2 grams twice per day, increasing to up to 6 grams three times per day. Inositol can be taken with or without food. Onset of clinical effect is usually observed in 2 to 4 weeks.

Inositol is generally well tolerated at doses of up to 20 grams per day (Settle, 2007). In children, the studied dose was 50 mg/kg per day (Alvarado et al., 2004). Common adverse effects are mild and include gastrointestinal upset, such as nausea, diarrhea, and flatulence. Few studies have reviewed possible interactions between inositol and other drugs, but the supplement is considered safe to use with other medications (Settle, 2007). Because of inositol's antidepressant effects, rare episodes of switching into mania have been reported. Patients with symptoms of agitation or depression who take inositol should be carefully monitored for signs of manic or hypomanic symptoms.

Choline and Dimethylaminoethanol

Choline (trimethylaminoethanol) is involved in the synthesis of the neurotransmitter acetylcholine. Dimethylanimoethanol is the immediate precursor of trimethylaminoethanol. Choline is involved in maintaining cell membrane integrity and regulating neuronal firing. Acetylcholine is an endogenous neurotransmitter that has not been directly implicated in symptoms of ADHD. Acetylcholine is involved in motor control, however, and disturbance in dopamine-acetylcholine balance is a well-known mechanism that underlies significant motor side effects of many medications (e.g., those seen with first-generation, low-potency antipsychotics, such as Thorazine and Mellaril). Thus, changes in acetylcholine activity may have some beneficial effects in improving symptoms of ADHD.

Dimethylaminoethanol, also known as dimethylethanolamine or DMAE, was once marketed in the United States as Deaner but was withdrawn in 1980 because the FDA required proof for its claims of efficacy in treating symptoms of minimal brain dysfunction (Arnold, 2002). Nevertheless, several placebo-controlled trials performed in the 1960s and 1970s showed that it was effective in improving symptoms of ADHD in children at doses of 500 mg/day or higher. Today, DMAE is not widely available, but choline supplements can be purchased from many drugstores and nutritional supplement vendors. There appears to be no difference in purchasing DMAE or choline, because one is converted to the other.

Choline is sometimes used with other supplements. For example, Alvarado et al. (2004) studied the joint benefits of inositol and choline and found a combination of the two to be effective in treating symptoms of ADHD. Because choline is generally well tolerated, supplementing inositol with choline may be an option to consider for patients who are candidates for treatment with inositol.

Doses of 3 mg/day of choline have been studied with adults and produced few side effects (Medical Economics, 2001). Usual effective doses are 425 to 550 mg/day for adults and 250 to 350 mg/day for children. Choline is generally regarded as safe, and pregnant mothers are sometimes encouraged to take choline to aid the brain development of the fetus. The most common side effects are nausea, diarrhea, and loose stools. High doses of choline have sometimes resulted in hypotension and increases in depressive symptoms. Those individuals who use choline jointly with inositol should stay within the lower levels of the therapeutic range for both compounds.

Pycnogenol

Pycnogenol is a generic name for a mixture of procyanidins extracted from the bark of the pine tree *Pinus maritima*, common to the Gascogne region of France. Pycnogenol has many active compounds, primarily consisting of dimmers of catechin, and oligomers of catechin and epicatechin. Similar compounds are also found in cocoa, chocolate, and some fruit. Their pharmacodynamic action primarily consists of antioxidant properties and possible anti-inflammatory effects. Pycnogenol may also influence the release of catecholamines (including dopamine and norepinephrine) and nitric oxide synthesis.

Some researchers have reported that odixative stress may underlie symptoms of Parkinson's disease (Olanow, 1996), and some have hypothesized that similar factors may underlie symptoms of ADHD. For many decades, pycnogenol has been used in Europe to treat symptoms of hyperactivity. Heiman (1999) reviewed many anecdotal reports and reported a case study where supplementation with pycnogenol for 4 weeks resulted in a significant decrease in hyperactivity and impulsivity in a patient with ADHD. A subsequent trial with 61 children and adolescents with ADHD also found beneficial effects after taking 1 mg/kg of pycnogenol for 1 month (Trebaticka, Kopasova, Hradecna, & Cinovsky, 2006). Notably, the treatment effects were more significant in boys than in girls. Another study also found that the treatment of ADHD with dextroamphetamine with the addition of pycnogenol was superior to the treatment of ADHD with the use of dextroamphetamine alone (Medical Economics, 2001).

Pycnogenol is generally supplied in tablets and capsules, and creams and lotions containing it are also available but have not been studied for their effectiveness. Pycnogenol is generally dosed at the ratio of 1 mg/kg, and adult doses range from 25 to 200 mg/day. Pycnogenol is generally well tolerated, and the available literature reports no adverse effects. Because it may produce vasorelaxation and inhibition of platelet activity, however, those who take blood thinners (e.g., aspirin) should exercise caution.

Rhodiola

Rhodiola rosea is a perennial plant that grows in the United States, Canada, Europe, and parts of Asia. Its root, also known as golden root, is commonly used in Asia and Europe to treat fatigue and cognitive blunting. Its pharmacology is complex and includes a large number of active compounds, such as flavonoids, monoterpenes, phenylpropanoids, triterpenes, phenolic acids, and phenylethanol derivatives. It has multiple effects, including antioxidant, anticarcinogenic, cardioprotective, and neuroendocrine properties. Its psychopharmacological effect may include agonist properties for serotonin and dopamine (perhaps secondary to monoamine oxidase inhibition), as well as influence on opioid peptides (such as beta-endorphins). Although the benefit of rhodiola in treating symptoms of ADHD has not been studied, it has been shown to have some antidepressant and psychostimulant effects (Darbinyan et al., 2007; Shevtsov et al., 2003). In addition, the use of rhodiola concomitantly with a stimulant has shown to have additive effects (Medical Economics, 2007).

Rhodiola is usually available in capsules or tablets that usually contain 100 mg of a mixture of 3% rosavins and 1% salidroside. Although other active compounds are found in the preparation, their role is unknown, and therefore rosavins and salidrose are generally sought. Rhodiola is given in 100 mg to 200 mg per dose, usually taken two to three times per day. Dosing for children has not been studied, but no contraindications exist, and therefore a dose of 100 mg one to twice per day can cautiously be tried and gradually titrated upward if well tolerated.

Rhodiola is presumed safe, and no adverse effects have been reported in available literature. Similarly, it is not presumed to interact with prescription medications (Medical Economics, 2007). Because of its antidepressant effects, however, it may pose a risk to individuals of their switching into manic or mixed-manic episodes in a manner that is similar to that of all compounds with antidepressant effects.

SUPPLEMENTS NOT LIKELY TO BE EFFECTIVE

It is not possible to review all the compounds that, at one time or another, have been tried to treat symptoms of ADHD and have not shown to be effective or lack sufficient rationale about how they may affect brain action to improve distractibility and/or hyperactivity/impulsivity. Some of these compounds continue to be marketed, however, and naturopathic zealots continue to espouse the benefits of some of these supplements despite the lack of evidence of efficacy. Clinicians who seek to practice in the area of naturopathic psychopharmacology should be aware of compounds that continue to be propagated in folklore or late-night infomercials, despite evidence to the contrary.

Saint-John's-Wort

Saint-John's-wort is an herb that exists in some 370 species found throughout the world, but it is originally endogenous to Europe. Saint-John's-wort contains a plethora of active ingredients, including dozens of flavonoids and acylphloroglucinols (especially hyperforin).

Saint-John's-wort is known to be an effective antidepressant, and hyperforin is thought to be responsible for most of its psychoactive activity. Saint-John's-wort increases the amount of serotonergic activity in the brain, and for this reason it also has anxiolytic properties. In addition, it may suppress monoamine oxydase, the enzyme responsible for the breakdown of all monoamines. Thus, in addition to its serotonergic effects, it may increase the activity of norepinephrine and dopamine (Schroeder, Tank, & Goldstein, 2004), and some clinicians have presumed that it may have beneficial effects in treating symptoms of ADHD.

Several studies, however, have found that Saint-John's-wort failed to improve symptoms of ADHD. Studies examining its effects on symptoms of ADHD in adults have not shown a significant effect (Barkley, 2006), and placebo-controlled research on children and adolescents with ADHD rendered similar results (Weber, Vander Stoep, McCarty, & Weiss, 2008). Although using this herb with adults who have comorbid symptoms of depression and ADHD may be beneficial, Saint-John's-wort is not likely to have much positive effect on symptoms of ADHD in individuals who do not exhibit depression, agitation, or anxiety.

Vitamin Therapy

Vitamin supplementation is generally administered in one of three strategies—daily multivitamin use that supplements daily intake to meet recommended daily allowances (RDAs), megavitamin cocktails that significantly exceed RDAs, or focused megadoses of a single vitamin. None of these have been shown to be an effective treatment for symptoms of ADHD.

The first of these strategies may be beneficial to overall health, but it has not been shown to improve symptoms of ADHD. Although supplementation of one-a-day multivitamin has been shown to improve cognitive functioning (Benton & Cook, 1991), presumed benefits exist only for those who exhibit vitamin deficiencies because of dietary deficits, and no additional benefits for individuals who consume normal, healthy diets have been shown in research (Benton & Buts, 1990). Thus, although the use of a multivitamin may help those who have poor diets, it is not a treatment to address symptoms of ADHD in boys, teens, or men with ADHD.

Megadose supplementation of multiple vitamins similarly has been found to be ineffective in double-blind, placebo-controlled studies that lasted up to 6 months (Arnold, 2002). A variety of combinations have been researched, but none seem to have any beneficial effects on symptoms of ADHD or learning disorders. In addition, some vitamins pose a significant risk when taken in excess. For this reason, megadoses of multivitamins not only are ineffective but may also be dangerous, especially when RDA levels of vitamins such as A or B_6 are significantly exceeded. Clinicians are encouraged to advise their patients and clients against trials of such unproven and potentially dangerous methods.

Focused megadoses of specific vitamins have not been adequately studied, but no reasonable rationale has thus far emerged as to the potential efficacy of those compounds to improve symptoms of ADHD. Again, it is important to observe daily RDA limits and not exceed those for many vitamins, because adverse effects may result in a variety of problems, from neuropathic effects to liver damage. Clinicians should advise their patients and clients against these approaches.

Focus Factor

A wide variety of multivitamin compounds exists on the market that purports to treat many disorders, including ADHD. One of the best known is Focus Factor, a cocktail of some 40 compounds that primarily includes RDA doses of multivitamins and small doses of dimethylaminoethanol (DMEA), trimethylaminoethanol (choline), and DHA, as well as other herbs with unproven pharmacology or efficacy. Various groups of ingredients have to be examined separately for the potential benefits of this preparation to be understood.

Essentially, Focus Factor is a multivitamin. As such, it is not likely to do any harm, but it is also unlikely to have any significant benefits in improving symptoms of ADHD unless the patient is on a diet that significantly restricts the intake of common nutrients. If that is the case, a drugstore multivitamin is likely to provide the same benefit at a fraction of the cost.

The second group of ingredients includes DMEA, choline, and DHA. The potential benefits of those ingredients are discussed previously, separately for each of them. To be potentially effective, each of those ingredients needs to be given in higher doses than are included in Focus Factor, and each of those ingredients can be purchased in a local pharmacy of nutritional supplement store for a smaller price.

The final group of ingredients includes rarely used herbs, such as huperzine and vinpocetine, which are scarcely studied and have no reasonable rationale about potential benefits in treating symptoms of ADHD. Overall, although there is no evidence that Focus Factor may be harmful, there is also no evidence that most individuals derive any benefit from this compound.

Iron

Iron is a chemical element involved in the anabolism of catecholamines. Iron is present throughout the body and is converted into amino acids. The vast majority of necessary iron intake is derived from the normal diet, and many iron-rich foods are commonly consumed in meats, cereals, fruits, and vegetables. Some members of at-risk populations may require iron supplementation, for example, those individuals who are malnourished, infants who are not breast-fed, or individuals who have lost a lot of blood. Iron supplementation in patients who are not iron deficient, however, is dangerous. Careful RDA limits must be observed, and excess iron intake has been associated with serious toxic effects, including death. Children are especially at risk for these problems, and iron supplementation should be undertaken only under the supervision (and recommendation) of a physician (Medical Economics, 2001).

Some studies have examined the effects of iron supplementation on symptoms of ADHD. For example, Sever, Ashkenazi, Tyano, and Weizman (1997) found some decrease in symptoms in boys with ADHD, and Burattini et al. (1990) found a decrease in symptoms of hyperactivity, but both studies used iron supplements with children who were initially found to exhibit iron deficiency, and iron supplementation generally has no positive effects on children with ADHD who do not exhibit iron deficiency. Because a vast majority of boys, teens, and men with ADHD probably do not exhibit iron deficiency, the effect of iron supplementation in this population is unknown. Given the risks of iron supplementation, clinicians should stay away from this practice unless it can be confirmed that the patient exhibits iron deficiency. Any iron supplementation should be given under close supervision of a physician.

Deleading

For decades, it has been known that children who experience lead poisoning exhibit symptoms of hyperactivity, poor self-control, and focusing difficulties. Consequently, a belief developed that deleading may be beneficial for those patients who exhibit these symptoms even if they are not known to suffer from lead poisoning. Unfortunately, results of research studies have clearly pointed out that this approach is not effective. True, studies have shown that chelation decreases hyperactivity (David, Hoffman, Sverd, Clark, & Voeller, 1976), but participants in the study were children who were shown to have abnormal lead levels in their blood. Although limits for acceptable lead levels in the blood have been steadily dropping, most children do not exhibit lead levels that are near the limit, even when conservative criteria are used. Deleading seems to provide no benefit for children who do not exhibit abnormal plasma levels of lead.

Chelation is not only useless but also very dangerous. Deleading is associated with dangers of kidney failure, bone marrow depression, shock, hypotension, convulsions, cardiac arrhythmias, and respiratory arrest. A number of deaths have been linked to chelation therapy. Although much of the unnecessary chelation is done with autistic children, some chelation is also done with children with symptoms of ADHD. Parents should be warned that chelation is potentially deadly and totally useless, unless it can be proved that the patient exhibits abnormally high levels of lead, in which case it must be done under very intensive medical supervision.

SUMMARY

Although many medications have been shown to be effective in treating symptoms of ADHD, a significant portion of the population is skeptical about prescription drugs, especially when used to treat psychological disorders. Many people prefer to use naturopathic supplements and presume that these are safer. Research literature has clearly revealed that supplements are neither safer nor more effective, and the lack of regulation has significantly limited the potential utility of these supplements, because buyers have no way of knowing if what is listed on the label is really included in the pill. In addition, most supplements are unrefined and contain a large number of active ingredients, only some of which have been studied, and the variety of active ingredients present in the same tablet can sometimes have contradictory and opposing actions.

That said, there are some supplements that can be potentially beneficial in treating symptoms of ADHD. Results of research studies have revealed that caffeine is the only supplement that has been shown in research studies to consistently be effective. Caffeine is a psychostimulant that primarily affects adenosine neurotransmission, but it may also affect the release of catecholamines. It has a relatively short duration of action, and multiple daily doses are likely to be needed. When used to address symptoms of ADHD, it should be ingested in tablets, rather than consumed in coffee, soft drinks, or other food products. Although the side effects generally are minimal, some clients experience an increase in anxiety when taking caffeine.

Compounds that are likely to be beneficial include omega-3 and SAMe. Both compounds may affect membrane fluidity and therefore may regulate neuronal firing. Studies are emerging that suggest beneficial effects on symptoms of ADHD, but the results of research are inconsistent. Both supplements may produce gastrointestinal discomfort and may exert anticoagulant properties. A long trial may be needed before clinical effects are evident, and dosing varies widely.

Inositol, choline, pycnogenol, and rhodiola may be effective, and a small amount of research is available that has suggested possible efficacy. Response varies widely, and dosing guidelines are not yet established. Much trial and error is likely. These compounds may be considered as third-line agents after others have failed to be effective, or they may be used to augment treatment with other supplements (e.g., omega-3) when partial improvement is evident. Clinicians and patients are advised to proceed cautiously, because little is known about the effects of these compounds.

Although they are sometimes advertised and propagated, Saint-John's-wort, vitamin therapies (including Focus Factor), iron supplementation, and deleading treatment have been shown in research to be ineffective in improving symptoms of ADHD. In addition, some of these treatments pose significant risks of toxicity, including death. Patients should be advised to stay away from these supplements.

REFERENCES

Abikoff, H. (2002). Matching patients to treatments. In P. S. Jensen & J. R. Cooper (Eds.), *Attention deficit hyperactivity disorder: State of the science, best practices* (pp. 15-1–15-14). Kingston, NJ: Civic Research Institute.

Achenbach, T. M. (2001). *Child behavior checklist*. Burlington, VT: Research Center for Children, Youth, and Families.

Aleman, S. R. (1991, December 5). *Special education for children with attention deficit disorder: Current issues* (Report No. 91-862). Washington, DC: Congressional Research Service.

Allsopp, L. A., Minskoff, E. H., & Bolt, L. (2005). Individualized course-specific strategy instruction for college students with learning diasibilites and ADHD: Lessons learned from a model demonstration program. *Learning Disabilities Research and Practice, 20,* 103–118.

Alvarado, A., Diaz, L., Sucre, Z., Perez, R., Veracoechea, G., Hernandez, M., & Alvarado, M. (2004). H magnetic resonance spectroscopy (MRS) assessment of the effects of eicosapentaenoic-docosahexaenoic acids and choline-inositol supplementation on children with attention deficit hyperactivity disorder. *Academia Biomédica Digital, 20.* Retrieved from www.vitae.com

Ambroggio, J. D., & Jensen, P. S. (2002). Behavioral and medication treatments for ADHD: Comparisons and combinations. In P. S. Jensen & J. R. Cooper (Eds.), *Attention deficit hyperactivity disorder: State of the science, best practices* (pp. 14-1–14-14). Kingston, NJ: Civic Research Institute.

American Psychiatric Association. (1980). *Diagnostic and statistical manual of mental disorders* (3rd ed.). Washington, DC: Author.

American Psychiatric Association. (1987). *Diagnostic and statistical manual of mental disorders* (3rd ed., Rev.). Washington, DC: Author.

American Psychiatric Association. (1994). *Diagnostic and statistical manual of mental disorders* (4th ed.). Washington, DC: Author.

American Psychiatric Association. (2000). *Diagnostic and statistical manual of mental disorders* (4th ed., Text rev.). Washington, DC: Author.

Anastopoulos, A. D., Rhoads, L. H., & Farley, S. E. (2006). Counseling and training parents. In R. A. Barkley (Ed.), *Attention-deficit hyperactivity disorder: A handbook for diagnosis and treatment* (3rd ed., pp. 453–479). New York: Guilford.

Anastopoulos, A. D., Spisto, M. A., & Maher, M. C. (1994). The WISC-III Freedom From Distractibility Factor: Its utility in identifying children with attention deficit hyperactivity disorder. *Psychological Assessment, 6,* 368–371.

Angold, A., Messer, S. C., Stangl, D., Farmer, E. M., Costello, E. J., & Burns, B. J. (1998). Perceived parental burden and service use for child and adolescent psychiatric disorders. *American Journal of Public Health, 88*, 75–80.

Arnold, L. E. (2002). Treatment alternatives for attention deficit hyperactivity disorder. In P. S. Jensen & J. R. Cooper (Eds.), *Attention deficit hyperactivity disorder: State of the science, best practices* (pp. 13-1–13-29). Kingston, NJ: Civic Research Institute.

Asarnow, J. (1988). Peer status and social competence in child psychiatric inpatients: A comparison of children with depressive, externalizing, and depressive and externalizing disorders. *Journal of Abnormal Child Psychology, 16*, 151–162.

Ballas, C. A., Evans, A. D., & Dinges, D. F. (2004). Psychostimulants in psychiatry: Amphetamine, methylphenidate, and modafinil. In A. F. Schatzberg & C. B. Nemeroff (Eds.), *The American Psychiatric Publishing textbook of psychiatry* (pp. 671–684). Washington, DC: American Psychiatric Publishing.

Bandura, A. (1976). Social learning theory. In J. T. Spence, R. C. Carson, & J. W. Thibaud (Eds.), *Behavioral approach to therapy*. Morristown, NJ: General Learning Press.

Bandura, A. (2000). Exercise of human agency through collective efficacy. *Current Directions in Psychological Science, 9*, 75–78.

Barkley, R. A. (1987). *Defiant children: A clinician's manual for assessment and parent training*. New York: Guilford.

Barkley, R. A. (1990). *Attention-deficit hyperactivity disorder: A handbook for diagnosis and treatment*. New York: Guilford.

Barkley, R. A. (1997a). *ADHD and the nature of self control*. New York: Guilford.

Barkley, R. A. (1997b). *Defiant children: A clinician's manual for assessment and parent training* (2nd ed.). New York: Guilford.

Barkley, R. A. (1998). *Attention-deficit hyperactivity disorder: A handbook for diagnosis and treatment* (2nd ed.). New York: Guilford.

Barkley, R. A. (2002). ADHD: Long-term course, adult outcome, and comorbid disorders. In P. S. Jensen & J. R. Cooper (Eds.), *Attention deficit hyperactivity disorder: State of the science, best practices* (pp. 4-1–4-12). Kingston, NJ: Civic Research Institute.

Barkley, R. A. (2006). *Attention-deficit hyperactivity disorder: A handbook for diagnosis and treatment* (3rd ed.). New York: Guilford.

Barkley, R. A., Guevremont, D. C., Anastopoulos, A. D., & Fletcher, K. E. (1992). A comparison of three family therapy programs for treating family conflicts in adolescents with attention-deficit hyperactivity disorder. *Journal of Consulting and Clinical Psychology, 60*, 450–462.

Baumgaertel, A., Wolraich, M. L., & Dietrich, M. (1995). Comparison of diagnostic criteria for attention deficit hyperactivity disorder in a German elementary school sample. *Journal of the American Academy of Child and Adolescent Psychiatry, 34*, 629–638.

Beck, J. S. (1995). *Cognitive therapy: Basics and beyond*. New York: Guilford.

Bellack, A. S., & Hersen, M. (Eds.). (1979). *Research and practice in social skills training*. New York: Plenum.

Benton, D., & Buts, J. P. (1990). Vitamin/mineral supplementation and intelligence. *Lancet, 335*, 1158–1160.

Benton, D., & Cook, R. (1991). Vitamin and mineral supplements improve the intelligence scores and concentration of six-year-old children. *Personality and Individual Differences, 12,* 1151–1158.

Berg, B. (1990). *The Self-Control Game.* Dayton, OH: Cognitive Counseling Associates.

Berg, B. (2000). *The Anger Control Game.* Los Angeles: Western Psychological Services.

Berliner, D. C. (1987). Simple views of effective teaching and a simple theory of classroom instruction. In D. C. Berliner & B. V. Rosenshine (Eds.), *Talks to teachers* (pp. 93–110). New York: Random House.

Bezchlibnyk-Butler, K. Z., & Jeffries, J. J. (2007). *Clinical handbook of psychotropic drugs* (17th ed.). Seattle, WA: Hogrefe & Huber.

Bezchlibnyk-Butler, K. Z., & Virani, A. S. (2004). *Clinical handbook of psychotropic drugs for children and adolescents.* Seattle, WA: Hogrefe & Huber.

Bhatia, M. S., Nigam, V. R., Bohra, N., & Malik, S. C. (1991). Attention deficit disorder with hyperactivity among pediatric outpatients. *Journal of Child Psychology and Psychiatry, 32,* 297–306.

Biederman, J. (2004). Impact of comorbidity in adults with attention-deficit hyperactivity disorder. *Journal of Clinical Psychiatry, 65*(Suppl. 3), 3–7.

Biederman, J., Mick, E., Faraone, S. V., Braaten, E., Doyle, A., & Spencer, T. (2002). Influence of gender on attention deficit hyperactivity disorder in children referred to a psychiatric clinic. *American Journal of Psychiatry, 159,* 36–42.

Biederman, J., Newcorn, J., & Sprich, S. (1991). Comorbidity of attention deficit hyperactivity disorder with conduct, depressive, anxiety, and other disorders. *American Journal of Psychiatry, 148,* 564–577.

Biederman, J., & Spencer, T. J. (2002). Nonstimulant treatments for ADHD. In P. S. Jensen & J. R. Cooper (Eds.), *Attention deficit hyperactivity disorder: State of the science, best practices* (pp. 11-1–11-16). Kingston, NJ: Civic Research Institute.

Biederman, J., Spencer, T. J., Newcorn, J. H., Haitao, G., Milton, D. R., Feldman, P. D., & Witte, M. M. (2007). Effect of comorbid symptoms of oppositional defiant disorder on responses to atomoxetine in children with ADHD: A meta-analysis of controlled clinical trial data. *Psychopharmacologia, 190,* 31–41.

Biederman, J., Wilens, T., Mick, E., Faraone, S. V., Weber, W., & Curtis, S. (1997). Is ADHD a risk factor for psychoactive substance use disorders? Findings from a four-year prospective follow-up study. *Journal of the American Academy of Child and Adolescent Psychiatry, 36,* 21–29.

Biederman, J., Wilens, R., Mick, E., Milberger, S., Spencer, T. J., & Faraone, S. V. (1995). Psychoactive substance use disorders in adults with attention deficit hyperactivity disorder (ADHD): Effects of ADHD and psychiatric comorbidity. *American Journal of Psychiatry, 152,* 1652–1658.

Biederman, J., Mick, E., & Faraone, S. V. (2000). Age-dependent decline of symptoms of attention deficit hyperactivity disorder: Impact of remission definition and symptom type. *American Journal of Psychiatry, 157,* 816-818.

Bird, H. R. (2002). The diagnostic classification, epidemiology, and cross-cultural validity of ADHD. In P. S. Jensen & J. R. Cooper (Eds.), *Attention deficit hyperactivity disorder: State of the science, best practices* (pp. 2-1–2-16). Kingston, NJ: Civic Research Institute.

Bolton, S., & Null, G. (1981). Caffeine: Psychological effects, use and abuse. *Orthomolecular Psychiatry, 10,* 202–211.

Bradley, W. (1937). The behavior of children receiving Benzedrine. *American Journal of Psychiatry, 94,* 577–585.

Brenesova, V., Oswald, L., & Loudon, J. (1975). Two types of insomnia: Too much waking or not enough sleep. *British Journal of Psychiatry, 126,* 439–445.

Breslau, N., Brown, G. G., DelDotto, J. E., Kumar, S., Exhuthachan, S., & Andreski, P. (1996). Psychiatric sequelae of low birth weight at 6 years of age. *Journal of Abnormal Child Psychology, 24,* 385–400.

Brickenkamp, R., & Zillmer, E. (1998). *d2 Test of Attention.* Seattle: Hogrefe & Huber.

Brown, T. E. (1996). *Brown Attention-Deficit Disorder Scales for Adolescents and Adults: Manual.* San Antonio, TX: Pearson Assessment.

Brown, T. E. (2001). *Brown Attention-Deficit Disorder Scales for Children and Adolescents: Manual.* San Antonio, TX: Pearson Assessment.

Brown, T. E. (2005). *Attention deficit disorder: The unfocused mind in children and adults.* Hew Haven, CT: Yale University Press.

Brown, T. E., Freeman, W. S., Perrin, J. M., Stein, M. T., Amler, R. W., Feldman, H. M., Pierce, K., & Wolraich, M. L. (2001). Prevalence and assessment of attention-deficit/hyperactivity disorder in primary care settings. *Pediatrics, 107*(Technical Suppl. 3), 1–11.

Buckley, A., & Buckley, C. (2006). *A guide to coaching and mental health.* New York: Routledge.

Burattini, M. G., Amendola, F., Aufierio, T., Spano, M., DiBitonto, G., Del Vecchio, G. C., & De Mattia, D. (1990). Evaluation of the effectiveness of gastro-protected proteoferrin in the therapy of sideropenic anemia in childhood. *Minerva Pediatrica, 42,* 343–347.

Burns, G. L., & Walsh, J. A. (2002). The influence of ADHD-hyperactivity/impulsivity symptoms on the development of oppositional defiant disorder symptoms in a 2-year longitudinal study. *Journal of Abnormal Child Psychology, 30,* 245–256.

Burt, S. A., Krueger, R. F., McGue, M., & Iacono, W. G. (2001). Sources of covariation among attention-deficit/hyperactivity disorder, oppositional defiant disorder, and conduct disorder: The importance of shared environment. *Journal of Abnormal Psychology, 110,* 516–525.

Butcher, J. N., Williams, C. L., Graham, J. R., Archer, R. P., Tellegen, A., Ben-Porath, Y. S., & Kaemmer, B. (1992). *Minnesota Multiphasic Personality Inventory–Adolescent.* San Antonio, TX: Pearson Assessment.

Carlson, C. L., & Mann, M. (2000). Attention-deficit/hyperactivity disorder, predominantly inattentive subtype. *Child and Adolescent Psychiatric Clinics of North America, 9,* 499–510.

Castellanos, F. X., Giedd, J. N., Elia, J., Mersh, W. L., Ritchie, G. F., Hamburger, S. D., & Rapoport, J. L. (1997). Controlled stimulant treatment of ADHD and comorbid Tourette's syndrome: Effects of stimulant and dose. *Journal of the American Academy of Child and Adolescent Psychiatry, 36,* 589–596.

Challman, T. D., & Lipsky, J. J. (2000). Methylphenidate: Its psychopharmacology and uses. *Mayo Clinic Proceedings, 75,* 711–721.

Chemers, B. (2002). The impact of attention deficit hyperactivity disorder on the juvenile justice system. In P. S. Jensen & J. R. Cooper (Eds.), *Attention deficit hyperactivity disorder: State of the science, best practices* (pp. 25-1–25-5). Kingston, NJ: Civic Research Institute.

Cheng, G., Chen, R., Ko, J., & Ng, E. (2007). Efficacy and safety of atomoxetine for attention-deficit/hyperactivity disorder in children and adolescents: Meta-analysis and meta-regression analysis. *Psychopharmacology, 194,* 197–209.

Childswork/Childsplay. (1999). *Circle of Friends Game.* Wilkes-Barre, PA: Author.

Chronis, A. M., Chacko, A., Fabiano, G. A., Wymbs, B. T., & Pelham, W. E., Jr. (2004). Enhancements to the behavioral parent training paradigm for families of children with ADHD: Review and future directions. *Clinical Child and Family Psychology Review, 7,* 1–27.

Clarfield, J., & Stoner, G. (2005). The effects of computerized reading instruction on the academic performance of students identified with ADHD. *School Psychology Review, 34,* 246–255.

Claude, D., & Firestone, P. (1995). The development of ADHD boys: A 12-year follow-up. *Canadian Journal of Behavioral Science, 27,* 226–249.

Claycomb, C. D., Ryan, J. J., Miller, L. J., & Shnakenberg-Ott, S. D. (2004). Relationship between attention deficit hyperactivity disorder, induced labor, and selected physiological and demographic variables. *Journal of Clinical Psychology, 60,* 689–693.

Colter, A. L., Cutler, C., & Meckling, K. A. (in press). Fatty acid status and behavioural symptoms of attention deficit hyperactivity disorder in adolescents: A case-control study. *Nutrition Journal.*

Conners, C. K. (2004). *Conners' Continuous Performance Test II: Technical guide and software manual.* North Tonawanda, NY: Multi-Health Systems.

Conners, C. K. (2008). *Conners 3rd edition: Manual.* North Tonawanda, NY: Multi-Health Systems.

Conners, C. K., Erhardt, D., & Sparrow, E. (1999). *Conners' Adult ADHD Rating Scales: Technical manual.* North Tonawanda, NY: Multi-Health Systems.

Connor, D. (2002). Preschool attention deficit hyperactivity disorder: A review of prevalence, diagnosis, neurobiology, and stimulant treatment. *Journal of Developmental and Behavioral Pediatrics, 23*(Suppl. 1), S1–S9.

Connor, D. F., & Steingard, R. J. (2004). New formulations of stimulants for attention-deficit hyperactivity disorder: Therapeutic potential. *CNS Drugs, 18,* 1011–1030.

Cruickshank, B. M., Eliason, M., & Merrifield, B. (1988). Long-term sequelae of water near-drowning. *Journal of Pediatric Psychology, 13,* 379–388.

Cuffe, S. P., Waller, J. L., Cuccaro, M. L., Pumariega, A. J., & Garrison, C. Z. (1995). Race and gender differences in the treatment of psychiatric disorders in young adolescents. *Journal of the American Academy of Child and Adolescent Psychiatry, 34,* 1536–1543.

Cunningham, C. E., & Cunningham, L. J. (1995). Reducing playground aggression: Student mediation program. *ADHD Report, 3,* 9–11.

Cunningham, C. E., Cunningham, L. J., & Martorelli, V. (2001). *Coping with conflict at school: The Collaborative Student Mediation Project manual.* Hamilton, Ontario, Canada: Community Parent Education Program.

Cunningham, C. E., Cunningham, L. J., Martorelli, V., Tran, A., Young, J., & Zacharias, R. (1998). The effects of primary division, student-mediated conflict resolution programs on playground aggression. *Journal of Child Psychology and Psychiatry, 39,* 653–662.

Darbinyan, V., Aslanyan, G., Amroyan, E., Gabrielyan, E., Malmström, C., & Panossian, A. (2007). Clinical trial of rhodiola rosea L. extract SHR-5 in the treatment of mild to moderate depression. *Nordic Journal of Psychiatry, 61,* 343–348.

David, D., & Brannon, R. (1976). *The forty-nine percent majority: The male sex role.* Reading, MA: Addison-Wesley.

David, O. J., Hoffman, S. P., Sverd, J., Clark, J., & Voeller, K. (1976). Lead and hyperactivity: Behavioral response to chelation; A pilot study. *American Journal of Psychiatry, 133,* 1155–1158.

Daviss, W. B., Bentivoglio, P., & Racusin, R. (2001). Buproprion sustained release in adolescents with comorbid attention-deficit/hyperactivity disorder and depression. *Journal of the American Academy of Child and Adolescent Psychiatry, 40,* 307–314.

deHaas, P. A. (1986). Attention styles and peer relationships of hyperactive and normal boys and girls. *Journal of Abnormal Child Psychology, 14,* 457–467.

Dews, P. B. (1984). Behavioral effects of caffeine. In P. B. Dews (Ed.), *Caffeine: Perspectives from recent research* (pp. 86–103). Berlin: Springer-Verlag.

Dixon, E. B. (1995). Impact of adult ADD on the family. In K. Nadeau (Ed.), *A comprehensive guide to attention deficit hyperactivity disorder in adults* (pp. 236–259). New York: Brunner/Mazel.

Donenberg, G., & Baker, B. L. (1994). The impact of young children with externalizing behaviors on their families. *Journal of Abnormal Child Psychology, 21,* 179–198.

Dossick, J. (1988). *Creative therapy: Fifty two exercises for groups.* Sarasota, FL: Professional Resource Press.

Dossick, J. (1990). *Creative therapy II: Fifty two more exercises for groups.* Sarasota, FL: Professional Resource Press.

Dossick, J. (1995). *Creative therapy III: Fifty two more exercises for groups.* Sarasota, FL: Professional Resource Press.

Drechsler, R., Rizzo, P., & Steinhausen, H. C. (2007). Decision-making on an explicit risk-taking task in preadolescents with attention-deficit/hyperactivity disorder. *Journal of Neural Transmission, 115,* 201–209.

DuPaul, G. J. (1991). Parent and teacher ratings of ADHD symptoms: Psychometric properties in a community-based sample. *Journal of Clinical Child Psychology, 20,* 242–253.

DuPaul, G. J., & Stoner, G. (2003). *ADHD in the schools: Assessment and intervention strategies.* New York: Guilford.

Ebaugh, F. G. (1923). Neuropsychiatric sequelae of acute epidemic encephalitis in children. *American Journal of Diseases of Children, 25,* 89–97.

Education of All Handicapped Children Act of 1975, 20 U.S.C. § 1400 *et seq.* (1975).

Enig, M. G. (2000). *Know your fats: The complete primer for understanding the nutrition of fats, oils and cholesterol.* Silver Spring, MD: Bethesda.

Enig, M. G., & Fallon, S. (1999). Tripping lightly down the prostaglandin pathways. *Price-Pottenger Nutrition Foundation Health Journal, 20,* 574–577.

Erford, B. T., & Hase, K. (2006). Reliability and validity of scores on the ACTeRS-2. *Measurement and Evaluation in Counseling and Development, 39*, 97–106.

Ernst, M., Kimes, A. S., London, E. D., Matochik, J. A., Eldreth, D., & Tata, S. (2003). Neural substrates of decision making in adults with attention deficit hyperactivity disorder. *American Journal of Psychiatry, 160*, 1061–1070.

Evans, S. M., & Griffiths, R. R. (1992). Caffeine tolerance and choice in humans. *Psychopharmacology, 108*, 51–59.

Exner, J. E. (2002). *The Rorschach: Basic foundations and principles of interpretation: Volume 1*. Hoboken, NJ: Wiley.

Fisher, M. (1990). Parenting stress and the child with attention deficit hyperactivity disorder. *Journal of Clinical Child Psychology, 19*, 337–346.

Flanagan, D. P. (2001). *Woodcock Johnson III assessment service bulletin number 1: Comparative features of the WJ III test of cognitive abilities and the Wechsler intelligence scales*. Rolling Meadows, IL: Riverside.

Fletcher, K. E., Fischer, M., Barkley, R. A., & Smallish, L. (1996). A sequential analysis of the mother–adolescent interactions of ADHD, ADHD/ODD, and normal teenagers. *Journal of Abnormal Child Psychology, 24*, 271–278.

Forehand, R. L., & McMahon, R. J. (1981). *Helping the noncompliant child: A clinician's guide to parent training*. New York: Guilford.

Frankel, F., Myatt, R., & Cantwell, D. P. (1995). Training outpatient boys to conform with the social ecology of popular peers: Effects on parent and teacher ratings. *Journal of Clinical Child Psychology, 24*, 300-310.

Frankel, F., Myatt, R., Cantwell, D. P., & Feinberg., D. (1997). Parent-assisted transfer of children's social skills training: Effects on children with and without attention deficit hyperactivity disorder. *Journal of the American Academy of Child and Adolescent Psychiatry, 36*, 1056-1064.

Frazier, T. W., Demaree, H. A., & Youngstrom, E. A. (2004). Meta-analysis of intellectual and neuropsychological test performance in attention-deficit/hyperactivity disorder. *Neuropsychology, 18*, 543–555.

Fredholm, B. B., Ijzerman, A. P., Jacobson, K. A., Klotz, K. N., & Linden, J. (2001). International Union of Pharmacology, XXV: Nomenclature and classification of adenosine receptors. *Pharmacology Reviews, 53*, 527–552.

Froehlich, T. E., Lanphear, B. P., Epstein, J. N., Barbaresi, W. J., Katusic, S. K., & Kahn, R. S. (2007). Prevalence, recognition, and treatment of attention-deficit/hyperactivity disorder in a national sample of U.S. children. *Archives of Pediatric and Adolescent Medicine, 161*, 857–864.

Fuster, J. M. (1997). *The prefrontal cortex* (3rd ed.). New York: Raven.

Garrett, B. E., & Griffiths, R. R. (1997). The role of dopamine in the behavioral effects of caffeine in animals and man. *Pharmacology, Biochemistry and Behavior, 57*, 533–541.

Gaub, M., & Carlson, C. L. (1997). Gender differences in ADHD: A meta-analysis and critical review. *Journal of the American Academy of Child and Adolescent Psychiatry, 36*, 1036–1045.

Gibson, A. P., Bettinger, T. L., Patel, N. C., & Crimson, M. L. (2006). Atomoxetine versus stimulants for treatment of attention deficit/hyperactivity disorder. *Annals of Pharmacotherapy, 40*, 1134–1142.

Glasser, W. (2001). *Counseling with choice theory: The new reality therapy.* New York: HarperCollins.

Golden, C. J., & Freshwater, S. M. (2002). *Stroop Color and Word Test.* Los Angeles: Western Psychological Services.

Golden, C. J., Hammeke, T. A., & Purisch, A. D. (1979). *The Luria-Nebraska Neuropsychological Battery: A manual for clinical and experimental uses.* Los Angeles: Western Psychological Services.

Goldstein, S., & Schwebach, A. J. (2004). The comorbidity of pervasive developmental disorder and attention deficit hyperactivity disorder: Results of a retrospective chart review. *Journal of Autism and Developmental Disorders, 34,* 329–339.

Gordon, M. (1983). *The Gordon Diagnostic System.* DeWitt, NY: Gordon Systems.

Gordon, M., & Mettelman, B. B. (1988). The assessment of attention: I. Standardization and reliability of a behavior-based measure. *Journal of Clinical Psychology, 44,* 682–690.

Gorman, C., & Park, A. (1994, October 10). Prozac's worst enemy. *Time Magazine.* Retrieved from www.time.com

Graetz, B. W., Sawyer, M. G., Hazell, P. L., Arney, F., & Baghurst, P. (2001). Validity of *DSM-IV* ADHD subtypes in a nationally representative sample of Australian children and adolescents. *Journal of the American Academy of Child and Adolescent Psychiatry, 40,* 1410–1417.

Grant, D. A., & Berg, E. A. (2003). *Wisconsin Card Sorting Test.* Lutz, FL: Psychological Assessment Resources. (Original work published 1948)

Gray, J. (1992). *Men are from Mars, women are from Venus.* New York: HarperCollins.

Greenberg, L. M., & Kindschi, C. L. (1996). *T.O.V.A. Test of Variables of Attention: Clinical guide.* St. Paul, MN: TOVA Research Foundation.

Greenhill, L. L. (2002). Stimulant medication treatment of children with attention deficit hyperacticity disorder. In P. S. Jensen & J. R. Cooper (Eds.), *Attention deficit hyperactivity disorder: State of the science, best practices* (pp. 9-1–9-27). Kingston, NJ: Civic Research Institute.

Greenwood, C. R., Delquadri, J., & Carta, J. J. (2002). *Classwide peer tutoring.* Seattle, WA: Educational Achievement Systems.

Griffiths, R. R., & Mumford, G. K. (1995). Caffeine: A drug of abuse? In F. E. Bloom & D. J. Kupfer (Eds.), *Psychopharmacology: The fourth generation of progress.* New York: Raven.

Gur, R. C., Turetsky, B. I., Matsui, M., Yan, M., Bilker, W., Hughett, P., & Gur, R. E. (1999). Sex differences in brain gray and white matter in healthy young adults: Correlations with cognitive performance. *Journal of Neuroscience, 19,* 4065–4072.

Hallowell, E. M. (1995). Psychotherapy of adult attention deficit disorder. In K. Nadeau (Ed.), *A comprehensive guide to attention deficit hyperactivity disorder in adults* (pp. 144–167). New York: Brunner/Mazel.

Halperin, J. M., Newcorn, J. H., Koda, V. H., Pick, L., McKay, K. E., & Knott, P. (1997). Noradrenergic mechanisms in ADHD children with and without reading disabilities: A replication and extension. *Journal of the American Academy of Child and Adolescent Psychiatry, 36,* 1688–1697.

Hathaway, S. R., & McKinley, J. C. (1989). *Minnesota Multiphasic Personality Inventory–2.* San Antonio, TX: Pearson Assessment.

Heaton, R. K., Miller, S. W., Taylor, M. J., & Grant, I. (1991). *Revised comprehensive norms for an expanded Halstead-Reitan Battery: Demographically adjusted neuropsychological norms for African American and Caucasian adults.* Lutz, FL: Psychological Assessment Resources.

Heiman, S. W. (1999). Pycnogenol for ADHD? *Journal of the American Academy of Child and Adolescent Psychiatry, 38,* 357–358.

Hesdorffer, D. C., Ludvigsson, P., Olafsson, E., Gudmundsson, G., Kjartansson, O., & Hauser, W. A. (2004). ADHD as a risk factor for incident unprovoked seizures and epilepsy in children. *Archives of General Psychiatry, 61,* 731–736.

Hibbeln, J. R., Umhau, J. C., Linnoila, M., George, D. T., Ragan, P. W., Shoaf, S. E., Vaughan, M. R., Rawlings, R., & Salem, N., Jr. (1998). Essential fatty acids predict metabolites of serotonin and dopamine in cerebrospinal fluid among healthy control subjects, and early- and late-onset alcoholics. *Biological Psychiatry, 44,* 243–349.

Hingle, M. (2007). Nutrition. In J. H. Lake & D. Spiegel (Eds.), *Complementary and alternative treatments in mental health care* (pp. 275–299). Washington, DC: American Psychiatric Publishing.

Hinshaw, S. P. (1992). Interventions for social competence and social skills. *Child and Adolescent Psychiatric Clinics of North America, 1,* 539–552.

Hinshaw, S. P. (2002). Is ADHD an impairing condition in childhood and adolescence? In P. S. Jensen & J. R. Cooper (Eds.), *Attention deficit hyperactivity disorder: State of the science, best practices* (pp. 5-1–5-21). Kingston, NJ: Civic Research Institute.

Hinshaw, S. P., & Erhardt, D. (1991). Attention-deficit hyperactivity disorder. In P. Kendall (Ed.), *Child and adolescent therapy: Cognitive-behavioral procedures* (pp. 98–128). New York: Guilford.

Hirayama, S., Hamazaki, T., & Terasawa, K. (2004). Effect of docosahexaenoic acid-containing food administration on symptoms of attention-deficit/hyperactivity disorder: A placebo-controlled double-blind study. *European Journal of Clinical Nutrition, 58,* 467–473.

Holtmann, M., Bolte, S., & Poutska, F. (2005). ADHD, Asperger syndrome, and high-functioning autism. *Journal of the American Academy of Child and Adolescent Psychiatry, 44,* 1101.

Homack, S., & Riccio, C. A. (2004). A meta-analysis of the sensitivity and specificity of the Stroop Color and Word Test with children. *Archives of Clinical Neuropsychology, 19,* 725–743.

Horrocks, L. A., & Yeo, Y. K. (1999). Health benefits of docosahexaenoic acid. *Pharmaceutical Research, 40,* 211–225.

Hunt, R. D., Minderaa, R. B., & Cohen, D. J. (1985). Clonidine benefits children with attention deficit disorder and hyperactivity: Report of a double-blind placebo-crossover therapeutic trial. *Journal of the American Academy of Child Psychiatry, 24,* 617–629.

Individuals With Disabilities Education Act of 1990, 20 U.S.C. § 1400 *et seq.* (1990).

James, J. J. (1991). *Caffeine and health.* London: Academic.

Janicak, P. G., Davis, J. M., Preskorn, S. H., Ayd, F. J. Jr., Marder, S. R., & Pavuluri, M. N. (2006). *Principles and practice of psychopharmacotherapy* (4th ed.). Philadelphia, PA: Lippincott, Williams and Wilkins.

Jensen, P. S., Kettle, L., Roper, M., Sloan, M., Dulcan, M., Hoven, C., & Bauermeister, J. (1999). Are stimulants overprescribed? Treatment of ADHD in 4 U.S. communities. *Journal of the American Academy of Child and Adolescent Psychiatry, 38,* 797–804.

Johnson, B. D., Franklin, L. C., Hall, K., & Prieto, L. R. (2000). Parent training through play: Parent–child interaction therapy with a hyperactive child. *Family Journal, 8,* 180–186.

Johnson, D. W., Johnson, R. T., Dudley, B., & Burnett, R. (1992). Teaching students to be peer mediators. *Educational Leadership, 50,* 10–13.

Johnson, M., Ostlund, S., Fransson, G., & Kadesjo, B. (in press). Omega-3/omega-6 fatty acids for attention deficit hyperactivity disorder: A randomized placebo-controlled trial in children and adolescents. *Journal of Attention Disorders.*

Johnston, C. (2002). The impact of attention deficit hyperactivity disorder on social and vocational functioning in adults. In P. S. Jensen & J. R. Cooper (Eds.), *Attention deficit hyperactivity disorder: State of the science, best practices* (pp. 6-1–6-21). Kingston, NJ: Civic Research Institute.

Johnston, C., & Mash, E. J. (2001). Families of children with attention-deficit/hyperactivity disorder: Review and recommendations for future research. *Clinical Child and Family Psychology Review, 4,* 183–207.

Jovanovic, H., Lundberg, J., Karlsson, P., Cerin, A., Saijo, T., Varrone, A., Halldin, C., & Nordström, A. L. (2008). Sex differences in the serotonin 1A receptor and serotonin transporter binding in the human brain measured by PET. *Neuroimage, 39,* 1408–1419.

Kapalka, G. M. (2001a). *Avoiding repetitions improves ADHD children's compliance with parent's commands.* Paper presented at the annual meeting of the American Psychological Society, Toronto, Canada.

Kapalka, G. M. (2001b). *Longer eye contact improves ADHD children's compliance with teacher's commands: II.* San Francisco: American Psychological Association.

Kapalka, G. M. (2002). Reducing ADHD children's management problems in out-of-class settings [Abstract]. In *Proceedings of the joint meeting of the Association for the Advancement of Educational Research and the National Academy for Educational Research* (Supplement, p. 6). West Monroe, LA: Association for the Advancement of Educational Research.

Kapalka, G. M. (2003a). Reducing ADHD children's management problems in out-of-home settings [Electronic version]. *Resources in Education.* (Document No. ED474462)

Kapalka, G. M. (2003b). *Reducing ADHD children's problems with interrupting at home.* Paper presented at the annual meeting of the American Psychological Association, Toronto, Canada.

Kapalka, G. M. (2004). Longer eye contact improves ADHD children's compliance with parents' commands. *Journal of Attention Disorders, 8,* 17–23.

Kapalka, G. M. (2005a). Avoiding repetitions reduces ADHD children's management problems in the classroom. *Emotional and Behavioural Difficulties, 10*(4), 269–279.

Kapalka, G. M. (2005b). Longer eye contact improves ADHD children's compliance with teacher's commands. *Journal for the Advancement of Educational Research, 1,* 69–78.

Kapalka, G. M. (2005c). *Reducing ADHD children's problems with interrupting in school.* Los Angeles: American Psychological Society.

Kapalka, G. M. (2005d). *Reducing ADHD children's problems with interrupting in school: II.* Washington, DC: American Psychological Association.

Kapalka, G. M. (2005e). *Reducing ADHD children's problems with transitions.* Paper presented at the annual meeting of the American Psychological Association, Washington, DC.

Kapalka, G. M. (2006a). *Efficacy of behavioral contracting with ADHD children.* Paper presented at the annual meeting of the American Psychological Society, New York.

Kapalka, G. M. (2006b). *Reducing problems with transitions that young students with ADHD commonly exhibit.* New York: Association for Psychological Science.

Kapalka, G. M. (2007a). Avoiding repetitions reduces classroom behavior management problems for students with ADHD. *Journal for the Advancement of Educational Research, 3*, 15–22.

Kapalka, G. M. (2007b). *Efficacy of behavioral contracting with students with ADHD: II.* San Francisco: American Psychological Association.

Kapalka, G. M. (2007c). *Parenting your out of control child: An effective, easy-to-use program for teaching self-control.* Oakland, CA: New Harbinger.

Kapalka, G. M. (2007d). *Reducing ADHD children's problems with home work.* Washington, DC: Association for Psychological Science.

Kapalka, G. M. (2008a). *Efficacy of behavioral contracting with students with ADHD.* Boston: American Psychological Association.

Kapalka, G. M. (2008b). Managing students with ADHD in out-of-class settings. *Emotional and Behavioural Difficulties, 13*, 21–30.

Kapalka, G. M. (2009). *Eight steps to classroom management success for teachers of challenging students.* Thousand Oaks, CA: Corwin.

Kapalka, G. M., & Bryk, L. J. (2007). Two to four minute time out is sufficient for young boys with ADHD. *Early Childhood Services, 1*(3), 181–188.

Kendall, P. C. (Ed.). (2005). *Child and adolescent therapy: Cognitive-behavioral procedures* (3rd ed.). New York: Guilford.

Kessler, R. C., Adler, L. A., Ames, M., Barkley, R. A., Birnbaum, H., & Greenberg, P. (2005). The prevalence and effects of adult attention deficit/hyperactivity disorder on work performance in a nationally representative sample of workers. *Journal of Occupational and Environmental Medicine, 47*, 565–572.

Klee, S. H., & Garfinkel, B. D. (1983). The computerized continuous performance task: A new measure of attention. *Journal of the American Academy of Child and Adolescent Psychiatry, 11*, 487–496.

Klein, M. (1963). *The psychoanalysis of children.* London: Hogarth.

Klein, R. G. (1987). Pharmacotherapy of childhood hyperactivity: An update. In H. Y. Meltzer (Ed.), *Psychopharmacology: The third generation of progress* (pp. 1215–1224). New York: Raven.

Kolberg, J., & Nadeau, K. (2002). *ADD-friendly ways to organize your life.* New York: Routledge.

Kroes, K., Kaliff, A. C., Kessels, A. G., Steyaert, J., Feron, F., & van Someren, A. (2001). Child psychiatric diagnoses in a population of Dutch school children aged 6 to 8 years. *Journal of the American Academy of Child and Adolescent Psychiatry, 40*, 1401–1409.

Lake, J. H. (2007). Omega-3 essential fatty acids. In J. H. Lake & D. Spiegel (Eds.), *Complementary and alternative treatment in mental health care* (pp. 151–167). Washington, DC: American Psychiatric Publishing.

Lambert, N. M. (2002). Stimulant treatment as a risk factor for nicotine use and substance abuse. In P. S. Jensen & J. R. Cooper (Eds.), *Attention deficit hyperactivity disorder: State of the science, best practices* (pp. 18-1–18-24). Kingston, NJ: Civic Research Institute.

Lambert, N. M., & Harsough, C. S. (1998). Prospective study of tobacco smoking and substance dependencies among samples of ADHD and non-ADHD participants. *Journal of Learning Disabilities, 31,* 533–544.

Lanau, F., Zenner, M., Civelli, O., & Hartman, D. (1997). Epinephrine and nor-epinephrine act as potent agonists at the recombinant human dopamine D4 receptor. *Journal of Neurochemistry, 68,* 804–812.

Laufer, M., Denhoff, E., & Solomons, G. (1957). Hyperkinetic impulse disorder in children's behavior problem. *Psychosomatic Medicine, 19,* 38–49.

Law, S., & Schachar, R. (1999). Do typical clinical doses of methylphenidate cause tics in children treated for ADHD? *Journal of the American Academy of Child and Adolescent Psychiatry, 38,* 944–951.

Lee, S. I., Schachar, R. J., Chen, S. X., Ornstein, T. J., Charach, A., Barr, C., & Ickowicz, A. (2008). Predictive validity of *DSM-IV* and ICD-10 criteria for ADHD and hyperkinetic disorder. *Journal of Child Psychology and Psychiatry, 49,* 70–78.

Legato, M. J. (2006, June 17). The weaker sex. *The New York Times.* Retrieved from www.nytimes.com/2006/06/17/opinion/17legato.html

Leon, M. R. (2000). Effects of caffeine on cognitive, psychomotor, and affective performance of children with attention-deficit/hyperactivity disorder. *Journal of Attention Disorders, 4,* 27–47.

Leung, P. W., Luk, S. L., Ho, T. P., Taylor, E., Mak, F. L., & Bacon-Stone, J. (1996). The diagnosis and prevalence of hyperactivity in Chinese schoolboys. *British Journal of Psychiatry, 168,* 486–496.

Levine, M. D. (2004). *The myth of laziness.* New York: Simon & Schuster.

Lewis, D., Linder, S., Kurlan, R., Winner, P., Dunn, D., Salee, F. R., Dure, L., Erenberg, G., Mintz, M., Milton, D., Schuh, K., Allen, A. J., & Kelsey, D. (2003). Atomoxetine for the treatment of attention deficit hyperactivity disorder and comorbid tics in children. *Annals of Neurology, 54,* S106.

Lifford, K. J., Harold, G. T., & Thapar, A. (2008). Parent–child relationships and ADHD symptoms: A longitudinal analysis. *Journal of Abnormal Child Psychology, 36,* 285–296.

Lindsay, S., Gudelsky, G., & Heaton, P. (2006). Use of modafinil for the treatment of attention deficit/hyperactivity disorder. *Annals of Pharmacotherapy, 40,* 1829-1833.

Lineberry, T. W., Bostwick, J. M., Beebe, T. J., & Decker, P. A. (2007). Impact of the FDA black box warning on physician antidepressant prescribing and practice patterns: Opening Pandora's suicide box. *Mayo Clinic Proceedings, 82,* 516–522.

Lombardo, J. A. (1986). Stimulants and athletic performance: Amphetamines and caffeine. *Physician and Sports Medicine, 14,* 128–140.

Loo, S. K., & Barkley, R. A. (2005). Clinical utility of EEG in attention deficit hyperactivity disorder. *Applied Neuropsychology, 12,* 64–76.

Luria, A. R. (1976). *Working brain: An introduction to neuropsychology*. Boulder, CO: Perseus.

Lynam, D. R. (1998). Early identification of the fledgling psychopath: Locating the psychopathic child in the current nomenclature. *Journal of Abnormal Psychology, 107*, 566–575.

Mandal, R. L. (2000). Test review of Brown Attention-Deficit Disorder Scales. *Psychology in the Schools, 37*, 196–200.

Manshadi, M., Lippmann, S., O'Daniel, R., & Blackman, A. (1983). Alcohol abuse and attention deficit disorder. *Journal of Clinical Psychiatry, 44*, 379-380.

Manuzza, S., Klein, R. G., Bessler, A., Malloy, P., & LaPadulla, M. (1993). Adult outcome of hyperactive boys. *Archives of General Psychiatry, 50*, 565–576.

Mattes, J. A. (1986). Propranolol for adults with temper outbursts and residual attention deficit disorder. *Journal of Clinical Psychopharmacology, 6*, 299–302.

McCarney, S. B. (1995). *The Early Childhood Attention Deficit Disorders Evaluation Scale*. Columbia, MO: Hawthorne Educational Services.

McCarney, S. B. (2003). *The Attention Deficit Disorders Evaluation Scale* (3rd ed.). Columbia, MO: Hawthorne Educational Services.

McDermott, S. P. (1999). Cognitive therapy of attention deficit hyperactivity disorder in adults. *Journal of Cognitive Psychotherapy, 13*, 215–226.

McDermott, S. P. (2000). Cognitive therapy for adults with attention-deficit/ hyperactivity disorder. In T. Brown (Ed.), *Attention-deficit disorders and comorbidities in children, adolescents and adults* (pp. 569–606). Washington, DC: American Psychiatric Press.

McGough, J. J., & McCracken, J. T. (2006). Adult attention deficit hyperactivity disorder: Moving beyond *DSM-IV*. *American Journal of Psychiatry, 163*, 1673–1675.

Medical Economics. (2001). *PDR for nutritional supplements*. Montvale, NJ: Author.

Medical Economics. (2007). *PDR for herbal medicines* (4th ed.). Montvale, NJ: Author.

Meichenbaum, D., & Goodman, J. (1971). Training impulsive children to talk to themselves: A means of developing self-control. *Journal of Abnormal Psychology, 77*, 115–126.

Michelson, D., Faries, D., Wernicke, J., Kelsey, D., Kendrick, K., & Sallee, F. R. (2001). Atomoxetine in the treatment of children and adolescents with attention-deficit/hyperactivity disorder: A randomized, placebo-controlled, dose-response study. *Pediatrics, 108*, E83.

Milberger, S., Biederman, J., Faraone, S. V., Chen, L., & Jones, J. (1997). ADHD is associated with early initiation of cigarette smoking in children and adolescents. *Journal of the American Academy of Child and Adolescent Psychiatry, 36*, 37–44.

Millon, T., Green, C. J., & Meagher, R. B., Jr. (1982). *Millon Adolescent Personality Inventory*. San Antonio, TX: Pearson Assessment.

Millon, T., Millon, C., Davis, R., & Grossman, S. (1993). *Millon Adolescent Clinical Inventory*. San Antonio, TX: Pearson Assessment.

Millon, T., Millon, C., Davis, R., & Grossman, S. (1996). *Millon Clinical Multiaxial Inventory–III*. San Antonio, TX: Pearson Assessment.

Mirsky, A. F. (1987). Behavioral and psychophysiological markers of disordered attention. *Environmental Health Perspectives, 74*, 191–199.

Moir, A., & Jessel, D. (1989). *Brain sex*. London: Michael Joseph.

Monastra, V. J. (2008). *Unlocking the potential of patients with ADHD: A model for clinical practice*. Washington, DC: American Psychological Association.

MTA Cooperative Group. (1999). A 14-month randomized clinical trial of treatment strategies for attention-deficit/hyperactivity disorder: Multimodal treatment study of children with ADHD. *Archives of General Psychiatry, 56*, 1073–1086.

Murphy, K., & Barkley, R. A. (1996a). Attention deficit hyperactivity disorder in adults. *Comprehensive Psychiatry, 37*, 393–401.

Murphy, K., & Barkley, R. A. (1996b). Prevalence of *DSM-IV* symptoms of ADHD in adult licensed drivers: Implications for clinical diagnosis. *Journal of Attention Disorders, 1*, 147–161.

Nadeau, K. G. (Ed.). (1995). *A comprehensive guide to attention deficit hyperactivity disorder in adults*. New York: Brunner/Mazel.

National Center for Health Statistics. (1994). National ambulatory medical care survey: Summary. *Vital Health Statistics, 13*, 116.

National Center for Health Statistics. (2002, October 8). Obesity still on the rise, new data show. *HHS News*. Retrieved from www.hhs.gov

Nay, W. R. (2004). *Taking charge of anger: How to resolve conflict, sustain relationships, and express yourself without losing control*. New York: Guilford.

Nehlig, A., Daval, J. L., & Debry, G. (1992). Caffeine and the central nervous system: Mechanisms of action, biochemical, metabolic and psychostimulant effects. *Brain Research Reviews, 17*, 139–170.

Nemzer, E., Arnold, L. E., Votolato, N. A., & McConnell, H. (1986). Amino acid supplementation as therapy for attention deficit disorder (ADD). *Journal of the American Academy of Child and Adolescent Psychiatry, 25*, 509–513.

Neville, K. (2006, April). Can omega-3 supplements help you reel in the health benefits of fish? *Environmental Nutrition*. Retrieved from www.environmentalnutrition.com

O'Dougherty, M., Nuechterlein, K. H., & Drew, B. (1984). Hyperactive and hypoxic children: Signal detection, sustained attention, and behavior. *Journal of Abnormal Psychology, 93*, 178–191.

Oehler-Stinnett, J. J. (1998). Review of the Gordon Diagnostic System. In J. C. Impara & B. S. Plake (Eds.), *Mental measurement yearbook* (13th ed.). Lincoln, NE: Burros Institute of Mental Measurement.

Olanow, J. P. (1996). Oxidative stress and the pathogenesis of Parkinson's disease. *Neurology, 47*(Suppl. 6), S161–S170.

Olfson, M., Marcus, S. C., Weissman, M. M., & Jensen, P. S. (2002). National trends in the use of psychotropic medications by children. *Journal of the American Academy of Child and Adolescent Psychiatry, 41*, 514–521.

Oskooilar, N. (2005). A case of premature ventricular contractions with modafinil. *American Journal of Psychiatry, 162*, 1983-1984.

Parker, J. G., & Asher, S. R. (1987). Peer relations and later personal adjustment: Are low-accepted children at risk? *Psychological Bulletin, 102*, 357–389.

Patterson, G. R. (1982). *Coercive family process*. Eugene, OR: Castalia.

Pelham, W. E. (2002). Psychosocial interventions for ADHD. In P. S. Jensen & J. R. Cooper (Eds.), *Attention deficit hyperactivity disorder: State of the science, best practices* (pp. 12-1–12-36). Kingston, NJ: Civic Research Institute.

Pelham, W. E., & Hoza, B. (1996). Intensive treatment: A summer treatment program for children with ADHD. In M. Roberts & A. LaGreca (Eds.), *Model programs for service delivery for child and family mental health* (pp. 193–212). Hillsdale, NJ: Lawrence Erlbaum.

Pfiffner, L. J. (1996). *All about ADHD: The complete practical guide for classroom teachers.* New York: Scholastic.

Pfiffner, L. J., McBurnett, K., Lahey, B. B., Loeber, R., Green, S., & Frick, P. J. (1999). Association of parental psychopathology to the comorbid disorders of boys with attention deficit hyperactivity disorder. *Journal of Consulting and Clinical Psychology, 67,* 881–893.

Pinker, S. (2002). *The blank slate.* New York: Penguin.

Rafalovich, A. (2001). Psychodynamic and neurological perspectives on ADHD: Exploring strategies for defining a phenomenon. *Journal of the Theory of Social Behavior, 31,* 397–417.

Ramsay, J. R., & Rostain, A. L. (2003). A cognitive therapy approach for adult attention-deficit/hyperactivity disorder. *Journal of Cognitive Psychotherapy, 17,* 319–334.

Ramsay, J. R., & Rostain, A. L. (2008). *Cognitive-behavioral therapy for adult ADHD: An integrative psychosocial and medical approach.* New York: Routledge.

Rappley, M. D., Mullan, P. B., Alvarez, F. J., Eneli, I. U., Wang, J., & Gardiner, J. C. (1999). Diagnosis of attention-deficit/hyperactivity disorder and use of psychotropic medication in very young children. *Archives of Pediatric and Adolescent Medicine, 153,* 1039–1045.

Ratey, N. A. (2002). Life coaching for adult ADHD. In S. Goldstein & A. T. Ellison (Eds.), *Clinician's guide to adult ADHD: Assessment and intervention.* San Diego, CA: Academic.

Ratey, N. A. (2008). *The disorganized mind: Coaching your ADHD brain to take control of your time, tasks, and talents.* New York: St. Martin's.

Ratey, J. J., Hallowell, E. M., & Miller, A. C. (1995). Relationship dilemmas for adults with ADD. In K. Nadeau (Ed.), *A comprehensive guide to attention deficit hyperactivity disorder in adults* (pp. 218–235). New York: Brunner/Mazel.

Rehabilitation Act of 1973, 29 U.S.C. § 701 *et seq.* (1973).

Reynolds, C., & Kamphaus, R. (2004). *Behavioral Assessment System for Children* (2nd ed.). Circle Pines, MN: American Guidance Service.

Richardson, A. J. (2003). The importance of omega-3 fatty acids for behaviour, cognition and mood. *Scandinavian Journal of Nutrition, 47,* 92–98.

Richardson, A., & Puri, B. (2002). A randomized double-blind, placebo-controlled study of the effects of supplementation with highly unsaturated fatty acids on ADHD-related symptoms in children with specific learning difficulties. *Progress in Neuropsychopharmacology and Biological Psychiatry, 26,* 233–239.

Ritchie, M. J. (1975). The xanthines. In L. S. Goodman & A. Gillman (Eds.), *The pharmacological basis of therapeutics* (pp. 367–378). London: Collier-Macmillan.

Robertson, J. M., & Shepard, D. S. (2008). The psychological development of boys. In M. S. Kiselica, M. Englar-Carlson, & A. M. Horne (Eds.), *Counseling troubled boys: A guidebook for professionals* (pp. 3–29). New York: Routledge.

Roid, G. H. (2003). *Stanford-Binet Intelligence Scales, Fifth Edition.* Rolling Meadows, IL: Riverside.

Rostain, A. L., & Ramsay, J. R. (2006). A combined treatment approach for adults with attention-deficit/hyperactivity disorder: Results of an open study with 43 patients. *Journal of Attention Disorders, 2,* 167–176.

Rucklidge, J. J., & Tannock, R. (2002). Validity of the Brown ADD Scales: An investigation in a predominantly inattentive ADHD adolescent sample with and without reading disabilities. *Journal of Attention Disorders, 5,* 155–164.

Safren, S. A., Otto, M. W., Sprich, S., Winett, C. L., Wilens, T. E., & Biederman, J. (2005). Cognitive-behavior therapy for ADHD in medication-treated adults with continued symptoms. *Behaviour Research and Therapy, 43,* 831–842.

Sanford, J. A., & Turner, A. (1995). *Manual for the Integrated Visual and Auditory Continuous Performance Test.* Richmond, VA: BrainTrain.

Schmidt, B. (2005). Methylxanthine therapy for apnea of prematurity: Evaluation of treatment benefits and risks at age 5 years in the International Caffeine for Apnea of Prematurity (CAP) trial. *Neonatology, 88,* 208–213.

Schrank, F. A., Becker, K. A., & Decker, S. (2001). *Woodcock Johnson III assessment service bulletin number 4: Calculating ability/achievement discrepancies between the Wechsler Intelligence Scale for Children–Third Edition and the Woodcock-Johnson III tests of achievement.* Rolling Meadows, IL: Riverside.

Schroeder, C., Tank, J., & Goldstein, D. S. (2004). Influence of St. John's wort on catecholamine turnover and cardiovascular regulation in humans. *Clinical Pharmacological Therapies, 76,* 480–489.

Settle, J. E. (2007). Nutritional supplements. In J. H. Lake & D. Spiegel (Eds.), *Complementary and alternative treatments in mental health care* (pp. 115–149). Washington, DC: American Psychiatric Publishing.

Sever, Y., Ashkenazi, A., Tyano, S., & Weizman, A. (1997). Iron treatment in children with ADHD: A preliminary report. *Neuropsychobiology, 35,* 178–180.

Sharp, W. S., Gottesman, R. F., Greenstein, D. K., Ebens, C. L., Rapoport, J. L., & Castellanos, F. X. (2003). Monozygotic twins discordant for attention-deficit/hyperactivity disorder: Ascertainment and clinical characteristics. *Journal of the American Academy of Child and Adolescent Psychiatry, 42,* 93–97.

Shaughency, E. A., Lahey, B. B., Hynd, G. W., Stone, P. A., Piacentini, J. A., & Frick, P. J. (1989). Neuropsychological test performance and the attention deficit disorders: Clinical utility of the Luria-Nebraska Neuropsychological Battery–Children's Revision. *Journal of Consulting and Clinical Psychology, 57,* 112–116.

Shekim, W. O., Masterson, A., Cantwell, D. P., Hanna, G. L., & McCracken, J. T. (1989). Nomifensine maleate in adult attention deficit disorder. *Journal of Nervous and Mental Disease, 177,* 296–299.

Shevtsov, V. A., Zholus, B. I., Shervarly, V. I., Vol'skij, V. B., Korovin, Y. P., Khristich, M. P., Roslyakova, N. A., & Wikman, G. (2003). A randomized trial of two different doses of a SHR-5 rhodiola rosea extract versus placebo and control of capacity for mental work. *Phytomedicine, 10,* 95–105.

Siegel, D. J. (1999). *The developing mind: Toward a neurobiology of interpersonal experience.* New York: Guilford.

Silva, R., Munoz, D., & Alpert, M. (1996). Carbamazepine use in children and adolescents with features of attention-deficit hyperactivity disorder. *Journal of the American Academy of Child and Adolescent Psychiatry, 35,* 352–358.

Singer, S., Brown, J., Quaskey, S., Rosenberg, L., Mellits, E., & Denckla, M. (1994). The treatment of attention-deficit hyperactivity disorder in Tourette's syndrome: A double-blind placebo-controlled study with clonidine and desipramine. *Pediatrics, 95,* 74–81.

Spencer, T., Biederman, J., Kerman, K., Steingard, R., & Wilens, T. E. (1993). Desipramine in the treatment of children with tic disorder or Tourette's syndrome and attention deficit hyperactivity disorder. *Journal of the American Academy of Child and Adolescent Psychiatry, 32,* 354–360.

Spencer, T., Biederman, J., & Wilens, T. (2004). Non-stimulant treatment of adult attention-deficit/hyperactivity disorder. *Psychiatric Clinics of North America, 27,* 373–383.

Spencer, T., Biederman, J., Wilens, T., Harding, M., O'Donnell, D., & Griffin, S. (1996). Pharmacotherapy of attention deficit hyperactivity disorder across the life cycle. *Journal of the American Academy of Child and Adolescent Psychiatry, 35,* 409–432.

Spencer, T. J., Heiligenstein, J., Biederman, J., Faries, D., Kratochvil, C., & Conners, C. (2002). Atomoxetine in children with ADHD: Results from two randomized, placebo-controlled studies. *Journal of Clinical Psychiatry, 63,* 1140–1147.

Stahl, S. M. (2000). *Essential psychopharmacology: Neuroscientific basis and practical applications* (2nd ed.). New York: Cambridge University Press.

Stahl, S. M. (2006). *Essential psychopharmacology: The prescriber's guide* (Rev. ed.). New York: Cambridge University Press.

Stevens, L., Zhang, W., & Peck, L. (2003). EFA supplementation in children with attention, hyperactivity, and other disruptive behaviors. *Lipids, 38,* 1007–1021.

Still, G. F. (1902). Some abnormal psychical conditions in children. *Lancet, 1,* 1008–1012, 1077–1082, 1163–1168.

Stewart, M. A. (1970). Hyperactive children. *Scientific American, 222,* 94–98.

Swanson, J. M., & Castellanos, F. X. (2002). Biological bases of ADHD: Neuroanatomy, genetics, and pathophysiology. In P. S. Jensen & J. R. Cooper (Eds.), *Attention deficit hyperactivity disorder: State of the science, best practices* (pp. 7-1–7-20). Kingston, NJ: Civic Research Institute.

Swanson, J. M., McBurnett, K., Christian, D. L., & Wigal, T. (1995). Stimulant medication and treatment of children with ADHD. In T. H. Ollendick & R. J. Prinz (Eds.), *Advances in clinical child psychology* (Vol. 17, pp. 265–322). New York: Plenum.

Tallamadge, J., & Barkley, R. A. (1983). The interactions of hyperactive and normal boys with their mothers and fathers. *Journal of Abnormal Child Psychology, 11,* 565–579.

Tannock, R. (2000). Attention-deficit/hyperactivity disorder with anxiety disorders. In T. E. Brown (Ed.), *Attention-deficit disorders and comorbidities in children, adolescents, and adults* (pp. 125–170). Washington, DC: American Psychiatric Press.

Tannock, R. (2002). Cognitive correlates of ADHD. In P. S. Jensen & J. R. Cooper (Eds.), *Attention deficit hyperactivity disorder: State of the science, best practices* (pp. 8-1–8-27). Kingston, NJ: Civic Research Institute.

Tapert, S. F., Baratta, M. V., Abrantes, A. M., & Brown, S. A. (2002). Attention dysfunction predicts substance involvement in community youths. *Journal of the American Academy of Child and Adolescent Psychiatry, 41*, 680–686.

Tarnopolsky, M. A. (1994). Caffeine and endurance performance. *Sports Medicine, 18*, 109-125.

Taylor, F. B., & Russo, J. (2001). Comparing guanfacine and dextroamphetamine for the treatment of adult attention-deficit/hyperactivity disorder. *Journal of Clinical Psychopharmacology, 21*, 223–228.

Tercyak, K. P., Lerman, C., & Audrain, J. (2002). Association of attention-deficit/ hyperactivity disorder symptoms with levels of cigarette smoking in a community sample of adolescents. *Journal of the American Academy of Child and Adolescent Psychiatry, 41*, 799–805.

Tercyak, K. P., Peshkin, B. N., Walker, L. R., & Stein, M. A. (2002). Cigarette smoking among youth with attention-deficit/hyperactivity disorder: Clinical phenomenology, comorbidity, and genetics. *Journal of Clinical Psychology in Medical Settings, 9*, 35–50.

Torrioli, M. G., Vernacotola, S., Mariotti, S., Bianchi, E., Calvani, M., DeGaetano, A., Chiurazzi, P., & Neri, G. (1999). Double-blind, placebo-controlled study of l-acetylcarnitine for the treatment of hyperactive behavior in fragile X syndrome. *American Journal of Medical Genetics, 87*, 366–368.

Trebaticka, J., Kopasova, S., Hradecna, Z., & Cinovsky, K. (2006). Treatment of ADHD with French maritime bark extract, Pycnogenol. *European Child and Adolescent Psychiatry, 15*, 329–335.

Trice, I., & Haymes, E. M. (1995). Effects of caffeine ingestion on exercise-induced changes during high-intensity, intermittent exercise. *International Journal of Sport Nutrition, 5*, 37–44.

Ullmann, R. K., Sleator, E. K., & Sprague, R. L. (2000). *ADD-H Comprehensive Teacher's Rating Scale: Teacher and parent forms manual*. Lutz, FL: Psychological Assessment Resources.

University of Illinois at Urbana–Champaign. (n.d.). *Out on a Limb*. Retrieved from http://www.urbanext.uiuc.edu/conflict/maria1.html

U.S. Census Bureau. (2003). *Statistical abstract of the United States: 2003*. Washington, DC: Author.

Van Brunt, D. L., Johnston, J. A., Ye, W., Pohl, G. M., & O'Hara, N. N. (2006). Factors associated with initiation with atomoxetine versus stimulants in the treatment of adults with ADHD: Retrospective analysis of administrative claims data. *Journal of Managed Care Pharmacology, 12*, 230–238.

Voigt, R., Llorente, A., & Jensen, C. (2001). A randomized, double-blind, placebo-controlled trial of docosahexaenoic acid supplementation in children with attention-deficit/hyperactivity disorder. *Journal of Pediatrics, 139*, 189–196.

Vygotsky, L. S. (1962). *Thought and language*. New York: Wiley.

Wagner, K. D. (2004). Treatment of childhood and adolescent disorders. In A. F. Schatzberg & C. B. Nemeroff (Eds.), *The American Psychiatric Publishing textbook of psychiatry* (pp. 949–1007). Washington, DC: American Psychiatric Publishing.

Walsh, W. (2003). *Commentary on nutritional treatment of mental disorders*. Retrieved from www.hriptc.org

Warshak, R. A. (1995). *Warshak Inventory for Child and Adolescent Assessment* (2nd ed.). Dallas, TX: Clinical Psychology Associates.

Weber, W., Vander Stoep, A., McCarty, R., & Weiss, N. (2008). *Hypericum perforatum* (St. John's wort) for attention-deficit/hyperactivity disorder in children and adolescents: A randomized controlled trial. *Journal of the American Medical Association, 299*, 2633–2641.

Wechsler, D. (2001). *Wechsler Individual Assessment Test, Second Edition*. San Antonio, TX: Psychological Corporation.

Wechsler, D. (2002). *Wechsler Preschool and Primary Scales of Intelligence, Third Edition*. San Antonio, TX: Psychological Corporation.

Wechsler, D. (2003). *Wechsler Intelligence Scale for Children, Fourth Edition*. San Antonio, TX: Psychological Corporation.

Wechsler, D. (2008). *Wechsler Adult Intelligence Scale, Fourth Edition*. San Antonio, TX: Psychological Corporation.

Weinstein, C. S., Apfel, R. J., & Weinstein, S. R. (1998). Description of mothers with ADHD with children with ADHD. *Psychiatry, 61*, 12-19.

Weinstein, D., Steffelbach, D., & Biaggio, M. (2000). Attention-deficit hyperactivity disorder and posttraumatic stress disorder: Differential diagnosis in childhood sexual abuse. *Clinical Psychology Review, 20*, 359–378.

Weiss, G., & Hechtman, L. (1993). *Hyperactive children grown up* (2nd ed.). New York: Guilford.

Weiss, M., Weiss, G., & Hechtman, L. (2002). *ADHD in adulthood: A guide to current theory, diagnosis, and treatment*. New York: Elsevier Science.

Wender, P. (1971). *Minimal brain dysfunction in children*. New York: Wiley.

Wender, P. H., Wood, D. R., & Reimherr, F. W. (1985). Pharmacological treatment of attention deficit disorder residual type in adults. *Psychopharmacology Bulletin, 21*, 222-230.

Weyandt, L. L., Linterman, I., & Rice, J. A. (1995). Reported prevalence of attentional difficulties in a general sample of college students. *Journal of Psychopathology and Behavioral Assessment, 17*, 293-304.

Whittaker, A. H., Can Rossem, R., Feldman, J. F., Schonfeld, I. S., Pinto-Martin, J. A., & Torre, C. (1997). Psychiatric outcomes in low-birth-weight children at age 6 years: Relation to neonatal cranial ultrasound abnormalities. *Archives of General Psychiatry, 54*, 847–856.

Wilens, T. E. (2002). Attention deficit hyperactivity disorder and substance use disorders: The nature of the relationship, subtypes at risk, and treatment issues. In P. S. Jensen & J. R. Cooper (Eds.), *Attention deficit hyperactivity disorder: State of the science, best practices* (pp. 19-1–19-17). Kingston, NJ: Civic Research Institute.

Wilens, T. E., Biederman, J., Brown, S., Tanguay, S., Monuteaux, M. C., & Blake, C. (2002). Psychiatric comorbidity and functioning in clinically-referred preschool children and school-age youth with ADHD. *Journal of the American Academy of Child and Adolescent Psychiatry, 41*, 262–268.

Wilens, T. E., Biederman, J., Prince, J., Spencer, T. J., Faraone, S. V., Warburton, R., Schleifer, D., Harding, M., Linehan, C., & Geller, D. (1996). Six-week, double-blind, placebo-controlled study of desipramine for adult attention deficit hyperactivity disorder. *American Journal of Psychiatry, 153*, 1147–1153.

Wilens, T. E., Faraone, S. V., Biederman, J., & Gunawardene, S. (2003). Does stimulant therapy of attention deficit/hyperactivity disorder beget later substance abuse? A meta-analytic review of literature. *Pediatrics, 11,* 179–185.

Wilens, T. E., McDermott, S. P., Biederman, J., Abrantes, A., Hahesy, A., & Spencer, T. (1999). Cognitive therapy in the treatment of adults with ADHD: A systematic chart review of 26 cases. *Journal of Cognitive Psychotherapy, 13,* 215–226.

Wilens, T. E., Spencer, T. J., & Biederman, J. (2002). A review of the pharmacotherapy of adults with attention-deficit/hyperactivity disorder. *Journal of Attention Disorders, 5,* 189–202.

Wilens, T. E., Spencer, T. J., Biederman, J., Girard, K., Doyle, R., & Prince, J. (2001). A controlled clinical trial of buproprion for attention deficit hyperactivity disorder in adults. *American Journal of Psychiatry, 158,* 282–288.

Wood, D. R., Reimherr, F. W., & Wender, P. H. (1985). Amino acid precursors for the treatment of attention-deficit disorder, residual type. *Psychopharmacology Bulletin, 21,* 146–149.

Woodcock, R. W., McGrew, K. S., & Mather, N. (2001). *Woodcock-Johnson III NU Complete.* Rolling Meadows, IL: Riverside.

World Health Organization (1992). *International Statistical Classification of Diseases and Related Health Problems* (10th rev.). New York: United Nations University Press.

Wozniak, J., Harding-Crawford, M., Biederman, J., Faraone, S. V., Spencer, T. J., & Taylor, A. (1999). Antecedents and complications of trauma in boys with ADHD: Findings from a longitudinal study. *Journal of the American Academy of Child and Adolescent Psychiatry, 38,* 48–55.

Yalom, I. D., & Leszcz, M. (2005). *Theory and practice of group psychotherapy* (5th ed.). New York: Basic Books.

Zubin, J., & Spring, B. (1977). Vulnerability: A new view of schizophrenia. *Journal of Abnormal Psychology, 86,* 103–126.

INDEX

A

Abikoff, H., 28
Academic achievement tests, 55–57
    Wechsler Individual Achievement
        Test (WIAT-II), 55–56
    Woodcock-Johnson III battery, 56–57
Academic assistance, 221–222
Academic records, 78–80
ACTeRS, 47–48
ADHD. *see* Attention deficit/
        hyperactivity disorder
        (ADHD)
Adjustment disorders, 88–89
Aggression, 3, 13–14
Agitation, 88
Allsopp, L. A., 144
Alpha-2 adrenergic agonists, 290–293
    adverse effects, 292–293
    dosing, 291–292
    evidence of efficacy, 290–291
    pharmacodynamics, 291
Alvarado, A., 319
Ambroggio, J. D., 28
Amphetamine and derivatives, 264–268
    adverse effects, 267–268
    dosing, 266–267
    pharmacodynamics, 265
    pharmacokinetics, 265–266
Anastopoulos, A. D., 39, 120
Anger Control Game, 193
Anger management, 110–112, 156–159,
        192–195, 202
Antidepressant medications, 273–274
    atomoxetine, 274–278

buproprion, 278–282
monoamine oxidase inhibitors
    (MAIOs), 287–288
serotonergic antidepressants,
    288–289
serotonin/norepinephrine reuptake
    inhibitors (SNRIs), 286–287
tricyclic antidepressants, 282–286
Antihypertensive medications, 289–294
    alpha-2 adrenergic agonists, 290–293
    beta-blockers, 293–294
Antipsychotic medications, 294–295
Anxiety disorders, 87–88
    obsessive compulsive disorder
        (OCD), 87
    other anxiety disorders, 88
    post-traumatic stress disorder
        (PTSD), 87–88
Anxiolytic medications, 296
Ashkenazi, A., 324
Asperger's syndrome, 69
Assessment, 43
    assessment instruments, 80–81
    behavioral checklists/inventories,
        43–49
Atomoxetine, 274–278
    adverse effects, 276–278
    dosing, 276
    evidence of efficacy, 274–285
    pharmacodynamics, 275
    pharmacokinetics, 275–276
Attention, 3, 141
    d2 Test, 60–61
Attention deficit disorder (ADD), 4
    pediatric data, 17–18